Herman Hanko

CONTENDING
FOR THE
The Rise of Heresy and the Development of the Truth

Reformed Free Publishing Association
Jenison, Michigan

All Scripture quotations by the author are taken
from the Authorized (King James) Version

Book cover and interior design by Jeff Steenholdt and Erika De Vries

REFORMED FREE PUBLISHING ASSOCIATION
1894 Georgetown Center Drive
Jenison, MI 49428 USA
Phone: (616) 457-5970
Fax: (616) 457-5980
Website: www.rfpa.org
Email: mail@rfpa.org

ISBN: 978-1-936054-01-5
LCCN: 2010921040

Dedicated to the memory of
George Martin Ophoff,
who taught me the glory
of the Reformed heritage
and the importance of defending it

"…and that ye should earnestly contend for the faith
which was once delivered unto the saints."
—Jude 3

CONTENTS

Preface   *xvii*
Introduction   *1*

PART I | ANCIENT PERIOD 100–476   7

CHAPTER I
Marcion: First Bible Critic   *9*
   Introduction
   Marcion's Life
   Marcion's Heresy
   The Church's Response

CHAPTER 2
Gnosticism: Synthesis Religion   *14*
   Introduction
   Various Gnostic Sects
   Gnosticism's Teachings
   Gnosticism's Main Characteristic
   The Church's Response
   The Meaning of the Battle against Gnosticism

CHAPTER 3
Montanus: First Charismatic   *22*
   Introduction
   Montanus and His Followers
   Montanism's Views
   Montanism's Significance

CHAPTER 4
Sabellius: First Unitarian   *28*
   Introduction
   The Problem
   Sabellius' Life
   Sabellius' Teachings
   The Church's Response

CHAPTER 5
Arius and the Council of Nicea   *34*
   Introduction
   Arius' Life
   The Calling of the Council of Nicea
   The Council Meeting
   The History after Nicea
   Conclusion

CHAPTER 6
Apollinaris and the Doctrine of Christ   *44*
   Introduction
   God's Greater Wisdom
   Apollinaris' Life
   Apollinaris the Heretic
   Apollinaris' Heresy

CHAPTER 7
Nestorius and an Unholy Squabble about Christ   *53*
   Introduction
   The Problem in the Church
   Nestorius' Early Life
   Troubles
   Nestorius' View of Christ
   Cyril's Intervention
   Subsequent Events
   Conclusions and Summary

CHAPTER 8
Pelagius and Celestius: Enemies of the Doctrines of Grace   *63*
   Introduction
   Pelagius and Celestius
   The Beginnings of the Conflict
   The Counterattack
   The End of the Matter
   Concluding Remarks

CHAPTER 9
Cassianus, Faustus, and Semi-Pelagianism   *72*
   Introduction

John Cassianus and Faustus of Riez
A Brief Statement of Augustine's Views
The Views of Cassianus and Faustus
Augustine's Response
The Synod of Orange

PART 2 | MEDIEVAL PERIOD 500–1517   83

CHAPTER 10
Gregory I: First Medieval Pope   *85*
  Introduction
  The Times in Which Gregory Worked
  Gregory's Early Life
  Gregory the Monk
  Gregory's Influence on Worship
  Gregory's Influence on Doctrine
  Gregory and the Growth of Monasticism
  Gregory the Theologian
  Gregory the Pope
  Gregory the Missionary

CHAPTER 11
Rabanus and the Victory of Semi-Pelagianism   *95*
  Introduction
  Rabanus' Life
  Gottschalk
  Synod of Mayence
  Synod of Chiersy
  Synod of Valence
  Two More Synods and the End of the Matter
  The Views That Prevailed
  Rome's Errors and the Doctrine of Merit

CHAPTER 12
Berengar and Transubstantiation   *104*
  Introduction
  The Presence of Christ in the Lord's Supper
  The First Controversy and Radbertus' Views
  The First Controversy and Ratramnus' Views

The End of the First Controversy
The Second Controversy and Berengar's Early Life
Berengar the Man
Berengar's Life of Controversy
The End of the Matter

CHAPTER 13
Abelard and the Doctrine of the Atonement   *113*
Introduction
Abelard's Rise to Fame
Abelard's Fall
Abelard's Heresies and Final Days
Abelard's Doctrine of the Atonement
The Church's Response

CHAPTER 14
Innocent III and Papal Hierarchy   *121*
Introduction
Innocent's Rise to Power
Innocent's Character
Innocent's View of the Papacy
The Fourth Lateran Council
Innocent's Struggle with Europe's Kings
Conclusion

CHAPTER 15
Thomas à Kempis and Medieval Mysticism   *132*
Introduction
Thomas à Kempis' Life
The Prevalence of Mysticism
Characteristics of Mysticism
The Explanation of Mysticism
How to Attain Communion with God
Mysticism's Attraction
True Emotions
Criticisms of Mysticism
The Greatest Evil

PART 3 | REFORMATION PERIOD 1517–1577   149

CHAPTER 16
Erasmus and Humanism   *151*
  Introduction
  Erasmus' Early Life and Education
  Erasmus' Later Life
  Erasmus' Interests
  Erasmus' Errors
  Erasmus' Writings
  Erasmus' Early Sympathy for the Reformation and Later Hesitation
  The Great Issue

CHAPTER 17
Melanchthon and Synergism   *162*
  Introduction
  Melanchthon's Life
  Melanchthon's Work
  The Relation between Melanchthon and Luther
  Melanchthon's Agreements with Calvin
  Melanchthon's Great Error
  Melanchthon's Heresy

CHAPTER 18
Agricola and Antinomianism   *171*
  Introduction
  Agricola's Life
  Agricola's Break with Reformation Thought
  Agricola's Antinomianism
  Conclusion

CHAPTER 19
Anabaptism: The Right Wing of the Reformation   *178*
  Introduction
  Carlstadt and the Zwickau Prophets
  Thomas Münzer
  John of Leiden
  Conclusion to the Struggle with the Radicals
  Early Swiss Anabaptism
  Anabaptism in the Netherlands and Menno Simons
  Anabaptist Errors

CHAPTER 20
The Nicodemites   *192*
   Introduction
   Nicodemites' Error
   Calvin's Condemnation of the Nicodemites
   Conclusion

CHAPTER 21
Bolsec and Predestination   *197*
   Introduction
   Bolsec's Life and Teaching
   The Resolution to the Conflict
   The End of the Matter
   Conclusion

CHAPTER 22
Servetus and the Denial of the Trinity   *205*
   Introduction
   Servetus' Early Life
   Servetus' Attempt at Theology
   Servetus' Career in Medicine
   Servetus' Return to Theology
   Servetus' Character
   Servetus' Arrest and Trial
   Servetus' Heresies
   Evaluation of Servetus' Death

PART 4 | POST-REFORMATION PERIOD 1577–1900   215

CHAPTER 23
Arminius and Arminianism   *217*
   Introduction
   Arminius' Education
   Arminius' Ministry in Amsterdam
   Arminius as Professor of Theology
   Arminius' Character
   Arminius' Views
   The Remonstrants

The Political and Ecclesiastical Situation
The Synod of Dordt

CHAPTER 24
Amyraut and Amyrauldism   *229*
  Introduction
  Amyraut's Life
  Amyraut's Views
  John Cameron and Developments in Scotland
  Reactions to Amyrauldism in Switzerland
  Conclusion

CHAPTER 25
Cocceius and Biblical Theology   *239*
  Introduction
  A Brief Sketch of Cocceius' Life
  Cocceius' Concerns
  Cocceius' Method
  Cocceius' Separation of the Testaments
  The Error of Biblical Theology
  The Importance of Systematic Theology
  The Dangers of Biblical Theology

CHAPTER 26
The Marrow Men and the Marrow Controversy   *248*
  Introduction
  Background
  The Marrow of Modern Divinity
  The Occasion for the Marrow Controversy
  The Problem with the Auchterarder Creed
  The Solution
  Where the Marrow Entered the Controversy
  Christ's Death and Preaching
  The Extent of the Atonement of Christ
  Wrong Interpretations of the Marrow Controversy
  The Concern of the Marrow Men
  An Implied View of Preaching
  The Erroneous View of Preaching Held by the Marrow Men
  Conclusion

CHAPTER 27
Wesley and Arminianism   *265*
   Introduction
   Wesley's Early Life
   Wesley's Life at Oxford
   Wesley's Conversion
   Wesley's Itinerant Ministry
   Wesley's Relation to Women
   Wesley's Relation to the Church
   Wesley's Relation to Others
   Wesley's Mysticism
   Wesley and Revivals
   Wesley's Arminianism

CHAPTER 28
Finney and Revivalism   *280*
   Introduction
   Finney's Pre-conversion Life
   Finney's Post-conversion Ministry
   The State of the Presbyterian Church
   Finney's Theological Views
   Finney's Mysticism
   Finney's Social Gospel
   Revivalism
   No Revivals in Scripture
   Revivals and the Church Institute
   Revivalism and the Covenant
   Revivalism and Preaching

CHAPTER 29
Darwin and Evolutionism   *295*
   Introduction
   Charles Darwin, Founder of Evolutionism
   Darwin's Life
   Darwin's Views
   Darwin's Atheism
   Summary
   Theistic Evolutionists
   Theistic Evolutionists and Scripture

A Wrong View of Faith
Why Faith?
Errors of Theistic Evolutionism

CHAPTER 30
Rauschenbusch and the Social Gospel   *308*
   Introduction
   Rauschenbusch's Background and Early Life
   Influences on Rauschenbusch's Thinking
   Rauschenbusch's Early History as a Social Reformer
   Rauschenbusch's Ideas
   Rauschenbusch's View of the Kingdom
   The Truth of the Matter

PART 5 | MODERN PERIOD 1900–2010   319

CHAPTER 31
Errors Concerning the Covenant   *321*
   Introduction
   Some History
   Dissenters
   Seriously Wrong Developments
   Consequences of a Conditional Covenant
   Justification by Faith and Works
   The Truth of God's Covenant

CHAPTER 32
Higher Criticism   *332*
   Introduction
   The Origin of Higher Criticism
   The Nature of Higher Criticism
   The Sinfulness of Higher Criticism
   Scripture's Inspiration

CHAPTER 33
Azusa Street Revival and Pentecostalism   *340*
   Introduction
   The History of Modern Pentecostalism
   Its Character

The Teachings of Pentecostalism
Criticisms of Pentecostalism

CHAPTER 34
Common Grace   *347*
   Introduction
   The Common Grace of the Gospel Offer
   Objections to the Gospel Offer
   The History of Kuyperian Common Grace
   The Nature of Kuyperian Common Grace
   Objections to Kuyperian Common Grace

CHAPTER 35
Federal Vision Theology   *356*
   Introduction
   Its Name and Origin
   The Teachings of the Federal Vision
   The Error of the Federal Vision

Notes   *363*

PREFACE

In 1999 the RFPA published my *Portraits of Faithful Saints*. It became evident in the lives of those who fought a good fight that a significant part of their lives was taken up in the defense of the faith: what Jude calls earnestly contending for the faith once delivered unto the saints (Jude 3). The mark their faithfulness left on history was the example of a courageous battle against heresy and, frequently, their willingness to die in the battle for the sake of the gospel of Jesus Christ.

Heresy has always been present in the church. It was present in the old dispensation when, already at Sinai, Israel worshiped a golden calf, which they said was the god who had delivered them from Egypt (Ex. 32:4). God's constant warning against false prophets could only have been due to the presence in Israel of men who were corrupting the truth, for example, in Deuteronomy 13:1–5.

The times of Christ and the apostles were no different. Christ repeatedly warned against the heresies of the scribes, Sadducees, and Pharisees, who took away the key of knowledge (Luke 11:52) and crucified the Christ, who is the way, the truth, and the life (John 14:6).

Paul frequently had to write his epistles to combat false doctrine: to the Colossians to ward off an incipient gnosticism; to the Galatians to defeat the Judaizers; and to the Thessalonians to correct errors in eschatology that they had learned from false teachers. Both Peter in 2 Peter 2 and Jude in his epistle warned against the evil men who were attempting to lead the church astray.

From the end of the apostolic era until the present, the church has never been free from the threat of false doctrine. Fighting false doctrine is so crucial a part of the church's existence in the world that to ignore it is to run the risk of not understanding church history at all. One cannot learn anything significant about a man from whose biography has been omitted the most important events in his life. One cannot understand the history of the church militant without understanding her battles against false doctrine.

A striking feature of heresy over the ages is the reappearance of false doctrines that had been taught in earlier times. Solomon tells us that there is nothing new under the sun (Eccl. 1:9). This is true of heresy as well as every other event. Heresy may appear in new clothing, but it remains the same heresy against which the church has fought many centuries earlier.

We can, therefore, learn from heresy and from the battle that the saints fought against it; the heresies are always very much the same. The church's calling today is no different from the calling of the church in past years: "Be thou faithful unto death" (Rev. 2:10).

If we live in ignorance of the church of past years, knowing nothing of its struggles, battles, temptations, and heresies it faced, we will be at a terrible disadvantage in our own time when heresy rises in our own church or denomination. False doctrine will seem to us to be only a new insight into the truth, and we will lose the benefit of the experience and struggle as well as the victory of our brethren from earlier centuries. We will be an easier prey for the enemy.

Knowledge of the past will give us knowledge to use in our own battles, give us assurance that Christ preserves his church against all the attacks of the enemy, provide us with skill in defending our faith, and make us joyful in knowing more fully its great truths as the Spirit of our ascended Christ has led the church to confess them.

May God be glorified through the story of the defense of his truth, and may the church be thereby strengthened in her calling.

HERMAN HANKO
Professor Emeritus
Theological School of the
Protestant Reformed Churches

INTRODUCTION

Throughout the history of the church of the Lord Jesus Christ, heretics have been present to trouble the church, to attempt to lead her astray, and to fight to destroy the church by robbing her of her dearest treasure and most important reason for existence.

The lives and teachings of these heretics are so closely interwoven in the life of the church that it is impossible to know anything about the church without knowing something of the heretics who periodically appeared and the false doctrines they proposed.

This book contains a series of biographical sketches of some of the church's most influential heretics; it describes the heresies they taught, and it gives some idea of what their role was in the larger picture of the history of the church. But before we actually get into the matter of writing about these heretics, it is well to say something about them in general and about the heresies they tried to pass on to the church.

A heresy is any teaching in the church of Christ that is contrary to Scripture and the doctrines established by creeds. The Greek word for "heresy" in the New Testament suggests that heresies create schism in the church. One attribute of the church is her unity; the unity of the church is the unity of the truth. Heresy destroys that unity.

The church has always made it her business to study the Scriptures. This studying has been done by all the members of the church, although especially by those who are in the offices of minister, elder, and deacon. The members of the church are, after all, though saints in Jesus Christ, also sinners as long as they are in this world. Sometimes in their study of Scripture they make mistakes in their understanding of God's word and begin to teach ideas that are not in harmony with Scripture.

There are several instances of such mistakes made by men in the past. Indeed, sometimes men taught wrong ideas that were even generally accepted in the church but that were proved wrong by later men of God who understood the Scriptures more perfectly. These mistakes are not really heresies.

An instance of this is Augustine's view of the sacraments. While Augustine was completely in harmony with Scripture in most of his teachings, especially when it came to his teachings on the doctrines of sovereign grace, he erred in viewing the sacrament of baptism as having itself the power of regeneration. This view was accepted by the church until the time of the Reformation.

But a heresy is different. One does not necessarily teach heresy when he sets forth a view born out of a less than full understanding of the truth. But once the church of which he is a part has shown a man that his view is wrong, that it is not in harmony with the teaching of Scripture, and that he should not, therefore, teach it—if he continues to teach it nonetheless, at that point he becomes a heretic.

Or if the church has already established a certain doctrine as being the teaching of Scripture, and if some man comes along and begins to teach something contrary to what the church has established as the truth of God's word, that man teaches heresy.

Heresy is, therefore, a teaching within the church of a doctrine contrary to what the church has officially declared to be the truth of the word of God.

It might be argued that this definition of heresy sets the declaration of the church above the word of God, but this conclusion is not true. The church is called to set forth the truth of the word of God against false doctrine, for only by doing this can the church successfully keep false doctrine from destroying the church. In fulfilling the calling to declare officially what Scripture teaches concerning the truth, the church is guided by the Spirit of Christ whom Christ promised to the church to lead her into all truth. While it is, of course, possible for a church at any given time to make a mistake in its declaration of what constitutes biblical truth, anyone at any time in the church—be he orthodox or heretic—has the right to challenge the church's decisions and call the church to compare a previous decision with Scripture. Heretics are especially bound to do this when they diverge from the church's teachings. Any decision of the church is subject to renewed study in the light of God's word.

How is it to be explained that heresy continually raises its head in the church?

If one would look at this question from the viewpoint of the man who himself teaches heresy, the question is somewhat difficult to answer. It is always possible for a man to make a mistake with respect to the truth and to teach something that is quite clearly wrong. Every man is sinful, and the imperfection of our natures makes heresy a distinct possibility. But when a man makes a mistake and the church points out that mistake to him, his obligation before God and the church is to confess that wrong, admit his error, and get clear in his own mind what the truth of Scripture is. This does not often happen. Man is too proud, as a general rule, to admit his wrong. He defends vigorously the error that he made, so that what was at first a mistake now becomes stubborn support of a wrong position. This happens repeatedly in the church.

Oftentimes men who are ministers of the gospel, professors in one of the church's schools or seminaries, or leaders in a certain area of the church's life deliberately begin to teach something that they know is wrong. They may do so in a very subtle way so that the heresy sounds as much like the truth as possible, but they make a conscious choice to teach something contrary to Scripture and the teachings of the church.

Why do they do this?

The reasons, I suppose, are legion. Perhaps they want to appear before men to be original theologians who come with new and amazing insights into the truth so that men will marvel at their intellectual prowess. Maybe they want to make a name for themselves as scholars whose masterful writings will appear in prestigious theological journals. Perhaps they simply want the preeminence within a congregation and choose to teach heresy as a way to gain a following.

But in every case, obviously, they consider themselves more important than the truth of God's word. They set themselves above the truth. The name, fame, reputation, and honor that they acquire for themselves are more important to them than God's truth and God's glory.

We must look at this matter of heresy from another point of view as well. Behind every heresy that lurks in the minds and hearts of men and that raises its ugly head in the church is Satan and his host of devils. They are the ones who sow the seeds of heresy and nourish these seeds until they become thorns and thistles in the life of the church.

Satan has his own reasons for bringing heresy into the church. He does so because he knows, better than men, that the surest and quickest way to destroy the church of Jesus Christ is through the introduction of heresy into her faith. The church is built on the foundation of the apostles and prophets, with Jesus Christ as the chief cornerstone (Eph. 2:20–22). That is, the truth, as it is centrally in Christ and as it is revealed through the apostles and prophets, is the foundation of the church. Take away the foundation, and the church collapses into a pile of rubble. The devil knows this.

Jesus referred to this idea when, in speaking of Peter's confession that Jesus was the Christ, the Son of the living God, he said that this confession was the rock on which he would build his church and that the gates of hell would not prevail against it. The gates of hell batter that rock on which the church stands, but the church cannot be overcome.

The struggle within the church between the truth and the lie, between heresy and the confession of the faith of Scripture, is never an intellectual battle only; it is profoundly and intensely a spiritual struggle. The very existence of the church is at stake. On the outcome rests the continued presence of the church in the world. It must never be forgotten that the devil will not consider himself to have accomplished his sordid purpose in this world until he has obliterated the church.

The church is the pillar and ground of the truth (1 Tim. 3:15). That is, the church proclaims loudly the truth found in the Holy Scriptures, for that truth is the truth of God. As long as the church is in the world, a sharp witness of God and Christ is present, and Satan considers the existence of the church as a dangerous threat to his purposes.

That the battle for the truth is a fight for the very existence of the church means also that the battle is spiritual. The greatest issues are always at stake. The eternal destinies of men are being decided, for in the confession and defense of the truth lies everlasting salvation, while in heresy and its promotion lie spiritual destruction and everlasting damnation. No battles in any war ever fought are as important as the battles fought in the defense of the faith on the battlefields of the church.

God is sovereign in everything and therefore no heresy can trouble the church without the will of God. Even Satan is under God's control and can do nothing without God's will.

Why does God so rule that heresy comes into the church, bringing with it all the pain and suffering that church struggles involve?

Although there are several answers to this question, we need only be brief, for the themes involved in this question are going to be the chief themes in the following chapters. The church throughout history has in it carnal and wicked seed. These come into the church from the outside, or they are in the church because even among the children of believers, not all that are of Israel are true Israel.

If they were permitted to continue to maintain their heresies with the church, they would so weaken the church that her position would become increasingly precarious. Heresy also forces the carnal element to reveal itself because it is forced to take a position in favor of heresy. If the church is faithful in repudiating heresy, the church undergoes purification and reformation. It may lose members—something distasteful to those who are not committed to the truth—but from struggle a stronger church emerges.

More importantly, it is always against heresy that the truth of the word of God is developed in a positive way.

There are, I think, two sides to this matter.

Generally speaking, the people of God are too spiritually lazy to be busy with developing the truth for its own sake. If no heresy ever appeared as a storm on the ecclesiastical horizon, the church would bask in the sunshine of peace and quiet, and the truth of God's word would go undeveloped. Heresy acts as a goad to push the church out of complacency and spiritual lethargy. When the truth is threatened, God uses the very threat of heresy to show his people that the existence of the church itself is in danger and that the church had better get to work to search the Scriptures so that the attacks of heresy may be fought off with the weapons of God's truth.

Christians are also called to live antithetically in the world. God has so ordained that their life in all respects is always a certain No to that which is wrong, and an emphatic Yes to that which is right. We cannot live any differently than that. We cannot serve God in any other way. When it comes to matters of the truth, we cannot say our Yes to the truth without first saying No to heresy. That is the way we serve God. It has been so ordained by God himself.

Therefore, heresy is always the spur to the development of the rich and glorious truth of Scripture. The weapons of spiritual warfare are not manufactured in the ivory towers of theological speculation; they are hammered out on hastily prepared forges set up right on the battlefield, where the din and noise of the conflict can be heard on every side.

All that the church is spurred on to do is through the power of the Spirit of truth, whom Christ promised and who leads the church into all truth. (See John 14, 15, and 16, which mention the Spirit of truth five times.) This Spirit works through the church in such a way that she defends the heritage of the church in the past, repudiates heresy, casts out heretics, and develops further the truth of the word of God.

To study the heretics is no virtue in itself. To study them with a view to seeing how in every case heresies resulted in a church stronger in the faith as it became more knowledgeable in the truth is to participate in an exciting and glorious endeavor.

Tolerance is the password in today's church world. Tolerance is stretched to the point where every heresy, ancient and modern, is allowed to remain in the church. The consequence is that the church slides rapidly backward into deeper and deeper apostasy. And tolerance or error very soon becomes intolerance of that church where the truth is truly confessed.

More importantly, the witness to the glory of God is stained until it is obliterated entirely and Christ removes that church from his candlestick (Rev. 2:5).

PART 1
ANCIENT PERIOD (100–476)

Contenders for the Faith and Historical Events		Promoters of Heresy
Death of apostle John c. 100	**100**	
		Marcion c. 110–c. 160
Tertullian c. 145–60–c. 220–40		
		Montanus c. 185–c. 254
		Origen c. 185–c. 254
		Sabellius birth and death unknown; excommunicated 220 and 260 or 261
	250	**Arius** c. 250–336
Partition of Roman Empire into west and east 285		
	300	
Reign of Constantine the Great over the Roman Empire 306–37		**Apollinaris** c. 310–c. 390
Edict of Milan officially tolerated Christianity in Roman Empire 313		
Council of Nicea 325		
	350	
Augustine 354–430		**Pelagius** c. 354–c. 420–40
		Cassianus c. 360–c. 435–48
Council of Constantinople 381		**Celestius** c. 380–c. 429
Synods of Hippo and Carthage approved canon of Scripture 393–94		
	400	**Nestorius** c. early 400s–c. 450
Sack of Rome 410		**Faustus** c. 410–c. 490
Nestorius chosen patriarch in Constantinople 428		
Council of Ephesus condemned Nestorianism and Pelagianism 431		
	450	
Council of Chalcedon 451		
Fall of Rome 476	**476**	

7

CHAPTER I

MARCION: FIRST BIBLE CRITIC

INTRODUCTION

The Scriptures are the word of God in which is found the truth of God as God makes himself known in Christ. Therefore, the Scriptures are the source of all the church knows of God and of his Christ. Take away the Scriptures, and the church has nothing. Rob the church of the Bible, and the church ceases to exist. All of the truth that was later to come under attack is found only in Scripture. No individual attack has to be made against any one doctrine if the Scriptures themselves are destroyed.

Marcion attempted to destroy Scripture, and he did it in much the same way that higher critics of Scripture still do it today. That is why I call Marcion the first Bible critic.

MARCION'S LIFE

Although the date of Marcion's birth is not known, it seems as if he was born shortly after the beginning of the second century. The apostle John had not been dead very long when Marcion entered the world, and Polycarp, the first martyr of the post-apostolic era and a friend of John, knew Marcion. Already in 139 Marcion was found in Rome spreading heresy.

Marcion was born in Sinope in the province of Pontus in Asia Minor, a city on the shores of the Black Sea. Proselytes from Pontus had been in Jerusalem on Pentecost, and converts may well have been responsible for bringing the gospel to this area. Marcion was born into a Christian family, for his father was a bishop (minister). Tertullian, a third-century church father, says that Marcion was a riverboat pilot.

Although almost nothing is known of his early life, there is some evidence that Marcion became a Christian only after long study, but that he was, soon after admission to the church, excommunicated by his father for teaching wrong doctrines. Apparently his father remained suspicious of him even when he later confessed his wrong, for his father refused him readmittance when he applied.

In about the year 139 Marcion went to Rome. There is some dispute among historians as to the precise order of events. Some say that he was refused admission to the church of Rome upon his arrival in Rome. Whether this refusal was because reports from Sinope had reached Rome or because Marcion was quick to promote his ideas in this city, it is impossible to tell. Others say that he was a member of the church for a while but was constantly the center of controversy and was excommunicated once again. They point to a story that Marcion gave the church in Rome 100,000 *sestertii* (Roman money) when he was admitted to membership, but the whole amount was returned to him when he was excommunicated.

Polycarp, who probably met Marcion while he was still in Asia Minor, called him "the first-born of Satan."[1] Indeed it was true that his heresies were deadly poison.

Marcion founded a church separate from the apostolic church and had considerable influence on many who flocked to him and joined his movement. In fact, his sect spread throughout the Mediterranean world as far east as Syria and Palestine. His church survived until the sixth century, a strong testimony to his influence.

Marcion was an extremely able man, skillful in presenting his ideas in the best possible light, charismatic in his influence on others, and a sufficiently profound thinker to construct something of a system of thought. But he was extremely bold and forward and was much like many today who think that they alone possess the truth. His views were so obviously contrary to the truth that none of the orthodox had any difficulty in detecting his heresy.

It must be remembered that the church was in her infancy and had, as a result, no systematic doctrine, no confessions, no body of truth to which to appeal in its defense of the faith. Not even the Apostolic Confession was in existence as yet. This lack may have been the reason that the orthodox of Marcion's day were more fearful of him and his influence on people than they were of those who persecuted the church.

MARCION'S HERESY

The heresy Marcion taught was an open and blatant attack on Holy Scripture. He took it upon himself to decide which books were to be included in Scripture and which were not. He concluded that the entire Old Testament and most of the New Testament that had not been written by Paul ought to be excluded. When he had finished with the New Testament, he had left only the epistles of Paul and a truncated gospel of Luke, which, he thought, had been written by Paul. In fact, Marcion did not even accept all the epistles of Paul as canonical because he denied the Pauline authorship of 1 and 2 Timothy and Titus.

Of course, there were reasons for his position. He had a certain "theology" that revealed his presuppositions, and on the basis of these, he rejected huge parts of God's word.

For one thing, Marcion held to some gnostic ideas.[2] But it was particularly his view of God that was corrupt. He believed that the God of the Old Testament and the God of the New Testament were two different and irreconcilable powers in the universe. The God of the Old Testament was the God of the law: harsh, critical, severe in judgment, and cruel in punishment. The God of the New Testament was the God of the gospel: kind, compassionate, loving, and merciful to those who do not measure up to his standards. Hence the God of the Old Testament was the author of suffering and misery in the world, while the God of the New Testament was the fountain of all that is good.

It is striking that in some modernistic circles a similar view of God is still taught and the Old Testament similarly rejected. But it is obvious that whether in the second century or in the twenty-first century, this view is an open attack on Scripture as the word of God.

THE CHURCH'S RESPONSE

God used the heresy of Marcion to prod the church into an extremely important aspect of her calling: to define carefully the doctrine of Scripture and to set down which books belong to the Bible and which books do not. Up to the time of Marcion, the church had not done this. The church's failure to do this was not neglect. There had been no need. The canon was only closed about four decades before Marcion when the apostle John completed the book of Revelation. Without a great deal of thought, the church had accepted the writings of the apostles as infallibly inspired.

Because the church had not defined the canon, some different opinions were held among the churches and saints on some relatively minor matters. Some held that other books were canonical, such as the epistles that Clement of Rome and Barnabas had written to various churches. Others questioned whether some books in the canon ought to be included.

This does not mean that the church had no idea of what the canon of

Scripture was. It is a testimony to Scripture's inspiration that from the beginning of her history, the church recognized that some books were inspired and others were not. The church had, of course, the Old Testament Scriptures, and prior to our Lord's earthly ministry, the Old Testament church had determined the Old Testament canon. Our Lord recognized this decision of the church by referring to those Scriptures as God's word (Matt. 11:13; Luke 16:16).

The history of the formation of the New Testament canon was briefly this. Almost as soon as the gospels were written, they were considered canonical and grouped together as such. Because the book of Acts carried on the history of the gospels, it too was considered canonical. When Paul's epistles were written, a *Corpus Paulorum* (Collection of Paul's Epistles) was soon circulated in the churches as writings inspired by God, and they were accepted as such by the whole church from the time they were written. Very early in the second century 1 John and 1 Peter were also accepted as canonical. Because the book of Revelation had been written by John, it was also received. But questions remained among some concerning a few other books. No one was sure who wrote the epistle to the Hebrews, and its canonicity was considered doubtful by some. The books of 2 Peter, 2 and 3 John, James, and Jude were not universally accepted, although the fact that they were not always mentioned in connection with the other books of the New Testament was because of the church's practice of including them with 1 Peter and 1 John. But since the canon of Scripture was not a source of controversy, no one gave much thought to disagreements on the matter.

Then came Marcion and his terrible heresies, and he launched his attack at a vulnerable point. It was as if through him God was saying to the church, "It is important that you study this question carefully and determine which books were inspired by me and which books were not."

A consensus quickly developed in the church on the disputed books. Marcion was condemned and his followers excommunicated. By the end of the second century, disagreement over the questions had ceased and all accepted the present canon.

In 352 Athanasius, bishop of the church in Alexandria, sent a pastoral letter to all the churches throughout the entire known world in connection with the date on which Easter was to be celebrated. In this letter he listed the sixty-six books of the canon, as we confess them today, to be the word of God. And in 393 and 397 the synods of Hippo and Carthage officially fixed the canon for the new dispensation.

Before the canon was finally fixed, the church had to settle a dispute over the criteria by which a book could be judged as canonical or non-canonical. For example, some thought that either an apostle or one closely connected to an apostle had to be an author for a book to be canonical. The canonicity of some books was questioned because the church was not certain that they had been written by apostles. But the church actually used the same criteria mentioned in the Belgic Confession of Faith, Article 5, namely, the objective testimony of the books themselves and the subjective testimony of the Holy Spirit in the hearts of his people. The former refers to the evidence the canonical books carry in themselves that they are inspired by the Spirit; the second criterion refers to the testimony of the Spirit of truth whom Christ promised to the church as the Spirit who would lead the church into all truth (John 14:17; John 15:26; John 16:13).

The objective testimony of Scripture itself was important. By this, the church meant that the Scriptures in every part *claim* to be authored by God. The proof for divine inspiration is not in only three or four texts, but is on every page of Holy Writ. That objective testimony of Scripture itself—the claim that Scripture makes for itself—is sealed on the hearts of those who believe by the Spirit of truth.

Since the eighteenth century, the higher critics of Scripture have followed in the footsteps of Marcion and have troubled the church with heresies similar to Marcion's. They, too, have their "theology" on the basis of which they pass their own judgments on Scripture. Their theology is a denial, to a greater or lesser degree, of the inspiration of sacred Scripture as the sole work of God the Holy Spirit and an insistence that Scripture, in whole or in part, is the word of man. This position is the direct development of their teaching that Scripture includes a human element alongside the divine. If Scripture is, in whole or in part, the word of man, then man can judge which part of Scripture he accepts and which part he rejects. That wicked men do this is not surprising. It is a sad but undeniable fact that higher critical views of Scripture have, more or less, infiltrated almost every seminary in the United States and abroad.

It was important for the church to establish which books were of God, because no possible development or defense of the truth could be made until this was done. God in his wisdom led the church to set the canon of Scripture first, for Scripture was to be the foundation of all the other truths the church would later confess. God's Scriptures are the rule of faith and life. God's word is the fountain from which all truth flows as a mighty stream. God also used Marcion's heresies as the occasion and the goad for the church's development of the truth concerning Scripture.

CHAPTER 2

GNOSTICISM: SYNTHESIS RELIGION

INTRODUCTION

There was a heresy in the early church so serious, so deadly, and yet so attractive that the church was engaged for many decades in a life or death struggle to overcome it. That heresy was known as gnosticism.

It was more like a movement than a departure from the truth on one specific point. It never resulted in a split of any significance in the church, nor were those who held this error of one united party. As a movement it could, perhaps, be compared with the "feminist movement" found in many denominations, which has its own theory about the place of women in society and which presses its own agenda. But one would never call "feminism" a separate church. So it was with gnosticism.

Early forms of gnostic teaching could be found in the apostolic church. It seems as if it was present especially in the churches of western Asia Minor. Paul warns against some early forms of gnosticism in his epistle to the Colossians, and the apostle John apparently had some early form of gnosticism in mind when he wrote his first epistle.

Gnostic teachings are difficult to understand and do not make much sense to our more modern minds. However, the deviltry that gnostics perpetrated is easy to understand. Gnosticism was interested in a religion of synthesis. That is, it vigorously promoted the idea that the one true religion takes the best elements out of Christianity, the old Judaism, Greek philosophy, and Oriental mystical religions and puts them all together into one system of belief that everyone is able to accept. While gnosticism is a very old heresy, it is also very new.[1]

VARIOUS GNOSTIC SECTS

Because gnosticism was a movement and not a heresy promoted by just one man or by a few men who worked together, the heresy also had many different proponents who differed widely from each other in their views. Their differences were so great that they represented different kinds of gnosticism. Those, for example, who emphasized Judaistic ideas were called Jewish gnostics; those who were more under the influence of pagan and Oriental religions were called pagan gnostics; and those who tended to stress the truths of Christianity were called Christian gnostics.

For this reason it is impossible in this sketch to offer biographies of all the leaders; as a matter of fact, not much is known of any of them.

Valentinus was perhaps the best known and most famous of all the gnostics. But even his birthplace and origin are lost in the murky past. What is known of him is learned from others and cannot, therefore, always be proved. But the following facts concerning his life seem to emerge.

He was an Egyptian and had been trained in Alexandria, Egypt's most important city. This in itself is significant, for Alexandria was, by virtue of its strategic location, one of the most important trading centers in the Mediterranean world. It was the place where East and West met and where trade routes from the Orient crossed the trade routes from the distant parts of the Roman Empire. It was a busy, bustling city, noisy with the babble of many languages spoken by its traders: a meeting place of different cultures, religions, and races and a bubbling cauldron of clashing ideas and philosophies. It was the one place where one would expect a heresy like gnosticism to emerge.

Jews were also present in Alexandria, and the LXX or Septuagint (the Greek translation of the Old Testament) had been prepared there before the birth of Christ. Christians were also present in the city in New Testament times, and the great Athanasius, the defender of the divinity of Jesus Christ, was bishop of the church there some 150 years after gnosticism had ceased to be a threat.

Valentinus went to Rome around 140 and stayed there until leaving for Cyprus in 165. Up to this point no one had had any reason to question his orthodoxy, but while in Cyprus he revealed his hatred of the church and became the leader of a heretical sect.

Valentinus was a man of great intellectual ability and vast oratorical powers. One story of an early church father says that his path to heresy was paved by disappointed ambition, for he had hoped to be chosen bishop of the church in Rome but had been passed over in favor of another.

Nothing more is known of him, and even these scraps are more than is known of most men who assumed leadership in the gnostic movement.

GNOSTICISM'S TEACHINGS

It is not possible, nor is it necessary, to give a complete sketch of the teachings of gnosticism in a short chapter. Nor would we be all that interested in these teachings, for they strike our ears as strange, esoteric, and hardly credible; we may very well wonder how it was that such a peculiar conglomeration of ideas could constitute a very real threat to the church. But such was the case.

In general, gnosticism was "a stealing of some Christian rags to cover heathen nakedness."[2] It taught that God was the great unknowable, a being more like the Mohammedan Allah than the triune God of the Scriptures. The gnostic God was cold, impersonal, pure being.

The great question of gnosticism was how the creation had come into existence. This was indeed a puzzling question, because gnosticism taught that the "matter" of which the creation was made was inherently evil, that is, was itself, in its essence, The Evil.

To explain this material world, gnosticism taught that from God proceeded a long chain of emanating "aeons" that themselves were divine creatures (sometimes identified with God's virtues), each proceeding from another, each weaker than its parent.

The church father Iranaeus, who fought fiercely against gnosticism, says in his description of what gnosticism believed that "the thirtieth and last of the aeons, wisdom, fell from the perfection of the pleroma [God] through an excess of passion, finally giving birth to a shapeless mass. And hence they declare material substance had its beginning from [wisdom's] ignorance and grief, and fear and bewilderment."[3]

The last aeon, therefore, was one "who, while powerful enough to create, was silly enough not to see that creation was wrong."[4] This aeon was sometimes called the "demiurge" and was identified either with the "Logos" of John 1 or the God of the Old Testament. This demiurge responsible for creation was, because of its own foolishness, imprisoned in the creation and needed redemption. In the entire creation, but especially in man, was this "spark" of divinity, which if freed would flow back to God to be eventually absorbed into the divine being.

How was this escape to be accomplished? The way was through *gnosis* —the Greek word for "knowledge"; hence the name gnosticism.

According to the gnostics, there are three kinds of people in this world: material people, who are beyond salvation; psychical people, who are capable of being saved although they lack the true gnosis; and spiritual people, who are the "inner circle" or the "elite." Those who possess true gnosis are therefore on the road to the liberation of the divine spark in them, which will fly heavenward to be absorbed into the being of God.

What role did Christ play in all this?

Obviously, Christ's human nature could not be real, said the gnostics, because that which is material is inherently evil, and Christ was sinless. And so Christ's human nature was only an illusion, a ghostlike wraith; it only seemed to be real. Out of gnosticism, then, rose docetism, a heresy that denies the reality of our Lord's human nature and an error perhaps referred to in 1 John 1:1–3.

But neither was Christ a redeemer. Most gnostics thought of him in terms of that divine spark, which having created the world through some misstep, became imprisoned in the world. This divine spark was to be found in all men and could and would be liberated through the mystery of gnosis.

This whole theory appealed to many people and laid its claim on the masses for many years. Gnosticism especially appealed to men with its seductive promise of a mysterious knowledge through which redemption would come, along with the use of ceremonies and rituals supposedly enabling men to open the door to heaven and union with God.

The secret knowledge that was the key to salvation involved the way of freeing the divine spark in man. It was thought that this liberation of the divine could come about only by a denial and suppression of the body. But how was one to suppress the body? That was the question. To that question two answers were given, depending on what form of gnosticism one adopted. One way was that of asceticism, a mortification of the body through denying it food and drink, making it suffer, and thus "crucifying the flesh." This idea was carried over into monasticism in the Romish church.

The other way, appealing to more adherents, was the way of giving one's body over completely and totally to an indulgence of all the lusts and pleasures of the flesh. The more such total licentiousness was practiced, the more the body was said to be denied. Therefore, some branches of gnosticism became wickedly evil. It was the ultimate expression of "Let us sin that grace may abound" (Rom. 6:1).

GNOSTICISM'S MAIN CHARACTERISTIC

If one is at all acquainted with ancient Greek philosophy, one can easily detect the remnants of it preserved and modified in the gnostic system. If one knows even a bit about the mysticism from India, China, and other parts of the Orient, one can see that such pagan religions influenced gnostic thinkers. Similarly, when one recognizes that a way gnostic leaders appealed to Christians was by preaching the teachings of Jesus, one can see that Christianity was intended to be a part of the gnostic system.

Gnosticism wanted a worldwide, eclectic religion to which everyone could agree and under the umbrella of which everyone could find a congenial religious shelter. It asked, "Why war over particulars and minute points when here is a religion that takes the best from every religion and makes one universal religion palatable to all?"

How could something like this appeal to so many in the church?

To answer this question, we ought to consider several things. Many if not most of the members of the church had come from heathenism and paganism and had not yet been fully taught in the Christian faith. Indeed, this was even true of some of the church fathers, who were reluctant to give up everything the philosophers had taught and that they had learned in the schools before their conversion. The inclination was to find good in all these things.

Gnosticism had some things about it that are always appealing to people, even members of the church. It spoke of a secret knowledge that one could attain and that would let one in on mysterious, esoteric things known only to a few: "inner circle" secrets. People are attracted to that sort of thing by virtue of its mysterious character.

Gnosticism also made skillful use of rituals and ceremonies, which always appeal to man's baser instincts because it is spiritually difficult to worship God "in spirit and in truth."

Gnosticism gave credence and support to the idea of tolerance in the area of religion. It taught that there is no need to insist on the unique character of the Christian faith since truth can be found in all religions, and it is possible to "get along" with many others whose faith differs from ours, for all have certain good points. In modern language it becomes a siren song that, although Arminianism may be defective theologically, it surely has this good that Calvinists lack: an enthusiasm and emphasis on holiness. That sort of a thing was appealing to the early church because it opened the door to the possibility of assuming a more tolerant position over against the culture of those early times. In this way it offered escape from persecution, which was the lot of the church.

One more appealing element in gnosticism, with its doctrine of aeons and its idea of salvation through the release in man of the divine spark, was that it was clearly pantheistic. That is, it taught that all is God and thus men, or at least the divine in man, are God. Pantheism, in all the ages in which it has been taught, including today's New Age movement, is a direct lie of the devil. This lie was first uttered in paradise and continues to be the lie by which Satan deceives many: "Ye shall be as God." Eve and a bit later Adam were deceived. Countless throngs today are deceived in a similar fashion.

The church had a fierce battle on its hands against gnosticism, and it took more than a century before the battle was won.

THE CHURCH'S RESPONSE

Why did God so govern in the affairs of men and saints that such an evil as gnosticism entered the church and threatened her very existence as the church of Christ? What was God's purpose? How did the church react and finally overcome the threat of gnosticism?

The first positive fruit of this great and terrible controversy in the church was this: the church was forced to give clear definition to her faith —to the truth that was her confession.

In the early life of the post-apostolic church, by virtue of the circumstances in which the church found herself, all the emphasis of her life fell upon the calling to live a holy and godly life that differed from the corruption of Roman civilization. All the emphasis fell on the need to live antithetically in the world, and all the thinking of the church was absorbed in this question: How does the Christianity that we have now embraced make our lives in every detail different from the wickedness of Roman culture? What is a Christian husband? May we be Roman soldiers after our conversion? How do we treat children? May we attend Roman shows? These and similar issues were on the top of the church's agenda.

Gnosticism, while certainly being an ethical system also, was primarily an intellectual system. One had to put on his thinking cap to understand the intricacies of its thought.

If Christianity was to defeat gnosticism on the battlefield of faith, it had to turn from ethical and moral questions to more basic questions involving the truth. What is the truth of God's word? What is the truth concerning God over against this cold and impersonal god of the gnostics? Who is Christ in distinction from this christ of the gnostics, whose human nature is only an illusion?

The Christian faith is exactly that: a *faith*, a system of doctrine, of doctrinal propositions that must be believed in order for a man to be saved. Faith is a unique way of life that is the necessary implication of what a Christian believes.

Gnosticism forced the church to begin thinking doctrinally. By doing this, the church came to realize that the only possible defense she had against gnosticism and the real claim that the Scriptures were making was *the unique character of the Christian faith.*

Gnosticism said that there is good in all religions. Gnosticism said that every religion is a way to God. Gnosticism said that the greatest religion unites all religions in some sort of spiritual hybrid under which all men can find a theological roof. Then the world will also be at peace.

But more and more it dawned on the church fathers who fought against gnosticism that the Christian religion was not like that. An absolute antithesis existed between the Christian faith and all other religions. Not only was the Christian faith the *only* true religion, but every other religion was totally false. If one believes the Christian religion, one will be saved because he believes the truth. If one believes anything else but the Christian faith, he will go to hell because he believes the lie. A mixture of lie and truth is the lie.

The reasons are clear why this vast and unbridgeable chasm exists between the Christian faith and all pagan thought and religion. Every pagan religion and every pagan philosophy is *man's invention.* It has its origin in man's sinful mind. It has in it no elements of truth, because there is no common grace to enlighten the wicked mind. It has no good about it, because there is no operation of the Logos of John 1 or of the Spirit operative in every man. Paganism is, in fact, the lie. It is the lie, not because wicked men who live far away from the gospel do not know about the truth and in their ignorance make mistakes, but because these men, thinking themselves to be wise and yet becoming fools, *change* the glory of the incorruptible God into images of their own imagination.

The Christian religion, on the other hand, has its origin in God—in God's mind and will. It is *revealed* and cannot be known apart from divine revelation. It is made known sovereignly by the Spirit in the hearts of God's elect because God hides his truth from the wise and prudent and reveals it unto babes, and this is his good pleasure. That truth, sovereignly made known, is the truth that saves.

The Christian is finally compelled, in faithfulness to God, to stand in the world and say, "What I believe is the only truth; what you believe is the lie. What I believe opens the doors of heaven; what you believe is from hell and carries its confessors into that dark place."

This takes a courage that few men have, but it is the courage of faith.

The Meaning of the Battle against Gnosticism

The battle that the church fought against gnosticism is never over in this life. Today we have the same thing. A Reformed body in the Netherlands shut down its mission work to the Jews because it is claimed that Judaism is an acceptable religion. Reformed ecumenical bodies openly approve of Buddhism, Hinduism, and pagan worship. "Reformed" teachers openly teach that God has provided many ways to himself, that each is entitled to his own way to God, and even that the way of the fetish worshiper may be better than the Christian way.

The New Age movement tells the world exactly what gnosticism said. That movement creeps into churches, seminaries, and Christian schools; weak and wishy-washy teachers, often scared half to death by the accusation of being intolerant, openly espouse New Age ideas.

There can be no question about it: to take the stand that the church took against gnosticism is to invite persecution. Let it be, then. Anything else is the destruction of the church. If you will, the salvation of the church lies in her intolerance—intolerance of all that is contrary to God's truth in Christ.

Our salvation lies in the truth of God's word.

CHAPTER 3

MONTANUS: FIRST CHARISMATIC

INTRODUCTION

Solomon told us in the book of Ecclesiastes that there is nothing new under the sun. How often has not modern history proved that to be true. It is so in the world; it is so in the church.

The charismatic movement is of recent origin, a phenomenon of the late twentieth century, and yet it is as old as the history of the new dispensation church. The evils of modern-day pentecostalism were found in the Montanist movement of the third century.

There is a kind of a pendulum that swings in the church from one extreme to the other. It swings between rationalism, which makes man's reason the final arbiter of truth, and mysticism, which makes feelings the final arbiter of truth. Both have in common that they abandon or add to the Scriptures as the sole authority of faith and life. The one puts reason in Scripture's place; the other puts feelings there.

Reason and feelings are opposed to each other, and this opposition makes the pendulum swing. Weary of the coldness of rationalism, the pendulum swings in the direction of mysticism; then, frightened at last by the quagmire of the shifting sands of mysticism, the pendulum swings wildly back toward rationalism. Both are reactions; both are wrong.

The great lesson to be learned by it all is simply *sola Scriptura,* the one great principle of the Reformation.

Montanism is the beginning of mysticism, the charismatic movement, and all revivalism. Yes, even revivalism, for it is not far removed from mysticism, and both share many common features, as we shall see.

MONTANUS AND HIS FOLLOWERS

Phrygia is located in central Asia Minor. In this general area a barbarian people, later known as the Galatians, settled. These people were the objects of the mission work of the church on Paul's first missionary journey. They were a volatile and excitable people, given to fanatical excesses, and some of these national traits remained after their conversion. Many strange heresies found in the early church arose in Phrygia. One of them was Montanism.

Montanus, after whom the heresy is named, was born a heathen and may have been a mutilated priest of the heathen goddess Cybele, whom the Galatians worshiped before their conversion. Around the middle of the second century, sometime between 150 and 170, Montanus was converted.

Soon after his conversion Montanus began to have some strange ideas about Christianity. He divided history into three periods. He was of the opinion that most of the Old Testament was the time of God the Father; that the first century in the new dispensation was the period of God the Son; and that with Montanus' birth and conversion, a new age dawned: the period of God the Holy Ghost.

Montanus' chief appeal to Scripture was to the lengthy discourse of Jesus to his disciples on the eve of his crucifixion, a discourse dealing chiefly with the Paraclete, the Spirit of truth whom Christ promised to send to the church. Montanus became convinced that perhaps he was the Paraclete, or if not the Paraclete, the inspired organ through whom the Paraclete spoke.

Usually the Paraclete—so Montanus claimed—spoke through him while he was in a trance or in a state of ecstasy, and what he (Montanus) spoke was infallible and had to be taken by men as from God.

Very soon he gained a following, and his influence spread rapidly. His views were adopted by many in the church, and because especially Rome and North Africa were affected by his teachings, the whole church was thrown into commotion, and his heresies became the occasion for the first synods to be held in the post-apostolic church.

I suppose that even then, Montanus' whole movement would not have attracted the attention that it did had it not been for the fact that Tertullian, one of the greatest of all the church fathers, joined the movement. This is always very difficult for me to understand, for Tertullian's writings are some of the most notable of all the church fathers, and his teachings on the Trinity were the clearest and most biblical of any writer prior to the Council of Nicea. Tertullian did more than any other single writer to shape the crucially important doctrine of God. Yet he joined the Montanist movement. It is a powerful lesson to us that the greatest of men in the church of Christ are prone to error and susceptible to false doctrine.

23

MONTANISM'S VIEWS

A vacuum is created in the church by some weakness in life or doctrine. Heresy rushes in to fill this vacuum.

So it was with Montanism. Before the sect arose, the church had enjoyed a long period of peace, of freedom from persecution, and of prosperity. The result was that the church had become in some measure very attached to this world; she possessed more material goods than had been the case since her beginning, was worldly-minded in her outlook, and lacked the spiritual characteristic of looking for the second return of Jesus Christ. She had accommodated herself to the world "for the long haul," so to speak. The result was moral laxity.

In addition to these characteristics, the balance of power was shifting in the church from the people of God functioning in the office of believers to an ordained clergy, an ecclesiastical priesthood that was to develop into the episcopal system of Roman Catholicism.

Against all these things Montanism reacted. It doesn't sound all that unfamiliar and does not strike one who knows the times in which we live as being excessively strange.

The chief characteristic of Montanism was, of course, its belief in continuous revelation. Ongoing revelation was accompanied by the special gifts of the Holy Spirit; the result was that miracles, too, became part of the proper exercises of those who possessed the Holy Spirit, even though prophecy was considered the main gift.

The Montanists believed that all those who are truly spiritual are endowed with these special gifts. No distinction was to be observed between clergy and laity, for men, women, and children alike were supposed to be prophets and prophetesses. Indeed, shortly after Montanus began his teachings in Phrygia, two women, Priscilla and Maximilla, left their husbands and homes to join Montanus and to become prophetesses in his group.

The prophecies given to the truly spiritual were usually given in ecstasies and trances, and Montanus described one who was in such a trance as a lyre or harp on which the Holy Spirit plays the melodious songs of heaven—a figure often used to this very day to describe the outpourings of those who claim to possess the gifts of prophecy.

While Montanism was intended to do away with the horrible sin of setting clergy above laity, it had its own levels of holiness. Only those who possessed the Spirit and could show the special gifts of the Spirit were the truly holy; the rest were looked down upon as "carnal."

This idea led the Montanists to another idea that has lingered through the centuries and that has had its own appeal: a "pure church." Montanists insisted that only the truly spiritual could belong to the church so that the church would be composed only of true believers. How often has it not been true that this notion of a church of true believers has dominated the thinking and life of the church? In fact, this very idea lies at the bottom of one tenet of Baptist thinking: believer's baptism. It is not surprising, therefore, that Montanism denied infant baptism and insisted on the baptism of believers only.

Such views of the church led, in turn, to a very rigid view of morality and discipline. The Montanists were, in their protest against worldliness and carnality, almost ascetic. They believed that in times of persecution believers ought actively to seek martyrdom. They had no sympathy for those who lapsed, that is, for those who under the pressure of persecution denied their faith but later repented and sought readmittance to the church. No lapsed member could ever again belong to the church here upon earth, said the Montanists. Tertullian went so far as to say that anyone who became guilty of any one of the seven deadly sins had forfeited all right ever to be a member of the church on earth.

Montanists viewed the institution of marriage with a great deal of suspicion. They were flatly opposed to remarriage, even when one's spouse died, and they generally considered marriage itself to be God's grudging consent to man's irresistible tendency to indulge in fleshly lusts.

In eating and drinking, in pleasures and dress, in demeanor and conduct, they were gloomy, sober, not given to anything that could be construed as the enjoyment of what belonged to this world. They were an unhappy lot who seem to have overlooked Paul's injunction, "Rejoice in the Lord alway" (Phil. 4:4). Gloominess and melancholy were the marks of true piety for them.

While the early church during the time of the apostles tended to believe that the Lord was coming within the lifetime of the saints then living (see Paul's epistles to the Thessalonians, for example), these hopes of Christ's imminent return tended to fade, and the church became increasingly aware that it was God's will that the church be on the earth for a great number of years. The loss of the hope of an imminent return of Christ soon left a mark of worldliness on the church. As Montanism rejected the worldliness of the church, it saw the church's salvation in a renewed emphasis on the immediate return of Christ. It became a sect that taught that Christ could come at any moment, and it attempted to persuade the church at large of the truth of this assertion.

Especially when persecution once again broke out under Antonius Pius, Montanism interpreted this persecution to mean that the final persecution had come and that the church was about to witness the return of Christ and the establishment of the millennium. It is strange that so often those two ideas seem to go hand in hand: special revelations from God and the imminent return of Christ, the date of which can be predicted.

Montanism's Significance

The ecstasies, trances, visions, and special revelations of Montanism were its chief characteristic. Nor were the Montanists able to keep this aspect of their teaching within reasonable bounds. Montanism was characterized by frenzied activities of those in trances, by extremely unusual and bizarre manifestations of the Spirit, by irrational behavior condoned on the basis of an appeal to the work of the Spirit, and by utterances in strange tongues and with strange noises that neither God nor man could understand. In a more modern period, the charismatic movement emphasizes the special gifts of the Spirit, and revivalism gives evidence of bizarre behavior as being manifestations of the Spirit's presence. The charismatic movement and revivalism show that they have much in common. To open oneself to revivalism is to cave in to the great evil of pentecostalism. The two came together in Montanism. Today's movements are no different.

Thus it is that Montanism, with its emphasis on special gifts, trances, and visions, was guilty of an excessive supernaturalism and an asceticism that deny the true character of the work of the Holy Spirit. Schaff is right when he says,

> The religious earnestness which animated it [Montanism] . . . and the fanatical extremes into which it ran, have since reappeared [in the church] under various names and forms, and in new combinations, in Novatianism, Donatism, . . . Anabaptism, . . . Puritanism, . . . Pietism, . . . by way of protest and wholesome reaction against various evils in the church.[1]

The antidote to all such error is the great Reformation principle *sola Scriptura*. This principle, so clearly and forcibly set down by Luther, means a number of things.

It means that the Holy Spirit, the author of all the life of the church, never works apart from the Scriptures. He binds himself to the Scriptures in all his work.

It means that the Spirit works in all of salvation by making known to the church the truth of Scripture, for he is the Spirit of truth. The truth of Scripture, though it has profound emotional overtones, is something appropriated by the intellect. The Spirit enlightens the mind so that it can understand ideas.

Only this can satisfy the child of God. A cold appeal to intellectualism is not enough, but an appeal to feeling is unsatisfactory also. God made man a whole being with mind and will, including the emotions. God saves the whole man. The pendulum of the Christian life hangs straight down, including both mind and will in the work of grace.

The Spirit works in such a way that the fruits of the Spirit are not speaking in tongues, healing, bizarre and unnatural behavior, or trances and visions; "The fruit of the Spirit is love, joy, peace, longsuffering, gentleness, goodness, faith, meekness, temperance: against such there is no law" (Gal. 5:22, 23).

The Spirit saves the church as the organism of the body of Christ. He saves believers and their children. All are part of the church. Because the lines of election and reprobation run through the lines of believers and their generations, there are always reprobate seed in the church: Esaus, bad fish in the net (Matt. 13:47–50), tares in the field (vv. 24–30).

The Spirit works in such a way that the believer, not knowing the time of the Lord's coming, walks always in the hope of that coming. That walk is the walk of a pilgrim and a stranger in the earth. It is the walk of one who knows that this world is not his home, but that the creation in which he lives is God's world, someday to be redeemed and given to the faithful, but now to be used to seek the kingdom of heaven and God's righteousness. The Spirit-filled believer is not one who flees the world, nor is he one who loves the world and makes this world his home. He is the heir of the world, but only in the kingdom of Christ.

CHAPTER 4

SABELLIUS: FIRST UNITARIAN

INTRODUCTION

The ways of God are always perfect and wise. Sometimes we are given a glimpse of this perfection and wisdom, and sometimes not. So it is in the development of the truth of Scripture through the ages. We are given such a glimpse into the wisdom of God's ways in the development of the doctrine of the Trinity. It was the first major doctrine of the Christian faith to be developed.

Once God shows us that the truth concerning himself is first, it is also evident to us why this had to be. That God is three in person and one in essence is the one great doctrine on which all other truth rests. Without establishing that doctrine near the beginning of her history, the church could not have gone on in the high calling of developing the other great truths of Scripture. The reason for this is very simple: all truth is the truth concerning God. What God is in himself, in his own divine being, is fundamental. What God does outside his own divine being is revelation of himself. The truth is always and only God's revelation of himself. So it was that God first led the church into a confession of the truth of the Trinity.

There is another aspect to this, however. The devil, probably better than we, recognizes the importance of the truth of God. It is not surprising that he attacked this truth first. If this truth about who God is could be destroyed, the church would not be the church of the living God, because the church would have no God to confess.

God is sovereign, also over the devil. God decreed that Satan should first launch a powerful attack against the truth of the Trinity and that the church, called to defend the truth, would develop it first.

The wisdom of God is also displayed in the fact that the truth of the Trinity took many years to develop and to be put in creedal form. It was not until the Council of Nicea in 325 that the doctrine of the Trinity was set down as the confession of the church. Even after this council, the battle continued for almost a century.

That it took so long to develop this doctrine is due to various important facts. One certainly was that the doctrine was difficult to understand. Maybe there is a wisdom even in this. God showed his church that the truth concerning himself was so great, so profound, so beyond all human comprehension, so utterly different from anything that could ever arise in the heart of man, that it took centuries before the church could even bring itself to say something about it.

Another reason the doctrine took so long to develop was because it was inseparably bound up with another doctrine: the absolute divinity of the Lord Jesus Christ. The doctrine of the Trinity and the doctrine of Christ's deity stand or fall together. Locked up in the doctrine of Christ's deity is our everlasting salvation. If we are saved, then it has to be that Christ is God. Only God can save. Thus Christ is our Savior.

THE PROBLEM

From the beginning of the new dispensational church, the saints never doubted that Christ was God. Some very early second-century writings prove this. Harnack says,

> The theology and christology of Athanasius are rooted in the thought of Redemption, and his views were not influenced by any subordinate considerations. Neither heathenism nor Judaism has brought men into fellowship with God, the point on which everything turns. It is through Christ that we are transported into this fellowship; He has come in order to make us divine, *i.e.,* to make us by adoption the sons of God and gods. But Christ would not have been able to bring us this blessing if He Himself had possessed it merely as a gift *secundum participationem,* for in this case He only had just as much as He needed Himself and so could not proceed to give away what was not His own. Therefore Christ must be of the substance of the Godhead and be one with it. Whoever denies that is not a Christian, but is either a heathen or a Jew. This is the fundamental thought which Athanasius constantly repeats.[1]

The problem arose from clear teaching of the gospel narratives that Christ ate, drank, suffered, and died. How could God eat and drink, suffer and die?

The gnostics solved the problem by saying that it was really impossible for God to eat and drink. So they proceeded to deny Christ's human nature and to teach that his human nature was only an appearance. He *seemed* to be human but really was not.

A prior question also troubled the church, a question still more funda-mental: What was the relation of the Son to the Father?

You must keep in mind that the church lived in a world in which poly-theism was the universal religion. The Greeks and Romans, and all nations everywhere, worshiped a whole temple full of gods—almost too many to be counted. The Christian religion insisted that all polytheism was wrong, blasphemously wrong. There is only one true God. All other gods are sim-ply idols, men's evil inventions, sinful corruptions of the truth.

The problem was that the church insisted that God was God alone. But Christ, the one who was sentenced by Pontius Pilate, who died in the year 33, and who arose from the grave—that Christ was also God! He was the Son of God, truly God. How could one avoid saying, after all, that the Christians had at least two gods?

The church's theologians proposed various solutions. One solution was that Christ was not the natural Son of God, but the *adopted* Son. The sta-tus of sonship was conferred on Christ either at his baptism or at his res-urrection. But this was unsatisfactory, for it denied that Christ was really God.

Another solution was that Christ was *derived from* the Father. In this view, the Father was greater than the Son, although great honor was as-cribed to the Son. Maybe he was a very high angel, maybe a spirit, maybe the Logos of which John speaks in the first chapter of his gospel narrative, or maybe just a son. But for all the greatness he possessed, he was still in-ferior to the Father. Maybe he was in some sense "divine," but his divin-ity was not the same as that of the Father.

Then a third solution was suggested. This one was really the gravest threat of all to the church in the third century. The theory suggested that Christ was *the same person as* the Father. There was really no difference be-tween the Son and the Father. Just the names given to God were different. Sometimes God was referred to as Father, sometimes as Son, and other times as Holy Spirit. The three names were only three different names for one God, three different ways to refer to him, three different ways of think-ing about the one and the same God.

A number of men in the early church held to this third solution. Al-though they disagreed on some minor points, they agreed that in order to distinguish Christianity from heathen polytheism, they had to maintain a rigid and strict monotheism at all costs. They could not sacrifice the truth that God is one God. They could not sacrifice the truth that God is one God for some heathen religion.

SABELLIUS' LIFE

Sabellius was the chief and best known proponent of this third solution, although he is not as well known as his heresy.

Many of these heretics were like meteors that flashed across the ecclesiastical heavens in one great burst of light—only to burn out in a short time, their graves unknown and their lives forgotten. So it was with Sabellius.

He was born in North Africa in the area of Pentapolis, probably in what is now Libya, but he did not stay there long. At the beginning of the third century, he was in Rome and had begun to ponder the mysteries of the Godhead. In fact, he was bold and brash enough to teach his views there, which brought him into conflict with Calistus, the bishop of Rome. Apparently Sabellius was not about to change his views, and he was excommunicated by Calistus in the year 220.

Sabellius ran into much the same troubles when he went to Egypt and began to propagate his views there. Dionysius, the bishop of Alexandria, called a council meeting of the churches in the city in 260 or 261, and this council excommunicated Sabellius.

One would think that two excommunications would have given the man pause, but the influence his views were beginning to have on others fed his pride.

Many in the church were not satisfied with the views of Sabellius. Dionysius, the bishop of Alexandria, fought strongly against Sabellius on the grounds that Sabellius made no distinction between God the Father and God the Son. In his criticism of Sabellius, however, Dionysius made such a deep distinction between Father and Son that he denied the essential unity of Father and Son and came close to teaching polytheism. In his distinction between Father and Son, Dionysius made Christ subordinate to the Father. Both were God; both claimed divinity; but the Son was inferior to the Father.

Sabellius saw in the overreaction of Dionysius an opportunity to get his views approved in Rome, which would have added enormous prestige to his heretical position. He appealed to the bishop of Rome against the views of Dionysius.

But his ploy did not work. The bishop of Rome called a synod in 262, the result of which was that Sabellius was condemned for his views, and Dionysius was condemned for teaching tritheism (three gods) and subordinationism (a Christ inferior to the Father). This decision in Rome effectively settled the controversy—at least for a few years.

31

To the credit of Dionysius, when his errors were pointed out by the bishop of Rome, he gladly retracted them.

SABELLIUS' TEACHINGS

The views of Sabellius, once referred to as Sabellianism, have become known as monarchianism.

While many heretics taught monarchianism, and while they differed somewhat from each other in certain emphases and peculiarities of their teachings, generally speaking they all insisted that there was only one God. They clung tenaciously to monotheism, but they insisted that the only way to protect the view that God is one is to deny any kind of "personal" distinction between Father, Son, and Holy Spirit.

I put the word *personal* in quotes because at this stage of the church's development, the theologians possessed no vocabulary to define the doctrine in the way we do today. Indeed, this was part of the problem, because Scripture itself gives us no vocabulary to use in connection with the doctrine of God. We say God is one in essence and three in person, but the early church had no biblical idea of the concepts "essence" and "person" and never thought to use these terms in connection with the doctrine of God.

Sabellius explained the names Father, Son, and Holy Spirit in Scripture as different "ways" or "modes" in which God revealed himself. He said that the one God, also one in person, revealed himself as a Father, as a Son, and as a Spirit. God revealed himself as a Father in the work of creation, as a Son in the work of redemption, and as a Spirit in the work of sanctification in our hearts. Thus Sabellius denied the Trinity.

THE CHURCH'S RESPONSE

Most in the church correctly confessed that the Father is God, the Son is God, and the Holy Spirit is God. Most also confessed that there is only one true God. But how to explain such seemingly contradictory ideas was beyond them.

The church knew that the views of Sabellius were wrong and with good reason, therefore, disciplined Sabellius wherever he attempted to propagate his views.

Although the church knew what was wrong, it did not know what was right. It was prepared to say to Sabellius and his henchmen, "You teach what is contrary to the Scriptures." It was not prepared to say, "The Scriptures teach this and this." Generally speaking, the church at this early day, did not know what the truth of Scripture was on the doctrine of God, although the western church understood the truth more clearly than did the eastern church. The bishop of Rome in the West understood exactly the error of Sabellius, while the bishop of Alexandria in the East strayed into other errors in his fear of Sabellianism.

What the West saw more clearly than the East could not be easily shared with the East because of the language barrier: the West wrote and talked in Latin, the East in Greek. The East did not know what the West was thinking and doing for the most part, although the West was more informed about the East because Greek was more common throughout the Mediterranean world than Latin.

The advanced ideas of the West on the doctrine of the Trinity were due, in large measure, to the work of Tertullian, who a century before Nicea came very close to defining what was to become the doctrine of the Trinity, and gave to the church a vocabulary that included the words *Trinity, person,* and *essence.* In fact, Tertullian was the first to define the error of Sabellius in a graphic and unforgettable way. Tertullian accused Praxeas, one of the monarchians, of driving away the Holy Spirit and crucifying the Father.[2]

These were all preliminary skirmishes in the great battles that were yet to be fought before the issues were settled. But they would have to be settled, because the doctrine of God is the basis of all truth.

The doctrine of the Trinity is not the abstract, difficult, icy cold doctrine of theologians. To mention only a few instances of how important the doctrine is, we must remember that the whole doctrine of the covenant rests upon the Trinity and the triune covenant life that God lives in himself. The absolute divinity of Christ rests on the truth of the Trinity, and on that doctrine of Christ's divinity rests all our salvation. The divinity of the Holy Spirit is the rock on which is to be built the whole blessed concept of our union with Christ—and union with God himself through Christ.

The condemnation of Sabellius could not be and was not the end of the struggle. It could only be settled by the church's answer to another heretic, Arius, whose teaching was the immediate occasion for the formulation of the Nicene Creed.

CHAPTER 5

ARIUS AND THE COUNCIL OF NICEA

INTRODUCTION

"I believe in . . . one LORD Jesus Christ . . . begotten of the Father before all worlds [God of God], Light of Light, very God of very God, begotten, not made, being of one substance [essence] with the Father."[1]

So read the lofty cadences of the first creed adopted by the church of the Lord Jesus Christ: the Nicene Creed. It sounds so familiar, yet it was born out of a fierce and bitter struggle that nearly tore the church to pieces.

God always leads his church to a knowledge of the truth by way of controversy. So it was also in the latter part of the third and the first part of the fourth centuries. And the controversy, lasting over fifty years, was fierce and bitter.

There were many complicating factors.

The church had no agreed-upon vocabulary to express the truth, and Scripture does not give such a vocabulary. This lack of a vocabulary confused and complicated the problem, especially because sometimes heretics would confiscate for their own use terms that the orthodox could have used and wanted to use. Another complicating factor was that heretics, attempting to solve the matter of Christ's divinity, were everywhere spouting their views and gaining a following. The church was thus troubled by many different doctrines.

One of the most influential heretics was Origen (c. 185–254). He was a strange man. When he was still a boy, his mother had to hide his clothes, because when his father was taken away to be killed for his faith, Origen wanted to be a part of this martyrdom and could be kept in the house only because he was too modest to appear naked in the streets. When he became a young adult, he mutilated himself, thinking that in this way he would be obedient to Christ and would become a eunuch for the kingdom's sake.

Origen was extremely brilliant and far ahead of his times in his theology. Though brilliant, he was also erratic, and many of the heresies that appeared in later years in the church can be traced back to him.

Origen had a direct role to play in the controversy that surrounded the heretic Arius. Origen was a man to whom both the orthodox and the heretics appealed—each with some justification. The orthodox appealed to him because he taught the absolute divinity of Jesus Christ and insisted that Christ was very God. The heretics, including Arius, appealed to him because he said that Christ's generation by the Father, though eternal, was an act of God's will. This was a serious error, because obviously this made Christ less than the Father. If Christ was begotten by an act of the Father's will, then Christ's will, according to his divine nature, could not be the same will as the Father's. Thus God and Christ would not be the same in essence, a view that is a denial of the unity of God.

Another factor in the troubles that plagued the church, though not directly related to the doctrinal aspect of the controversy, was jealousy and competition between the two major seminaries in the eastern part of the church. In the course of the years, two seminaries had been established in the Greek-speaking church: one in Alexandria and the other in Antioch. Alexandria was in Egypt; Antioch was in Syria, the city from which Paul and Barnabas had been sent in their first missionary journey. Both were prestigious schools, Alexandria because of its important position in the empire and Antioch because of the prestige of its teachers.

It may seem somewhat surprising, but probably Alexandria was the more orthodox of the two. This was not true, however, when it came to biblical interpretation. Alexandria used the allegorical method of biblical interpretation, which gives direct spiritual meaning to every part of Scripture and treats Scripture as if it were composed of countless allegories. Antioch, on the other hand, was much more sober; in fact, the method of interpretation still used today in seminaries where correct principles of hermeneutics are taught was developed early in Antioch.

When it came to the doctrine of Christ, however, Alexandria was much nearer Scripture than Antioch. This was partly because the outstanding theologian of Antioch, Lucian, was a believer in a form of Sabellianism.

This jealousy between the two seminaries not only played an important role in the controversy that would swirl about the person of Arius, but it also was a jealousy that was to affect the church in her struggles for another two hundred years.

Against the background of all this confusion, the Arian controversy began, and in the very center of it was the man for whom this heresy is named: Arius.

ARIUS' LIFE

The birthplace of Arius is unknown, although it is thought to be the province of Libya in North Africa, to the west of Egypt. Arius appears the first time on the stage of history as a member of the church in Alexandria of Egypt. The bishop of this church was Alexander, a firm and unwavering defender of the doctrine of the divinity of Christ.

Even though Arius appeared first in Egypt and in the church of Alexander, there is much evidence to suggest that he was under the influence of Lucian from Antioch—so much so that if it had not been for Lucian's teachings, Arius would never have thought of his heresies.

Arius was a tall, very thin man with a look of deep asceticism. He was not a profound thinker, although he was learned and eloquent, charismatic in speech and in personal relationships. He was also proud and artful, restless and disputatious, and not above devious dealings to attain his ends.

His more distasteful characteristics were not widely known when he was ordained a deacon in about 311 and when he arose to the position of presbyter (elder) in 313.

Arius' views came to light when he was attending a class for presbyters, bishops, deacons, and interested laity. Alexander conducted the class and was speaking at length on, and emphasizing as strongly as possible, the divinity of our Lord Jesus Christ. Suddenly, in the midst of the discourse, Arius interrupted his bishop and began to charge him with heresy. In support of this challenge, Arius stated his own views. With an obvious reference to Origen, Arius said that because Christ was son, he was begotten; because he was begotten, he had a father; because a begetting father is before a begotten son, so God was before Christ; because God was before Christ, Christ could not possibly be equal with God the Father; and because Christ was not equal with God the Father, he was less than the Father.

This heresy could not be tolerated, and Alexander called a synod of Alexandrian and Libyan bishops to consider the matter and deal with it. One hundred bishops came together and in 321 condemned Arius' teaching, deposed him from office, and excommunicated him.

As is so often the case with heretics, Arius paid no attention to this discipline by the church but continued to meet with his followers and supporters and to teach at worship services and religious assemblies.

This conduct could not be tolerated either, and so, in keeping with practices in those days, Arius was driven from Alexandria, and a circular letter was sent to all the bishops in the empire warning them to beware of the teachings of this heretic.

In spite of these warnings, Arius moved to Palestine and Nicomedia in Asia Minor, where he taught his views widely and gained a considerable following, including some of the most influential bishops in that part of the world. Arius even incorporated his views into a memorable prose-poem called "The Banquet," parts of which are still extant in the writings of others who quoted him.

All of this turned the church, especially in the East, into an ecclesiastical battlefield. Bishops were set against bishops, churches against churches, and people against people. And in the middle of it all stood the proud Arius, oblivious to the horror of a divided church, intent on having his own way.

His errors became increasingly clear as he wrote in defense of his position. He did not deny the divinity of Christ as such, and he was prepared to admit that Christ was in fact divine. But he also insisted that Christ was not eternal, that he was created, and that therefore there was a time when Christ was not. Arius was prepared to say many nice things about Christ: he was higher than all creatures; he was before time and existed long before the worlds were created; he was divine in a way in which no other creature was divine, the greatest of all under God. But he was not God; he was a creature. He was less than the Father and subordinate to him. Arius was a dreadful heretic.

Into all this stepped the Emperor Constantine.

Constantine had come to the throne of the Roman Empire at the beginning of the fourth century. He was supposed to have seen a sign of the cross in the sky just before the crucial battle that gave him the emperor's throne in the West. The cross was supposed to have inscribed on it the words *In hoc signo vinces* ("In this sign conquer"). Constantine interpreted that sign to mean that Christianity would conquer and that he would do well to become a Christian. This he did, although most probably in name only, for even after his "conversion" he committed some atrocious crimes.

But we are not writing about Constantine. Whether the man was a Christian or not, he brought persecution of Christians to an end, formally accepted the Christian religion, and proceeded not only to give Christianity his approval but also to promote it in various ways.

Constantine touches on our narrative because the colossal controversy launched by Arius was a bitter disappointment to Constantine. There is reason to believe that his adoption of Christianity was for political purposes, one of which was to bring unity and some moral energy to a divided, morally bankrupt, and decadent empire. Relying heavily upon Christianity as a political and unifying force in the empire, he now discovered to his astonishment and dismay that even the Christians could not get along but were fighting fiercely and locked in controversies that threatened to tear the church apart, and with it the whole fabric of society. His last hope for a united empire was fading. What a disappointment these squabbling Christians were to the emperor! What could be done?

Constantine showed his failure to understand Christianity by attempting to heal the rift by diplomacy. If he had known about ecclesiastical affairs, he would have known that church controversies are not settled by diplomacy or political involvement, and that, in fact, such interference would only make matters worse. He finally realized the hopelessness of treating church matters as if they were matters of state.

THE CALLING OF THE COUNCIL OF NICEA

Constantine saw a ray of hope in calling a council of the entire church to discuss and settle an issue that seemed to him to be much ado about nothing, or as Constantine himself put it, a debate over unanswerable and unsolvable riddles.

He summoned the bishops of the church together in the small town of Nicea in northwestern Asia Minor, about twenty miles from Nicomedia, the seat of the royal residence. Each bishop was instructed to take along two presbyters and three servants. All expenses were to be paid out of the imperial treasury, and transportation would be provided by the emperor so that the bishops could come from every part of the Mediterranean world.

Three hundred and eighteen bishops came together, which was one-third of the total number of bishops in the church. If one would count all the office bearers present at Nicea, the total number of delegates was between fifteen hundred and two thousand. Most of them were from the eastern or Greek church. The western or Latin church sent only seven delegates, although their influence was far greater than their number.

The council met from around June 14 to July 25, 325.

Many bishops took the opportunity to bring to the emperor's attention their own personal grievances and problems, but the emperor was not interested. He burned all their papers in one huge bonfire and exhorted them instead to unity. The attention of the bishops was thus concentrated on the matter at hand.

THE COUNCIL MEETING

One delegate described the opening ceremonies in this way:

> After all the bishops had entered the central building of the royal palace, on the sides of which very many seats were prepared, each took his place with becoming modesty, and silently awaited the arrival of the emperor. The court officers entered one after another, though only such as professed faith in Christ. The moment the approach of the emperor was announced by a given signal, they all rose from their seats, and the emperor appeared like a heavenly messenger of God, covered with gold and gems, a glorious presence, very tall and slender, full of beauty, strength, and majesty. With this external adornment he united the spiritual ornament of the fear of God, modesty, and humility, which could be seen in his downcast eyes, his blushing face, the motion of his body, and his walk. When he reached the golden throne prepared for him, he stopped, and sat not down until the bishops gave him the sign. And after him they all resumed their seats.[2]

Among the many delegates were some worthy enough to have attention called to them. Perhaps the most notable of all, apart from the emperor, was Alexander from Alexandria, the bishop who had first opposed Arius. With him came his deacon, a man by the name of Athanasius. Although at this time only a deacon and a young man, Athanasius made such careful arguments on the floor of the council that he had more influence on the formation of the creed than any other delegation. And Athanasius, in the years following the council, became the man whose name was synonymous with Nicene orthodoxy.

Some delegates present still bore in their bodies the marks of the cruel persecution that the church endured under Diocletian. Polamon had had his right eye dug out. Paul of Neo-Caesarea had been tortured with red-hot irons and had been crippled in both hands.

Some were ascetics. Jacob of Nisibis had spent years and years living in forests and caves, eating roots and leaves like a wild animal. Spyridion, although ordained as a bishop, had never abandoned the life of a simple shepherd, even while attending to preaching and the needs of his congregation.

At the outset of the council, the delegates were divided into three groups. The orthodox group, numbering less than a dozen and led by Alexander and Athanasius, was undoubtedly the most able. The Arians, who were devoted to Arius their leader, numbered only about twenty. The middle party was the largest group, but it was split into numerous factions. The group was finally persuaded to support the orthodox position.

After preliminary maneuverings, a creed was presented for consideration that represented the Arian position and attempted to get the assembly to approve the heresy of Arius. This creed was shouted down with raucous shouts and torn to pieces. Assemblies were somewhat more volatile in those days than they are now.

This paved the way for the presentation of another creed, which was in all respects sound and which most of the delegates were willing to sign. The difficulty with it was that it lacked one word that the orthodox wanted incorporated. Transliterated from the Greek, it is *homo-ousion* and means "of the same essence." It was an important word, and it became yet more important in the years after Nicea. It expresses the idea that the Lord Jesus Christ is "of the same essence" as the Father, that is, that he and the Father are one in essence.

The word might have been excluded from the creed altogether if it had not been for the fact that Arius expressed himself as willing to sign the creed without the word. This readiness of Arius to sign the creed made the orthodox suspicious, and they fought long and hard to get it included in the creed. They finally succeeded.

And so we have the beloved Nicene Creed.

The pertinent part originally read as follows:

> I believe in . . . one Lord Jesus Christ, the only-begotten . . . of the Father before all worlds [God of God], Light of Light, very God of very God, begotten, not made, being of one substance [*homo-ousion*] with the Father.[3]

Almost all present signed the creed, especially when the emperor announced that any who refused to sign it would be banished. Finally only two Egyptian bishops, plus Arius himself, refused to sign. They were banished to Illyria, and the books of Arius were burned. This was by direct order of the emperor, who now had set a precedent for imperial involvement in all matters of the church.

THE HISTORY AFTER NICEA

If the emperor or anyone else thought that the decisions of the council would settle the matter, they were sadly mistaken. The controversy continued with renewed bitterness shortly after the bishops returned to their churches, and fighting continued without letup.

The issues became more complicated, and we need not go into them in detail here. They revolved chiefly around the one word the council had insisted on: *homo-ousion.*

The strict Arians had insisted on the word *hetero-ousion,* which means "of a different essence," but their numbers were almost zero after the council. A new party arose that wanted to use another word than Nicea had used, although not the *hetero-ousion* of the Arians. It was the word *homoi-ousion*. The only difference between this word and the word Nicea had used is a small letter "i." It is not much of an exaggeration to say that the more than fifty years of terrible struggle that followed were over the question of the "i." Many might be inclined to say, as Constantine often said, "This is evil wrangling over unimportant differences." But it was not. The "i" made all the difference in the world: *homoi-ousion* means that Christ was only "like" the Father in essence; "similar to," but not "the same as." On that "i" hung the whole truth concerning our Savior.

The reasons the controversy continued were many. Many who signed the Nicene Creed had done so because they feared banishment, though they were not convinced of its truth. Many of the issues that Nicea had attempted to settle were not yet clearly defined in the minds of some bishops. Many enemies of the truth were still roaming the sheepfold of Christ as ravening wolves. And Constantine himself, unable to understand the issues, was not the firm and dauntless defender of Nicea that he should have been.

Constantine's own ambivalence paved the way for Arius to return from exile. He was recalled because he had presented a creed to the emperor that the emperor approved. In fact, Arius even signed the Nicene Creed, most probably with some sort of mental reservations, or perhaps while giving in his own mind a meaning to the creed acceptable to him that the creed itself would not bear.

The emperor forced the churches to receive Arius back. Athanasius, now bishop because of the death of Alexander, flatly refused to do so on the grounds that another synod was the only body able to lift the ban imposed on Arius. It was, said Athanasius, an ecclesiastical matter, not an imperial decision. The bishop of Constantinople was forced to admit Arius to the table of the Lord against his better judgment. But God saved the table from being profaned when Arius died in 336, one day before the Lord's supper was to be administered.

Athanasius, for his strong defense of Nicea, was banished from his church no less than five different times. He suffered much for the cause of the truth. In fact, it seemed at times as if Arianism was sure to gain the victory after all. "The whole world," said Athanasius, "has gone Arian," and he was not far from wrong. In fact, this remark of his was the occasion for history to give Athanasius the honorable name *Athanasius contra mundum* (Athanasius against the world).

So bitter was the battle that even the lowliest fishmonger in the marketplace and the chimney sweep in his sooty clothing could discuss intelligently the issues involved.

Orthodoxy did finally win. God often works that way. When the night is the darkest, then the dawn is about to break. God must show that the preservation of his church is his work, not man's. And God saves his church when, from a human point of view, all is hopeless. So it happened in the second half of the fourth century.

A new generation of theologians arose in the East, able men, committed thoroughly to Nicene orthodoxy. They defined the issues with clarity and biblical discretion. The West, always orthodox, began to exert more influence on the East, especially through such men as Augustine. The horrible notions of Arianism had reached their high tide and were beginning to wane.

Another council, the second great ecumenical council, met in 381 in the eastern capital of the empire: Constantinople. It reaffirmed Nicene orthodoxy and made some changes in the Nicene Creed that particularly affirmed the divinity of the Holy Spirit. The Nicene Creed had, in connection with the Holy Spirit, said only, "I believe in the Holy Ghost." Constantinople stated it like this: "And [I believe] in the Holy Ghost, the Lord and Giver of Life; who proceedeth from the Father . . . ; who with the Father and the Son together is worshiped and glorified; who spake by the Prophets."[4] In 589 at a synod in Toledo, Spain, the words *and the Son* were added after *proceedeth from the Father.*

So the truth of the absolute divinity of Christ and the doctrine of the holy Trinity was established as the foundation of all the confessions of the church.

CONCLUSION

One striking and extremely important aspect of the controversy was the fact that Athanasius, in his defense of the divinity of Christ at the Council of Nicea, had consistently argued his point on the grounds that the question involved *salvation.* He never permitted himself or the council to discuss the question as abstract theology but insisted that it had to do with the salvation of the church.

Athanasius' argument, in brief, was this: Our lost condition makes salvation impossible for us to accomplish. Only God can save. And because salvation comes to us through Jesus Christ, Christ must himself be very

God. This insistence of Athanasius on looking at the divinity of Christ as related to our salvation is reflected in the Nicene Creed:

> I believe in...one Lord JESUS CHRIST...who, for us men and for our salvation, came down from heaven, and was incarnate by the Holy Ghost of the Virgin Mary, and was made man; and was crucified also for us under Pontius Pilate; he suffered and was buried; and the third day he rose again, according to the Scriptures; and ascended into heaven, and sitteth on the right hand of the Father; and he shall come again, with glory, to judge both the quick and the dead; whose kingdom shall have no end.[5]

How important is this biblical approach, for the divinity of Christ is connected directly with our salvation, something already evident in Christ's name given to him by the angel: "Thou shalt call his name JESUS [Jehovah saves]: for he shall save his people from their sins" (Matt. 1:21).

When the eastern church, some years later, failed to follow the example of Athanasius and argued over the questions of Christ's divinity apart from the question of salvation, it fell into barren and fruitless speculative argumentation and spawned every heresy under the face of the heavens. For that sin the judgment of God came upon the eastern church, a judgment that all but destroyed it in the Mohammedan conquests.

Christ himself had affirmed that he would build his church on the foundation of the confession of Peter: "Thou art the Christ, the Son of the living God" (Matt. 16:16). In this way salvation as a work of God alone is maintained. Athanasius stood for sovereign grace.

Arminianism, a heresy of the seventeenth century, makes salvation partly the work of man. Let it never be forgotten that Arminianism is incipient modernism and leads churches back to Arianism. Denying that salvation is of God alone, Arminianism will ultimately deny that Jesus Christ is the eternal Son of God, very God of very God.

The apostle John warns us to beware of those spirits that do not confess that Jesus Christ has come into the flesh, for the spirit that denies this truth is of antichrist—not of Christ (1 John 4:1–3).

Salvation is of God!

CHAPTER 6

APOLLINARIS AND THE DOCTRINE OF CHRIST

INTRODUCTION

After a long and bitter struggle in the early Christian church over the heresy of Arianism, the truth of the absolute divinity of Jesus Christ had been established. That truth had been established and incorporated into a creed of the church by the Council of Nicea, which met under the auspices of the Emperor Constantine the Great in the year 325. The doctrine had been reaffirmed by the Council of Constantinople in 381. From that time it has been confessed by the church of Christ in every age, even though throughout the centuries others have denied it.

But these decisions did not mean that the controversies over the truth of Christ were at an end. Although the church had declared as scriptural that the Lord Jesus Christ was divine, very God of very God, nothing had been said about the fact that he was also like us in all things, except for our sin.

The church was forced to face specific questions involving the doctrine of Christ. How was our Lord like us? It could hardly be denied that the Scriptures describe Christ as one who was born just as we are; he ate, drank, grew, walked the roads of Palestine, talked with many, and did the same things we do. How could that be when he was very really God?

Further, the church emphatically agreed that the divine nature could not suffer, and yet our Lord, who was God, suffered. How was that possible?

The questions did not end here. Perhaps more importantly, all knew that only God can save us from our sins, and that salvation by the power of one who was truly God was obviously sound doctrine. But the church had also a clear understanding of what the Heidelberg Catechism later set down as truth: he who saves us from our sins must be truly man, for "God will not punish, in any other creature, that of which man has made himself guilty."[1]

It was, of course, easy to answer these questions by simply saying that Jesus Christ was both God and man, which in itself is true. But the fact remains that such a statement could not be satisfactory, for one must still find some answers to the burning question, How could one person be both God and man at the same time? And in what way was Christ God, and in what way was he a man? These questions were difficult, and the church did not immediately see how they could be answered.

Other questions arose as well, questions that had to do chiefly with the worship of the church. How was Christ present in the Lord's supper? Was he present as divine, or was he present as a human? When the saints partook of the Lord's supper, did they partake of Christ's divinity, and/or of his humanity?

Another question involved the worship of Christ. If Christ is divine, and he is, surely we must worship him. But if he is human, may we nevertheless worship him, considering that it is wrong to worship a man?

By this time in history, many monks were present in the church. They had a special knack for complicating things. The monks in Egypt especially, where the idea of asceticism arose in the first place, developed a rather elaborate doctrine of Mary. Perhaps because they themselves had taken vows of celibacy, they gave much attention to Mary, the mother of the Lord, and said many great and wonderful things about her. In fact, the whole Romish doctrine of Mariology really arose among the monks in Egypt.

In their veneration of Mary, they exalted her and applied a term to her that gave her honor. The term was the Greek *theotokos,* which literally means "mother of God." While it is not now the time to go into the term and its proper or improper use, the fact is that this term was to cause almost endless grief in the church for more than one hundred years. Monks had a way of doing that.

The term *theotokos* added confusion to an already confusing situation. If Mary was the "mother of God," was she also the mother of a man?—the man Jesus? If so, how could she be the mother of both at the same time?

All these questions simply came down to one great question: How could our Lord Jesus Christ be at the same time both God and man?

These questions triggered the great Christological controversies of the fourth and fifth centuries, which were finally settled in creedal form by the Symbol of Chalcedon in 451.

This chapter on Apollinaris is only one chapter in the long and involved story. It does not bring us to the final answer of the church, but it is the story of one man's solution to the problem and the story of the church's rejection of that solution as an answer insufficient and inadequate to do justice to all that Scripture says concerning our Savior.

GOD'S GREATER WISDOM

I must mention one other aspect of the controversy. It is an aspect not of just this controversy, but of all the controversies that followed. It has to do with what strikes me as an amazing display of God's wisdom.

While heresy in the church was to be explained as Satan's way of destroying the truth and the church, which needs the truth to survive, at the same time God used heresy to goad the church to develop the truth. A striking demonstration of this is found in these controversies over the doctrine of Christ.

The truth that the church has confessed concerning the Lord Jesus Christ since the time of Chalcedon is this: he united the divine nature and the human nature in his one person, the person of the Son of God. Therefore, he was personally the eternal Son of God, the second person of the holy Trinity. He united in his one person the whole of the divine nature, so that he is indeed, as Nicea confessed, very God of very God, and he had a complete human nature, so that he was like us in all respects, except for sin.

Before this truth was confessed and set down by the Council of Chalcedon, it was preceded by every possible heresy that one could imagine. One gnostic heretic taught that the humanity of Christ was not real but had only ghostlike characteristics. Another said that Christ had one person, a divine person, and had only one nature, a kind of mixture of divine and human, making him a sort of God-man. Another said that Christ possessed two natures, a divine nature and a human nature, but that this was possible only because Christ also was two persons, a divine person and a human person.

God led the church to consider mistaken ideas and denials of the truth concerning the relation between the two natures of Christ before he guided the church by his Spirit into the truth, so that only by considering what was wrong could the church finally see what was right.

This is a wisdom of God to help us poor mortals who are so hard of hearing and dull of understanding that we find it almost impossible to know the great mysteries of the works of almighty God.

APOLLINARIS' LIFE

It is almost embarrassing to write about the lives of these early men. If one is expecting an interesting and exciting biography, one is bound to be disappointed, because so little is known that one has difficulty filling a single page with the actual facts of one man's life. Yet history has provided us with a few interesting details of the life of Apollinaris.

Apollinaris was born somewhere around 310. He was fifteen years old when the Council of Nicea was held. His father must have named him after himself, because the father is known as Apollinaris the Elder, and the one in whom we are interested is known as Apollinaris the Younger.

Father and son were apparently very close and collaborated for many years in various writing projects. They were both confessing Christians, and Apollinaris the Elder served as presbyter (elder) in the church for many years.

Apollinaris the Younger received a classical education and went on to teach rhetoric in the city of Laodicea. In that city was a church, whose bishop (minister) was Theodotus.

Now that in itself was interesting. You will recall that around the end of the first century when the apostle John was banished to the island of Patmos, a church already existed in Laodicea. It was one of the seven churches to which our Lord wrote the letters that are recorded in Revelation 2 and 3. These seven churches were all in western Asia Minor, in the province of Asia. It is probable that they were all organized while Paul was working in Ephesus, and laborers in the gospel went into that area to bring the gospel.

In less than fifty years, the church in Laodicea had become all but apostate. In his letter to them, the Lord threatened to spew them out of his mouth. But here, three hundred years later, a church was still in that city. It may have been that the church of Laodicea repented of its sin in obedience to the command of the Lord and thus continued to exist as a church; or it may be—and this is more likely—that the faithful in this apostate church heard and obeyed the call of Christ, who was standing at the door of the church knocking and calling his faithful out. After leaving a church that had become the false church, the faithful may have reorganized the church, and that may have been the one mentioned here in our story of Apollinaris.

Apollinaris the Younger also became a presbyter in the church of Laodicea, which would seem to indicate that both father and son were men of exceptional ability. But both had the same flaw: they were deeply involved in the reading and study of pagan philosophy. They both loved pagan learning, and they both gave themselves too much to it. About this time both were closely associated with and became friends of some pagan philosophers in the city who were sophists. As a result they were excommunicated by their church, but they repented of their sin and, after confession, were received back into the fellowship of the church.

However, they never completely shook free from their love of pagan culture, and in the course of the years, they collaborated in the writing of a great deal of secular prose and poetry. Their gifts of writing were so great that they gained something of an international reputation among scholars and authors.

Eventually Apollinaris the Elder died, and Apollinaris the Younger became bishop (minister) of the church in Laodicea. It was about the year 346 that Apollinaris the Younger met and became a lifelong friend of the great Athanasius, the powerful defender of Nicene orthodoxy who suffered so much because of the truth. From that time on, Apollinaris joined forces with Athanasius and was himself an influential defender of the truth of the divinity of Jesus Christ.

Although Apollinaris did not stand in the shadow of the great Athanasius, he acquired a good reputation by his own superb accomplishments. He was a gifted Hebrew scholar, mastered that language, and became a skilled exegete who put the books from Genesis to 1 Samuel into poetry and drama. His exegetical abilities shown brightly in the firmament of the church, for he was known everywhere as a sober and sensible expounder of the word of God who avoided that dreadful allegorizing that was characteristic of so many preachers in his day. He was famous as a theologian, and some claimed that his theological abilities were greater than those of Athanasius himself. Apollinaris was a prolific writer and penned some thirty books that defended the Christian faith against various heresies. He was one of the great theological writers of all time, although, sad to say, almost none of his works have survived the destructive forces of time. He was a wise and respected minister in the church where God had placed him.

For all these accomplishments and more, he was held in high esteem by friend and foe alike. In fact, when he began to teach erroneous views of Christ's person and natures, those who attacked his views rarely, if ever, mentioned him personally and by name. But in spite of all his accomplishments, he became a heretic. And that is sad.

Apollinaris the Heretic

Apollinaris was not, I think, a heretic when he first began to propound his views. A heretic is one who teaches doctrines contrary to those that have been officially established by the church as the truth of Scripture.

This may sound somewhat strange, but it must be remembered that it has often happened in the hard work of developing the truth that one of the church's theologians, in struggling with a difficult theological or exegetical problem, came up with a solution to the problem that turned out to be wrong. This is not surprising, for all men in the church of Christ have imperfect understanding, and any one of the saints can come up with wrong ideas about theological problems.

Incidentally, that is why we need each other in the church and why no one can ever develop theology by himself. We need each other, because only the church as a whole is guided by the Spirit into the truth rather than by one individual. And so the saints are "checks" on each other, necessary correctors, and together guardians of the truth who keep the truth running in the channel of Scripture.

Apollinaris came up with a solution to the problem, not yet understood by the church, of our Lord's humanity and divinity and the relation between them. It was a wrong solution, and the church as a whole demonstrated unmistakably that he was wrong and that his views could not be sustained by Scripture.

At that point he became a heretic. If only he had had the grace and humility to admit that he had erred and that the solution to the problem had to be sought elsewhere. If only he had said, "Yes, I see that. I see that what I proposed will not do. I shall abandon that position and continue to study in the confidence that the church will come to an understanding of the truth." If he had said something like that, all would have been well.

But such humility is rare, even in the church. We "discover" our own solution to a difficult problem, and our own solution becomes a kind of "sacred cow" with us, so that anyone who dares to attack our view is considered by us guilty of something profane. Every attack on our view we see as an attack on ourselves. Such is pride. This is what often happens. It happened with Apollinaris.

So insistent on his own position was Apollinaris that when the church officially condemned his views, he still clung to them, left the church of which he had been a part, and organized several congregations of his followers in the area of Laodicea.

We may hope that Apollinaris repented before he died, although there is no evidence of it.

APOLLINARIS' HERESY

What was the heresy of Apollinaris?

It seems to me that the problem with this man was that he had spent too much time with, and had thought too highly of, pagan philosophy. He was something of a rationalist. That was his downfall.

It did not seem rational to him that Jesus Christ could be wholly God and wholly man at the same time, and still be just one Lord Jesus Christ. One cannot, Apollinaris argued, take two wholes which remain two wholes and make of them one whole. On the surface that is nonsense. One cannot (the figure is mine) take a whole orange and a whole apple and unite them in such a way that one has just one piece of fruit while that piece of fruit remains both an orange and an apple. It might be an orange; then the apple would be gone. It might be an apple; then the orange would be gone. It might even become some kind of an orange-apple, a third kind of fruit, neither orange nor apple but a combination of both. It cannot be one piece of fruit that in every respect is an orange and in every respect is also an apple.

In a similar way the Lord Jesus Christ could not be wholly God and wholly man, and still be one Lord Jesus Christ. He might be wholly God without being a man; he might be wholly a man without being wholly God; or he might be some kind of God-man, as indeed some proposed. But for God to be both God and man at the same time, and remain both, would be impossible. So reasoned Apollinaris.

His approach was rationalistic, not scriptural. It was an attempt to solve a problem by applying reason without paying attention to Scripture. One may never do this. Apart from the problem facing Apollinaris, the fact is that the doctrine of Christ teaches us that what man can never do, God is able to do. What never entered the heart of man is God's perfect wisdom. God's works are great, and no work is greater than the work of Immanuel ("God with us"). Whatever else one is going to say, this had better be his starting point.

It is rather interesting—and we may just as well introduce the whole matter here, although it played a more important role in later controversies—that there was serious division in the church over the problem Apollinaris faced. In an earlier chapter we pointed out that there were two seminaries of importance in the church: one in Antioch of Syria, and the other in Alexandria of Egypt. And these two did not get along very well. They were always at each other, sometimes in unseemly ways.

In keeping with a certain spirit of competition between the two seminaries, they both had a different solution to the question of how Christ could be both God and man at the same time. The seminary at Antioch tended to emphasize the notion that this was possible only because Christ was two "persons." The seminary in Alexandria wanted to solve the problem by going in the direction of some kind of merger of the two natures of Christ, so that the human and the divine nature were mixed together to form a third kind of nature.

What I write here is a simplification of the views of these two schools, because no one at that time understood very clearly what the terms *person* and *nature* meant, and it was necessary to understand them to come to an understanding of the truth. But the fact is that these two seminaries tended to go in the very directions that I described, and later they would go precisely in those directions.

Apollinaris was more under the influence of Alexandria than of Antioch, which is not surprising when one thinks of the fact that his good friend Athanasius was also from Alexandria.

Here, once again, Apollinaris had listened too much to Greek philosophy. He taught that man is composed of three parts: a body; a lower or animal soul, which is the power in man of the baser emotions, instincts, thoughts, and desires; and a higher soul or spirit, which is the power in man of logic, higher and nobler thoughts, more powerful and significant ideas, and the like.

Apollinaris taught that in Jesus Christ, the "Logos," who is truly God and is spoken of in John 1:1–14, took the place of the human spirit in a man. Apollinaris said that the divine Logos assumed the nature of a man, but did so by eliminating one part of this man, the spirit, and taking its place. So the Lord Jesus Christ was one Savior but with a human body and lower soul, and a divine higher soul or spirit. Thus Christ was a mixture of human and divine, not wholly human, not wholly divine.

But Apollinaris' notion would never do. It is possible that already in 362 a synod in Alexandria condemned his views. But surely several synods emphatically rejected what he taught: two synods in Rome in 377 and 382, one synod at Antioch, and several later synods. Three men—Apollinaris' friend Athanasius, Gregory of Nazianzus, and Gregory of Nyssa—wrote against Apollinaris. Yet though he was so often condemned, these synods did not once mention him by name, nor did those who wrote against his views. He somehow retained the respect of those who opposed him even though he clung tenaciously to his errors. He should have listened to them.

One powerful argument was brought against his views, especially by Athanasius. It was so simple, yet so profound. It struck at the heart of the problem, and more importantly, it took the problem out of the arena of philosophical speculation and put it right where it ought to have been: in the arena of the doctrine of salvation. The objection was this. Since our sins have corrupted us in body, soul, and spirit, we need to be saved in body, soul, and spirit. Therefore, if Christ has saved us, he had to be like us in all things except our sin. He, too, had to be a man with body, soul, and spirit. That is, he who was the eternal Son of God had to have a human body, and a human soul, and a human spirit. If that is not true, our salvation is impossible.

Apollinaris died some time before 392. He is now long forgotten. His story is only one chapter in the long book of the struggle for the truth. But it is an important chapter. It showed so clearly that our Lord Jesus Christ, to save us poor sinners, had to be like us *in all things*—except that he had no sin. Only then could he be truly Immanuel, God with us, our Redeemer.

CHAPTER 7

NESTORIUS AND AN UNHOLY SQUABBLE ABOUT CHRIST

INTRODUCTION

Controversies are frequently present in the church of Christ because the church is called to fight the good fight of faith in defense of the truth of Scripture. But controversies are not pleasant, and sometimes they are very ugly.

It is not surprising that controversies should be ugly when one thinks of the fact that they are fought by men who are sinners, although they are a part of the church of Christ. The redeeming element is usually that some who are engaged in the fight are defenders of the faith and are fighting that the truth of God may be preserved. One can overlook a great deal of individual wrong in controversy if it is clear that the truth is at stake and that there are those who are fighting valiantly for it. In the throes of controversy people frequently are offended by the character, and perhaps character faults, of those who stand for the truth. They end up following heretics in their failure to see that the truth is more important than the faults of a man.

Once in a while it happens that the spectator to a controversy, as he observes the battle, mutters to himself, "A plague on both your houses," and he turns away in disgust. Such a controversy took place in the fifth century in the Mediterranean world between a heretic by the name of Nestorius and a man named Cyril, who although his views were vindicated at the time, was not himself as orthodox as one would have liked him to be.

The controversy was over the doctrine of our Lord Jesus Christ. That is what makes it all so sad. It involved the doctrine of the incarnation of Christ, the truth of him whom the Scriptures call Immanuel, God with us. And it was so violent, so unchristian in every sense, so brutal, so ugly, that it is difficult even to talk of it. When I was teaching church history, I found this topic to be one of the more distasteful ones. Yet the Lord used the controversy to bring the church nearer to the truth concerning the union of the divine and human natures of the Savior. The result of the controversy was the Symbol of Chalcedon.

The Problem in the Church

In the last chapter I mentioned that the church was having a most difficult time defining precisely who Christ is. In 325, at the great Council of Nicea, the church had emphatically confessed the doctrine of the Trinity, especially as it was connected to the absolute divinity of Christ. Christ Jesus our Savior is, in the memorable words of that creed, "true God of true God."

Although the church readily acknowledged that Christ was also a man, like us in all things, except our sin, no one was prepared to say precisely in what way Christ was a man. And granted that he was indeed a man, what was the relation between his divinity and his humanity? These are vexing questions.

Apollinaris had given his opinion by which he attempted to answer both questions. He had concluded, under the influence of Graeco-Roman philosophy, that the divine Logos had taken the place of the human spirit in the man Jesus Christ. But the church told him that he was wrong and that he would be branded a heretic if he insisted on his position. He was wrong, so said the great Athanasius, because Christ had to have a human soul in order to save us in both body and *soul*. Apollinaris would not admit his wrong and was branded a heretic.

But the questions remained.

The story of Nestorius is one of two other attempts to answer these questions about Christ and of the final answer of the church.

Nestorius' Early Life

Nestorius was born in the early part of the 400s in Germanicia, Syria, on the northeast coast of the Mediterranean Sea. Its most important city was Antioch, the city from which Paul the apostle set sail on his missionary journeys. Nestorius went to Antioch for his education. While attending school and in his early post-graduate years, he lived in a cloister hard by the walls of the city. In the cloister he learned about the ascetic life and learned to love it.

Nestorius had considerable ability. He not only found it relatively easy to master his subjects, but after his schooling he showed a vast theological learning and a sound and practical judgment that set him apart from most of his peers. These gifts soon came to the attention of the leaders in the church, and he was ordained a presbyter in the church at Antioch. In that church he practiced a rigid austerity in keeping with his love of the ascetic life, and he became a fervent and powerful preacher whose oratory attracted hundreds. He became accustomed to preaching to a church crowded with people.

Such a man soon drew wider attention to himself, and it was not long before an emperor took notice of him. When the patriarchate of Constantinople fell vacant, this emperor was responsible for filling the post.

To appreciate fully what happened one must understand the importance of Constantinople, a city that occupied a strategic position on the Strait of the Bosporus as the western door that connected Asia on its eastern side and Europe on its western side. Constantinople had received its name from Constantine the Great, who, when he became ruler of the Roman Empire, moved the capital of the empire from Rome to this city on the Bosporus. Because the church in Constantinople was so closely associated with the center of political power, it grew rapidly in importance as well, especially when the emperors were devoted to the task of supporting the church and, when possible, also ruling it. As a result, Constantinople became the most important church in the eastern part of the Mediterranean world and was rivaled only by Rome itself.

The patriarch of Constantinople was the most important man in the eastern church, the equal in the East to the pope who was bishop of Rome. In fact, the two tended to squabble a great deal over who was really ruler of whom. Both wanted the top spot. The controversy continued until 1054, when the church split between east and west. The patriarch of Constantinople was in a position to influence all ecclesiastical affairs in the East; he was able to influence the emperor himself and give him counsel and advice on how best to rule in church and state; he was, under the emperor, the most powerful man in Asia.

It is some measure of the high reputation of Nestorius that the emperor passed over the leading clerics in Constantinople and chose Nestorius to be the new patriarch. The year was 428. Nestorius could not have been much more than twenty-five years old.

TROUBLES

The church was embroiled in controversy over the relation between the human and divine natures of the Lord Jesus Christ. One complicating element in the controversy was the use of a rather strange term, *theotokos,* which means "God-bearer," or less literally, "mother of God." The church applied the term to Mary, the mother of Jesus; therefore, Mary was *theotokos,* the mother of God.

There were many who did not like the term, refused to use it, and sometimes fought vehemently against its use in the churches. They complained that it was not biblical, that it did not accurately express Mary's relation to Christ, and that it was a dangerous term that could easily leave the impression that God himself was not only born from the virgin, but also suffered and died on the cross. One can sense the force of these objections.

The differences over the use of *theotokos* were also present in Constantinople at the time Nestorius moved from Antioch to take over his prestigious post.

Something happened to Nestorius when he received this appointment from the emperor. I think what happened was something latent in Nestorius' character that had not had opportunity to come to expression until he had the reins of power in his hands. From the very day he assumed his duties, he became a proud and arrogant man who was a religious fanatic of the worst sort. He seemed to think that God had appointed him to be patriarch of Constantinople for no other reason than that he might be God's sole avenging angel against every heresy that appeared on the horizon.

From day one, Nestorius moved with intolerant zeal and bigotry against every little sect that had a corner in the teeming mass of people who inhabited the imperial city. On day five after his inauguration, he ordered the burning down of a small Arian church in a poor quarter of the city. I suppose a zeal against heresy can be approved, but the methods that Nestorius used were harsh and cruel even by the standards of his day. Condemnation was not enough. The heretics had to be run out of the city or destroyed. Their property had to be confiscated and their voice silenced. Nestorius began to deliver impassioned speeches against heresy that roused the people to fury until riots became everyday occurrences in the city and blood began to be spilled.

What made Nestorius' frenzy and inordinate zeal all the more distasteful was the fact that when the western church condemned Coelestius and Julian of Eclunum for the heresy of Pelagianism, and when these two men fled to Constantinople, Nestorius was the one who was tolerant of their view and supported them in their heresy of the free will of man. He was even willing to appeal to the pope on their behalf in an effort to get their condemnation undone.

Nestorius hated the term *theotokos* and regarded the use of it as the greatest of all heresies.

It is not so easy to determine exactly why Nestorius hated the term. One reason was his opposition to a "Mary cult" in the church. The cult was found chiefly among the monks in their waste desert places, and it was intended to lead to the worship of Mary, because of her exalted position in heaven. Another reason, it seems, was Nestorius' pride. The church was deeply divided over the use of the term when Nestorius came to office, and many looked on him as one who could, with his sound and practical judgment, unite the church by finding common ground between those who opposed the term and those who wanted it. The most serious reason for Nestorius' opposition to *theotokos,* however, was his hatred of the doctrine that the term implied and that became the real issue in the controversy.

We may sum up Nestorius as a thoroughly unlikable office bearer in the church of Christ. He was gifted to a considerable extent with ability to learn and with wide theological knowledge. He was a powerful orator and effective preacher. He was entrusted with a position of great responsibility. But rather than use his gifts in caring for the sheep Christ had placed under him, Nestorius saw his sole work as the rooting out of every idea that he deemed heresy, and he did so with vehemence and ruthlessness. He became a rather nasty man.

NESTORIUS' VIEW OF CHRIST

While the Council of Nicea had settled the matter of Christ's divinity, it had not said much about Christ's human nature. In what sense was Christ like us in all things? And how was it possible for Christ to be both "true God of true God" and "like us in all things" at the same time? Apollinaris had given his opinion and had been declared heretical. It was now Nestorius' turn.

Nestorius did not doubt the absolute divinity of Christ, nor did he in any sense deny it. He was also persuaded that Christ was indeed fully human, except that Christ did not sin. But Nestorius erred badly when he described the relation between Christ's humanity and his divinity. Nestorius claimed (because of his opposition to the word *theotokos*) that the human and the divine natures are united in Christ in much the same way as a man and a woman are united in marriage. Husband and wife become "one flesh," an expression that defines their unity; yet they remain distinct and separate individuals.

So the union, according to Nestorius, was a *moral* union. Nestorius

57

spoke of Christ's human nature as the "temple" in which dwelt the divine nature. He refused to accept the idea that Mary was the mother of God and spoke of her as the mother of a man only. He used the rather strange expression, "God passed through Mary's womb," but she was in no sense God's mother.

This error of speaking of the union of Christ's two natures as a moral union implied (though Nestorius probably never said it in so many words) that Christ had both a human person and a divine person. His divine person was the person of the Son in the holy Trinity, but his human person was born of Mary. Two persons were united in Christ much like two persons are united in marriage.

This would, of course, never do, and the church recognized it.

The error of Nestorius is relatively common today. An instance of this comes to mind. In defense of the error of the well-meant offer of the gospel, one theologian defended the well-meant offer with the following line of reasoning. In his human nature, Jesus was under the law. The law requires that we love all men as our neighbors. In his human nature Jesus loved all men, although in his divine nature he loved only the elect. This minister was correctly charged with Nestorianism.

CYRIL'S INTERVENTION

Nestorius' opposition to the idea of Mary as the mother of God aroused fierce opposition to him and to his views. If you would like to have some idea of how strong the worship of Mary was already in the days of Nestorius, then consider a quote from a sermon of Proclus, one of the bishops in Constantinople who did not agree with Nestorius and who defended the term *theotokos*.

> The Virgin . . . [is] "the spotless treasure-house of virginity; the spiritual paradise of the second Adam; the workshop, in which the two natures were annealed together; the bridal chamber in which the Word wedded the flesh; the living bush of nature, which was unharmed by the fire of the divine birth; the light cloud which bore him who sat between the Cherubim; the stainless fleece, bathed in the dews of Heaven, with which the Shepherd clothed his sheep; the handmaid and the mother, the Virgin and Heaven."[1]

So violent did the opposition to Nestorius become that Nestorius himself was forced to call a synod in Constantinople in 429 that was firmly under his control and that followed his directives. That synod declared his views correct and deposed some of the more violent members of the clergy who opposed him.

However, it was not the end of the battle. It increasingly involved the entire eastern church, especially the church in Alexandria of Egypt over which Cyril ruled.

Cyril was the defender of orthodoxy in the struggle and the chief opponent of Nestorius' heresy. Cyril was, in comparison with Nestorius, the greater and more profound theologian. He was also a man of lower character. He was vain and haughty and loved the trappings of his office. But worse, he believed and put into practice the adage "The end justifies the means." He stopped at nothing to defeat Nestorius and considered any method of attack to be justified by the rightness of his cause.

Other factors were involved in what became a bitter war between these two. Alexandria was also a patriarchate in the eastern church, and the rivalry between Alexandria and Constantinople for supremacy added fuel to the controversy.

Cyril took it upon himself to correct Nestorius and began what became a rather lengthy correspondence. As the correspondence continued, it became violently bitter and brought no solution. Cyril took the opportunity to write to many other bishops throughout the church, filling them with evil stories about Nestorius and the horror of his heresy.

Nestorius and Cyril appealed to the emperor for help, but Nestorius, friendly to the emperor and a frequent visitor to the imperial court, gained the emperor's approval. In disgust, Cyril appealed to the pope, who was elated that his supreme jurisdiction in the church was so recognized. The pope called a synod in Rome, which proceeded to excommunicate Nestorius unless he retracted his views within ten days of the receipt of the synod's decision.

Cyril took it upon himself to execute the papal decree, and he issued, on his own, the bull of the excommunication of Nestorius. This did not solve anything, and the next years were spent in their excommunicating each other and hurling anathemas at each other, while both tried in every way to gain the support of the populace.

It all culminated in an ecumenical synod held in Ephesus in 431. It was a strange synod. For one thing, the great Augustine had been asked to preside. But he could not, for God took him to heaven in 430. One wonders what would have happened had he been there. I suspect that God made it impossible for Augustine to come because the whole controversy was an unholy mess.

For another thing, a large group of bishops from the eastern Mediterranean countries (Syria and Palestine) were late for one reason or another.

Most of them were supporters of Nestorius. The delegates waited fourteen days and then met in solemn session without the eastern bishops. Nestorius was there, but the wave of opposition to him was so great that he needed police protection. Cyril was also there with a large number of Mary-worshiping monks. The synod condemned Nestorius and his views: "The Lord Jesus Christ, who is blasphemed by him [Nestorius], determines through this holy council that Nestorius be excluded from the episcopal office, and from all sacerdotal fellowship."[2] Because it met without a large contingent of tardy bishops, the synod has gone down in history as the "Robbers' Synod."

No sooner had the synod passed its condemnation than the other bishops arrived. But it was too late; the synod had spoken. Yet this did not deter Nestorius' supporters, and they proceeded to hold their own synod at which all the decisions of the Robbers' Synod were nullified, Cyril excommunicated, and Nestorius exonerated.

Thus the unhappy controversy ended in what can only be called a stalemate.

SUBSEQUENT EVENTS

Finally, the emperor tipped the balance against Nestorius. For whatever reasons, he approved of the decisions of the Robbers' Synod. The pope did the same. This was an unbeatable combination against which opposition was broken.

Nestorius retreated to a cloister in Antioch, perhaps the same in which he had lived while in that city, and he may very well have been happy to spend the rest of his life there. But his choice of location was not trusted since he had many supporters in the city. Therefore, he was banished to an oasis in the Upper Nile River, far from church activities and too isolated to have any influence.

Here Nestorius wrote his autobiography entitled *Tragedy*. Even in isolation, he was given no peace. "The unhappy Nestorius was dragged from the stillness of his former cloister, the cloister of Euprepius before the gates of Antioch, in which he had enjoyed four years of repose, from one place of exile to another, first to Arabia, then to Egypt, and was compelled to drink to the dregs the bitter cup of persecution which he himself, in the days of his power, had forced upon the heretics."[3] Nestorius died about 450, at approximately age fifty, shortly before the Council of Chalcedon.

Conclusions and Summary

Throughout history until the present, debate has raged over whether Nestorius was truly a heretic or whether he was condemned for views that he did not teach. Sometimes sympathy can make one blind. Let it be clear: Nestorius was wrong, and his refusal to retract his views made him a pernicious heretic. Regardless of what one may think of his treatment, sympathy for him must not obscure his sin of holding erroneous views. Nestorius taught a view of the union between the two natures of Christ that led inevitably to the conclusion that Christ possessed a human person in addition to a divine person. This is serious and destructive of the faith.

The truth, arrived at later, was that Christ was one divine person who included in his divine person both the human nature and the divine nature.

However much we may dislike Cyril, and however strongly we wish to condemn his tactics, he was right in his opposition to Nestorius. What his views were is difficult to say. He seemed to be correct for the most part, but the flaw in his views may have been an overemphasis on the *union* of the two natures of Christ. I say that because shortly after Cyril died, the church in Alexandria itself became heretical. In its fierce opposition to Nestorianism and the separation of the two natures, the church there (or at least many in it) began to go to another extreme and teach a union between the human and the divine natures of Christ that merged the two natures in such a way that Christ was neither wholly God nor wholly man, but some kind of God-man. The divine and human so mixed with each other that what emerged was one single nature neither completely human nor completely divine. For them, Christ was, therefore, one person with one nature. That, too, is heresy, and I suspect Cyril had a lot to do with influencing the church in Alexandria to go in that direction. In some sense, then, we can surely say, "A plague on both your houses."

The term *theotokos* was the bone of contention. May Mary be properly called the "mother of God"?

Quite frankly I do not care for the term. It has its origin in wrong views of Mary. It is not found in Scripture, and it is subject to wrong interpretations. Nevertheless, it can be interpreted correctly. The person of the Son of God, the second person of the holy Trinity, united the human nature that came from Mary with the divine nature at the very moment of conception in Mary's womb. The Son of God was the Lord Jesus Christ from the moment of his conception. The Son of God in our flesh was indeed in Mary's womb. How that was possible is the great mystery of God become flesh—Immanuel, God with us. But it is true and the clear teaching of Scripture.

The controversy between Nestorius and his supporters, and Cyril and his supporters—along with all the struggles that followed—was finally settled in 451 by the Synod of Chalcedon. That synod taught the following:

> Christ, the same perfect in Godhead and also perfect in manhood; truly God and truly man . . . begotten before all ages of the Father according to the Godhead, and in these latter days, for us and for our salvation, born of the Virgin Mary, the Mother of God, according to the Manhood; one and the same Christ, Son, Lord, Only-begotten, to be acknowledged in two natures, *inconfusedly, unchangeably, indivisibly, inseparably;* the distinction of natures being by no means taken away by the union, but rather the property of each nature being preserved, and concurring in one Person and one Subsistence, not parted or divided into two persons, but one and the same Son, and only begotten, God the Word, the Lord Jesus Christ.[4]

You will notice that the creed uses the expression "Mother of God." It is imbedded for all time in our creedal heritage. So God has ordained.

The Belgic Confession, while it mentions in Article 9 the Apostles' Creed, the Nicene Creed, and the Athanasian Creed, does not mention the Symbol of Chalcedon. This is striking, and one wonders whether this is due to the fact that Guido de Brès, the chief author of the Belgic Confesson, disliked the term *theotokos,* especially because he had just come out of Roman Catholicism with its idolatrous doctrine of Mary.

Whatever may be the case, Article 19 of the Belgic Confession does incorporate in it the same teaching as is found in the Symbol of Chalcedon, and the same doctrine may be found in the Athanasian Creed.

What makes us pause in adoration and worship is God's wonderful way of providence by means of which he, the sovereign Lord of the church, brought truth out of such an unholy and oftentimes wicked battle. That truth is no less than the truth of our Lord Jesus Christ. Upon the truth of Chalcedon rests our only hope of salvation.

CHAPTER 8

PELAGIUS AND CELESTIUS: ENEMIES OF THE DOCTRINES OF GRACE

INTRODUCTION

With the adoption of the Symbol of Chalcedon, the trinitarian and Christological controversies were brought to an end. Many different controversies continued to perplex the church, especially in the East, but they were vain and useless, mostly due to philosophical speculations of men who were more out to promote their own private agendas than to learn the truth of Christ. Chalcedon established for the church of the new dispensation the doctrine of the person and natures of Christ.

The controversies that next plagued the church after those of the doctrine of Christ (Christology) were over entirely different doctrines: the doctrines of man (anthropology) and of salvation (soteriology). The controversy over the person and natures of Christ overlapped somewhat the controversy over the doctrine of salvation. The Council of Ephesus in 431, for example, made decisions about Nestorianism, but also about Pelagianism, the heresy against which Augustine fought.

PELAGIUS AND CELESTIUS

We will discuss Pelagius and Celestius together, for their lives were intertwined in the controversies that they stirred up when they promoted Pelagianism.

Little is known about the early life of either of them—just as little is known of their final end. Most likely Pelagius was born in England (or Ireland) around 354. He became a monk and spent most of his early years in a monastery. Celestius was probably born in Scotland, but nothing other is known of him until he appeared in Rome. These two men became the closest of friends.

Although Celestius was a disciple of Pelagius and had learned his heresies at Pelagius' feet, Celestius was theologically the superior of the two. He was the theologian of Pelagianism; he set forth and developed the doctrines that became known as Pelagianism. Pelagius wrote a one-volume work on the epistles of Paul, in which Pelagius set down his views, such as they were. However, he depended on Celestius to be his spokesman. Celestius could set down the views that Pelagius never understood sufficiently well enough to explain.

Benjamin Warfield dismisses Pelagius with this off-handed remark:

> He was...constitutionally averse to controversy; and although in his zeal for Christian morals, and in his conviction that no man would attempt to do what he was not persuaded he had natural power to perform, he diligently propagated his doctrines privately, he was careful to rouse no opposition, and was content to make what progress he could quietly and without open discussion. His methods of work sufficiently appear in the pages of his "Commentary on the Epistles of Saint Paul," which was written and published during these years, and which exhibits learning and a sober and correct but somewhat shallow exegetical skill. In this work, he manages to give expression to all the main elements of his system, but always introduces them indirectly, not as the true exegesis, but by way of objections to the ordinary teaching, which were in need of discussion.[1]

Pelagius was a very learned man if one considers the breadth of his education, but he was shallow and superficial in thought and in feeling. As a monk, he gave himself over to ascetic practices (although one of his contemporaries spoke of him as somewhat chubby), and he lived a moral life. He never married, and while not disapproving of marriage, he considered it to be a kind of concession to the flesh. Although Pelagius seemed to have no understanding of the difference between morality and holiness, no one had ever charged a moral fault against him. He was blameless in conduct, but coldly and dispassionately so. He had no sense of the struggles with sin that characterize the life of a saint. He fought no inner battles, struggled with no temptations, knew not a holiness that comes from denying oneself, taking up one's cross, and following Christ. Outward morality was all he considered. A morally upright life was a breeze. To gain the holiness of Christ through the deep way of sin—of that he had no conception.

THE BEGINNINGS OF THE CONFLICT

Pelagius moved to Rome about 400, the year Augustine finished writing his *Confessions*. Probably in Rome Celestius was converted by Pelagius and became his disciple and friend. Although Pelagius openly preached his views in Rome for nearly ten years, he never had any trouble with the church or the theologians there.

In 411 Pelagius and Celestius were in North Africa, where Augustine was already bishop of Hippo. The date they went to North Africa is hard to determine. Probably Celestius went first, around 409. In 410 Rome was sacked by the barbarian Alaric. In 411, it seems, Pelagius moved to North Africa. But he soon went on to Palestine and was warmly received by Jerome in Bethlehem, where Jerome had established a seminary of great repute.

Celestius remained in North Africa. He decided that he wanted to be a presbyter (elder) and applied for the office. But the church in North Africa was strong. Those who were considered for presbyter were subjected to a rigorous exam and a careful scrutiny of their views. During the exam, Paulinus, a deacon from Milan, came to the conclusion that Celestius was a heretic and that he ought not to be ordained.

The following six charges made against Celestius give us an idea of the very heart of Pelagian heresy: that Adam was created mortal and would have died whether or not he had sinned; that Adam's sin injured only himself and not the human race; that newborn infants are in the same condition in which Adam was before his transgression; that since by neither the death nor the transgression of Adam the whole human race dies, so neither will the whole human race rise again from the dead on account of Christ's resurrection; that the law as well as the gospel is able to guide into the kingdom of heaven; and that there were men who lived without sin before the advent of Jesus Christ.

Two additional heresies complete the summary of the doctrines of Pelagianism: the grace of God is not absolutely necessary to lead men to holiness and grace is given to men in proportion to their merit.

The six charges were brought against Celestius at the Synod of Carthage in 412. Celestius argued that the differences between him and his accusers were minor and unimportant to the faith, had not been settled in the church, and thus were open for discussion. Hence he thought he ought not to be condemned for his views. His defense was ineffective. The synod, without hesitation, condemned as contrary to Scripture every one of his propositions and ordered Celestius to recant. When he refused, he was excommunicated from the church.

That did not deter Celestius, however. He promptly moved to Asia Minor, where he soon was ordained a presbyter in the church of Ephesus.

Soon the news of what the Synod of Carthage had done came to Bethlehem, where Pelagius was enjoying himself. Because it was widely known that Celestius was a student of Pelagius, the views of Pelagius came under attack. But in 415 a Jerusalem council under the direction of John, bishop of Jerusalem, completely exonerated Pelagius.

The reasons for this vindication of Pelagius' views give us insight into the state of the church at that time.

First, the East was strong on the doctrine of the freedom of the will. Pelagius made it clear that defending this doctrine was all that really interested him.

Second, Pelagius was not forthright in the explanation of his views that he offered the council. As is so characteristic of heretics everywhere, he equivocated, used ambiguous terminology, tried to present his views in the best possible light and in agreement with the accepted doctrines of the church, and never forthrightly stated what his own position was.

This point is worth emphasizing. Warfield writes concerning Pelagius' evasiveness:

> Pelagius escaped condemnation only by a course of most ingenious disingenuousness, and only at the cost both of disowning Celestius and his teachings, of which he had been the real father, and of leading the synod to believe that he was anathematizing the very doctrines which he was himself proclaiming. There is really no possibility of doubting, as any one will see who reads the proceedings of the synod, that Pelagius obtained his acquittal here either by a "lying condemnation or a tricky interpretation" of his own teachings; and Augustin is perfectly justified in asserting that the "heresy was not acquitted, but the man who denied the heresy," and who would himself have been anathematized had he not anathematized the heresy.[2]

Third, animosity between the East and the West already was dividing the church. The East took this attitude: "What do we care what the West decides? We are determined to show our independence, and we are not about to let the West lead us around by the nose." So true was this that when it was pointed out to the Jerusalem council that Augustine had joined in the condemnation of Pelagius, one delegate scornfully shouted, "And what is Augustine to me?" The East, I suspect, took a great deal of delight in making a decision that contradicted the decision taken at Carthage.

Thus Pelagius' vindication continued. When two presbyters from Gaul (France) were present in Palestine and warned the church there of the disastrous consequences of Pelagius' views, another council was called, and again Pelagius was completely exonerated. Almost the entire eastern church agreed with these decisions, and it appeared as if Pelagianism would win the day there.

Although most of the East agreed with Pelagius, this was not entirely true of Jerome. Jerome was a noted scholar in his own right, he was deeply devoted to the church, and he was in almost constant communication with Augustine. Jerome is probably most noted for his translation of the Bible into Latin, a translation that became known as the Vulgate and that became the official Bible of the Roman Catholic Church. Nevertheless, Jerome's condemnation of Pelagius was weakened by Jerome's insistence on the freedom of the human will and on conditional predestination.

THE COUNTERATTACK

The West was not about to take these decisions in Palestine sitting down. The theologians in the West poured out a stream of books and pamphlets showing how the views of Pelagius (and Celestius) were contrary to Scripture and the historic faith of the church. Augustine concentrated almost exclusively on the Pelagian heresy in his writings during the last twenty years of his life.

Two synods were also held in North Africa in 416, one in Carthage and one in Mileve, which condemned Pelagius and Celestius *in absentia*. Gradually the course of the struggle began to tip in favor of the West. Among the more serious and biblical theologians in the East, the light began to dawn that Pelagianism could hardly be separated from Nestorianism. As the tide turned against Nestorianism, and as the church came to realize that the two heresies of Nestorianism and Pelagianism were related, Pelagianism came more and more into disrepute.

One additional event brought the matter to a certain climax.

The two synods in North Africa appealed to Pope Innocent I for support of their decisions. He approved of what they had decided and commended the African bishops for their diligence in remaining faithful to the truth and for their zeal in combating heresy. But Innocent died, and the opportunity was lost to make his decisions stick. Zosimus came to the papal throne in his place.

Pelagius, having heard of his condemnation by the North African synods, and confident of the backing of the synods in Palestine, wrote a letter to Innocent to defend himself against the excommunication that had been imposed on him, but the letter came instead to Zosimus, the new pope. At about the time that Pelagius' letter arrived, Celestius appeared in Rome, also in an effort to defend himself before the pope. Zosimus read Pelagius' letter and heard Celestius' plea, and he decided that both had been unjustly treated, that their condemnation was wrong, and that the views they taught were in perfect keeping with the teachings of the church. He ordered their excommunication to be lifted and ordered the North African bishops to remove their condemnation of Pelagius and Celestius.

But the North African bishops were convinced of their position and were not at all inclined to pay any attention to the dictates of Zosimus. In 418 they very carefully drew up their case against Pelagius and Celestius, stated their own position on the doctrines in question as clearly as they could, and politely but emphatically informed Zosimus that he had better change his mind because they were not going to change theirs.

Zosimus concurred. He changed his mind, informed the bishops in North Africa, and ordered all the bishops to sign a declaration of condemnation of Pelagius and his cohorts. Thus the fortunes of men are changed in a moment as God executes his counsel.

It is interesting to note that one year after Augustine died Zosimus approved of heresy, a bit of church history that the Roman Catholic Church has difficulty defending in the light of their view of papal infallibility.

All the bishops in the West (not all in the East) agreed with the decisions of the African bishops except eighteen from Italy, who were promptly excommunicated. They fled to Constantinople, where they were welcomed by Nestorius. Some of them later recanted their support of Pelagius and returned to Italy, where they were once again accepted into the church. The followers of these eighteen bishops were ordered excommunicated and banished from the empire, and all their goods were ordered confiscated by imperial decree.

One of the bishops who refused to sign the papal condemnation of Pelagius was Julian. He became the most articulate spokesman of Pelagianism, a bitter opponent of Augustine, and wrote extensively against his views. Augustine considered Julian's writings so significant that he wrote a book entitled *Against Julian* in response to him.

Julian objected to sovereign predestination because, he said, it makes God the author of sin, it is deterministic and fatalistic, and it teaches that God respects persons. More interestingly, he objected to Augustine's emphasis on sovereign grace because Julian believed that God seeks the salvation of *all* men. In support of this contention, he appealed to 1 Timothy 2:4 and Romans 2:4.

THE END OF THE MATTER

Because Nestorius took under his wing those from the West who refused to repudiate Pelagius and Celestius, the teachings of these heretics were soon associated in the public mind with Nestorius' heresy concerning the natures of Christ. However, one year after Augustine died, the Council of Ephesus finally condemned Nestorianism and Pelagianism in the same breath.

Celestius was not heard of again and very little was heard of Pelagius. Some say that Pelagius died in exile somewhere in Gaul. Others say that he returned to Jerusalem and lived there until he died at the age of seventy. But no one knows for sure.

The heretical position of Pelagius and Celestius had this good effect: it caused Augustine to refute these men and bring out the truth of the matter.

CONCLUDING REMARKS

Augustine emphatically taught everything concerning the doctrines of grace that Calvinists hold dear today. He believed in sovereign predestination—both election and reprobation. He believed that Adam's fall brought both the guilt of sin and the corruption of sin on the whole human race. The result of the fall was the total depravity of man, so that Adam's descendants are unable to do any good. Christ died on the cross only for the elect. By his death Christ earned grace for the elect and for them only. Grace is sovereignly given and bestowed only on God's elect. Grace provides the power for all the good that the people of God do. The elect are preserved throughout all their lives and brought faithfully to glory. In short, Augustine held to what are now called the five points of Calvinism.

The Roman Catholic Church, however, never accepted Augustine's teachings. This is another story, which we will tell in the next chapter, for there were good reasons why the Romish church found it impossible to accept Augustine's views. The irony is that while Rome hails Augustine as its spiritual and theological father and even canonized him, it repudiates what was the most important part of Augustine's theology.

The issues raised in the Pelagian controversy are the great issues over which countless battles have been fought in the history of the church and which still today are the great issues of our times. Calvin especially reached back beyond the Rome of his day to that time a millennium earlier when Augustine had taught the great truths of sovereign grace. Calvin made them his own and gave them as his heritage to the church that followed him.

Warfield has correctly written, "The chief controversies of the first four centuries and the resulting definitions of doctrine concerned the nature of God and the person of Christ; and it was not until these theological and Christological questions were well upon their way to final settlement that the Church could turn its attention to the more subjective side of truth."[3]

It is important to see the relation between the controversies over the doctrine of man's salvation and the doctrine of Christ. The church could not have dealt properly with the doctrine of salvation without first settling the doctrine of Christ. The truth of salvation is based on the truth of Christ. To get soteriology straight, one must understand Christology correctly. We cannot save ourselves; only God can save us. Salvation comes through Christ. Hence Christ must be God—in the ringing words of Nicea, "true God of true God."

The doctrine of man and the doctrine of grace are also related to each other. The Pelagian heresies really were errors in the doctrine of man. Pelagius denied original sin and the corruption of the human nature, but this denial naturally affected the doctrine of salvation as well. If man is not a sinner, totally depraved, he does not need Christ to save him. He can save himself. Thus soteriology and anthropology had to be treated together.

Prior to the time of Pelagius and Augustine, the church had really not understood very well either the doctrine of man or the doctrine of salvation. In a way this is understandable, because the church had been occupied with the defense of the truth concerning Christ and had not examined the doctrines of man and of salvation. But serious errors were present, primarily in the eastern church.

The church as a whole surely understood that man is a sinner and needs salvation. The church also understood that Christ had come into the world to save his people from their sins. These truths were too clear and too frequently mentioned in Scripture to doubt them. But when it came down to specifics, errors kept cropping up. The chief of these errors was the doctrine of the freedom of the human will to choose between good and evil.

The question of human freedom was the pivotal point on which the whole Pelagian controversy turned. How amazing it is that people will never learn the lessons of history. Still today most of the church world clings tenaciously to the doctrine of human freedom, even though it is the downfall of salvation by grace alone.

From a certain point of view, it is not surprising that the church held to the doctrine of the freedom of the will. The theologians who did consider the matter thought this doctrine was important in order to defend Scripture against other errors. The church had to do battle with paganism, and paganism held strongly to the idea that Fate, which it really deified, irresistibly controls the lives of men, so that they are helpless pawns in Fate's hands. The paganism of Augustine's time even held to the idea that Fate controlled the lives of the gods. It was thought that only if a man possessed a free will could the fatalism of paganism be resisted.

In addition to such pagan thought, heresies had appeared in the church. Gnosticism and Manicheanism taught that sin was inevitable and that matter itself is sinful. Because man is composed of matter, at least in part, they argued that man is sinful by virtue of his creation. They believed that the human body is inherently evil. Over against this erroneous doctrine, the church thought it necessary to teach that man has a free will, and that sin is not inevitable but the result of human choice.

The church also pointed to the fact that the Bible speaks of choice. And in connection with choices we have to make, the Bible speaks of rewards for good choices and punishments for bad choices. It seemed obvious that man by his own power could resist temptation. Man could exercise himself to do good. He could make choices that would bring the promised rewards or the justly given punishment.

Many believed in the doctrine of original sin, even though they did not clearly understand it. This was especially true in the western church (Italy, Spain, France, and North Africa), where Latin was the main language, in distinction from the eastern church (Greece, Asia Minor, Palestine, and Egypt), where Greek was mainly spoken.

Two other doctrines of the Christian faith seemed to many theologians in the West to make a doctrine of original sin necessary. One doctrine was that of the virgin birth of Christ. The theologians in the West argued correctly that Christ's virgin birth was necessary to preserve his sinlessness.

Appeal was also made to a wrong doctrine of baptism. An error in the thinking of some in the church was that baptism washed away sins committed prior to baptism. If the Bible commanded infants to be baptized, and baptism washed away sin, infants were sinful. How could infants be sinful? Only by original sin; all infants shared in Adam's sin.

So advanced was the conception of some of the western theologians that they already struggled with the difference between original guilt and original pollution. Augustine taught both. The church, which in large measure repudiated Augustine's teaching, lost the doctrine of original guilt. It was not recovered until the time of the sixteenth-century Reformation one thousand years later.

CASSIANUS, FAUSTUS, AND SEMI-PELAGIANISM

INTRODUCTION

The attack against the doctrines of sovereign grace that had been made by Pelagius and his disciple Celestius were answered by the great bishop of Hippo, Augustine. But Augustine was only one individual in the church. He was its greatest thinker; he was its soundest theologian; he towered over his age like Colossus. But what he believed and taught, while influential in the lives of many others, could not become official church dogma until the church adopted his position.

Would the church do this? That was the crucial question of the age. Sooner or later the church was going to have to say something about the matter. It could not turn its eyes the other way and act as if a controversy did not exist. The differences of opinion were too sharp, the divisions too deep. A doctrine of "one, holy, catholic church" required a statement on this divisive issue of sovereign grace.

If one knew nothing about the outcome of the controversy and had no idea of what the church ultimately decided, one would almost certainly predict that Augustine would lose, that his views would be rejected, and that his position would be repudiated. And so it happened. However, there is irony here: Rome has canonized Augustine and written his name in large letters in its book of saints. But Augustine's name is written in Rome's annuls as one who attained sainthood in spite of terrible heresies, for according to Rome, his theology was all mixed up. This anomaly Rome has yet to explain.

The story of how and why Rome repudiated Augustine is a long and interesting one that lasted four hundred years. For three reasons Augustine's story is interesting and worth telling. First, his struggle was long and bitter, ending in the brutal murder of one of Augustine's most eloquent defenders. Second, when one carefully considers the problem Rome faced, Rome had no choice but to repudiate Augustine's views; Rome could not be Augustinian and remain Rome. This was true already in Augustine's lifetime, but it became abundantly clear in the centuries following Augustine. Third, in an astonishing way the controversy shows how the issues that faced the church a millennium and a half ago are issues that still divide the church today. For example, the defenders today of the well-meant offer of the gospel raise the same objections in its defense that the enemies of Augustine raised in his day against his teachings. Although the church discussed many different issues in Augustine's day, we can say with certainty that the real issue was whether the grace of almighty God is sovereign or resistible.

JOHN CASSIANUS AND FAUSTUS OF RIEZ

The two men we will describe—Cassianus and Faustus—are not, taken by themselves, very interesting or important men. Not a whole lot is known of their lives, nor did they contribute anything substantial to the history of the church of Christ or to the history of the development of the doctrine of Scripture. Their importance lies strictly in this: they both were sharp opponents of Augustine's doctrines.

John Cassianus was born in or near Marseilles in southern France, then known as Gaul. Although he received some education in his home town, he traveled to the East, where he entered a monastery in Bethlehem and came under the tutorship of Germanus, the head of the monastery and an extremely influential man in Palestine and Egypt.

Apparently both Cassianus and Germanus were fascinated with the concept of monasticism because they traveled together to Egypt to visit with Egyptian monks. They stayed there for seven years and learned the theory, practice, and doctrine of monasticism.

Monasticism was based on a certain theology, primarily ethical. Monasticism taught that one who practiced celibacy, self-denial through various ascetic practices, and poverty lived on a higher level of holiness than the child of God who married, brought up a family, and earned a living. Because the monks (and nuns) lived on a higher plane of holiness, closer to heaven and God, they were considered saints of a higher caliber. It is not difficult to see that such thinking would inevitably result in the notion that such saints, practicing self-denial, were more pleasing to God than the ordinary Christian who struggles with raising his children, loving his wife, and earning his daily bread. But if God were more pleased with the monk who starved himself rather than one who enjoys his evening meal after a day of hard work, then some works merited favor in God's sight. The determinative word here is *favor*. Out of monkery came the idea of the meritorious value of good works. Monks, quite generally, believed they were meriting with God. So did John Cassianus.

After seven years in Egypt, John and Germanus traveled to Constantinople. Nothing much happened there of importance, except for two things. One was that John met Chrysostom, the golden-tongued preacher, and studied under him. Chrysostom also ordained John as a deacon. The other event was that when Chrysostom was exiled because he attacked the wickedness of the empress, John and Germanus, as friends of Chrysostom, thought it the better part of wisdom to leave the city.

John returned to southern France and spent the rest of his life in his home town.

John's name has gone down in Roman Catholic history as the real founder of monasticism in the West. He had learned his lessons well in Bethlehem and Egypt. Upon returning to France, he founded two monasteries, one for men, one for women. The monastery for men became in time one of the most famous monasteries in Europe, the Abbey of St. Victor. Over these monasteries he exercised his rule, and for these monasteries he drew up a set of rules.

The dates of John's birth and death are obscure. He was apparently born around 360, although even that is in question. He died anywhere from 435 to 448, but he is said by at least one historian to have died when he was ninety-seven years old. Some quick figuring will show that this doesn't come out very well.

Faustus of Riez was, like Pelagius, a native Englishman. Faustus was born around 410 or so and also chose the monastic life. He soon moved to Brittany, and from Brittany to southern France. He is said, by his contemporaries, to have been a very pious and self-sacrificing man who devoted his life to helping others. His reputation as a pious man, a preacher, and a writer soon earned him a bishopric in Riez. One outstanding event in his life (in our judgment, at any rate) was the fact that at the Synod of Lyon he was instrumental in having Lucidus condemned for his views on predestination. Lucidus closely followed the teachings of Augustine, but that kind of adherence to Augustine could not be tolerated. In fact, Faustus had the dubious honor of persuading Lucidus to retract his "heresy."

Other honors came his way. Faustus was chosen by the emperor to engage in negotiations with Euric, king of the Visigoths, a barbarian tribe and a threat to Rome. The barbarians had already made several successful incursions into Italy and had even sacked Rome, but efforts were being made to keep the empire intact. Faustus loved politics.

A Brief Statement of Augustine's Views

We would probably call Augustine a Calvinist if he had lived in our day, at least as far as the truth of God's grace is concerned.[1] He held firmly to the five points of Calvinism although he lived more than one thousand years before the Synod of Dordrecht (Dordt). Augustine not only taught total depravity, but he also specifically denied the freedom of the will and the concept of merit. He insisted that because man is totally depraved, grace is absolutely essential for salvation. God has to take the initiative, for man can do nothing of himself. Grace is irresistible in its operations, so that God's intentions and purposes are always accomplished. And grace is particular, rooted in the eternal decree of predestination.

Some have challenged the assertion that Augustine taught double predestination (election and reprobation). There can, however, be no doubt that he taught both. Augustine taught a sovereign reprobation that reflects God's own purpose and will; he did not teach a conditional reprobation based on God's prediction that man in unbelief would reject the gospel.

I have searched many of Augustine's writings to learn what his teachings on predestination were. I have in my file numerous quotes in which Augustine speaks emphatically and unequivocally of reprobation. The conclusion I have come to is the conclusion of other scholars of Augustine as well, even some who disagree violently with Augustine's position.

It nevertheless remains a fact that Augustine, while believing in all the truths of sovereign grace from the beginning of his controversies with Pelagius and Celestius, sharpened and clarified his position when Cassianus and Faustus attacked him and he had to defend his teachings against their attacks.

The Views of Cassianus and Faustus

Three remarks are necessary before I spell out the specific views of these two heretics.

First, these men did not write personally to Augustine and express disagreement with his position. They attacked him in the churches in France where they worked. They not only taught views directly opposite those of Augustine, but they repudiated what Augustine taught and condemned him by name as well as the doctrine he taught. This was not honest on their part, even though no official stand had been taken on these issues by the church.

Second, although they disagreed with Augustine on many points, they centered their attacks on the doctrine of sovereign predestination, and particularly on the doctrine of reprobation. In a way, this is not surprising. The enemies of sovereign grace have always attacked the doctrine of reprobation more than any other. They seem to consider reprobation the Achilles' heel of sovereign grace. Election, yes. They claim to want election. But reprobation—that is another matter. That doctrine takes the brunt of the attack, in large measure because it is inescapably a doctrine that emphasizes God's sovereignty.

Third, one must not conclude from what I have written about John Cassianus and Faustus of Riez that these men were Pelagians. They attacked Pelagius and his views with just as much vehemence as they attacked Augustine and his views. However, they proposed the middle way of reconciling Augustine's radical position with Pelagius' equally radical views as the solution to a knotty problem. They rejected a bit of both, accepted a bit of both, and recommended their middle way to the church.

Their urging the church to adopt a middle way has led to a strange controversy over names that has attracted the attention of some historians. Some people want to call the views of Cassianus and Faustus semi-Augustinianism. They do this to underscore that some parts of Augustine's position were accepted by these men. Others insist that these men ought to be called semi-Pelagians. The idea is that they tipped toward Pelagianism more than toward Augustinianism.

We call these men semi-Pelagians. But let it be understood that this is for purposes of identification only. In the doctrine of sovereign grace, there is no halfway position. One is either for or against: for or against Augustine, for or against Christ. There are no semi-Christians, semi-Reformed, semi-Calvinists, semi-Arminians, or semi-Protestant Reformed. The fathers at Dordt called the Arminians teachers of a modified semi-Pelagianism, or Pelagians who were resurrecting the errors of Pelagius from hell. That kind of language is not a semi-condemnation.

In attacking predestination, and particularly reprobation, Cassianus and Faustus had three main objections.

First, they argued that predestination did not do justice to human responsibility. These two gentlemen who hated predestination claimed that there was contradiction in Scripture between man's responsibility, which was rooted in the freedom of the will, and God's sovereignty. Faustus wrote, "If you pay careful attention, you will recognize clearly and abundantly how through the pages of the Scriptures sometimes it is the power of grace and at other times it is the assent of the human will that is asserted."[2]

It is interesting that in connection with human responsibility, one of the main objections to Augustine's teachings was that his view denied the invitation of Christ in the gospel. This so-called invitation necessarily implies the desire of God to save all men.

Second, Cassianus and Faustus branded Augustine's views as fatalism in the heathen sense. His view was interpreted to mean that "by God's predestination men are compelled to sin and are driven to death by a sort of fatal necessity." Thus the doctrine of predestination was characterized as nothing short of the heathen worship of Fate. One is struck by the fact that the Arminians accused the fathers at Dordt of the same sin.[3]

Third, especially Cassianus brought up some other objections that included a charge that Augustine made the baptism of the reprobate of none effect since the reprobate were predestined to destruction. He argued that evangelism becomes a useless endeavor if predestination is true. He claimed that the call to repentance becomes meaningless in Augustine's view, because a true call implies both divine grace and human freedom. If Cassianus had known the term *hyper-Calvinist,* he would have used it against Augustine. Even prayer becomes useless if predestination is true, he said. He argued on the basis of his conviction that the free will of man had to take some initiative in salvation. "By the goodness of the Creator there still remained the capacity to initiate the will for salvation." Cassianus also claimed that predestination destroys all morality because it instills in man a spirit of disregard for God's law; that is, it makes men careless and profane.[4]

How wearyingly familiar it all sounds to those who hear the arguments of today's Arminians. Even the so-called universalistic texts appealed to today, such as 1 Timothy 2:4 and Matthew 23:37, were already quoted against Augustine back in the fifth century. I mention only two here because it is important to quote Augustine's answer to these men who appealed to such texts in support of their position.

In short, Cassianus and Faustus believed that though man was born depraved, some remnants of good remained in him. These remnants, they said, were strengthened by baptism, which restored a free will in man. The result was that man was not dead, but very sick. The possibility of the healing of his sickness lay in calling the great physician. Christ could heal. But Christ would not heal unless the sinner called for him, for Christ would heal no man against his will. In the healing process, the sick sinner was said to cooperate with the physician—sometimes Christ taking the initiative, sometimes the sinner. But Christ would save only those who call upon him to come to their aid, because Christ died for all men and desired that all men be saved. Yes, already then, the doctrine of a universal atonement was introduced.

The whole thing was a modification of the crass views of Pelagius, but was only an attempt to dress up a terribly ugly heresy in a more attractive suit of clothes.

AUGUSTINE'S RESPONSE

Augustine sharpened his views on sovereign grace and predestination in his battle with semi-Pelagianism. At this time he wrote two important books concerning the truth of sovereign grace. They are *A Treatise on the Predestination of the Saints* and *The Gift of Perseverance*.

This is not the time or the place to go into detail on Augustine's views, but I want to give two enlightening quotations from Augustine's book *Enchiridion*.

The first quotation is from Augustine's comments on Matthew 23:37: "But even though she [Jerusalem] was unwilling, He gathered together as many of her children as He wished: for He does not will some things and do them, and will others and do them not, but 'He hath done all that He pleased in heaven and in earth.'"[5]

On 1 Timothy 2:4 Augustine writes,

> But that we are to understand by 'all men,' the human race in all its varieties of rank and circumstances,—kings, subjects; noble, plebeian, high, low, learned, and unlearned; the sound in body, the feeble, the clever, the dull, the foolish, the rich, the poor, and those of middling circumstances; males, females, infants, boys, youths; young, middle-aged, and old men; of every tongue, of every fashion, of all arts, of all professions, with all the innumerable differences of will and conscience, and whatever else there is that makes a distinction among men. . . . we are not compelled to believe that the omnipotent God has willed anything to be done which was not done: for, setting aside all ambiguities, if 'He hath done all that He pleased in heaven and in earth,' as the psalmist sings of Him, He certainly did not will to do anything that He hath not done.[6]

No one can doubt that Augustine would have repudiated any notion of the well-meant offer of the gospel, although the idea was being taught in his time by Cassianus and Faustus. Augustine wanted no part of it.

THE SYNOD OF ORANGE

After Augustine's death the controversy continued, although Augustine's views had few supporters. Most of the debate concerned various modifications of the views of Cassianus and Faustus. The differences of opinion in Gaul were sufficiently great to warrant the calling of the Synod of Orange, which met in 529.

The synod, in itself, was of very minor importance. It was a local gathering attended by only thirteen or fourteen bishops. It could not speak for all of Gaul, much less the whole western church. What makes it important is Pope Boniface II's endorsement of its decisions, making them binding on the western church. Pope Boniface II thereby officially committed the Roman Catholic Church, at least in the West, to semi-Pelagianism, and Pelagianism has remained official Roman Catholic doctrine.

Even before the synod met, a certain consensus emerged among Gaul's theologians. The consensus acknowledged, generally speaking, that election was indeed true and that grace was necessary to salvation because of man's sinful condition with which he was born. But having tipped the hat, so to speak, toward Augustine, the consensus also thought reprobation to be wrong. It made a caricature of Augustine's views by condemning the idea that men are predestined to evil and that damnation belongs to the will of God apart from sin. Such views, which Augustine never taught, attempted to make the doctrine of sovereign reprobation, which he did teach, to be reprehensible in the minds of men. The theologians mostly agreed that even though predestination in a limited sense is true, nevertheless God wills the salvation of all men, and baptism enables a person to do what is necessary for the salvation of his soul.

The Synod of Orange went in the direction of this consensus. As if to prove its orthodox character, the synod insisted on original sin, total depravity, and the inability of the natural man to do any good. It felt perfectly free to anathematize anyone who denied these truths. But in the same decision, with a complete about-face, the synod also spoke of the ability of any baptized person to work out his own salvation. And so the synod said that God gives the beginning of faith and charity, with an emphasis on the word *beginning,* which made it clear that the synod meant to teach that from thereon in, salvation was up to man.

More crucially, the synod refused to adopt the doctrine of reprobation and would only pour its anathemas upon the heads of all who taught the doctrine. With this thundering anathema, the synod anathematized its own Augustine, whom the Roman Catholic Church had declared a saint.

Herman Hoeksema makes this comment on the Synod of Orange: "It appears very clearly that they were afraid to maintain the strict doctrine of Augustine. The synod assumed an apologetic attitude. And although it opposed the doctrine of the semi-Pelagians, it nevertheless was far from maintaining the positive doctrine of predestination and sovereign grace."[7]

PART 2

MEDIEVAL PERIOD (500–1517)

Contenders for the Faith and Historical Events		*Promoters of Heresy*
	500	
Synod of Orange 529		
		Pope Gregory I c. 540–604 (pontificate 590–604)
	700	
Battle of Tours stopped Arab advance in Europe 732		
		Rabanus c. 776–856
Charlemagne crowned emperor of the Holy Roman Empire 800	**800**	**Radbertus** c. 800–c. 865
Gottschalk 806–68		
Ratramnus birth unknown; died after 868		
Berengar 1000–88	**1000**	
Anselm 1033–1109		**Lanfranc** 1005–89
Schism of western and eastern parts of the church 1054		**Abelard** 1079–1142
First Crusade 1096–99		
	1100	
Synod of Soissons condemned Abelard for antitrinitarian teaching 1121		
Synod of Sens tried Abelard for his heretical view against the inspiration of Scripture 1141		
Second Crusade 1145–53		
		Pope Innocent III 1160–1216 (pontificate 1198–1216)
	1200	
Fourth Lateran Council made transubstantiation official doctrine and established the Inquisition 1215		
	1300	
Beginning of Black Death in Europe 1347		**Thomas à Kempis** 1380–1471
	1400	
Fall of Constantinople to Seljuk Turks 1453		
	1517	

CHAPTER 10

GREGORY I: FIRST MEDIEVAL POPE

INTRODUCTION

The most important institution in the Middle Ages, roughly from the time of the death of Augustine (430) to the Protestant Reformation (1517), was the Roman Catholic papacy. It dominated all the history of the western Mediterranean world and Europe, and its influence was inescapable in the eastern church until the great schism between East and West in 1054.

During this millennium the papacy determined, more than any other institution, the political, economic, and ecclesiastical life of Europe. The man who, more than any other, shaped the medieval papacy was Pope Gregory I, known throughout history as Gregory the Great. Although he was a child of the ancient period of church history, he stood with one foot in that period and the other foot in the medieval period. And by shaping the medieval papacy, Gregory formed the medieval Romish church. He determined its direction and set the pattern for the entire medieval period in the exaltation of the power of the papacy, in its political rule of the nations, in its liturgy, and in its theology.

Gregory was, in fact, the first pope. Other men who were called popes preceded him and made the same extravagant claims for the papacy as Gregory. Others exerted some influence on the affairs of men and nations from their position in the see of Rome, but Gregory was not called "the Great" without reason. He was the first true pope.

It is interesting to know something of the life of the man and of his views on various ecclesiastical matters, simply because the medieval period of church history never departed significantly from what Gregory had taught and promoted. Traveling the distance from Gregory to the Reformation, one feels the hand of Gregory wherever he turns. Gregory is a man worth looking at.

THE TIMES IN WHICH GREGORY WORKED

One could hardly imagine worse times than the years of Gregory's life. The great barbarian migrations had resulted in the near death of all civilization in the West, whereas the eastern Roman Empire survived in the Byzantine Empire until the capture of Constantinople in 1453.

The barbarian migrations had overrun and almost destroyed what is now Europe. Philip Schaff writes,

> Italy...was exhausted by war and overrun by the savage Lombards, who were still heathen or Arian heretics, and burned churches, slew ecclesiastics, robbed monasteries, violated nuns, reduced cultivated fields into a wilderness. Rome was constantly exposed to plunder, and wasted by pestilence and famine. All Europe was in a chaotic state, and bordering on anarchy. Serious men...thought that the end of the world had come.[1]

Gregory himself, in one of his sermons, said,

> What is it...that can at this time delight us in the world? Everywhere we see tribulation, everywhere we hear lamentation. The cities are destroyed, the castles torn down, the fields laid waste, the land made desolate. Villages are empty, few inhabitants remain in the cities, and even these poor remnants of humanity are daily cut down...We see how some are carried into captivity, others mutilated, others slain.[2]

The times were grievous indeed.

Yet in all the chaos of the barbarian conquests and the repeated sack of Rome, though the empire disintegrated in the West, the church remained the one surviving institution.

GREGORY'S EARLY LIFE

Gregory was born in 540, 110 years after the death of the great Augustine. He was born from the ancient Roman nobility, for his ancestors for many years had belonged to the senatorial class in the Roman Empire. Over the years the family had acquired vast holdings, immense wealth, and a huge castle for a home.

The home was also a Christian home, and the early influences on Gregory were religious, even though his education prepared him for governmental services. When Gregory's father Gordianus died, his mother Sylvia entered a convent. She gave herself over so completely to an ascetic life and to piety and godliness that the Romish church later canonized her.

Gregory seemed to be destined for a life of governmental work and was, in fact, appointed by the emperor in the East to the office of Imperial Prefect, the highest government post in Rome and in the entire West. The year was 574; Gregory was only thirty-four years old.

GREGORY THE MONK

Apparently the religious influences of Gregory's childhood and youth continued to work on him, for shortly after his appointment to Rome's most prestigious post, he renounced the world completely, changed his father's palace, which he had inherited, into a monastery, and became a monk in it. The enormous wealth that he had inherited he used partly to found six monasteries in Sicily, all of which were given land holdings; the remainder of the wealth of his ancestral patrimony he gave to the poor. He was a penniless monk in a lonely monastery that had once been his home.

But he soon attracted attention. Others joined him in his ascetic life, and a monastic community was established. Gregory was so completely a monk that, because of his frugal meals and self-discipline, he permanently harmed his health.

Even though he had turned his back on political service, the government would not let him alone. In 579 the church appointed him as a deacon, and the government sent him as an ambassador to the court in Constantinople. In the seven years he continued there, he did invaluable service for the government.

In 585 he returned to Rome and became abbot of the monastery that he had founded. Although Gregory continued in government service, the direction of his life had fundamentally changed. One interesting aspect of this change was his sudden interest in missions. The event reads like a story.

One day, while in the slave market in Rome, Gregory saw three Anglo-Saxon boys offered for sale on the slave block. He was struck by their appearance, for they had light hair, fair complexions, and sweet faces. After some inquiry he learned that they were heathen idolaters from another country and nation. "When he discovered that they were Angles, he said: 'Right, for they have *angelic* faces, and are worthy to be fellow-heirs with angels in heaven.'"[3] Gregory learned that the name of their king was Ella, to which he responded, "*Hallelujah*... the praise of God the Creator must be sung in those parts."[4]

Gregory rushed from the slave market to the papal residence and pleaded with the pope to send missionaries to "Angle-land" (England). He offered to go himself and even started out for that land. But he never arrived because he was summoned back to Rome. He could not be spared in the holy city. In 590, by the popular acclaim of the clergy and the people, he was elected pope.

From all outward appearances, Gregory did everything in his power to escape being pope. He considered himself unworthy of this exalted position and would have, if possible, escaped from its responsibilities. It seems as if he was coerced into accepting the election. Yet one ought to be a bit cautious. Gregory was not always the man he seemed to be—as we shall learn.

The papacy did not change his manner of living, however. He continued to live frugally and, faithful to his monastic vows, he practiced the ascetic life even while pope. Because the papacy already then had vast land holdings, the revenue was enormous. But he refused to allow this revenue to be used to satisfy the covetous greed of those who surrounded him; rather, he used the resources of the church to engage in acts of charity. It was not uncommon to see Gregory out in the streets personally distributing food and money to those in need. And through others, he fed hundreds, cared for the sick, clothed the beggars, and alleviated the suffering of those around him.

He became a powerful pope.

Schaff describes Gregory in the following way:

> He is one of the best representatives of medieval Catholicism: monastic, ascetic, devout and superstitious; hierarchical, haughty, and ambitious, yet humble before God; indifferent, if not hostile, to classical and secular culture, but friendly to sacred and ecclesiastical learning; just, humane, and liberal to ostentation; full of missionary zeal in the interest of Christianity and the Roman see, which to his mind were inseparably connected. He combined great executive ability with untiring industry, and amid all his official cares he never forgot the claims of personal piety.[5]

GREGORY'S INFLUENCE ON WORSHIP

Gregory's accomplishments were many—some good, some bad. We shall take a look at both.

Gregory took an interest in the worship of the church. To a certain extent, worship, especially in the West, had developed extensively over the centuries and had assumed some fixed form. But Gregory, a skilled liturgist who was sensitive to the nuances of worship, made some changes, fixed for all time some aspects of worship, and added some elements heretofore ignored.

He introduced into the church the chant, and to this day those chants, known as Gregorian chants, are popular and common. The technical aspects of the music are beyond my understanding, but it is clear that Gregory introduced these chants, in part at least, in an effort to introduce music into the drab lives of the monks and to give the singing to choirs within the church by taking it away from the congregation.

Gregory was also a preacher. In fact, he was a very popular preacher who loved to preach and who, through preaching, influenced the thinking of the people in Rome.

But one aspect of his preaching requires special notice. Although allegorical preaching was characteristic in certain parts of the church for many centuries, Gregory perfected and codified the art. Gregory did not know Hebrew and Greek and therefore could not work with the original languages. Nor did he have any training in grammatical and historical interpretation. His allegorizing is an exegetical curiosity.

Gregory was able to find, either between or beneath the lines of Scripture, the history of Jesus Christ and a natural and revealed theology.

> The names of persons and things, the number, and even the syllables, are filled with mystic meaning. Job represents Christ; his wife the carnal nature; his seven sons (seven being the number of perfection) represent the apostles, and hence the clergy; his three daughters the three classes of the faithful laity who are to worship the Trinity; his friends the heretics; the seven thousand sheep the perfect Christians; the five hundred yoke of oxen and five hundred she-asses again the heathen, because the prophet Isaiah says: "The ox knoweth his owner, and the ass his master's crib: but Israel doth not know, my people doth not consider."[6]

In a way, Gregory canonized this form of interpretation. Because of his influence and because of his success as a preacher, this type of exegesis became a kind of norm for preaching. It even developed into a form of exegesis that required the exegete to find a fourfold meaning in the text. The church of Rome utilized this type of exegesis to take the Scriptures away from the people of God.

The Reformation, and particularly Luther, brought the church back to the literal interpretation of Scripture, for it is the literal interpretation that allows God's people to understand the Scriptures whether they be young or old, educated or uneducated, wise or simple. God writes Scripture for all his people.

Allegorical interpretation remains the curse of much exegesis in the church to the present.

GREGORY'S INFLUENCE ON DOCTRINE

Of even greater importance is Gregory's development of the doctrine of the mass and of transubstantiation. It is true that much controversy would continue to swirl around these questions for several centuries, and it is true that the Romish doctrine of transubstantiation would not be fixed as dogma for several more centuries; but Gregory began its real development. He taught that the sacrifice of Christ on the cross, though a completed sacrifice, nevertheless continues in the mass. When the priest celebrates the mass, therefore, he reenacts the atonement on Calvary. To do this, the priest changes the bread and wine into the body and blood of Christ. And because of that change in the substance, the church, through the mass, is able to bring various influences to bear on God in connection with the sins of the people. Gregory is, in fact, known as the father of the mass and of transubstantiation.

Because of the importance given to the mass, the entire liturgy was organized around it. While preaching continued in the church, the mass became more and more the important thing. As the ages rolled by, preaching was gradually to go into total eclipse, and the mass alone, with all its rituals and ceremonies, constituted the worship service. This practice did not end until the Reformation.

GREGORY AND THE GROWTH OF MONASTICISM

Gregory was the first monk to sit on the throne of the see of Rome. He became a monk early and never forsook his monastic ways. In fact, Gregory was partly instrumental in giving form and shape to medieval monasticism.

Gregory did much to formulate rules governing monasteries; he also used his enormous influence to regulate monasteries throughout the western church and to enforce the rules that had been made. Monasticism, in its very nature, can be conducive to a very ascetic life given over to many outward forms of piety. Monasteries can also become, by their very nature, cesspools of corruption. The efforts to observe the vows of poverty and celibacy can (and did) result in drunkenness, gluttony, and fornication. Gregory imposed strict discipline upon wayward monasteries and ordered wicked monks thrown out of the movement—and, if necessary, the church.

In order to achieve his goal, Gregory made clerical celibacy the rule in the church. It had been widely practiced; it had been extolled as particularly virtuous; it had been enforced in some parts of the church. But many married priests could be found—that is, until Gregory. From Gregory's time, celibacy was required. In more evil times, concubinage was tolerated, but marriage was forbidden.

More than these things, Gregory, in his favor toward monasticism, gave to the monks the status of a kind of quasi clergy. They were not exactly clergymen, but they were not laymen either. They moved about somewhere in between. Because all monastic movements and orders were directly authorized by the pope and directly responsible to only the pope, they became a kind of papal army. Future popes knew how to manipulate these monks to serve their own purposes. Monks became a plague on the church. Europe was full of them. They often wandered around, interfered in the affairs of others, preached, administered the sacraments, enforced papal decrees, defended the by-the-pope-defined doctrines, and generally made a colossal nuisance of themselves. It was Gregory who began this practice.

GREGORY THE THEOLOGIAN
Although not original in his thinking, Gregory numbered among his extensive gifts the abilities of a theologian. In fact, his writings became standard textbooks in theological schools for several centuries.

Yet his theology was sadly deficient. Gregory maintained, of course, the decrees of the great councils of Nicea, Constantinople, and Chalcedon; he was orthodox in all matters for which these councils stood. Nevertheless, he was a semi-Pelagian. This is particularly distressing, for Gregory was in a position to choose otherwise. It is true that the compromising Synod of Orange (529) had adopted a kind of semi-Pelagianism, and it is true that Benedict II had fixed these decisions for the church as dogma. But the question was still being discussed, and Gregory could have used his influence for good.

But Gregory was a monk. As we noticed in an earlier chapter, monasticism and the doctrine of merit are two sides of the same coin. Augustine had no room for merit in his theology; for him, all was of God in the work of salvation. Semi-Pelagianism did have room for human merit, and Gregory led the church into this devilish error.

Gregory was a vigorous defender of ecclesiastical orthodoxy—in some instances. He fought tooth and nail against the Donatists in North Africa. Would to God he had been as courageous in his battle against the Pelagians. But Gregory wanted the doctrine of merit. He wanted it for his precious monks to make their life of self-sacrifice worthwhile. He wanted it for all the people of the church. And so he spoke of the value of good works because of their meritorious nature. By virtue of the merit earned through good works and penance, one could atone for the sins that a person committed and so earn favor with God.

It is not strange that this idea led Gregory to two other ideas. The first was the doctrine of purgatory, for a place had to be invented for those people who had done insufficient good works to atone for their deficiencies in life. The second was the doctrine of works of supererogation, for there were some who did so many good works that they did not need them all to atone for their moral lapses and falls. Hence a bank of good works was built up, the assets of which could be used for others. Everyone who knows anything about the Reformation knows what a lucrative business this became for Rome, which raked in much of the wealth of Europe by its preposterous and blasphemous doctrine of indulgences.

Thus Gregory was not averse to denying the doctrines of sovereign grace. He taught freely a conditional predestination, a love of God for all men, and a universal cross of Christ.

GREGORY THE POPE

Gregory always appeared in public as a humble man. He cultivated humility. He attempted to avoid becoming pope at all. He constantly referred to himself as servant of servants. He refused the title Universal Bishop and protested every effort to be ruler in the church and among the nations.

However, his protestations shall remain forever suspect, for his actions belied his words. One of the outstanding characteristics of the medieval papacy was its insistence that the pope was not only the head of the church, but also the Vicar of Christ in the political arena, and thus the king of kings. While it took centuries for the popes to realize this dream, there can be no question that Gregory began it.

The half-barbarian Lombards were a constant threat to Italy, and Gregory was the one most involved in defeating them. He fought the Lombards by obtaining troops and sending them against the barbarians. He engaged in negotiations with them and signed a peace treaty. Thus he assumed responsibility for the political peace of the land.

Through various events in earlier centuries the church owned vast tracts of land throughout Italy, Sicily, Dalmatia, Gaul, and North Africa. As the pope became increasingly powerful, he became the overseer and ruler of all these possessions. The government of these areas fell upon the pope, the revenues entered his coffers, the problems came to his desk, and the decisions had to be made in his study. The result was that he became a temporal sovereign over a private kingdom known as the *patrimonium petri* (the patrimony of Peter).

The pope claimed his enormous powers on the basis of the Lord's words: "Thou art Peter, and upon this rock I will build my church" (Matt. 16:18). In other words, Gregory claimed to be the successor of Peter and taught that Peter was the head of all the apostles and of all the church.

It can be argued that when the barbarians sacked Rome and destroyed the Roman Empire in the West, the church was the only surviving institution. It can be argued that the pope was the most influential man in the western church and that he was in the best possible position to deal with barbarian threats. But one cannot stretch Scripture so far that one finds in it the right of any cleric to exercise political power. This remains a papal claim; and, if it were possible, the pope would today, once again, claim rule of the nations.

For many years conflict and controversy had raged between the bishop of Rome and the patriarch of Constantinople concerning the question of who had preeminence in church matters. At Gregory's time, the patriarch of Constantinople was claiming to be universal bishop. Gregory hated that and did all in his power to stop Constantinople's head primate from calling himself by a title that indicated the patriarch's claim to universal rule.

Gregory always railed against this practice of his rival in the East with many professions of humility and assurances that he wanted no part of such arrogance and blasphemy. At the same time, his very ferocity revealed that Gregory considered himself to be what he was condemning in another.

Here Gregory acquired one of the worst stains upon his character. In order to get Constantinople's patriarch to cease calling himself universal bishop, Gregory enlisted the aid of Phocus, who was an absolute monster of sin and evil. He had murdered the previous emperor in the East and his six children, and he had set himself on the throne. Phocus so debauched the throne and the palace that the people rose in rebellion against him, dragged him from his throne, mutilated him, and cut off his head. But Gregory, during Phocus' reign, enlisted the aid of such a monster by calling him high and lofty names, giving him honorable titles, and fawning over him.

On another occasion Gregory did something similar. When the church in Gaul seemed unwilling to surrender its independence to papal control, Gregory enlisted the help of Brunhilda, a notoriously wicked woman, but one of considerable power. His theory was that the good she could (and did) do for the church merited sufficient forgiveness to cover her many and monstrous sins.

Popes after Gregory followed the same ethical rule: the end justifies the means. As long as something was good for the church, it mattered not what means were used to attain that goal.

GREGORY THE MISSIONARY

It is better to end on a more positive note, although also here things take a sour turn.

Gregory was deeply interested in missions, especially in Great Britain. He pursued missionary labors after he became pope and did much to promote the Christianizing of barbarian Europe. Gregory adopted two mission policies that were to affect all future mission work.

The first policy was that missionaries were to adapt themselves to pagan practices while giving these practices a Christian meaning and facade. Today that would be called cultural or transcultural adaptation in missions. The second policy was that missionaries were to convert the ruler of a land and work through the ruler to make the entire country Christian. This was done in England, for example. King Ethelbert married a Christian wife, was himself converted and baptized, and gradually influenced his entire nation to become Christian. It was a successful policy.

Gregory died on March 12, 604, at the age of sixty-four and after being pope only fourteen years. But Rome and Europe were never the same.

Only at the Reformation did God deliver his church from Rome's tyranny.

CHAPTER II

RABANUS AND THE VICTORY OF SEMI-PELAGIANISM

INTRODUCTION

The battle over the doctrine of sovereign grace between Augustine, on the one hand, and Cassianus and Faustus, on the other, continued for one hundred years after the death of these men until official decisions were made by the Synod of Orange in 529 and approved by Pope Boniface II.

Even these decisions of Orange did not settle the matter. There continued to be defenders of Augustine and defenders of semi-Pelagianism for another three hundred years. The controversy climaxed in the life of Rabanus, who, though an extremely gifted man, proved a terrible enemy of the doctrine of sovereign grace. In fact, he was the man who, more than any other, was responsible for the murder of Gottschalk, a courageous defender of sovereign grace and double predestination.

One wonders sometimes why the battle was so prolonged. There was something inevitable about the adoption of semi-Pelagianism by the Roman Catholic Church. Given its prior history, especially its approval of monasticism, it could hardly have adopted the theology developed by Augustine. Yet the Lord prolonged the controversy for four hundred years.

It is probably impossible to determine why the Lord worked in this mysterious way. God's ways are always higher than our ways, and the mysteries of his providence are the mysteries of the works of one who knows the end from the beginning, who does all things perfectly from the beginning to the end of time, and who sees the perfect pattern into which every event must be fit.

But two ideas regarding the four centuries of controversy suggest themselves. First, the prolonged battle demonstrates vividly that even as the clouds of apostasy lowered on the Romish church, God preserved a faithful remnant ready to defend, at the cost of their lives, the truths of sovereign grace. Second, Rome had abundant opportunity to know the terrible error to which the church was determined to commit itself, yet it persisted in its evil way. Rome has no excuse for its terrible denial of salvation by grace alone. One is reminded of what the Lord says of Judah: "What could have been done more to my vineyard, that I have not done in it?" (Isa. 5:4). Yet Judah brought forth wild grapes.

Our story is centered on Rabanus and Gottschalk.

RABANUS' LIFE

Rabanus lived during the time of the great Frankish king, Charlemagne, who carved out a kingdom from the wilds of France and Germany, and who was the founder of what became known as the Holy Roman Empire. Rabanus was born around 776 in Mainz, Germany. He was educated in the abbey at Fulda and thus destined for monkhood. He entered the Benedictine Order, became a deacon in 801, and went to Tours in France to study theology and the liberal arts under Alcuin, the great educator in Charlemagne's empire.

Rabanus completed his education and returned to Fulda to teach in the school that was connected with the abbey. His administrative and teaching abilities were so great that the school grew rapidly. Attending it were many sons of noblemen, but also future ministers and teachers who, upon completing their studies, fanned out into all parts of Charlemagne's domain.

In 814 Rabanus became a priest and in 822 the abbot of the abbey in Fulda. The choice proved to be a good one, for Rabanus ruled the abbey well and supervised its rebuilding. He encouraged and promoted the building of many churches in the surrounding area and ruled the monks with wisdom, discretion, and firmness. He helped artistic monks to develop their talents and instructed them to use their artistic abilities to decorate the new churches built in the area. He increased the property holdings of the monastery and made it one of the leading monasteries in Europe. He taught and preached regularly and produced an enormous amount of material. He wrote a commentary on all the canonical books of the Bible and on all the apocryphal books.

In 842 Rabanus retired to spend his time in a nearby church where he could concentrate on devotional activities and writing. However, in 847 he was called out of retirement to become archbishop of Mainz. It was during this period of his life that Rabanus showed how deeply he was committed to Roman Catholicism in its most virulent forms.

GOTTSCHALK

I must at this point remind our readers of Gottschalk, who—in my judgment—was one of the great men of medieval times. I cannot give you here his entire biography, but the interested reader can find more of it in my book on the church fathers.[1]

Gottschalk was born in 806 and was placed by his parents in the monastery at Fulda when he was a child. Upon arriving at years of discretion, he asked to have his monastic vows cancelled because he had had no choice in making them when still a child. This request was first granted, but it was vetoed by Rabanus, the abbot of the monastery.

Rabanus was an ardent and radical defender of monasticism and all the theology implied in that strange Roman Catholic institution. Rabanus firmly believed that once someone had taken a monastic vow, that vow was absolutely unbreakable. He could not, therefore, grant Gottschalk a release. Instead, Rabanus sent Gottschalk to Orbais to be ordained as a member of the Benedictine convent there.

Because Gottschalk saw no hope of ever being delivered from a monastic life, he devoted himself to a study of Augustine and became persuaded of Augustine's teaching concerning the sovereignty of grace, including Augustine's doctrine of double predestination. He was so enthralled with these views and their biblical character that he traveled through the Mediterranean world bringing the gospel of sovereign grace to all who would hear.

Such practices as this soon got him into trouble with the church authorities. A bishop from Verona took exception to Gottschalk's teaching and referred the matter to Rabanus in Mainz, who was, after all, Gottschalk's superior. Rabanus condemned Gottschalk's views out of hand, but Gottschalk had the courage to stand up to Rabanus and condemn Rabanus' views as being semi-Pelagian. The controversy between the two soon reverberated throughout Europe.

SYNOD OF MAYENCE

Because of Gottschalk's refusal to kowtow to Rabanus' judgment, Rabanus called a synod to meet in Mayence in 848. Gottschalk, a bit naive, was convinced that when he had shown to the synod that his teachings were pure Augustinianism and in keeping with Scripture besides, he would be completely exonerated. He set forth his views at the synod "in the joyous conviction that it was in accordance with the one doctrine of the church."[2] But the poor monk had no conception of ecclesiastical politics. The synod condemned him, and Rabanus handed him over to Hincmar of Rheims,

France, with this paragraph in the accompanying letter: "We send to you this vagabond monk, in order that you may shut him up in his convent, and prevent him from propagating his false, heretical, and scandalous doctrine."[3]

Gottschalk was now at the mercy of Hincmar, a man noted for his cruelty. Gottschalk never escaped from the convent or from the prison into which he was eventually thrown. Beaten, starved, cruelly treated, he finally died in 868. But he never denied his faith.

SYNOD OF CHIERSY

While Gottschalk still lived, his courageous stand continued to stir up discussion, and various other synods were forced to meet to consider the matter. One such synod was the Synod of Chiersy in 849. It made every effort to persuade Gottschalk to retract his views, but it failed miserably. Gottschalk was convinced that the truth he confessed was the truth of God.

The synod did make some notable decisions about doctrine. Concerning predestination the synod said two things: God elected a people out of the fallen human race to eternal life; and God did not predestinate the rest that they should perish, but he predestinated them to eternal punishment because he foreknew they would not believe. This is the doctrine of conditional reprobation, taught later by the Arminians and held by many today who still claim to believe in reprobation.

The synod also said that grace works in such a way that man's will is made free, so that the depravity of man's nature is mitigated by the power of grace. This is the doctrine of preparatory grace, a grace given to all who hear the gospel.

Further, the synod decided that God wishes all men to be saved and expresses that wish in the preaching. So also, Christ died for all; but the fact that his death did not set all men free "is the fault of those who are unbelieving, or who do not believe with the faith that works love."[4] So salvation was said to be dependent upon the choice of man's will made free by preparatory grace.

Gottschalk had some supporters who were appalled at his cruel treatment and who were in basic agreement with his views. Ratramnus (later famous for his arguments against the Roman Catholic doctrine of transubstantiation) insisted that God is the "ruler" although not the author of sin. In this way he insisted on the sovereignty of God over sin. Prudentius repudiated the idea of a universal atonement and insisted that Christ died only for the elect whom it was God's purpose to save. Although Lupus was weak on the doctrine of reprobation, he agreed with Gottschalk that 1 Timothy 2:4 refers to different kinds of people and to a limited number, not to all men head for head. Lupus also held, against those who charged that Gottschalk's doctrine of sovereignty created carnal Christians, that the elect can never be carnally secure because they see their need of Christ and go to him.

All this led to another synod.

SYNOD OF VALENCE

The Synod of Valence in 855 was a surprise. In some important respects it upheld Gottschalk. Its decision reads as follows:

> We confess a predestination of the elect to life, and a predestination of the wicked to death; but that, in the election of those who are to be saved, the mercy of God precedes good merit... and in the condemnation of those who will perish, evil merit... precedes the righteous judgment of God. But that in predestination God has determined only those things which he himself would do, either from gratuitous mercy or in righteous judgment... But that in the wicked he foreknew the wickedness because it comes from them; and did not predestinate it, because it does not come from him.[5]

The synod also said those teachers in the church "are condemned who think that some are predestinated to evil by divine power, *i.e.,* so that, as it were, they cannot be anything else."[6]

The clause in the above decision that reads "in the condemnation of those who will perish, evil merit *precedes* the righteous judgment of God" is the sticky one. The Canons of Dordt do not say that; nor has any Reformed man ever agreed to that. The statement, as it stands, seems to teach conditional reprobation after all. It seems to say that God reprobates those who make themselves worthy by their unbelief, but this is not true. The matter is different. The Reformed have always refused to say that reprobation means only God's sovereign determination to punish man for sin. But they have refused to teach the corollary of this as well: that God determines that some should go to hell because he foresees that they will reject the gospel and live in unrepentant sin. This is a conditional reprobation that does not do justice to God's sovereignty. Rather, the very careful language that has always been employed is this: God determines to damn some to hell in the way of their sin. This formulation may not be exhaustive, but it does take into account the two truths that God is sovereign over sin and that man is responsible for his own sin, so that he justly suffers eternal damnation because of it.

Two More Synods and the End of the Matter

Quite understandably, the enemies of Gottschalk were not satisfied with the decisions of Valence. Another synod was held in Savonieres in 859 that attempted to make compromise decisions, but every effort failed.

The final synod to deal with the matter was held in Touchy in 860. All went against Gottschalk. The decisions of Chiersy were reaffirmed, and the decisions of Valence were altered and revised to fit the decisions of Chiersy. Gottschalk's views had no support. But the synod did have its moments when its conscience was pricked. That became evident in the fact that every man at the synod took his turn to profess solemnly his loyalty to Augustine. It was something similar to a husband spending five minutes every day professing his faithfulness to his wife. She might, I suspect, begin to wonder a bit about him.

The Views That Prevailed

The views that finally prevailed in the Roman Catholic Church are best defined by the views of Rabanus himself, for they reflect what became standard Roman Catholic teaching. When I speak of the views of Rabanus, I mean not only his positive teachings, but also the points at which he condemned Gottschalk. What were these views?

The objections to Gottschalk's teachings were chiefly against the doctrine of predestination. This is not surprising, because this was the truth that Gottschalk so strongly emphasized. Rabanus brought up many objections, all of which have been repeatedly heard and have become old and tired tirades against the Reformed faith. Gottschalk makes God the author of sin, said Rabanus. And further, God is unjust in his actions toward the wicked when he sends them to hell for doing things that they were destined to do. And, as far as election is concerned, the doctrine that Gottschalk teaches leads people into carnal security or despair.

But concerning the atonement, Rabanus made a surprising statement that proved conclusively that anyone who teaches an atonement for all men must necessarily also believe that the atonement is ineffectual; it cannot accomplish salvation. Rabanus complained that Gottschalk denied that Christ's blood was shed in vain for the lost. This means that Rabanus insisted that Christ did die in vain for those who are lost. Rabanus taught that Christ died for all men because God willed the salvation of all. God could not, Rabanus insisted, will the salvation of all men unless that salvation was actually available for all men in the cross.

Hence, said Rabanus, the determining factor in salvation was man's faith or unbelief. His faith in Christ's death saved him; his unbelief doomed him to hell. Because the decisive element in salvation was man's choice, this choice became the condition for predestination. God elected those whom he foreknew would believe; and God rejected those whom he foreknew would not believe. Predestination thus became conditional.

These views became the position of the Roman Catholic Church. At least it is a consistent position. One could wish that those who defend a well-meant offer of the gospel would be as consistent as Rome. Rather, they say that God wills the salvation of all men and that God wills the salvation of some men; that Christ died for all men in one sense and that Christ died for his people in some other sense; that salvation depends on man's acceptance of the gospel offer and that salvation is by grace alone. When such flat contradictions are protested, the defenders of the well-meant offer fall back on apparent contradiction and paradox.

Rome's Errors and the Doctrine of Merit

We face another issue. It is an important one, for it uncovers the deepest evil of Rome's position, and of course the evil of those who agree with Rome on these matters. I made the assertion in chapter 9 that Rome was compelled to reject Augustine and to adopt semi-Pelagianism. It really could do nothing else without ceasing to be Rome and changing the whole structure of Roman Catholicism from the ground up. This Rome would not, and in a sense could not, do.

What do I mean by this?

Monasticism had become an integral part of the life of the church. It had not only received the church's approval, but monasticism was encouraged by the church as the ideal life for the Christian.

Monasticism was built foursquare on the doctrine of merit. Without the doctrine of merit, monasticism not only lost its appeal, but also became a useless exercise in self-denial, which really made one who practiced it a fool. The monastic life was supposed to be a life of superior holiness. The man who ate stale bread and drank old water once a day was holier than the man who ate and enjoyed potatoes and roast beef. The man who lived alone in his cell and slept on a narrow stone bench was holier than the man who slept with his wife. The man who wore borrowed or donated clothes was holier than the man who purchased a new dress for his wife and a new suit for himself.

One living a life of self-denial was considered to be more obedient to Christ's command and thus holier than the normal mortal who lived his life to God's glory in his daily calling. Because greater holiness was nearer to the will of Christ and more approved by God, it also brought a greater reward because it merited more of Christ's favor.

Monasticism is a denial of Scripture, which warns that such beliefs are characteristic of those "who depart from the faith" and give "heed to seducing spirits and doctrines of devils" (1 Tim. 4:1). Those who deny the faith forbid to marry and command to abstain from meats. These are hypocritical lies of men whose consciences are "seared with a hot iron" (vv. 2, 3). We must confess the great truth that "every creature of God is good, and nothing to be refused, if it be received with thanksgiving, for it is sanctified by the word of God and by prayer" (vv. 4, 5).

Rome introduced the whole concept of merit with its doctrine of monasticism. This was early—in fact, before Augustine's time. It was imbedded in the very fabric of the life of the church. Man merited with God.

Other factors contributed to Rome's dilemma when confronted with Augustine's teaching. Rome's view of the sacraments was a contributing factor. Rome taught that baptism, in itself, conveyed grace; that is, all who received baptism received grace. How, then, was it to be explained that some who received grace went lost? The only answer could be that the grace of baptism enabled a man to choose either for or against the gospel. Interestingly enough, Augustine himself held to this same view of the sacraments but never seemed to have faced the contradiction in his own views. He could teach that baptism gave grace to all baptized, and yet he also taught that grace is sovereign (that is, it always saves) and particular (saving whomever God has chosen and no others). But Rome made baptism crucial to its doctrine. We can thank God that Augustine taught God's sovereignty despite his views on baptism.

Another factor was the long-held view in the church of the freedom of the will. Augustine was very close to singing a solo when he insisted that the will of fallen man was totally incapable of choosing good. The doctrine of free will won, however. I know that Rome taught a will made free by baptismal grace. That makes no difference. God frees every man's will, they said. The choice of salvation is now up to him.

And so all errors followed upon the first errors: a conditional predestination; not only conditional reprobation, but also conditional election; a universal will of God that all men be saved; a cross of Christ for all; and salvation dependent upon man's will. Merit! Man merits salvation by a choice of his own.

And so Rome committed itself to salvation by grace *and works.* From this it never wavered. It does not waver from this position today. Evangelicals may sign their documents of agreement with Rome, but by their signatures they are selling the truth for a mess of pottage.

It is well to conclude with an observation and a warning. We may talk all we please about salvation by grace alone without human merit, but when we teach a universal love of God rooted in a universal cross, we make salvation dependent upon man's will. All the shouting in the world to the contrary does not change that basic truth. And when salvation is dependent upon man's will in any sense of the word, salvation is no longer of grace but of merit. Man merits his salvation. He earns it by his acceptance of the gospel offer. He has made himself worthy of being saved. He can claim salvation as his own because of his works.

The issue always is one of merit. Can man merit with God? To a Reformed Augustinian (I do not now say "Calvinist" although the two are the same) this very idea of merit is abhorrent. It is not only wrong, but it is a repulsive notion that the believer throws as far from him as he can. Merit repels him because to the extent that man introduces the concept of merit into the work of salvation, he denies God's glory. "By grace are ye saved, through faith." Salvation by grace through faith is not of ourselves; it is the gift of God. All of it. There is nothing of man. Why must it be all of God? Because salvation by works gives man reason to boast, and boasting deprives God of glory (Eph. 2:8, 9).

You ask, "Well, what about our good works?" This, too, Paul puts in unmistakably clear language. We are God's workmanship, created in Christ Jesus for the purpose of doing the good works that are prepared by God from all eternity and earned in the cross. God has even sovereignly determined that we should walk in good works. They do not merit. Good works are given by grace as a privilege to God's people that they should walk in them (v. 10).

This is the legacy of Augustine.

After Rome murdered Gottschalk, Augustine's eloquent defender, Rome had the gall to give to Augustine not only sainthood, but the honorable title *Doctor Gratiae* (Doctor of Grace). Such hypocrisy does not go unnoticed in heaven.

CHAPTER 12

BERENGAR AND TRANSUBSTANTIATION

INTRODUCTION

Although I have included the name Berengar in the title of this chapter, there are two reasons why this choice of names is wrong.

The first reason is that Berengar was not by any means the only one to enter the debate over the doctrine of transubstantiation. In fact, in this chapter we will be talking about two others: Paschasius Radbertus and Ratramnus. Both are important names in the struggle over the meaning of the Lord's supper.

The second reason is that Berengar was, as a matter of fact, not the heretic in this controversy. He was the one who held a correct view of the sacrament of the Lord's supper. He fought long and hard against transubstantiation. And, after all, these chapters are about heretics.

I have chosen Berengar because his life is the most interesting one, and the story of his life best illustrates the controversy over this doctrine.

Radbertus, Ratramnus, Berengar, and Lanfranc represent two different controversies separated by about two hundred years. The first controversy was during the lifetime of Gottschalk in the middle of the ninth century. Gottschalk's opponents were Paschasius Radbertus and Ratramnus. The second controversy took place in the middle of the eleventh century, and the two antagonists were Berengar and Lanfranc.

THE PRESENCE OF CHRIST IN THE LORD'S SUPPER

We must have a clear understanding of the issues around which debate swirled in order to understand the lives and views of the men who battled over transubstantiation.

The basic question was this: How is Christ present in the bread and wine of the Lord's supper?

While there were some variations in the two answers given to this question, the difference centered on whether Christ's presence in the bread and wine of the Lord's supper was physical or spiritual. Some said that Christ was present in the elements literally and corporeally, so that his body and blood were communicated through the mouth. Others said that Christ was present spiritually and that he was communicated through faith.

The same controversy divided Rome from the reformers in Switzerland and finally divided Calvinists from Lutherans.

THE FIRST CONTROVERSY AND RADBERTUS' VIEWS

The view that ultimately prevailed in the Roman Catholic Church—that the bread and wine are changed into the body and blood of Christ—was taught in some simple forms almost from the beginning of the new dispensation church. But it never had any prominence, at least not in the first five or six centuries. Augustine repudiated the whole notion and taught emphatically that Christ's presence was a spiritual presence only.

Two monks carried on the controversy that developed in the ninth century, and two monks carried on the controversy in the eleventh century. In fact, all the work in theology in the Middle Ages was the work of monks, whether they defended the truth or the lie.

The reason for this is that the majority of people were trained in monastic schools, that is, those established, supported, administered, and staffed by monks from particular monasteries. This did not necessarily mean that one had to join a monastery as a monk to attend the school, but the education in a monastic school was, in itself, a powerful incentive to join the monastery.

Further, the education in those days was almost exclusively for a life in the service of the church. Whatever one may have studied, it was to prepare him for a career in the church. Quite naturally, therefore, those who had sufficient education to be busy in theology were also directed into careers in the church, the most available one being a career as a monk.

The view on transubstantiation that later prevailed in the Roman church was defended by Paschasius Radbertus. He lived from about 800 (the year Charlemagne was crowned emperor of the Holy Roman Empire) to about 865.

Radbertus was a very learned and devout monk, but he was also superstitious, as most monks were. He was a native of Soissons in France and soon rose in the Benedictine Order to become abbot of the monastery in Corbie.

Prior to becoming abbot he had been a teacher in a monastic school, and because of his ability he was sent on various ecclesiastical missions, especially involving the Benedictine Order.

In 831 Radbertus began to teach his views on transubstantiation, although that term was not used until almost the thirteenth century. He developed his ideas in a book that he dedicated to Charles the Bald, son of Charlemagne, who ruled over France upon the death of his father.

Radbertus taught that the bread and wine of the Lord's supper were so completely changed into the body and blood of Christ that nothing remained of bread and wine at all, even though the figure of bread and wine was present to the senses of sight, touch, smell, and taste.

While Radbertus attempted to find proof for his views in the teachings of the fathers and in Jesus' words in John 6, he also appealed superstitiously to other lines of proof. Schaff describes him as follows:

> He appealed also to marvellous stories of the visible appearances of the body and blood of Christ for the removal of doubts or the satisfaction of the pious desire of saints. The bread on the altar, he reports, was often seen in the shape of a lamb or a little child, and when the priest stretched out his hand to break the bread, an angel descended from heaven with a knife, slaughtered the lamb or the child, and let his blood run into a cup.[1]

THE FIRST CONTROVERSY AND RATRAMNUS' VIEWS

Ratramnus was a contemporary of Radbertus. He was a monk in the same monastery in Corbie. He was only a simple monk, and Radbertus was his superior. That did not deter him from taking issue with his abbot.

Ratramnus was a friend of Gottschalk and was also a defender of Augustine. Ratramnus wrote a book entitled *Concerning the Predestination of God* in which he taught double predestination. He wrote this book, strangely enough, at the request of Charles the Bald.

Why Ratramnus was not condemned and punished as severely as Gottschalk is something of a mystery. I suspect that one major reason was that Gottschalk was much more outspoken in his defense of the truth than Ratramnus. Gottschalk vigorously promoted Augustine's views at every opportunity. Ratramnus was more discreet. I do not say this to point to Ratramnus' discretion as a virtue. It was not. When the truth of God is at stake, one ought to defend that truth with vigor and enthusiasm—even if one must suffer for it, as Gottschalk did.

Ratramnus was a man of astonishing literary ability. His gifts of writing were widely recognized. Probably for this reason Charles the Bald, after receiving Radbertus' book on transubstantiation, which had been dedicated to him, asked Ratramnus to write a response.

Ratramnus complied, setting forth his views of the presence of Christ in the bread and wine as a spiritual presence only. Ratramnus had it all straight. He taught that Christ was appropriated by the participant at the Lord's table not by the mouth, but by faith. Hence only those who had faith were also able to appropriate Christ, while unbelievers were unable to receive Christ. The sacrament of the Lord's supper, therefore, was a commemorative celebration to assure believers of their redemption in the cross of Christ.

Such a view was in keeping not only with the views of Augustine, but also with Ratramnus' view on sovereign predestination. Believers are elect, and the power of their faith lies in election. Unbelievers are reprobate, and they can receive no blessing from the sacrament.

THE END OF THE FIRST CONTROVERSY
The views of Ratramnus did not prevail in the church of Rome. They did not prevail any more than did the views of Gottschalk. The views of both men were ultimately condemned.

It would seem, therefore, that all the work of Ratramnus was in vain, that his remarkable understanding of the sacrament of the Lord's supper and his defense of it—even though he had to disagree with his superior in the monastery of Corbie—was of no account and amounted to nothing.

But God works in unexpected ways, and man's time is not God's time. More than five hundred years later, during the heated discussions in England over the Reformation, the works of Ratramnus on the Lord's supper were discovered. They were republished, were widely read, and powerfully influenced the development of the views of this sacrament in the English Reformation. The English reformers saw the clear and unequivocal arguments Ratramnus had raised against Rome's position, and they were persuaded by much of Ratramnus' interpretation of the presence of Christ.

God's truth is always victorious.

THE SECOND CONTROVERSY AND BERENGAR'S EARLY LIFE
Without any resolution, the controversy between Ratramnus and Radbertus finally died with the death of the two antagonists. Both views continued to be taught in the church, although little by little, the views of Radbertus gained ground.

A second controversy, also between two monks, took place in the eleventh century. In a way, it was more important than the first controversy, because it led directly to the adoption of transubstantiation as official church dogma. It took place between Berengar and Lanfranc, although Berengar was the principal character.

Berengar was born in or near the city of Tours in the year 1000. Tours was an important city in France because Charles Martel defeated the invading Moslems near Tours in 732, slammed the southern door of Europe in their faces, and prevented Mohammedanism from overrunning Europe.

Berengar was early committed to the monastic life and rose quickly in the Benedictine Order. He became canon and director of the cathedral school in Tours, in which school he sharpened his teaching skills. Soon he was elevated to the rank of archdeacon in Angers, but he retained his love for teaching. Berengar was a popular teacher whose fame soon spread throughout France, and students from every part of France flocked to him.

BERENGAR THE MAN

Berengar was something of an enigma, however. As a monk, he was deeply devoted to monasticism. Yet he could understand that monastic life did not enable one to escape from the world. He saw the inherent dangers in a life of seclusion. He wrote to his fellow monks:

> The hermit...is alone in his cell, but sin loiters about the door with enticing words and seeks admittance. I am thy beloved—says she—whom thou didst court in the world. I was with thee at the table, slept with thee on thy couch; without me, thou didst nothing. How darest thou think of forsaking me? I have followed thy every step; and dost thou expect to hide away from me in thy cell? I was with thee in the world, when thou didst eat flesh and drink wine; and shall be with thee in the wilderness, where thou livest only on bread and water. Purple and silk are not the only colors seen in hell,—the monk's cowl is also to be found there. Thou, hermit, hast something of mine. The nature of the flesh, which thou wearest about thee, is my sister, begotten with me, brought up with me. So long as the flesh is flesh, so long shall I be in thy flesh. Dost thou subdue thy flesh by abstinence?— thou becomest proud; and lo! sin is there. Art thou overcome by the flesh, and dost thou yield to lust? sin is there. Perhaps thou hast none of the mere human sins, I mean such as proceed from sense; beware then of devilish sins. Pride is a sin which belongs in common to evil spirits and to hermits.[2]

Berengar was a man of rare learning and deep piety. He also was brave —up to a point. He was not afraid to challenge church authority when he believed it was wrong. Nor was he afraid to stand up for his views, as long as it did not mean suffering. Twice he recanted when faced with the threat of death. Twice he regretted it. Finally he died in sorrow for betraying the truth that he believed.

His writings show him to be "a worthy man, a loving Christian, and a man of tender and placable nature."[3] His learning was vast, and he was an ardent student of the church fathers. He was a physician and was a theologian among theologians. He was admired as an orator and a preacher. He was friend and counselor to some of the foremost men in France and occasionally moved in the highest circles without losing his humility.

But he was, in all respects except one, a man of the church. He agreed with church doctrine, good and bad, and only opposed the general teachings of the church on the question of Christ's presence in the sacrament.

BERENGAR'S LIFE OF CONTROVERSY

After careful study of the church fathers and the teachings of Scripture, Berengar came to the conclusion that the view of the Lord's supper that was later called transubstantiation was a vulgar superstition contrary to Scripture, to most of the church fathers, and to reason. It was contrary to Scripture, because when Jesus referred to himself as "the bread of life" in John 6:35, he clearly meant this in a symbolic sense. Although a few of the fathers had taught what Rome was teaching, many more, including Augustine, had repudiated such notions. It was unreasonable to believe that something that looked like bread, felt like bread, and tasted like bread was not bread, but a human body.

Berengar could have saved his breath. While here and there a few agreed with him, his views were in the minority.

His most influential opponent was Lanfranc, one of the great Roman Catholics of the Middle Ages. He was born in 1005 and entered a monastery early in life. In 1045 he became prior of the prestigious convent in Bec, located in the French region of Normandy. In 1070 he was appointed to the highest ecclesiastical post in England, Archbishop of Canterbury, where he served until 1089. From that position he carried on a running battle with the English kings in a relentless defense of papal claims against the struggles of the kings to free themselves from papal rule.

Berengar's views concerning the symbolic presence of Christ in the sacrament of the Lord's supper frightened the church. This is evident from the fact many regional synods met to condemn Berengar. They followed upon each other in such rapid succession that sometimes two or three were held in the same year.

Berengar was condemned by Pope Leo IX at a synod in Rome in 1050. He was summoned to a synod at Vercelli, to which he did not come, and was condemned *in absentia* without being granted a hearing. In 1051 a synod in Paris threatened Berengar with death if he did not recant.

An interesting thing happened at a synod in his home city of Tours in 1054. Present at the synod was Hildebrand, who became one of the great medieval popes, Gregory VII. He listened intently to Berengar's views, became convinced that Berengar was correct, and persuaded the synod to rebuke him mildly but to tolerate his views.

But Berengar was summoned to Rome in 1059, where the Lateran Council condemned him, ordered him to recant on his knees, and throw his books into the fire. Fearful of what would happen, he complied and went against his own conscience.

Back in France, Berengar recanted his recantation and began to teach his views again. Lanfranc answered Berengar in a treatise of twenty-three chapters on the eucharist that served to establish transubstantiation as official church dogma.[4] The weight of almost the whole church was against Berengar. At a synod in Poitiers in 1075 he was almost killed.

Hildebrand had become Pope Gregory VII, and in 1078 he summoned Berengar to Rome in an effort to protect him. But another Lateran Council a year later would not even be persuaded by the pope, and in its fury condemned Berengar once again. Basest of all, Gregory abandoned Berengar when he appealed for help. The pope was fearful that his own orthodoxy would come into question. Berengar submitted and once again recanted.

But returning to France, he again regretted what he had done and publicly announced that he was of the same opinion as formerly. Pondering Gregory's betrayal, and his own recantation, Berengar wrote,

> Confounded by the sudden madness of the pope, . . . and because God in punishment for my sins did not give me a steadfast heart, I threw myself on the ground and confessed with impious voice that I had erred, fearing the pope would instantly pronounce against me the sentence of excommunication, and that, as a necessary consequence, the populace would hurry me to the worst of deaths.[5]

Berengar could hardly live with himself after this, and he retired to a lonely life of strict monastic seclusion on the island of St. Come. There he lived in regret for his cowardice but died in peace in 1088.

THE END OF THE MATTER

Transubstantiation won the day. Berengar was the last voice raised in protest against such a monstrous view as Rome wanted. That view, as horrible as it is, became official Romish doctrine in 1215 at the Fourth Lateran Council under Innocent III, and it remains the official teaching of Rome.

Transubstantiation is not a doctrine that stands by itself. It leads to and is connected with other doctrines.

The view of transubstantiation developed along with the idea that the clergy were *priests* who offer sacrifices. In the early church, when it was first suggested that clergy be called priests, the sacrifices they brought were considered spiritual sacrifices of thanksgiving. But the sacrifices were connected to the Lord's supper. In the minds of the people and eventually in the entire church, these sacrifices were considered sacrifices of atonement.

How was that to be explained? The answer lies in the Romish doctrine of the mass. When a priest performs the mass, that is, administers the Lord's supper, he miraculously but very really changes the bread and wine into Christ's body and blood. By doing this he performs the sacrifice that Christ offered for sin on the cross. Golgotha is reenacted. Calvary takes place in every mass. Christ dies a million times at the hand of the priests. And the people, eating this bread and wine, participate in the sacrifice of Christ and eat his body and drink his blood.

No wonder the reformers could not find strong enough words to condemn this view. They pointed out, correctly, that such a view denied the completeness and perfection of Christ's one sacrifice for sin. Just as wrongly, it introduced a terrible sin into the worship, the sin of idolatry. The Heidelberg Catechism says that the mass is "an accursed idolatry."[6] Many evangelicals, lusting for union with Rome, think this language too strong and want to remove it. But let that never happen. Ursinus and Olevianus were right.

Other terrible doctrines followed.

Rome taught the doctrine of concomitance. That is, the people need only eat the bread and need not drink the wine (lest the blood of Christ be spilled) because Christ's body and blood are present in both bread and wine.

The bread and wine were worshiped by the throngs in exactly the same way pagans bow before gods of wood and stone. And this worship of the elements became a crucial part of Rome's liturgy.

Because a sacrifice took place at the mass, it was necessary to have an altar. The result was a priest, an altar, and a sacrifice. It was all in place. But a priest took the place of the preacher and a sacrifice took the place of God's word. The altar took the place of the pulpit, and the words of consecration (spoken in Latin so that none understood) took the place of preaching.

None had to understand what was said because the sacraments worked automatically (if I may use that word). If one actually ate Christ's body and drank his blood, then Christ was communicated to the participant even though no faith was present. A person received Christ by virtue of eating, not necessarily believing. The doctrine was called *ex opere operato*. This Latin expression means that the sacrament has, in itself and apart from faith, "power to work" grace.

The whole wretched system, cloaked in superstition of the worst kind, became a key building block in Rome's mighty sacerdotal system by which God's people were held in bondage.

It took the Reformation to restore the truth. And the Reformation was a vindication of Berengar's views, for Calvin taught the same as Berengar. Christ is present spiritually, and Christ becomes the possession of the child of God by faith, worked by the Holy Spirit.

The Belgic Confession of Faith also states the Reformed view:

> In the mean time we err not when we say that what is eaten and drunk by us is the proper and natural body and the proper blood of Christ. But the manner of our partaking of the same is not by the mouth, but by the Spirit through faith. Thus, then, though Christ always sits at the right hand of his Father in the heavens, yet doth he not, therefore, cease to make us partakers of himself by faith. This feast is a spiritual table.[7]

CHAPTER 13

ABELARD AND THE DOCTRINE OF THE ATONEMENT

INTRODUCTION

It is a bit difficult to make choices concerning the individual about whom to write when many others taught the same heresy as we will describe in this chapter. The heresy has to do with our Lord's atoning work on the cross. The choice of Abelard is, therefore, somewhat arbitrary. Yet there are reasons I have chosen to write about Abelard and not others who held to the same heresy. The first reason, probably the most important, is that Abelard was a contemporary of Anselm and, in fact, studied briefly under him.

That may not immediately strike one as being a good reason to choose Abelard, but Anselm was not only the sole defender of a sound and biblical doctrine of the atonement in the entire last half of the Middle Ages, but he was also a man whom God used to make an important and significant development to the doctrine. In fact, one really looks in vain for any significant development of the truth in the entire period from Augustine to the Reformation—a period of over one thousand years. Anselm is the exception. He did what no other medieval churchman did. He developed the truth in a crucially important area.[1]

The second reason for choosing Abelard as the representative of heretical views on the atonement is that Abelard represented an extreme position. The question that was at issue in medieval times was the *necessity* of the atonement. That is, was Christ's atoning sacrifice necessary for salvation? Or could God have saved people without Christ's suffering and death on the cross?

Anselm insisted on the absolute necessity of the atonement for salvation. Almost all the medieval theologians denied the necessity of the atonement. Some said that the atonement was partially necessary, but not completely so; others said that it was not necessary at all, but served a different purpose. The latter view is the extreme view of Abelard.

Another reason for writing on Abelard is that his life was extremely interesting. His life also gives an insight into church life during the Middle Ages, into the activities of a genuine, though heretical, scholar. His life even has the spice of romance about it. It makes for fascinating reading.

Abelard was not only heretical in his views of the atonement; he was also heretical in many other respects. He had a wrong doctrine of the inspiration of Scripture, of the Trinity, and of faith and knowledge. For these views he was condemned by his own church. However, for his views on the atonement he was never condemned. That says a lot about the state of Roman Catholicism at the time in which Abelard lived.

ABELARD'S RISE TO FAME

Although Abelard went through life with the name Peter, at birth he was given the French version of the name, Pierre. To designate the place of his birth, he was called Pierre de Palais, for he was born in Palais, a small village in Brittany, in the year 1079.

Abelard was born of nobility, and his father, Berengar (not the Berengar of the transubstantiation controversy), was lord of the village and a knight. Abelard gave up his prerogatives among the nobility in favor of a life of study and teaching. He was intellectually qualified for this, for he was a brilliant student, a gifted teacher, and an original thinker—somewhat too original for his own good.

His first teacher was Roscelin, an able teacher in his own right. In those days a good teacher would simply begin teaching somewhere and draw paying students to him. Sometimes he was connected to a school (usually a cathedral school), but not always. The more able he was, the more students he attracted, the greater grew his fame, and the fuller were his pockets.

After a brief stay with Roscelin, Abelard wandered about for a time engaging in some teaching. Eventually he moved to Paris and studied under William of Champeaux, a man with a reputation that extended to the far corners of Europe.

During these years of study under William, one of Abelard's chief personality traits appeared—a towering pride that plagued him all his life. Perhaps pride was bred into him by his birth among the nobility, but it was fed by his intellectual acumen and success in studies. Pride is common to all men who have fallen in Adam, but intellectual pride is a curse on those who are responsible for studying and teaching, and it is as great a barrier to salvation as riches are to a wealthy man. Abelard had plenty of intellectual pride.

Abelard set himself up as a rival to William and began to teach views differing from William's in an obvious attempt to steal his students. Abelard was remarkably successful, drawing students by the hundreds from all parts of Europe. He claims in his autobiography, though probably with a bit of exaggeration, that he took all of William's students from him.

Intellectual pride was not limited to Abelard; William also had his share of it. Because of his position and "seniority" in academic circles in Paris, William was able to force Abelard out of the city in 1113 while he was still relatively young.

At this point Abelard studied for a short time under Anselm.

Schaff makes an interesting comparison of the two men:

[Abelard's] fame was derived from the brilliance of his intellect. He differed widely from Anselm. The latter was a constructive theologian; Abelard, a critic. Anselm was deliberate, Abelard, impulsive and rash. Anselm preferred seclusion; Abelard sought publicity. Among teachers exercising the spell of magnetism over their hearers, Abelard stands in the front rank and probably has not been excelled in France. In some of his theological speculations he was in advance of his age...A man of daring thought and restless disposition, he was unstable in his mental beliefs and morally unreliable.[2]

Soon Abelard took issue with Anselm also and left him to seek greener pastures elsewhere. He was sufficiently arrogant to describe Anselm as a man with a wonderful flow of words, but not thoughts; as one who lights a fire, but fills the house with smoke.

The years that followed were his glory years. He went to Paris because William, who had retired, was no longer a threat, and he was invited to preside over the cathedral school. Schaff also has an interesting description of these years.

All the world seemed about to do him homage. Scholars from all parts thronged to hear him. He lectured on philosophy and theology. He was well read in classical and widely read in sacred literature. His dialectic powers were ripe and, where arguments failed, the teacher's imagination and rhetoric came to the rescue. His books were read not only in the schools and convents, but in castles and guildhouses. William of Thierry said they crossed the seas and overleaped the Alps. When he visited towns, the people crowded the streets and strained their necks to catch a glimpse of him. His remarkable influence over men and women must be explained not by his intellectual depth so much as by a certain daring and literary art and brilliance. He was attractive of person . . . To these qualities he added a gay cheerfulness which expressed itself in compositions of song and in singing.[3]

ABELARD'S FALL

The Scriptures warn that pride goes before destruction and a haughty spirit before a fall (Prov. 16:18). So it was with Abelard.

His fall came about through what has become known as the "Heloise affair." Heloise was the daughter of a canon, attractive, younger than Abelard by many years, and in need of instruction. Abelard persuaded her father that he was eminently suited to be her tutor. The end was a passionate love affair, an illegitimate child, a hasty marriage that really never was a marriage, and disgrace for them both. In a fury over Abelard's deceptiveness, Heloise's father conspired with others to have Abelard castrated, and both he and Heloise ended in monasteries.

Abelard never changed from the proud man he had always been. He really wanted no part of marriage, fearful that it would spoil his career. He insisted on being married in secret, and he spoke disparagingly of this divine institution:

> What accord . . . has study with nurses, writing materials with cradles, books and desks with spinning wheels, reeds and ink with spindles! Who, intent upon sacred and philosophical reflections could endure the squalling of children, the lullabies of nurses and the noisy crowd of men and women! Who would stand the disagreeable and constant dirt of little children![4]

ABELARD'S HERESIES AND FINAL DAYS

In a way it was not his fornication that brought Abelard down, but his heresies. It is well to be reminded of the fact that heresy in the church is deliberate. When an office bearer in the church or a teacher in the school begins to teach false doctrine, it is not ignorance that leads to this sorry state. It is a deliberate perversion of the truth. Such deliberate distortion of the truth is almost always, if not always, rooted in intellectual pride. Pride in one's knowledge, acumen, intellectual abilities, and vast learning leads to the desire to promote oneself. What better way to promote one's great gifts than to be original in one's thinking? And what better way to demonstrate one's originality than by teaching doctrines that have not been taught before—at least in the form in which one now proposes them? Or what better way to show one's independence from other great theologians in the history of the church than by taking issue with them at certain points? This great temptation comes to all who occupy positions

116

of leadership in the church of Christ. It is a devil, for ministers at least, often worse than riches.

Abelard denied the Trinity. We do not need to go into the heresy here, for his heresy was an old one. He identified various virtues of God with the persons in the Holy Trinity and thus denied the personal distinctions in God altogether. It was a kind of modalism, which teaches that God, one in person and one in being, reveals himself in three different ways.

He was condemned in 1121 by the Synod of Soissons. He was required to burn his own books. And he was sentenced to read the Athanasian Creed in public.

Abelard became the abbot of a monastery in Brittany, but he was unable to control the wild behavior of the monks who lived in gluttony, drunkenness, and immorality. In fact, on two different occasions these monks, chafing under his efforts to reform them, tried to kill him, once by putting poison in his wine.

For a time he became the counselor of the monastery to which his wife Heloise had retired as a nun. But this did not work, and public opinion, scandalized by the idea, forced him to flee once again.

Much of his life from this time on is obscure, because his autobiography breaks off at this point, and he seems to have become a lost man. He wandered about from place to place, staying in each place for a while, teaching and gathering a circle of students, but his influence was gone.

Abelard was tried once again for other heresies—this time by the Synod of Sens in 1141. He refused to defend himself but appealed to the pope. He was, however, condemned by Innocent II, who ordered him to be silent and to retire to a monastery. Innocent ordered Abelard's books to be burned and his followers to be excommunicated.

Abelard spent his last days in his studies. "He read continually and prayed fervently."[5] But he was broken by his sufferings and died in 1142. He was buried in the monastery where Heloise lived, and when she died, she was buried alongside of him.

The heresies for which he was condemned by the Synod of Sens were chiefly denials of the inspiration of Scripture. He taught that the same inspiration that brought into existence the Bible was present in the great Greek and Roman philosophers as well as in pagan holy writings. Degrees of inspiration, he said, are present in all writings, and the degree of divine influence varies from one writing to another. Scripture, therefore, contained many human errors.

How modern Abelard was. Those who deny Scripture's inspiration today have not advanced much beyond him.

ABELARD'S DOCTRINE OF THE ATONEMENT

The real issue in the controversy over the atonement of Jesus Christ was the *necessity* of the atonement.

It seems that the controversy involved the relation between some of God's attributes and the suffering and death of Christ. For example, these questions were asked: Could not an omnipotent God have saved men by his power without sending his Son to suffer on the cross? Could not a merciful God have forgiven sin out of his mercy rather than through the means of the death of Christ?

Abelard answered these questions by appealing to God's benevolence and teaching that only God's benevolence was important in a consideration of the atonement of Christ. The death of Christ on the cross was not necessary to accomplish salvation. God was sufficiently benevolent simply to forgive sin. Thus no satisfaction for sin with its fruits of pardon is necessary. Pardon was granted to a man on the basis of repentance alone. When a man turned from his sin, showed proper sorrow for his sin, and resolved to walk in obedience before God, he was pardoned of his wrong.

One is compelled to ask, What about Christ's death? If it is true that Christ did not have to die to obtain salvation, why did he die? Abelard's answer was that the death of Christ on the cross was intended only to have a beneficial moral influence on men and to produce sorrow for sin. The love revealed by Christ in his willingness to suffer on the cross was intended to awaken in us a similar love. This love, awakened in us by the example of the love of Christ, liberates us from the power of sin so that we can walk in obedience.

Abelard's position, completely the contrary of the position of Anselm, sparked great controversy in the church.

THE CHURCH'S RESPONSE

It was immediately apparent to many that the church could not adopt Abelard's position because it was a complete repudiation of the significance of the cross of Christ. If Christ died as an example only, the cross of Christ has no saving value.

What was the church to do about this?

It was important that the church adopt Anselm's position that salvation could only be given through a cross that satisfied for sin. Christ's suffering and death had to have propitiatory value. That is, the suffering and death of Christ had to be satisfaction for sin if it was truly to redeem.

The word *satisfaction* was the key word in the controversy, and it later became a key word in the doctrine of the reformers and in the Reformation confessions.[6] The same issues lie at the heart of all controversies in our day as well over the extent of the atonement.

Yet the Romish church could not swallow the doctrine of satisfaction, either. Its theologians were caught between the devil and the deep blue sea. They were trapped between two "impossible" positions.

The Romish theologians could not accept Anselm's doctrine of an absolute necessity of the atonement because the Roman church was totally and fatally committed to the doctrine of human merit. This commitment to the doctrine of human merit had been adopted officially at the Synod of Orange when pure Augustinianism had been repudiated. It had been sealed when Gottschalk, an ardent defender of Augustinianism, had been martyred. It was now part and parcel of Romish theology.

The doctrine of the absolute necessity of the atonement ruled out human merit entirely because to the extent that man is able to contribute to his salvation and to earn merit with God, he does not need the atoning sacrifice of Christ. If man contributes, say, 10 percent to his salvation, that 10 percent is not found in the atoning death of Christ but in the will of man and his ability to do something to save himself.

The Arminians at a later date understood this all too well. Because salvation hinged on the free will of man, salvation was not efficaciously earned in the cross of Christ. So the Arminians developed a theory of the atonement much like that of Abelard.

The opposite is true as well. If Christ's suffering and death are *absolutely necessary* for salvation, this can be true only because all the salvation of all the elect church is in Christ alone. This leaves no room for human endeavor, human contribution, or a free will of man upon which hangs the efficacy of salvation. All human merit is expunged from the records.

If Christ's death on the cross is for all men, and yet all men are not saved, the cross of Christ has no saving power. Then the cross is ineffective for salvation in every respect. Then there is no *necessity* for Christ's suffering and death.

So Roman theologians were caught between the obvious doctrine of the absolute necessity of Christ's death and the church's teaching of merit. The only way to extricate themselves from this dilemma was to teach a *relative necessity,* that is, the atonement is necessary, but only relatively so.

Rome's theologians set about the difficult task of defining what they meant by *relative necessity.*

The theologian Bonaventura spoke of Christ's atonement as a satisfaction because it was the most fitting way to restore the sinner, the most in keeping with God's attributes, and the most calculated to arouse sorrow for sin. Thus, though necessary, it was only relatively so.

Even the great theologian Thomas Aquinas did not want an absolute necessity for the atonement of Christ because of his commitment to the doctrine of merit. He spoke of the atonement as being necessary in a relative way because it was in keeping with God's justice. This was an important point, because when one speaks of satisfaction, the question is satisfaction of what? The satisfaction of *God's justice* must be the answer. Aquinas also hedged when he taught that God could save in another way by overlooking his justice.

One theologian opted for this much necessity; another spoke of that much necessity; but all of them denied an absolute necessity. Anselm stood alone.

Anselm's doctrine is clear and biblical. Whether he understood that his doctrine necessarily ruled out all human merit is another question. He was a man of his times; he lived within the church of his day and its teachings on merit. Nevertheless, he was right on Christ's atonement.

He believed that God's attributes are one in God. He insisted that if the cross of Christ revealed God's mercy, it had to reveal God's justice also. God's justice requires *satisfaction* for sin. If God overlooks his justice, he denies himself. He cannot do that.

Sin is of infinite demerit. An infinite price is required to pay an infinite debt. That price cannot be paid by a man because he is a sinner who increases his debt to God rather than being in a position to pay for it. He is like a man who owes $50,000 on his credit card. He is required to pay off the debt at $1,000 a month. But he can afford to pay only $100 a month, so that every month his debt gets bigger, not smaller.

But man cannot pay at all. Thus the debt becomes infinite, and only he who is both man and God can pay that awful debt.

We cannot enter into the whole argument here, nor is it necessary. It is all found in the Heidelberg Catechism in Lord's Days 4–6. It is the doctrine of the reformers and of the Reformed churches to the present. It was Anselm's doctrine.

Abelard, the heretic, paved the way for many present-day heresies.

If we are to be saved, the atonement is an *absolute necessity.* Then all human merit is excluded. We are saved by grace.

CHAPTER 14

INNOCENT III AND PAPAL HIERARCHY

INTRODUCTION

Not all heresies in the history of the church of Christ involve matters of doctrine. Sometimes the heresies are matters of church government and the corporate worship of God in the church.

These heresies are also corruptions of the truth. A corruption of church government is, for example, a denial of the truth of the kingship of Christ over the church. An aberration in worship involves the doctrine of the nature of God and the obligation to worship God in such a way that the truth concerning his divine being is preserved.

In this chapter we will explain the Roman Catholic corruption of church polity.

To illustrate this corruption, I will discuss the pontificate of Innocent III, whose papal rule extended from 1198 to 1216. He is acknowledged by all students of church history as the most powerful pope who ever lived and occupied the see of Rome. He was closer to the Roman Catholic idea of the papacy than any single man in the history of the church. Therefore, he is an ideal figure to demonstrate Roman Catholic church polity.

Innocent III was not alone in his efforts to concentrate ecclesiastical power in the papacy. Papal power had slowly developed in the church from a very early date. It had grown through the centuries bit by bit. Weaker popes were often unable to make papal claims stick, and papal power decreased under their rule. Stronger popes not only held firmly to earlier developments, but often built upon what had already been done to expand papal power. It is not necessary to trace that development over the centuries.

A discussion of this matter, however, does leave us with one difficult problem. I refer to the fact that we are confronted with the question of why God allowed the church to remain under a terribly wrong church government for most of the history of the new dispensation church. Tendencies toward the papal system appeared in the church as early as the third century. After Innocent III, they continued in the church until the time of the Reformation, another three hundred years after Innocent. Therefore, of the twenty centuries of the history of the church since Pentecost, more than thirteen of them were centuries in which the church lived under a less than biblical church government. The question is, Why?

There is not a satisfactory answer to that question. In this respect, too, the ways of God are inscrutable. One idea suggests itself, however, as a possible answer.

Innocent III came closer than any individual in the new dispensation to being antichrist. This may surprise some, though we are all acquainted with the worldwide power of the Roman Empire with the rule of cruel Caesars who extended their authority over large areas and many countries and who attempted to crush and destroy the church. The Roman Empire was the last political picture of antichrist, the legs of iron in the image of Nebuchadnezzar's dream (Dan. 2:33). The papacy was the ecclesiastical side of antichrist's union of political and church rule.

I am saying that papal claims come closer to the final claims of antichrist than any other institution in the world. It just might be that through all those years God was teaching his people, as John puts it, that antichrist is always in the world and that part of the church's life is to live, if not under, at least present with and influenced by antichrist.

I leave it to the reader to evaluate what I say.

INNOCENT'S RISE TO POWER

Innocent III was born of noble parents in 1160 in Anagni, a city well-known in Italy because it served as the favorite summer home of the popes. His parents named him Lothario, a name that he kept until he adopted the name Innocent III at his coronation as pope.

It seems that Lothario lived the life of the scholarly son of a wealthy family. He went to the best universities in Italy and France: Bologna and Paris. But Lothario was not the idle and spoiled son of nobility. He was an extremely gifted scholar and quickly mastered his subjects. Bologna was famous as a center in the study of canon law, and Paris was the center of study in theology. In both Lothario excelled.

Early in his studies he began a literary career. His first book was a stern, dark book on the ascetic life. It was a reflection of his own devotion to asceticism and the importance of living the life of a monk. The book gave him a reputation as a gifted young man who was dedicated to the welfare of the church.

The result of this reputation was an appointment to the College of Cardinals at the early age of twenty-nine. He was, however, too young to make it to this exalted position on his own merits, even as brilliant a man as he was. He had three uncles who exerted influence on his behalf and paved his way into the Roman curia. We ought not to consider this strange. Simony (the purchase of offices in the church), bribery, and political influence were more important than abilities and gifts in those days.

The College of Cardinals was the highest level of the hierarchy in the church under the pope. It was the administrative body in the church responsible for advising the pope and carrying out papal directives and decisions. It was to the pope what a president's cabinet is today in the executive branch of government in the United States. It was also the body that chose a new pope when the incumbent died. It was enormously influential, and in it Innocent learned thoroughly how the church operated and where the reins of power were.

When the man who was pope at the time died, Innocent entered the College of Cardinals. A new pope was chosen from another branch of Italian nobility, and he turned out to be an enemy of the noble house from which Innocent came. Innocent was forced to retire under the pressures of this antagonistic pope. But the time of retirement was well spent in studying literature and writing.

Innocent became pope in 1198. He was chosen by the College of Cardinals, of which he had been a member and was called out of retirement to assume the papal chair and tiara or crown. The crowning of a pope was a glittering pageant.

> At the enthronization in St. Peter's, the tiara was used which Constantine is said to have presented to Sylvester, and the words were said, "Take the tiara and know that thou art the father of princes and kings, the ruler of the world, the vicar on earth of our Saviour Jesus Christ, whose honor and glory shall endure throughout all eternity." Then followed the procession through the city to the Lateran. The pope sat on a white palfrey and was accompanied by the prefect of the city, the senators and other municipal officials, the nobility, the cardinals, archbishops, and other church dignitaries, the lesser clergy and the popular throng—all amidst the ringing of bells, the chanting of psalms, and the acclamations of the people . . . Arrived at the Lateran, the pope threw out handfuls of copper coins among the people with the words, "Silver and gold have I none, but such as I have give I thee." The silver key of the palace and the golden key of the basilica were then put into

his hands, and the senate did him homage. A banquet followed, the pope sitting at a table alone.[1]

It is interesting to spend a few moments pondering what Peter would have thought of such pomp, though the pope considered himself to be a successor to the humble fisherman from Galilee who suffered martyrdom for the cause of the gospel.

Innocent became pope at the age of thirty-seven, the youngest in the line of popes up to that time. Upon hearing that Innocent was pope, a contemporary plaintively expressed his fear about Innocent's relative youth and what it meant for Christendom: "Alas! the pope is so young. Help, Lord, thy Christian world."[2]

INNOCENT'S CHARACTER

Schaff describes Innocent as

> well-formed, medium in stature, temperate in his habits, clear in perception, resolute in will, and fearless in action. He was a born ruler of men, a keen judge of human nature, demanding unconditional submission to his will, yet considerate in the use of power after submission was once given—an imperial personality towering high above the contemporary sovereigns in moral force and in magnificent aims of world-wide dominion.[3]

It appears as if all the emphasis ought to be placed on one characteristic of the man: he was a man of iron will. He had control of himself and his own life. In an age when popes were fornicators, gluttons, drunkards, and murderers, not one moral stain has ever been attached to his character.

He also had an iron will in dealing with the curia so that he bent it completely to his wishes. His will was a rod in his hand to wield as he saw fit. He allowed no opposition, no dissent, no individual initiative in the actions of others.

That iron will extended to his dealings with the kings and princes of Europe. So adamant was he in his purposes and so forceful in his determination to have his way that at the end of his reign, every ruler in Europe, no matter how powerful, bowed before his throne.

Innocent was totally dedicated to the church and was determined to make the church over which he ruled the dominating institution in Europe. He not only attempted to accomplish this goal through his own personal diplomacy and iron-fisted rule, but he also preached at every opportunity and wrote countless letters of which five hundred are extant. In his sermons and letters he promoted the hierarchical view of church government and advanced the power of Roman Catholicism.

He was a startling picture of what antichrist will ultimately be.

INNOCENT'S VIEW OF THE PAPACY

Innocent did not invent the theory of the papacy that he promoted and that is still official Roman Catholic policy. The theory was held by his predecessors and practiced by them insofar as they were able to extend their rule. But Innocent developed the theory and succeeded in putting it into practice.

At the time of his coronation, he spoke on the faithful and wise servant who did his lord's will. So early in his pontificate he tipped his hand by these words: "Ye see... what manner of servant it is whom the Lord hath set over his people, no other than the vicegerent of Christ, the successor of Peter. He stands in the midst between God and man; below God, above man; less than God, more than man. He judges all and is judged by none."[4]

The arrogance of such statements leaves one gasping. Innocent defines his office as that of mediator between God and man, a position which the Lord Jesus Christ occupies. Does not the very name *antichrist* mean not only "one opposed to Christ," but also "one who claims to be in Christ's place"?

But such arrogance is quickly covered by a show of humility. Innocent went on to say, "But he, whom the pre-eminence of dignity exalts, is humbled by his vocation as a servant, that so humility may be exalted and pride be cast down; for God is against the high-minded, and to the lowly He shows mercy; and whoso exalteth himself shall be abased."[5]

In spelling out his views concerning the papacy, Innocent made himself equal to Christ. He did not hesitate to say that God gave all authority to Christ at the time of his exaltation; but he insisted that Christ conferred authority on Peter, and following Peter, on the popes who are Peter's successors. In conferring authority on the popes, Christ, in effect, made the popes as great as himself. *All* the authority of Christ is given to the popes. This means, as anyone can see, that authority in the church and *over the nations* is given to the pope.

Innocent put himself on a level with Christ also with respect to Christ's offices. He claimed not only to be prophet (teacher in the church) as Christ is; he claimed also to be king and priest. Nor did he mean by that merely (though extravagantly enough) that he combined in himself the offices of minister, elder, and deacon. He meant that Christ's office of priest enabled him to exercise sole authority in the church, and Christ's office of king conferred on him rule over the nations.

THE FOURTH LATERAN COUNCIL

The council meeting called the Fourth Lateran Council effectively extended Innocent's rule over the entire church. It was the largest council meeting that had ever been held in the West.

It met on November 11, 20, and 30 in the year 1215 and was totally dominated by Innocent himself. It was controlled so completely by him that not one matter was treated except those introduced by Innocent, and not one decision was made without his consent.

The council was held in the Lateran in Rome and was attended by 412 bishops, 800 abbots and priors, a large number of delegates representing absent prelates, and representatives of Emperor Frederick II and Emperor Henry. The kings of England, France, Aragon (Spain), Hungary, Jerusalem, and others were also present.

The council did many things. In various doctrinal pronouncements, it set down the orthodox teachings of the church. It established transubstantiation as official church dogma in the universal church of Rome "outside of which there is no possibility of salvation." It condemned various heresies present in the church, particularly a heresy that was a denial of the Trinity.

The council did more. It authorized the fourth crusade. This crusade, though executed by Innocent, accomplished nothing in its efforts to take the Holy Land from the infidel Mohammedans. All it really accomplished was to widen the breach between the western church and the eastern church when the crusaders decided to sack Constantinople on their way to Palestine.

Perhaps the most ominous decision of the council was the establishment of the Inquisition. This institution, under the direction of the pope, was set up to enforce the church's teachings throughout the whole of Europe. It was an ecclesiastical court in which prelates of various kinds served as police, prosecutors, juries, judges, and executioners. Its powers went far beyond anything acceptable in civil law in the present day. It could make use of mere suspicion, torture to extract confession, confiscation of goods, exquisitely painful methods of execution, and indescribable cruelty in its efforts to make every person conform to the teaching of the church.

The Inquisition was used to exterminate the Albigensians, a sect mostly in southern France that diverged from the teaching of the church. It was brought to bear in all its horror against the Waldensians, that group of saints who suffered untold cruelty for their doctrines of Scripture. Some Waldensians, however, endured for several hundred years hidden in the Alpine valleys of France and Italy, and many of them joined the Reformation when it dawned in the sixteenth century.

Under the Inquisition's bloody work countless people of God suffered torture and death during the time of the Reformation, especially in the Lowlands.

Innocent was the one who instituted this apparatus, gave it its power, and forever branded the Romish church as the one that "persecutes those who live holily according to the Word of God, and rebuke her for her errors, covetousness, and idolatry." Rome thus bears the mark of the "false church."[6]

INNOCENT'S STRUGGLE WITH EUROPE'S KINGS

Scripture says that the rule of antichrist will be a worldwide rule in which all the nations of the earth are united in one political world power. To this political world power will be joined the false church. Revelation 13 and 17 depict this union of church and state.

No institution comes closer to that description than the papacy, and no single man came closer to realizing that goal than Innocent. This happened in Innocent's struggle with Europe's kings in what has become known as the Investiture Controversy.

Europe's kings and the pope carried on the controversy. By the time Innocent put on the papal tiara, the controversy had been going on for at least four hundred years. The issue was this: Who has the authority to consecrate to office the clergy in the Roman Catholic Church? Does this right belong to the church or to the king?

It appears at first glance to be an easy question to answer. Why, of course, the church. In the Middle Ages that meant the pope. Are not the clergy office bearers in the church? Should not the office bearers, therefore, be appointed and consecrated by the church?

This would seem to be true. But there was one difficulty. Many clerics, especially of the higher clergy (bishops and archbishops), had become owners and rulers of huge tracts of land. This had happened over the years as wealthy men had willed their estates and land to the church in an effort to buy their way out of purgatory. Thus clerics ruled vast domains over which they were sovereign, in which they had absolute authority, from which they organized armies of knights to wage war, and by means of the revenues of which estates they lived like royalty.

In other words, within various kingdoms there were sub-kingdoms ruled by the clergy who, although they may have expressed loyalty to the king, nevertheless owed their first allegiance to the church and fed into the church's coffers vast amounts of money on which Rome lived and maintained its extravagant lifestyle.

The pope argued that he had the right to appoint clerics because they held ecclesiastical office. The kings argued that they had the right to appoint these clerics because they were political rulers and owed allegiance to the crown.

As is usually the case, the bottom line was money. Who was going to get the money? The pope or the king?

It was a problem of no little importance, especially if we consider that at one time the church owned more than one-half of the landed estates of Europe.

Innocent's solution to the problem was simple. Make the pope the sole ruler in Europe, even over kings. And this he set about doing.

It is useless to go into all that went on in France, Germany, and England during this struggle. It is complicated and not edifying. But the result was that all the kings of Europe were brought to heel, one by one, until only England remained.

England was ruled by the powerful, usually able, but thoroughly corrupt Plantagenet kings. They were sometimes called Angevin kings because they traced their dynasty back to William the Conqueror, the Frenchman from Anjou who had conquered England and put England under the rule of his line. The power of the Plantagenets was something with which to reckon.

However, the pope was by no means without any power of his own. He could make decrees, issue edicts, and aim directives at Europe's kings, and he had various tools at his disposal to enforce his will. There were three such tools.

One was the horde of monks who lived in all Europe, were a drain on every country, inhabited the monasteries, but were totally loyal to the pope. He controlled them, manipulated them, and used them as a standing army to enforce his will. In every country they numbered in the thousands.

The second weapon was excommunication, and along with it, the anathemas that so frightened Europe's superstitious throngs. It was a decree of the pope that declared a man outside the church, outside of which was no salvation. Also excommunication in those days, when society was entirely under the control of the church, meant ostracism from society itself. An excommunicated person could not get a job. He could not buy or sell. He could not have any kind of intercourse with his fellow men. He was an outcast in the literal sense of the word.

Kings could be and were excommunicated when they defied the pope. Frederick II of Germany must have been excommunicated three or four times at least. But when the pope excommunicated a king, the people were automatically freed from submission to that king. The people could, of course, give their loyalty to the king in spite of what the pope said or did, but two things often prevented that. One was that army of monks roaming the land to enforce the pope's edicts.

The third tool was the interdict, which in the pope's hand was perhaps the most feared of all. When the pope put a region or a country under the interdict, that region or country could not have any religious exercises or ceremonies performed in it until the interdict was lifted. During the interdict no churches were open, no sermons were preached, no babies were baptized, no masses were performed, no marriages took place, no deaths were followed by church burial, and no consecrated burial grounds could be used.

In medieval Europe this was spiritual suicide. Rome had taught, and the people believed, that the church alone could give its members entrance into heaven. The church determined their salvation. The church regulated and directed their religious life. The church determined their stay in purgatory. The church released them from purgatory so that they might enter heavenly bliss. Without the church's work the people went to hell.

If the pope could make an interdict stick, it was almost a guarantee of the success of papal policies.

This is what happened in England in the days of King John, that monstrously wicked Plantagenet who was guilty of every crime under heaven and whose arbitrary tyranny was even too much for the people. It was this King John who, after the issue of investiture was solved, was brought to heel by the barons and forced to sign the Magna Charta on the plains of Runnymede.

The controversy was over the ordination of Stephen Langton as Archbishop of Canterbury. The pope wanted him; King John did not. The struggle was fierce. The pope excommunicated John. John thumbed his nose at the pope. But then the pope put all England under the interdict, and the people, weary of John's brutal reign, threatened to take matters into their own hands. The dukes and earls, the powerful nobility of England, all agreed that John had better knuckle under.

He gave all England to the pope, and the pope returned it to him, but as a papal fief. That is, John was, from henceforth, a minor lord ruling in the pope's name. And most galling of all, he had to pay an enormous sum into the papal treasury, thus depleting his own wealth and curbing sharply his own luxurious lifestyle.

Hence all Europe bowed before the papal throne. Innocent had won. Hungary, Bohemia, Sicily, France, England, Denmark, Spain, Germany and the Holy Roman Empire, Bulgaria, Sweden—all Europe submitted to the pope and acknowledged him as their head. The only exception to this universal rule was the eastern church.

Innocent's rule was complete. He was sole head of the church and sole ruler of Europe.

Conclusion

Innocent's tremendous power did not last. Europe's kings were becoming more and more powerful, and no subsequent popes were as strong as Innocent. Gradually the papal power began to crumble, and by the time the Reformation dawned, though the pope still tried to exert his will, he was stymied by independent rulers who simply refused to do what he said. Frederick the Wise is a case in point, for Luther's work would have been impossible from a human point of view without the defiance of papal edicts by Luther's ruler and sovereign in Saxony.

Within the context of the work of the Reformation, the true government of the church was restored to the church. It is not our purpose to go into this in detail, but the time-tested Church Order of Dordrecht was forged in the fires of the Reformation, especially the Reformation under Calvin.

Central to all biblical church order are the headship of Christ over the church and the office of believers, both of which Rome, in the papal hierarchy of its day, had denied. Christ, not the pope, is the sole head of the church. All God's people, through the anointing of Christ's Spirit, are prophets, priests, and kings in the church of God. We can, I think, scarcely imagine what an ocean of difference lies between that simple concept and Rome's hierarchy. It was Luther who laid this foundation.

God has established special offices in the church to reflect the threefold office of Christ: ministers (prophets), deacons (priests), and elders (kings).

By their work in the congregation, Christ is present in the congregation as the true prophet, priest, and king. Thus every congregation is autonomous.

Yet the church is called to express its unity in Christ. And so broader assemblies are formed, and denominations come into being. And denominations of like precious faith throughout the world seek each other to work together and have fellowship together.

The unity of the church is not only the external unity of an institution, as Rome taught. It is also the unity of the body of Christ, the unity of one faith, one hope, one calling, one baptism. In short, it is the unity of Christ's body itself come to visible manifestation in the congregation of believers.

The church had seen what the tyranny of hierarchical Rome could do to the church. God led the reformers into an understanding of the Scriptures in matters of church polity over against Rome's corruptions. These truths are precious principles, so important that for them, too, we ought to fight and in defense of them to be willing to die.

Over against these truths stand Rome's claims. Can it be denied that Rome's claims bear all the resemblances of the claims of antichrist himself? Whether antichrist as he finally reveals himself is one who arises out of the political sphere, which Revelation 13 and 17 seem to indicate, or whether he is predominantly a religious figure, makes no difference in the end. He does claim to be Christ and sets himself up in the temple of God claiming that he is God.

But God's people acknowledge Christ as their head and give their unswerving and joyful loyalty to him.

CHAPTER 15

THOMAS À KEMPIS AND MEDIEVAL MYSTICISM

INTRODUCTION

The error of mysticism has never been absent from the church of Christ in the new dispensation. It appeared early in the Montanist movement in the third century and has, in a remarkable way, maintained itself to the present. The church has always had to fight off mysticism.

Not a single period in the Middle Ages was without its mystics. Sometimes they were present in multitudes; sometimes only individual mystics kept the flame of mysticism burning; but never did the church free itself from them. In the Middle Ages, in fact, the church had no interest in condemning the mystics; they were never considered heretics. One gets the impression, on the contrary, that the church encouraged them. I suspect there were good reasons for such encouragement. The mystics were, almost without exception, faithful and loyal members of the church and supporters of the hierarchy. Perhaps more importantly, the church seemed almost unconsciously to recognize that in the cold formalism of Roman Catholic liturgy, the warm and experiential piety espoused by the mystics was a necessary and healthy counterbalance.

Mysticism is a word with a vague and fuzzy meaning. It covers a wide range of views and practices and describes a broad spectrum of people. In some instances mysticism cannot be distinguished in any significant way from genuine orthodoxy. In other instances it is radical, extreme, and as far removed from orthodoxy as pantheism is from the truth of creation. Indeed, some mystics were pantheists, a heresy that identifies God with the creation. In between these two extremes was such a wide diversity of opinion that no single book could contain all the differences and nuances among various branches of mystical thought.

That makes our present task a daunting one and forces us to limit our discussion, for the most part, to the main ideas that mysticism of every sort has in common.

It is also for this reason that I have chosen Thomas à Kempis as an example of medieval mysticism. He was by no means the worst of the mystics. In fact, he was a late mystic from the Netherlands and part of a group of mystics who had an influence on the reformers and the Reformation. His book, *The Imitation of Christ,* is considered a classic and is still read by Protestants as well as Roman Catholics.

He is, therefore, ideally suited for our purposes. From him we can learn what mysticism is all about and what the dangers in mysticism are against which we have to fight.

THOMAS À KEMPIS' LIFE

The surname à Kempis means "from Kempen." That was the name of the village in which Thomas was born in 1380, a little less than two hundred years before the beginning of the Reformation. The village of Kempen is near Cologne, Germany. Thomas' birthplace helps us explain, I think, the mysticism to which he was committed, for Cologne and Kempen are both in the Rhine River valley, and the fog-shrouded valley was the center of the mystical life.

Thomas was born of poor parents who were unable to provide any kind of education for him. Their surname was Hemerken, a name almost totally unsuited to Thomas, for it means "Little Hammer." Thomas was about as gentle a man as it is possible to find.

A biography of Thomas à Kempis would hardly fill ten pages, for he was determined that nothing would happen to him in his life, and so, under God's providence, it turned out to be.

He was a studious young lad and very serious-minded. He resolved, therefore, at about thirteen years old, to seek an education someplace where he could receive it at an affordable cost. Such a place was to be found in the circles of the Brethren of the Common Life. One community of these Brethren was to be found near Deventer in the Netherlands, a city straight east of Amsterdam and on an arm of the Rhine.

In a sense one could call the Brethren of the Common Life a community of mystics, but that designation would not be entirely accurate. They were made up of a fairly large number of communities stretching from Strassburg all the way to Rotterdam. They were loosely tied together with little or no organizational unity, but they were brought together by a common desire to cultivate the Christian life and emphasize genuine piety. These communities put a great deal of emphasis on establishing schools for children and educating them in the knowledge of godliness. They built hospitals and were assiduous in caring for the poor. The Brethren were very influential, produced some outstanding theologians in the tradition of mysticism, and influenced the Reformation in Germany and the Netherlands.

During the years of his study, Thomas developed his skills as a copyist and used these skills to support himself. All his life he continued in this work, copying books for the libraries of theologians of the Brethren of the Common Life, copying various manuscripts of importance to the community, and copying Scripture. There was as yet no such thing as a printing press although the invention of a moveable-type printing press was just around the corner. In his lifetime Thomas made four copies of the Scriptures, one of which is still extant.

While in Deventer, Gerhard Groot observed the studious and pious ways of the young boy and took him into his own house. This put Thomas in the center of the life of the Brethren, for the house of Gerhard Groot was the headquarters of the community located in the city. The influence of the mysticism of the Brethren molded Thomas' entire life.

After completing his studies, and attracted to the ascetic life, Thomas entered an Augustinian convent in Zwolle, twenty or thirty miles north of Deventer. Thomas' brother was prior of this convent, and in it Thomas found a congenial home. He was ordained a priest in the Roman Catholic church in 1413, and in 1429 he became sub-prior. After his brother died, he was prior for a short time, but he found the administrative work too burdensome and asked to be relieved of that position.

From that point on, his life can be summed up in a few sentences. He spent his time in three activities: copying, devotional exercises, and writing. It was a quiet life, removed from the bustling world about him, placid and serene, noiseless and routine, without any variation in the activities of the day. He himself wrote, "In all things I sought quiet, and found it not save in retirement [from all aspects of life in the world] and books."[1] Thomas died in Zwolle in 1471 and was buried in the convent cemetery.

Although Thomas possessed a prolific pen, he is remembered for only one book, *The Imitation of Christ,* which has been called "the pearl of all the mystical writings of the German-Dutch school."[2] It has been given a highly honored place among Augustine's *Confessions* and John Bunyan's *Pilgrim's Progress* as one of three great devotional books of all time.

Today there are more than two thousand editions of *The Imitation of Christ,* more than one thousand of them in the British Museum in London.[3] It was written originally in Latin, in which more than 545 editions exist. It was translated into many languages, including English. There are more than nine hundred editions in French alone.[4] Its English editions are available today and are read by many. Dr. Samuel Johnson, the great English lexicographer and friend of James Boswell, learned Dutch by reading *The Imitation of Christ.*[5]

Schaff says,

> [*The Imitation of Christ*] consists of four books... It seems to have been written in metre... The work is a manual of devotion intended to help the soul in its communion with God. Its sententious statements are pitched in the highest key of Christian experience. Within and through all its reflections runs the word, self-renunciation... The life of Christ is presented as the highest study it is possible for a mortal to take up... Over the pages of the book is written the word Christ. It is for this reason that Protestants cherish it as well as Catholics.[6]

At the same time, it was written by a Roman Catholic mystic and has references in it to the merit of good works, transubstantiation, purgatory, and the worship of saints, although these references are few in number and easily ignored.

A few scattered sentences from the book will give the reader a taste of its contents.

> Love is to be unknown and to be reputed as nothing.

> Where the crowd is, there is usually confusion and distraction of heart.

> Love solitude and silence, and thou wilt find great quiet and good conscience.

> Choose poverty and simplicity.

> Humble thyself in all things and under all things, and thou wilt merit kindness from all.

> Let Christ be thy life, thy reading, thy meditation, thy conversation, thy desire, thy gain, thy hope and thy reward.

> Zaccheus, brother, descend from the height of thy secular wisdom. Come and learn in God's school the way of humility, long-suffering and patience, and Christ teaching thee, thou shalt come at last safely to the glory of eternal beatitude.

THE PREVALENCE OF MYSTICISM

Already in the early church, the Montanists, to which Tertullian joined himself late in life, represented a mystical tendency to which many in the church were inclined.

The medieval period of church history was filled with mystics. In the years just prior to the Reformation, many communities of mystics were crowded into the Rhine River valley in Germany and the Netherlands.

Mysticism did not stop with the Reformation. Very early in the history of Luther's Reformation, he was confronted by the Zwickau prophets in particular and Anabaptism in general, each of which possessed its own brand of mysticism.

John Wesley was heavily influenced by medieval mysticism. He translated books of the mystics and infused Methodism with his mysticism.[7]

In the Netherlands the *gezelschappen* (conventicles that arose during the *nadere Reformatie,* or later Reformation) were often characterized by a mystical tendency from which the Dutch churches never completely escaped.

Mysticism has reached new heights in the modern-day charismatic movement.

CHARACTERISTICS OF MYSTICISM

Searching around for a general definition of mysticism, especially that of the medieval church, I found the following paragraph in *Mysticism in the Wesleyan Tradition.* Tuttle writes,

> Perhaps as good a definition as any could begin with the statement that mysticism is anything that gets one in touch with reality beyond the physical senses. Furthermore, mysticism embraces a "right brain" awareness of God and all mystics stress (more or less) the essential unity of God, nature, and humankind; therefore, union with God can be achieved (more or less) through the mystical contemplation of that unity. More specifically, mysticism is in essence that "deep sense of union with God in the inmost depths of the soul," an immediate awareness of a unique relationship with God. "It is religion in its most acute, intense, and living state."[8]

Tuttle also writes,

> Several characteristics have been listed as common to all mystical experience. First of all, mysticism defies expression, and its ineffable character makes it virtually impossible for mystics to describe their experiences adequately. Another characteristic of mysticism lies in its "noetic quality." To understand mysticism one must experience mysticism. Its thoroughly esoteric nature plunges the soul into depths of truth unplumbed by the discursive intellect. The mystical experience is also transitory because the mystical heights cannot be sustained for long, but this is

not to imply that no growth has taken place. Ideally, after each experience the mystic returns to a level of devotion even higher than before. In fact, these "mystical heights" are nonessential to mysticism and can be justified only if the mystic returns to the senses with a higher level of devotion.[9]

It is easy to understand how mysticism in many cases began to emphasize dreams, visions, and other forms of revelation that one would receive directly from God apart from the Scriptures. When the Zwickau prophets boasted of the revelations they had received from the Holy Spirit, Martin Luther responded, "I slap your spirit on the snout."[10] Luther's point was that the Holy Spirit speaks only through the objective Scriptures.

It is also easy to see how in many instances some sort of mystical experience was considered the decisive determination of the Christian life.

THE EXPLANATION OF MYSTICISM

We can find, I think, an explanation for mysticism and its constant attractiveness. In a sense, mysticism is an effort to pay unpaid bills. Mysticism arises when the church does not preach the full gospel of Jesus Christ, or at least does not live fully the gospel that she preaches. Mysticism fills the vacuum.

Man is created by God as a creature with a soul. The soul includes mind and will. The will, in turn, includes the powers of choice and the powers of emotions. God has determined that fellowship with him through Jesus Christ includes the whole man in body and soul, in mind and will. The first words of the Heidelberg Catechism are, "[My] only comfort in life and death... [is] that I, *with body and soul*...am not my own, but belong to my faithful Saviour Jesus Christ."[11] A true religion that is undefiled satisfies the whole man in body and soul. Basically that means that a true religion satisfies man's mind and will—both. It brings the whole man into fellowship with God.

The church has had trouble maintaining that proper balance, however. When Montanism arose and Tertullian chose to become a part of it, the reason was partly because during a period of rest from persecution, the church had become worldly. Eusebius, a contemporary of Nicea in the early part of the fourth century, makes this point in his *History of the Church.*

In the Middle Ages the Roman Catholic Church developed a religion that reduced the worship of God to outward liturgical forms and actions. The inward worship of the heart was slighted, if not ignored. One needed only to go through the motions of the ecclesiastically prescribed liturgy.

When scholasticism was in favor, the appeal of religion was to the intellect, to the person able to make the subtlest distinctions. The most difficult analysis of intellectual propositions was regarded as being the most religious. There was no passion, no intensity of feeling, no emotional content, and no concern for godly living; religion was in externals or intellectual attainment.

Mysticism flourished as a reaction to what was often a cold, formal religion without heart. Man is more than a head that thinks. He is also a soul who feels, loves, hates, grieves, and sings; this part of man also has to be caught up in his religion.

Then again, when mysticism flourishes and religion is reduced to nothing but feeling and emotion, the mind is left empty. The child of God has nothing to chew on with his mind, nothing to think about, nothing to remember, nothing to learn. How does he feel? Does his religion make him feel good? These seem to be the only questions that count.

So the pendulum in the church swings back and forth. It swings toward mysticism during periods of worldliness and dead orthodoxy, and it swings toward intellectualism when religion is reduced to feeling. But both are reactions. Mysticism is the swing of the pendulum toward feeling.

Mysticism also takes on other characteristics. It often arises out of a genuine concern about a life of godliness and piety, especially when worldliness and carnal-mindedness capture the church. When dead orthodoxy is present, many within the church worry that religion is only outward. People go to church, but worship in spirit and in truth is often lacking. People have their confessions but know almost nothing about them. People claim to have the truth but seem unwilling to defend it, or perhaps unable to defend it as they perish for lack of knowledge.

What counts, therefore, are not these outward forms of religion, but the true religion of the heart: true piety, true godliness, and a genuine devotional life. Mysticism is concerned about the cultivation of the devotional life, the development of piety and holiness, the life of prayer and meditation. These are hailed as the true marks of Christianity. This was the mysticism of Thomas à Kempis. This was the mysticism so prevalent among the mystics of the Rhine River valley.

But this rather naive mysticism, too, develops along a certain line. The church is composed of many types of people. Many of them are only outwardly religious. Who are the truly religious? Who are truly godly, truly pious, truly holy? Who are true believers? Who are genuinely converted? How can one tell? How can one tell for others? How can one tell for himself?

So often, precisely here, questions that could be proper, necessary, and important become the bridge to mysticism in its worst forms. It is not wrong to pursue piety and godliness. It is not wrong to cultivate inner holiness. These are necessary parts of true religion. But the next step is dangerous. True piety and true religion are, after all, close fellowship with God. But how does one know whether he truly has fellowship with God? Does this knowledge come by way of mystical experiences of closest and most intimate contact with the divine being in which there is indescribable and yet overwhelmingly sweet communion? The mystic says that dreams, visions, revelations, overwhelming joy, and feelings that transport one beyond life are part of the fellowship with God that marks genuine piety and that is, finally, the mark of the true believer.

How to Attain Communion with God

We are back now to what we described earlier as being the essence of mysticism: "a deep sense of union with God in the inmost depths of the soul."

The Middle Ages developed a lengthy process through which one had to pass in the attainment of that deep sense of union with God. It is worth our while to go through these steps to try to see what the mystics were talking about. The process had five distinct steps, although two things must be remembered about these steps: one is that all five were not always necessary, nor did all agree on exactly the five that I shall mention; the other is that the order might differ from one mystic to another. But this is generally the ladder one had to climb to reach union with God.

The first step was awakening. A man would come to the awareness that while he had been religious in an external and ultimately meaningless way, this was far from genuine religion. More was required. Study, reading devotional materials, and looking into what others had said would show one how he was missing the very heart and core of true religion and what had to be done about it. It was like a lifelong attendee at church suddenly realizing that the outward worship of God is not enough. Something more had to be there. This was surely true if, in addition to such an outward form of religion, one lived an essentially worldly life. To acquire what was missing, and how to attain what was missing, was part of the "awakening."

The second step was purgation. I guess we would be inclined to call this "conversion," although it was often carried beyond the boundaries of what we consider conversion to be. Purgation involved freeing oneself from his former way of life. If one was a soldier, he ought to leave the army. If one was worldly, he ought to abandon his worldliness. If one's interest in spiritual things was minimal and peripheral, he ought to rid himself of all that formerly distracted him and concentrate solely on spiritual things. In the Middle Ages this step often included selling all his possessions and living a life of poverty. It included renouncing marriage to live a celibate life. It included entering a monastery so that the external world could not intrude and all his life could be devoted to spiritual things. It was a "purgation" of his former life. It was often radical and extreme but absolutely necessary on the ladder to union with God.

The third step was illumination. Different ideas were meant by this term. Sometimes it referred to a period in which one gradually came to the awareness of what was involved in coming to true union with God. It was a sort of study of the devotional life. It could be a study of something extremely complicated as all aspects of a genuinely devout and pious life were explored, understood, and put into practice. At other times, by illumination was meant brief and occasional glimpses of the transcendent glory of a true union with the divine. It was not that union itself; it was a fleeting glimpse of the ineffable blessedness that awaited one who attained to it. It was intended to prepare one for the next step, the most difficult and agonizing of all.

The fourth step was the dark night of the soul. This step was considered absolutely essential, for without it no union with God was possible. It was somewhat patterned after the Scripture's emphasis on the believer's personal knowledge of his sin, which is expressed in a broken spirit and a contrite heart. It had the overtones of a genuine part of the believer's life. But it was also taken over by revivalism (much of which is sheer mysticism). It was a period of intense suffering of soul in which the darkness of sin, guilt, and hell dragged one lower and lower into depths of despair, hopelessness, and utter awareness of one's unworthiness and damnworthiness. The deeper and more intense that it was, the better and more likely to lead to God. The Puritans made a great deal of this aspect of the Christian's life, and they were followed by others. But oftentimes this period was such a "dark night" that it manifested itself in convulsions, long periods of rigidity of the body, unconsciousness, even screaming and hollering in terror because of visions of demons and the fires of hell. This fourth step was most difficult.

The final step was the union with God himself. As I mentioned in describing mysticism, this step is really indescribable. It is totally a matter of feeling. The mind does not function in any sense of hearing, reading, studying, or mastering intellectual propositions. It is beyond thought. It is beyond—far beyond—all knowing, all understanding, and all thinking. It is transcendent, unreal (when by "real" is meant anything pertaining to this world). It is beyond the five senses because it is direct, immediate (without means), intense, all-absorbing union with God himself. It is to be swallowed up in and engulfed by the brilliant light of the infinite ocean of the divine being. It is pure and unalloyed joy. It is to be oblivious to anything and everything except God's engulfing and consuming love. It is the apex of the Christian life. It is said to be the ultimate of all that is right and good and genuinely pious.

Because some mystics emphasized union with God via union with Christ, this union with God could be so complete that the very marks of the nail holes in Christ's hands came into the hands of the mystic. Such a one was so closely absorbed into Christ that the hole in Christ's side made by the soldier's spear came into the side of the mystic. The blood that Christ had spilled in the dust of Gethsemane now rolled off the brow of one who had been completely absorbed by Christ, and thus by God. These were called the stigmata of union with Christ, which many mystics claimed to bear, although others never could see them.

It is not difficult to see that such mysticism could become outright pantheism. And it often did. Pantheism is that terrible heresy, the ultimate expression of the devil's lie, "Ye shall become like God." Pantheism identifies God with the creation and speaks of man as the highest expression of the divine essence. The whole notion of union with God is only a small jump from such pantheism.

MYSTICISM'S ATTRACTION

The attraction of mysticism is great and not easy to resist. Especially when the church of which one is a member falls into dead orthodoxy or confessional carelessness, the spiritual lack of a fervent and heartfelt religion weighs heavily on the soul of a believer. When worldliness lays an icy grip on the lives of the people in church (there is a close relation between dead orthodoxy and worldliness), then those who are concerned for themselves and others to walk a life of obedience to Christ search about for an alternative to the spirituality of their own church home.

There is a fervency in religious matters, a zeal for holiness, a delight in walking in covenant fellowship with God that characterizes mystics and makes one lacking these things envious of what mystics possess.

One who understands that the deepest reality of the godly life is walking with God, as Enoch and Noah walked with him, can easily be enchanted by the claim of a mystic that he has attained this goal.

When mysticism puts all the emphasis of religion on emotions and feelings, few of us would deny that there is an attractiveness that tugs at our souls. To think about theological problems is often hard work and, so it seems, spiritually dry toil. To master doctrinal propositions may be intellectually stimulating, but it does little or nothing for our experience of what true religion is all about. Heavy tomes on Reformed dogmatics are far less able to nourish our spiritual life than devotional writings or biographies of unusual people who have had moving spiritual experiences. "It doesn't do anything for me!" is the plaintive cry of one who has just listened to a doctrinal sermon. And what is meant is that the preacher has not moved us emotionally either to weeping or to hallelujahs. A "feel good" religion is the thing of the day, in which all the emphasis falls on the word "feel."

TRUE EMOTIONS

These things and more drove the mystics in whatever age they appeared.

That there is an emotional aspect to true religion can never be denied. We are to love the Lord our God with all our hearts, and love is intensely emotional. We are to be sorry for our sins, and sorrow is heavily emotional. We are to rejoice in the Lord always, and rejoicing is an emotional thrill.

To put it differently, religion is experiential. The Lord has ordained that the eternal life, which he defines as the *knowledge* of the only true God and Jesus Christ whom he has sent (John 17:3), is an experiential knowledge. It is not knowledge like that of knowing a textbook on solid geometry. It is not even the knowledge of Abraham Lincoln, which one gleans from Bruce Catton's biography. It is an experiential knowledge, very similar to the knowledge a man has of his wife when he has lived with her in love for thirty years.

God gives us the gift of salvation so that we experience the rich blessedness of salvation and experience it over against the horror and hopelessness of our own personal hells. The Spirit witnesses with our spirit that we are the children of God.

It is this experiential aspect of religion that the mystic wishes to retain or recover, but he goes about recovering it in a wicked and unbiblical way.

CRITICISMS OF MYSTICISM

Various criticisms of mysticism can be made that, as serious as they are, do not come to the heart of the matter. We mention these first. Some have said that in the quest for union with God and absorption into the divine being, the mystic bypasses Christ. There is an element of truth in this, although it is not true of all mystics. However, when one reads the mystics, one cannot help but think that the union with God that the mystic holds up as the ideal religion is such complete absorption into the divine essence that Christ is no longer the only way to the Father. One goes directly to God and hurls himself into the brilliantly shining ocean of the divine being without coming to Christ. Such a bypassing of Christ happens because one forgets the words of Christ himself: "I am the way, the truth, and the life" (John 14:6). The meaning is that Christ is the way to the Father *because* he is the truth and the life.

In the interests of a genuine godly life, devotional exercises, meditations, solitude, and a life of prayer are held high as the ideal for one who would be saintly. It is, so the mystic says, better for a mother to read Augustine's *Confessions* than to wash the dirty dishes. It is better for a father to spend the day on his knees than to pick up his lunch pail and punch the time clock at a place of employment.

It all brings to mind an incident from my youth. It was in grade school where we often had chapel speakers who were missionaries or missionary helpers. One particular speaker warned us with unmistakable premillennial emphasis (which I did not recognize at the time) that because Christ could come back at any time, we ought to spend our time reading our Bibles so that Christ would find us doing this when he returned. Being a bit puzzled by the question of how I could spend my time reading my Bible and get my arithmetic finished in time to please my teacher, I questioned my father about it. "Well," he said, "You ought really to hoe the corn in the garden this afternoon. And even if you and I knew with absolute certainty that the Lord was coming back this afternoon, you ought still to go out and hoe the corn and keep right on hoeing until you saw Christ and he took the hoe out of your hands."

While the contemplative life of prayer and meditation is to be a part of our daily existence, we are given other tasks to perform as well. The position taken by mystics often led to monasteries and cubicles far removed from life—as happened to Thomas à Kempis. We have work to do. We must do our work to God's glory, but we had better *do* the work.

THE GREATEST EVIL

One evil in mysticism is greater than all others: it divorces Christian experience from the objective word of God. It speaks of communion with God through contemplation of the Godhead itself. When mystics speak of meditation or a life of contemplation, often they do not refer to meditating on Scripture or contemplating God's revelation in Holy Writ; they mean direct, immediate contemplation of God himself without any intervening mediating means. They just sit and think about God. They do not think about various propositions concerning God, and by means of these, think about God. They do not pay attention to any objective truth that God has revealed. They just think about God vaguely, ethereally, wordlessly, thoughtlessly, much in the same way one would think about a bright light: not thinking about why the light is bright, where it gets its energy to give light, how it is able to be so bright, or what is the nature of the light it emits. Instead, it is just thinking about light so that the light floods one's mind simply as light. That, someone once told me, is a good way to go to sleep.

The mystic tips his hand when he describes his experience of God as so high, so otherworldly, so exalted, that it is pure experience, beyond description in human words, ineffable (a word that means "indescribable"), of the sort that lies beyond thought, beyond our senses, beyond cognitive powers and the rational operation of the mind. Pure experience is what it is.

That experience can easily embrace, therefore, trances, visions, dreams, special revelations, direct speech of God to the consciousness, and the like. In any case, the word of God is abandoned.

To set aside the word of God is always very wicked. Some claim, and in my judgment with considerable justice, that Luther adopted the theory of consubstantiation (Christ's bodily presence in, with, and under the elements of the sacrament of the Lord's supper) because he was desperately afraid of the Zwickau prophets and their dreams, visions, and special revelations. In his view of consubstantiation Luther gave an objectivity to the word of God that, he believed, kept one from the subjectivism of mysticism.

As a side light, this is extremely interesting because Luther was influenced in his formative years by German mysticism. He was able, however, to throw it off completely and do fierce battle with the right wing of the Reformation, the mystical Anabaptists.

We must insist on an important truth that is being sacrificed on the altar of today's versions of mysticism. The truth is that the only way we are able to know God is through his revelation to us. He is the transcendent one, so highly exalted above us that we can never climb any ladder, not even the ladder of the mystics, to contemplate him as he is. He must first speak. He must speak in a language that we are able to understand. Calvin talked about God speaking to us in baby talk because we are so small. God speaks of himself in his speech. He speaks of who he is, what kind of God he is, what he does, how he works, and so on. He also tells us that because he is the kind of God he is, we are to be the kind of people he demands. He is holy, so we must be holy. We can know this only because God speaks in such a way that he tells us these things in words we understand.

So true is this that, on the one hand, God's speech is always a miracle, whether that speech be in creation or in Scripture. These two speeches of God are not really two speeches, as the theistic evolutionist insists; they are one speech saying the same thing about Christ and salvation as the great work of God, but we are able to hear this speech in creation only when God gives us the "hearing aids" of his word in Scripture.

On the other hand, God's speech to us is always limited, finite, only a part of the whole, only a dribbling of God's infinite depths. We can never know everything in the Scriptures and in creation. Even if we could, we would still possess less than a thimbleful of knowledge in comparison with all the oceans of this world.

That word of God is the *only* way to know God. There is no shortcut. There is no direct path. There is no speech of God directly to the soul—not even the assurance of our salvation. The Spirit indeed witnesses with our spirit that we are the sons of God, but the Spirit speaks of our sonship only through the Scriptures. The Spirit chains himself to the Scriptures. The Spirit confines all his work to the holy word of God in the Bible. Where no Bible is, there is no Spirit.

Thus we know God before we can "feel" him. What kind of nonsense is it to speak as some do: "I felt the closeness of God"? How does one do that apart from Scripture? We must *know,* with our heads and in our minds, definite intellectual propositions found in Scripture in order to know him. It is true that the more I know of Reformed dogmatics, the better I know God—not simply know about him, but know *him!*

This is not intended to imply that the mere knowledge of Scripture in itself guarantees the delightful experience of God. The devil knows more about God than you and I do. Hell is populated with learned theologians. Although it is true that not all who know about God actually experience

145

God, it is also true that those who experience God know him, first of all. And that knowledge of him is intellectual, cognitive knowledge.

God saves the whole man, body and soul, mind and will and emotions. But the emotions are part of the mind and will and not a power in themselves. When religion becomes an emotional matter, as it ought to become, this is so only because we appropriate its truths with the mind and desire its truths with the will.

This amazing work of the transformation of our minds takes place by means of the work of the Spirit. The Spirit causes the truth of the Scriptures to be indelibly impressed upon our consciousness in such a way that these truths are reflected in our conscious experience. This is an amazing work, but it is part of God's way of saving us so that we know our salvation and can praise him for it.

All religious life is rooted in, based upon, empowered by, and in conformity with God's word in Scripture. Do we desire to make confession of faith in our church? It is not enough to feel one is a Christian and to have some sense of Christ in one's heart. No. One had better be able to give an account of the Reformed faith as contained in Scripture and the confessions. Do we want to have the sweet consciousness of fellowship with God? Then we had better pore over his word and meditate upon its truths. There is no other way. Do we want such fellowship that God speaks to us and we to him? His speech comes only and always through the Bible. Is God speaking to me? Yes, he is, because Psalm 27:1 says, "Jehovah is my light and my salvation." And that is all that God says to me at the moment I am pondering that text. He may and does say that to me when I am surrounded by enemies who seek to destroy me with threats and fierce hatred. He says it to me when I need to know it and when my response is also his word to me: "Whom shall I fear?" But it is there in the Bible, and my sitting down and reading it is the only way God speaks to me.

Do I have problems needing the solutions that divine guidance alone can provide? Then, foolishly and wickedly, I do not say, "God put it on my heart to do this or that." I do not ask for the prayers of others so that I may know the will of God. Perhaps I ask for the prayers of others, but then it is only that others may pray that I put my nose more deeply into the Bible and receive a willingness to do what the Bible says. I do not wait for some direct word of God, subjectively heard, spoken in my soul, to do this or that. This is nonsense and results only in doing, after all, what I had wanted to do all the time, regardless of what the Bible says.

The Holy Spirit binds himself in all his work to the word. We can do no less. To separate ourselves from the word or to separate the Spirit's work from the word is to get trapped in the quicksands of subjectivism. If anyone claims that the Holy Spirit speaks directly to him apart from the word, he can make the Holy Spirit say anything that he wants the Spirit to say; indeed, this is precisely what he does. In these subjective revelations, the Holy Spirit is always in full agreement with anything the receiver wants or thinks. There is never any dissent from above.

Our subjective assurance of our salvation is also inseparably tied to the word. The Spirit speaks to us through the word, and never apart from it. The Spirit does not use experiences, dreams, visions, inner voices, or anything of the like. The word speaks. The Spirit speaks through that word, also in our own consciousness.

The close inner communion of the soul with God in which we are caught up in the rapture of union with the divine may seem the ideal of the Christian life, but it is the siren call of Satan, who would lead us away from the word in which alone our souls ought to be anchored.

Every child of God has times of great spiritual drought when God is very distant and the inner life of the soul seems barren. The same thing happens to churches where zeal has been lost, love has grown cold, and piety seems a distant dream. The solution to the problem is not to pray for revival with special outpourings of the Spirit apart from the word, outpourings resulting in bizarre behavior reminiscent of medieval mysticism. The solution is not to seek revival through some mystical contemplation of the divine. The solution is not to follow the five steps to union with God. The solution for the church is the lively and faithful preaching of the word. And the solution for the child of God wandering in a wasteland is to tie himself to the word and await times of spiritual refreshing.

Mysticism is wrong in every form it takes. Let us cling to the word.

PART 3
REFORMATION PERIOD (1517–1577)

Contenders for the Faith and Historical Events		Promoters of Heresy
		Desiderius Erasmus 1466 or 1469–1536
		Andrew Carlstadt 1481–1541
Martin Luther 1483–1546		Thomas Münzer 1490–1525
		Johann Agricola 1494–1566
		Menno Simons 1496–1562
		Philip Melanchthon 1497–1560
John Calvin 1509–64		John of Leiden 1509–35
		Michael Servetus 1509 or 1511–53
Charles V ruled over the Holy Roman Empire 1516–55		
Luther posted his ninety-five theses in Wittenberg 1517	1517	
Seljuk Turks threatened Europe early 1520s		
Diet of Worms 1521		
Inquisition brought to Lowlands by Charles V 1522		Jerome Bolsec birth unknown; died c. 1584
First edition of Calvin's *Institutes of the Christian Religion* 1536		Nicodemites condemned by Calvin 1537–62
Calvin banished from Geneva 1538		
Council of Trent 1545–63	1545	
Final edition of Calvin's *Institutes of the Christian Religion* 1559		
Belgic Confession of Faith 1561	1561	
Heidelberg Catechism 1563		
St. Bartholomew's Day massacre of French Huguenots 1572		
Formula of Concord 1577	1577	

CHAPTER 16

ERASMUS AND HUMANISM

INTRODUCTION

It is time to turn from the medieval period in the history of doctrine and to concentrate on the time of the Reformation. The medieval period, with a few exceptions, was a barren period theologically, and little can be learned from it when one is pursuing the development of the truth of God's word. Heretics abounded, but the answers to heretics were not to be found.

The Reformation is a different kind of period. During the time of the first generation reformers, God, through them, restored his truth in the church and restored the church itself to what it ought to be. In the beginning of the Reformation, the work that especially Luther did in leading the church of Christ back to the fountain of all truth in the sacred Scriptures was work that had to, and did, point out the truth over against Roman Catholicism. But once that had been done, the reformers were forced to deal with heretics of many different stripes, some of whom fought against Reformation doctrine from within the citadel of the Romish church, and some of whom joined the Reformation movement but in the course of time betrayed it.

One of the more interesting heretics was Desiderius Erasmus, sometimes referred to as the Prince of the Humanists. He was a contemporary of Luther, in fact sixteen years older than the German reformer, but he played a major role in the development of Reformation truth.

ERASMUS' EARLY LIFE AND EDUCATION

Erasmus was born out of wedlock, the youngest child of a Roman Catholic priest by the name of Gerard and a physician's daughter named Margaret. How many children these two had is not known. Erasmus was born in

Rotterdam, the Netherlands, where his father served as a priest. His birth date was October 27, either 1466 or 1469.

Erasmus was well cared for by his parents until their death, which occurred while Erasmus was yet a young boy. He was robbed of his inheritance by a guardian and was forced into a convent. In spite of these sad events, he received the best education available in his land. This education was first in the cathedral school in Rotterdam, then in Deventer with the Brethren of the Common Life. Education among these people left an indelible mark on Erasmus.

He early showed a love for the ancient Latin classics and an amazingly retentive memory. These classics were, of course, the pagan classics by old Roman authors: Cicero, Livy, and the like. The school in Deventer was, though emphasizing inner piety, not averse to the study of pagan authors.

Nor ought it to surprise us that such studies occupied Erasmus. The Renaissance had taken Europe by storm, and the movement had been embraced by the church, presumably in an effort to baptize classical pagan culture with the religion of Rome. The Renaissance was characterized by a return to Greek and Roman classical culture, particularly the literature of those long-gone centuries. Many within the church were not only attempting to incorporate the ideas of pagan thought into the theology of the church, but even saw in classical learning the means whereby the church could be cleansed from its corruption and reformed in morals and worship.

Taken in by the lofty thoughts of pagan philosophers, poets, litterateurs, and essayists, Erasmus found himself in the camp of those who wanted classical learning included in the church. Erasmus was a man of the Renaissance.

ERASMUS' LATER LIFE

After completing his studies with the Brethren of the Common Life, Erasmus was ordained to the priesthood. This was about 1490, when he was twenty-five years old. Although he remained an ordained priest all his life, he neither did the work of a priest, nor performed even one priestly function. He never had a parish of his own, and the work of the parish ministry was totally foreign to him. He did, however, receive a papal dispensation to abandon his position as a monk and his oath to remain a member of the monastery. Perhaps the only good thing he gained from his life in a monastery was an intense dislike of monastic life and a bitter hatred for the corruptions he had seen all about him among the monks.

He chose instead to pursue his studies, chiefly in Paris at the famous University of Paris, where he earned his doctorate. By that time Erasmus became so enamored with his studies and with learning for its own sake that he resolved to spend the whole of his life as a free and independent scholar. And this is what he did the rest of his life until he died in 1536.

ERASMUS' INTERESTS

Erasmus boasted of his devotion to scholarship. He boasted of the fact that he was free from home life, free from attachment to any school, free from family, free from any occupation, free from citizenship in any country, and free from the toils of daily work. He was a scholar, a professional scholar, one who could spend all his time developing his intellect and pursuing his studies in any direction he chose. He could write at leisure and never under the pressures of deadlines. He could write as he pleased and what he pleased, and he needed to give account to no one for what he wrote. He once said to a friend that the little money he acquired he preferred to spend on books rather than on food or clothes. He was what Paul would proba- bly call a man "ever learning and never able to come to the knowledge of the truth" (2 Tim. 3:7). He claimed to be and was a man of the world, a true cosmopolitan. No country could claim him. The church could not snare him, not even when he was offered a cardinal's hat. He spoke and wrote in Latin. He never learned another language, not even French, Ger- man, or Italian. In fact, he spoke his native tongue, Dutch, with difficulty and poorly. But his Latin was elegant and stylish, and that was, after all, the language of Europe's intelligentsia.

This did not mean that Erasmus did not travel. He traveled to Italy, where he spent a few years and published a few works. He lived chiefly in Venice and came to think of it as the most beautiful city in the world. He made two trips to England, during the first of which he met such leading English humanists as John Colet and Thomas More. During his second visit he occupied the chair of Lady Margaret Professor of Divinity at Cam- bridge, one of the more prestigious chairs in England's universities. He was offered a permanent appointment to this chair, and the whole of En- gland would have been flattered if he had accepted. But he declined in the interests of maintaining his freedom.

Because Switzerland was the one country more than any other that wel- comed freedom of thought, he finally settled in Basel on the German- French border. There Erasmus made a life-long friend in Forbet, who became his printer and published the works of his confidant and friend.

ERASMUS' ERRORS

The life of a scholar may appeal to some people; indeed, it appealed to Calvin, who nearly had to be dragged into the work of the Reformation by Farel, the reformer of Geneva. But Paul is not being complimentary when he speaks scornfully of those who are ever learning and never coming to the knowledge of the truth. A man is given his place in the church to work on behalf of the cause of Christ and his own fellow saints. Study is good, but study without work is useless in the maelstrom of the church militant here on earth.

Erasmus would perhaps agree with what I have said, but he would also refuse to apply such a characterization to himself. He was persuaded that the many evils in the Romish church could be rooted out through genuine scholarly learning, preferably learning rooted in the past. But this is not true. It is a humanist principle that man's improvement is rooted in education, a theory tried repeatedly in a foolish world, which perpetually looks to its schools to solve the moral, ethical, and social problems of life. Erasmus was content to apply his principle to the church, and he was persuaded that a thoroughly educated clergy, with the roots of its learning in Aristotle and Cicero, would automatically bring about morally upright priests and genuine reform in the church. He was dead wrong. It is a Pelagian heresy that leads men to think this.

Freedom to live as one pleases, to write and teach without any constraint, to be independent of any institution or country, may seem to some like an idyllic life, but it is wicked for all that and is rooted in pride. The simple fact is that, especially in the church, God gives us the communion of the saints for a good purpose. Every one of us needs the others in the household of faith. We may not and cannot be independent. If we insist on our independence, we will go astray. The church of which we are a part, our responsibilities in it, our work on its behalf, our labors with others in the church: all act as a check on our natural tendency to dart off in this theological direction or that moral error. Erasmus' pride was also his intellectual downfall.

But his most serious flaw was his humanism. In what is probably an oversimplification, humanism teaches that man is the center of the universe, that he is given the world for his own benefit, that he has the means to control it, that it is here for his personal enjoyment, and that his own personal welfare is the only legitimate goal of all human activity.

This humanism in the men of the Renaissance gave them a love for classical learning that lifted the writings of mere pagans to the level of God's own truth. In these pagan writers, so it was said, was to be found right knowledge, high moral standards, truth concerning God and man, and a rich mine of learning that could be integrated with the Christian faith to the enrichment of theology. The Roman Catholic Church as a whole accepted this view, and some of the leading patrons of such learning were Rome's popes.

It is not so surprising that Erasmus, along with his fellow humanists, should think this; the same view is held today by those who hold to common grace. A grace of God operative in pagan men and women, they say, enables them to produce works of culture pleasing to God and of use to the church. Such grace in the arena of thought and ideas produces truth, no, Truth with a capital T. Already in my college days the students were given instruction on how to bring about the marriage of Athens and Jerusalem.

Let it be clear. This is humanism, and humanism destroys the church of Christ.

All of this does not mean that Erasmus did not gain fame, honor, and wealth in his lifetime. He was the most famous man in Europe. Every university, with the exception of those that hated his efforts to reform, coveted his presence on the faculty. The learned and mighty of Europe counted it an honor if he would deign to answer their correspondence. Kings and princes sought his advice, and even they thought that a personal interview with Erasmus was the epitome of honor. Popes and prelates did homage to his learning and wanted his counsel on ecclesiastical affairs. He was recognized as Europe's most learned man and so adored that some came perilously close to deifying him.

Although in his earlier years he had to teach and depend on the kindness of wealthy friends for his livelihood, as his fame increased, so did his wealth. The rich and the famous, the powerful and the mighty, showered him with gifts and money until he was so wealthy that he could, upon his death, leave a sizeable estate.

Schaff writes of Erasmus, "He combined native genius, classical and biblical learning, lively imagination, keen wit, and refined taste. He was the most cultivated man of his age, and the admired leader of scholastic Europe from Germany to Italy and Spain, from England to Hungary."[1]

Erasmus was, beyond doubt, the most highly educated man in Europe. He was Europe's greatest scholar, bar none; his gifts for writing in elegant and effective Latin surpassed the gifts of any other man who put pen to paper. He was the counselor and advisor of Europe's mighty in church and state. The professors and teachers in the universities listened to his words and read his works with awe. He was urbane, witty, serious, forceful, erudite—a true Renaissance man. He was showered with honors and money until he became wealthy.

> The humanists were loudest in his praise, and almost worshiped him. Eoban Hesse, the prince of Latin poets of the time, called him a "divine being," and made a pilgrimage on foot from Erfurt to Holland to see him face to face...Zwingli visited him in Basel, and before going to sleep used to read some pages of his writings. To receive a letter from him was a good fortune, and to have a personal interview with him was an event.[2]

ERASMUS' WRITINGS

We might mention here a couple of Erasmus' more popular books. Perhaps the best known is *The Praise of Folly,* in which he took dead aim at the terrible evils in monasticism, ruthlessly exposed these evils, and criticized the institution for fostering these evils. He was particularly opposed to the follies of monks and friars and mocked them with biting sarcasm. With this book he made the world laugh.

A more sober and constructive book was his *Handbook of a Christian Soldier* in which he laid out the pattern for the life of one who wanted to live faithful to Christ.

Erasmus edited and published many of the church fathers but, tellingly, did not like Augustine. Augustine was too sharp a defender of God's sovereign and free grace.

Perhaps his greatest accomplishment was the first publication of a critical edition of the Greek New Testament. He gave scholars the New Testament in its original language in the place of the Vulgate, a Latin translation by Jerome. He hurried to get this published because he wanted to get his edition on the market before the Spanish Cardinal Ximenes, who was also known to be working on such an edition. God uses the work of wicked men for his purpose as well as the labors of the faithful. With the Greek New Testament in their hands, the reformers could work with the original languages and prepare accurate translations for God's people. They could work with the original languages in their preaching, teaching, and writing. It was a great gift to the church. It came one year before Luther's reformatory work began.

In all his writings, Erasmus opposed formalism, traditionalism, and the moral evils of the church, which in his judgment obscured the teaching of Christ.

Erasmus' Early Sympathy for the Reformation and Later Hesitation

Erasmus wanted reformation in the church. There can be no question about that. He was dismayed at the many evils prevalent in the church.

When Erasmus saw that Luther was bent on bringing reformation to the church, Erasmus was delighted. His correspondence with Luther began early, and he was very sympathetic with Luther's aims. On his part, Luther wanted Erasmus to join with him in his quest for reformation in the church.

It would have meant a great deal if Erasmus had taken a stand with Luther. Erasmus, with his enormous prestige, could have brought many of Europe's universities and scholars to the side of the Reformation and have made the Reformation a credible and powerful force in the social, political, and ecclesiastical life of Europe. The pressure on the church to reform itself would have been far, far greater than any pressure exerted by an obscure monk in the dirty little town of Wittenberg. But Paris, Cologne, London, Cambridge, Rotterdam—who knows what great forces could have been unleashed to bring reformation to Europe if only Erasmus had joined the movement.

Yet it did not happen. Luther was suspicious of Erasmus from the start, although he expressed admiration for Erasmus' work and urged him to join the Reformation. Erasmus equivocated and finally demurred. He decided not to go that way. He was sympathetic to Luther's work, but only to a point. When Frederick the Wise asked Erasmus for his opinion of Luther, Erasmus acted as if he hadn't heard the question. But when Frederick pressed him, he paused thoughtfully and could finally come up with nothing better than this: "Luther has committed two sins—he has touched the Pope on the crown, and the monks on the belly."[3]

There were reasons for his reluctance.

Erasmus saw the need for reformation but insisted that it had to take place *within the church,* not by separation from it. He was like so many today who remain within a corrupt and apostate church, always hoping for change and meanwhile becoming weakened by the downward slide of the church they hope to save.

Erasmus basically took an entirely different view of reform than Luther. Erasmus was, for the most part, in full agreement with the church's doctrine; he wanted reformation of morals only. Granted that moral reformation was necessary, such reformation had been attempted for more than two hundred years by others more concerned even than Erasmus, and all without success. Moral decay arises out of doctrinal error, and moral reformation is born from doctrinal renewal. It does not work to try to bring about reformation in a church by calling attention to errors of the church in practical matters of life without insisting on a return to the truth of Scripture.

Erasmus was offended by Luther's sharp, angry, condemnatory language and his insistence on describing things as they were. Anyone who has read even a smattering of Luther knows the Luther of violent language and sharp invective. Erasmus was the scholar, witty, polished, polite, and learned. He had no time for Luther's crudities. He thought them irresponsible, uncultured, unscholarly, unkind. When Erasmus was charged with having "laid the egg, which Luther hatched,"[4] Erasmus replied that perhaps this was true, but he had expected a different kind of a bird.

I am on Luther's side on this matter. It not only took such language as Luther spoke to shake the citadel of Rome to its foundation, but also his language, though brutal and forthright, was honest in every respect. Luther described things as they were. This wakes up lethargic and sleeping people of God and demonstrates the seriousness of church struggles. It takes the controversy out of the ivory tower of scholarly research and dignified disagreement and puts the struggle on the battlefield where, in fact, it belongs. The church needs neither learned scholars (although Luther was such) nor nice people who discuss with mutual respect for each other various differing viewpoints in quiet and hushed voices. Such are to the detriment of the church and the truth of God, for they deal with God's truth itself as if it is nothing but an interesting theological question. In times of apostasy, the church needs trumpet blasts, sharp unambiguous language, men willing to "say it as it is," fearless men who love God and his word above all else.

Herein lay Erasmus' problem. To stand with Luther would have ended his high standing in Europe's scholarly circles, in king's courts, in papal palaces. He could not bear the thought of this. It was, at last, a matter of pride, of wanting to be recognized, of coveting the respect of his peers, of fearing the condemnation of others, and of suffering for Christ's sake. Erasmus recognized that suffering was the price to pay for reformation: he bluntly said that he was not made of the stuff of martyrs. But it takes those willing to suffer for Christ's sake and to stand alone bearing the reproach of Christ to do the work of God.

The nature of the Reformation made it necessary for Europe to choose one side or the other. Erasmus was caught in this dilemma but was unwilling to take sides on issues not defined by him or to enter into controversies not controlled by him. This is Schaff's evaluation, and it is true.[5]

Erasmus' pride! That was finally the thing. And strangely enough, that pride became a matter of theology. I think Luther knew it. He forced Erasmus to spell out his position on one of the most important theological questions of the Reformation: the question of the free will of man. That, finally, brought the break.

Luther wrote the following to Oecolampadius, the reformer of Basel:

> [Erasmus] has done what he was ordained to do: he has introduced the ancient languages [a reference to Erasmus' critical edition of the Greek New Testament—HH], in the place of injurious scholastic studies. He will probably die like Moses in the land of Moab . . . but to reveal the good and to lead into the land of promise is not his business.[6]

THE GREAT ISSUE

It seems to me that Luther himself forced the issue. He was early suspicious of Erasmus. As early as 1516, prior to the beginning of the Reformation proper, Luther expressed his fear that Erasmus understood far too little of the grace of God. Luther was concerned that Erasmus was interested more in a demonstration of Romish error than of biblical truth, and as a consequence, had a greater love for peace than a love of the cross.

With Erasmus' equivocation, Luther grew more impatient. Under prodding from Luther and others, Erasmus made up his mind, broke openly with Luther, and declared all-out war against the Reformation. But the issue, strikingly and providentially, was over grace. Erasmus made his public announcement of war against Luther in a book in which he attacked the doctrine of total depravity. The book was *The Freedom of the Will.* In it Erasmus spelled out in detail his views: the doctrine of total depravity destroys moral responsibility; to teach total depravity makes useless the commandments of God, repentance from sin, and reward in heaven. It was a fiery attack against Augustine and what Erasmus knew was the heart and soul of Luther's position. Man, said Erasmus, has a free will. That enables him to choose for or against God. That makes him morally responsible for his deeds, enables him to repent of his sins, and earns for him a reward for his merit.

It is not surprising that Erasmus took this position, if one thinks about it. He was, first of all, deeply committed to pagan thought and was sure that pagan philosophers spoke truth. How did they do this if they were unregenerated? The possibility lay in their ability to do good, find truth, express it eloquently, and teach it to others. Such possibility of good for these pagans was the grace of God toward them. That grace resulted in something less than total depravity. Luther would make Erasmus give up his darling pagans, a price far too high for Erasmus to pay.

Erasmus' pride also showed itself when he allowed Europe to worship him. He clung to his pride when to go with Luther would mean the loss of the respect of the whole world of scholarship. To join the Reformation would be to take up a cross. Erasmus did not want a cross; he wanted an earthly crown. His pride led him to exalt his own spiritual powers. Every effort on the part of man to salvage some tattered remains of his own goodness is in order to enable him to make his own contribution to salvation and thus earn merit with God. Pride led Erasmus away from the dark horror of Calvary to bask in the sunshine of the favor and praise of Europe's scholars.

Finally, Erasmus was from the start, and would always remain, a son of the church. Centuries earlier, in the interest of maintaining that precious doctrine of human merit, Rome had condemned Augustinianism, killed Gottschalk, its leading defender, and committed itself to the hellish error of semi-Pelagianism. Erasmus was content with, and indeed believed, this gross, God-denying heresy.

I am thankful that under God's providential direction, the issue was man's free will. There is no defender of free will today, although defenders number in the millions, who can maintain his haughty, man-exalting doctrine and claim to be a son or daughter of the Reformation, whether in Calvinistic circles or in the Lutheran tradition.

When all is said and done, the issue in the church of Christ is always this: Is salvation from God alone, and therefore without human aid, assistance, or cooperation? Is salvation by sovereign and particular grace, or does the almighty God wait on puny man and remain dependent on him in order to save? God or man? Erasmus was for man. Luther stood for God.

Luther waited a year before he answered. This was not because there was any doubt in Luther's own mind. The issue was defined, and Luther had taken his position much earlier when he found peace with God in the doctrine of justification by faith alone. The issue, however, was so crucial that Luther prepared his answer with care.

Think of the matter from Luther's side. Most claimed the issue was only a minor point of doctrine. Conceding depravity, Erasmus wanted a bit of good in man. Conceding justification by faith, Erasmus demurred at the word "alone." If Luther had been willing to make that minor concession, Europe would have fallen at his feet. The doors of the universities would have swung open. The numbers following him would have been greatly multiplied. He could have laid aside the cross of persecution and taken on a cardinal's hat. He could have been a force in the church for the moral reform so desperately needed. The bull of excommunication would never have been written. The lonely stand at Worms and isolation in the castle at Wartburg would never have been necessary. The pope himself would have placed a crown on his head.

But there was the matter of God's glory and the truth of his word; from that, Luther would not and could not budge. So he wrote his *Bondage of the Will*, that magnificent and powerful defense of all the doctrines of grace —as strong as or stronger than anything Augustine had written or that Calvin would later write. It was a bold and challenging defense of God's honor and salvation by grace alone. It is the one book that Luther said was the most important book he had written. It is the one book that anyone who loves the Reformation must read.

The Bondage of the Will gave right direction to the entire Reformation. The consequence was the alienation of most of Europe's intelligentsia. For Luther it meant denying himself and taking up the cross of Christ. But through it, Luther was Christ's disciple, and he pointed the way for all those who followed him in the path of true faithfulness to their Lord.

Erasmus was finally forsaken by friend and foe. That happens sometimes to men who try to sit on the fence. It happened to him. The criticism came from all sides: Pelagians faulted him for his equivocation and sympathy for reform; the faithful, for whom the gospel of sovereign grace had been opened, despised him for his willingness to sell his soul for a mess of human praise. He died alone.

It was the parting of the ways between humanism and godliness, between the Renaissance and the Reformation, between sovereign, particular grace and common, general grace. It remains the parting of the ways today.

CHAPTER 17

MELANCHTHON AND SYNERGISM

INTRODUCTION

Anyone interested in the great Reformation of the sixteenth century readily acknowledges that Martin Luther was the outstanding reformer of all those who engaged in this great work. Followers of John Calvin, while recognizing that Calvin's theological writings were, in a sense, more thoroughly biblical in his theological approach to the truth in distinction from Luther's soteriological emphasis and his doctrine of the presence of Christ in the Lord's supper, nevertheless recognize that God used Luther to begin the Reformation and to assail and demolish the bulwarks of Roman Catholic doctrine and practice with roaring cannon shots from Scripture that shook Europe to its foundations. On the fundamental doctrines of Scripture both Luther, Calvin, and the other reformers were agreed.

This agreement was especially evident in the doctrines of salvation by grace alone through faith alone. All the reformers hated Romish Pelagianism with a passion, and all, with great power, set forth the doctrines of the sovereignty of God in salvation. Double predestination, sovereign hardening, irresistible grace: all the doctrines of grace can be found sharply and with emphasis in Luther's *Bondage of the Will.*

How is it, then, that Lutheranism worldwide no longer holds to these teachings of the great man after whom their churches are named? Is the case the same in Lutheran circles as in Reformed circles: that the churches that are heirs of the Reformation have simply departed from the teachings of their spiritual fathers? In part, this is true of course. In matters of the truth, a denomination must move, and movement can be only in two directions: backward or forward. A church either develops the truth or loses it. There is never any standing still. The tendency is usually backward.

The departure from Luther's teachings took place very shortly after

Luther died. In fact, it can be proved that departure began already, in spite of Luther's best efforts, before the great reformer breathed his last. The evidence of such departure is, furthermore, embodied in the official creed of worldwide Lutheranism, the Augsburg Confession. The departure is known as "synergism." It was introduced into Lutheran theology by Luther's respected colleague and fellow reformer, Philip Melanchthon. One reads the story and weeps.

MELANCHTHON'S LIFE

From a certain viewpoint, Melanchthon is in the same list as the greatest of the reformers. His intellectual gifts exceeded those of Luther. He was, from the viewpoint of his theological accomplishments, nearly the equal of John Calvin. He shone with greater light than Knox, Zwingli, Oecolampadius, Farel, Bucer, or any other reformer of the first and second generation. Nor were Melanchthon's powers strictly intellectual; he was a man known throughout all Europe for his Christian piety, his humility, his utter disregard for the comforts of life, his devotion to his wife and family, his total commitment to the cause of Christ, and his unceasing labor on behalf of the gospel. He worked so hard and such long hours that in exasperation Luther himself (no slouch when it came to unbelievable amounts of work and long hours) bellowed at Melanchthon that if he did not quit working so hard, he, Luther, would excommunicate him.

Melanchthon was born in Bretten, in the lower Palatinate of Germany, on February 16, 1497, just over thirteen years after the birth of Luther and about twelve years before the birth of John Calvin. His surname was Schwarzerd (black earth). Melanchthon is only the Latinization of his German name. While Luther was born of peasant stock, Melanchthon was born in better circumstances. His father was such a skilled maker of armor that his work was sought by the princes and knights of the surrounding country.

The Palatinate was, geographically, all that Wittenberg was not. Wittenberg, at the time of the Reformation, was little more than a cluster of hovels and a monastery built on a huge sand pile with little to commend it other than the university that Frederick the Wise had erected there. Melanchthon often complained that he could not even get a decent meal in the town, and he frequently expressed a longing for the beauties of his homeland. The Palatinate, on the other hand, boasted a nicer climate, was filled with forests rich in game, and had fertile fields and lush meadows. Its peaceful and beautiful valleys followed the meandering Neckar River.

Melanchthon's great-uncle was the famous and influential Reuchlin, the outstanding Hebrew scholar of his day. Reuchlin was a humanist on the order of Erasmus. While working for reform in the Romish church, Reuchlin was not interested in doctrinal reform and consequently remained a member of Rome's church to the end. But his work in Hebrew enabled the reformers to work with the Old Testament Scriptures in their original language, and his grammar was used in most of Europe's universities for centuries after it was written. Reuchlin took responsibility for Melanchthon's education. Melanchthon's intellectual gifts were astounding, even by the reckoning of that great age of intellectual giants.

Melanchthon earned his master's degree in 1514 when he was seventeen years old. He was knowledgeable in almost every subject known throughout Europe: philosophy, rhetoric, astronomy, jurisprudence, mathematics, Greek grammar, classical writings, medicine, and dialectics. Some of these subjects he may have mastered on his own. He studied in Pforghum in 1507, the University of Heidelberg in 1509, and Tubingen in 1513. In Tubingen, at the tender age of eighteen, he began to teach. In 1516 he concentrated his studies on theology. He wrote and spoke Latin and Greek better and more fluently than his native German.

In 1518 he accepted an appointment to the University of Wittenberg, even though many prestigious universities throughout Europe sought him. His salary was 100 guilders, a sum doubled after the first year but an increase he would accept only after Luther's most strenuous efforts to persuade him to take it. He was appointed to the chair of Greek but soon took over the chair of theology. When the professors and students then present in Wittenberg saw him for the first time, they were uneasy. Melanchthon was short, thin, unimposing, youthful, and seemingly altogether unsuited for the work. It was like calling a junior in high school to occupy a prestigious chair at Yale University.

But at his inauguration, Melanchthon spoke on "Reforming the Studies of Youth." His speech was a masterpiece. Not only was it delivered in impeccable Latin, not only was it scholarly and thorough, but it also broke such new ground in the field of higher education that it set the tone for Europe's universities for centuries to come. Luther himself was so pleased that he could not speak highly enough of his new colleague.

MELANCHTHON'S WORK

Upon assuming his post at the university, Melanchthon literally hurled himself into the work of the Reformation.

The list of his labors and achievements is long and impressive. His teaching abilities were so great that he attracted students from all over Europe. He himself said that at one time eleven different languages were spoken in his classroom. The lecture hall in which he taught was filled, sometimes with as many as fifteen hundred to two thousand students crammed into one place.

His writing was extensive and influential. He wrote books on almost every subject, although his books on theology were the most popular. He was the first of the reformers to write a systematic theology. It was called *Loci Communes,* and it had an influence on systematic theologies for many years after he died.

Melanchthon was frequently the representative of Luther and the Lutheran Reformation at meetings, colloquies, conferences, and assemblies of various kinds. Considering that travel was difficult and time-consuming in those days, and considering that these meetings were held in many different places in Germany, vast quantities of time were consumed simply in traveling. He was present with Luther in Leipzig where Luther debated with the great John Eck in 1519 and where Luther came to the realization that Scripture alone is authoritative for all of faith and life. Melanchthon provided Luther with arguments and quotations from the fathers to the annoyance of Eck, who finally told him to shut up. Melanchthon was present with Luther at the great Colloquy of Marburg, where representatives from the Lutheran and the Swiss Reformation met in an effort to come to agreement on the presence of Christ in the Lord's supper. He was also present at some of the great meetings of Protestant princes and rulers who met to defend themselves against the armies summoned by the pope to fight against Lutheranism. He played major roles in meetings with the Roman Catholics when efforts were made to heal the breach struck by the Reformation. The story of these meetings, too lengthy to tell, is filled with heroism, excitement, danger, and just plain hard work.

Melanchthon played a greater role than any other single man in the writing of the Lutheran confessions that arose out of the Reformation. He was the competent and superbly qualified linguist who could give his invaluable assistance to Luther (and a few others) in the preparation of the German translation of the Bible.

In addition to all these labors, he was a faithful and busy husband and father. At the urging of Luther, Melanchthon married Katherine Krapp on November 25, 1520. It was a tranquil marriage, blessed with four children, although often filled with sorrow (the parents lost two children early in life). Melanchthon, scholar that he was, could often be found in the cozy kitchen rocking the cradle, although inevitably with one hand on the cradle and the other holding a book. How different from Erasmus' views of parenthood!

THE RELATION BETWEEN MELANCHTHON AND LUTHER

Probably no two men have ever been closer to each other in the work of the church than Luther and Melanchthon. Luther relied heavily on Melanchthon and frequently praised his work. Publicly he said that his colleague's writings were better than his own. But they complemented each other. Luther was rough, blunt, fierce, forceful, and unafraid of devils, kings, or the pope. Melanchthon was mild, timid, scholarly, irenic, and altogether too willing to compromise.

Melanchthon was Luther's co-reformer. They worked together during the violent years of the early Reformation. They respected each other, loved each other, labored together in harmony, and complemented each other. It is fair to say that each needed the other and that the Reformation would not have been what it was without the one or the other.

In eloquent terms Schaff defines their relationship and how they complemented each other:

> [Luther] differed from Melanchthon as the wild mountain torrent differs from the quiet stream of the meadow, or as the rushing tempest from the gentle breeze, or, to use a scriptural illustration, as the fiery Paul from the contemplative John. Luther was a man of war, Melanchthon a man of peace. Luther's writings smell of powder; his words are battles; he overwhelms his opponents with a roaring cannonade of argument, eloquence, passion, and abuse. Melanchthon excels in moderation and amiability, and often exercised a happy restraint upon the unmeasured violence of his colleague...
>
> Luther was a creative genius, and pioneer of new paths; Melanchthon, a profound scholar of untiring industry. The one was emphatically the man for the people, abounding in strong and clear sense, popular eloquence, natural wit, genial humor, intrepid courage, and straightforward honesty. The other was a quiet, considerate, systematic thinker; a man of order, method, and taste, and gained the literary circles for the cause of the Reformation.[1]

Luther himself said of their relationship,

> I am rough, boisterous, stormy, and altogether warlike. I am born to fight against innumerable monsters and devils. I must remove stumps and stones, cut away thistles and thorns, and clear the wild forests; but Master Philippus comes along softly and gently, sowing and watering with joy, according to the gifts which God has abundantly bestowed upon him.[2]

Calvin himself, fully aware of Melanchthon's weaknesses, nevertheless wrote a glowing eulogy at the time Melanchthon died.

Melanchthon died on April 19, 1560, in Wittenberg and was buried alongside Luther in the church where they both had worshiped. Melanchthon's last words, spoken to himself, were a firm testimony of his faith and a summary of the burdens of his life in the struggles of the Reformation: "Thou shalt be delivered from sins, and be freed from the acrimony and fury of theologians... Thou shalt go to the light, see God, look upon his Son, learn those wonderful mysteries which thou hast not been able to understand in this life."[3]

Calvin, upon hearing of Melanchthon's death, cried out,

> O, Philip Melanchthon! I appeal to thee who now livest with Christ in the bosom of God, and there art waiting for us till we shall be gathered with thee to that blessed rest. A hundred times, when worn out with labors and oppressed with so many troubles, didst thou repose thy head familiarly on my breast and say, "Would that I could die in this bosom!" Since then I have a thousand times wished that it had been granted to us to live together; for certainly thou wouldst thus have had more courage for the inevitable contest, and been stronger to despise envy, and to count as nothing all accusations. In this manner, also, the malice of many would have been restrained who, from thy gentleness which they call weakness, gathered audacity for their attacks.[4]

MELANCHTHON'S AGREEMENTS WITH CALVIN

In the swirling vortex of the Reformation that engulfed both Luther and Melanchthon, the stresses and anxieties were many and great. One of Melanchthon's great griefs was the division within the Lutheran camp itself. There were those who, even shortly before Luther's death but with great boldness after he was gone, became suspicious of their fellow Lutherans and charged them with being unfaithful to Luther's teachings.

A view that Melanchthon held contributed to this division in Lutheranism. Already before Luther died, Melanchthon had expressed sympathy for the Zwinglian view of the spiritual presence of Christ in the elements of the Lord's supper. Luther had a view very similar to Rome—that the real body and blood of Christ were present in, with, and under the bread and wine. Zwingli held to the idea that the presence of Christ was spiritual and that one did not chew Christ's flesh with his teeth. Melanchthon tended to agree with Zwingli over against Luther.

When Calvin developed his views and expressed Scripture's doctrine on this question more clearly than Zwingli, Melanchthon was persuaded that Calvin was right. He openly said so and wrote in support of Calvin's view.

This position of Melanchthon, along with the controversy over antin-omianism, created deep divisions in the Lutheran camp. The hostility was great and the battle fierce. It was Melanchthon's greatest grief. Those who followed him were branded with his name: "Philipists." To these struggles he referred when on his deathbed he longed for deliverance from "the fury" of theologians.

In spite of Melanchthon's more correct view on the presence of Christ in the sacrament, Lutherans did not follow him in this respect.

MELANCHTHON'S GREAT ERROR

As great a man as Melanchthon was, he erred in one crucially important respect. It was a serious enough error, since it caused Lutheranism to fol-low Melanchthon and not Luther. It cast a long and dark shadow over all Melanchthon's accomplishments.

Scholars and church historians have pondered why Melanchthon went in the direction he did. It is probably impossible to answer this question, and only God, who judges righteously, knows the heart. But we can best rely on the testimony of Calvin, who knew better than today's scholars what kind of a man Melanchthon was. The remarks Calvin made at the time of Melanchthon's death suggest in so many words that if Melanch-thon and Calvin had lived together, Melanchthon would have been "more valiant to face danger, and stronger to despise hatred, and bolder to disre-gard false accusations." While the statement may not be true (Melanchthon had Luther at his side, after all), Calvin meant to say that Melanchthon's timid nature and love of peace made him weak in the storms of opposition that blew against the reformers. Calvin was right.

Melanchthon, great man that he was, did not have the spiritual forti-tude to stand the barrage of hatred and criticism to which the reformers were subjected. He was, at every opportunity, willing and ready to com-promise for the sake of peace. This spirit of compromise was not only pres-ent in his dealings with fellow Protestants, but also came to the surface in meetings with papal delegates. In fact, if it had not been for the haughty, uncompromising spirit of Rome, which rejected his compromises as inad-equate (Rome wanted all or nothing), Melanchthon would have sold the Reformation down the river.

As early as 1540 Melanchthon was ready to accede to articles that were so ambiguous that the doctrine of justification by faith alone was as good as denied. It reminds one of so many evangelicals in our day who are willing to sell the great truth of justification by faith alone as they fall over each other in their mad rush to make peace with Rome.

In 1542 and 1543 Melanchthon prepared a book for instruction that was so wishy-washy it incurred the wrath even of Luther, who generally was almost too patient with his colleague.

But in his negotiations with the papists, Melanchthon was at his compromising worst. He was intent on some sort of reunion with Rome. Schaff writes,

> So far was he carried away by his desire for reunion, and fears of the disastrous results of a split, that he made a most humiliating approach to the papal legate, Campeggi, who had advised the Emperor to crush the Protestant heresy by fire and sword, to put Wittenberg under the ban, and to introduce the Spanish Inquisition into Germany. Two weeks after the delivery of the [Augsburg] Confession, he assured him that the Lutherans did not differ in any doctrine from the Roman Church, and were willing to obey her if she only would charitably overlook a few minor changes of discipline and ceremonies, which they could not undo.[5]

At the Augsburg conference Melanchthon set his dark mark on subsequent Lutheranism. Luther was not present for fear of his life, but was nearby. It was all Luther could do, by messenger and letter, to hold Melanchthon back from scurrying into the arms of Rome.

Sad to say, the church has always been plagued with these great compromisers. They are almost more dangerous than outright heretics, for they sell the truth under the guise of toleration, love for brethren, and desire to be known as peacemakers. They are like a man who hears others unjustly accuse his wife of harlotry, and who in negotiations with these slanderers and because he fears them, is willing to settle for the possibility that his wife committed adultery. Some theologians thus deal with the truth of God.

Melanchthon's Heresy

It was, in my judgment, this spirit of compromise, even with Rome, that led Melanchthon to his synergism.

The word *synergism* comes from two Greek words that mean "to work with." Melanchthon, on the great doctrines of sovereign grace, taught exactly that. Conversion, he said, is the cooperating work of the Holy Spirit, the word, and the will of man. When these three work together in harmony, salvation is accomplished. Uncaring about Luther's bitter struggle with the freewillism of Erasmus, Melanchthon adopted Erasmus' heresy —to his perpetual shame.

Of course, one who chooses this path must pay the price. There are other sacred doctrines of Scripture that must be abandoned. Predestination was, in Melanchthon's thought, reduced to foresight, namely, that God foresees who will believe and who will reject the gospel, and that he elects and reprobates on the basis of this foresight. Those who in our day are intent on speaking of justification by faith and works would have found Melanchthon congenial company. He insisted that the keeping of the law played a role in salvation.

These views, in turn, have something to say about God's purpose, which Melanchthon defined in the familiar terms of the well-meant gospel offer: God's desire is to save all men. One ponders in dismay why so many, under the name of Reformed, can defend so ferociously such historical heresies.

In perfect keeping with Melanchthon's view of the gospel offer, he also taught that the suffering and death of Christ had universal implications and accomplished atonement for all men.

These views, later expounded more fully by Jacob Arminius, were embodied in the Lutheran confessions and explain why Lutheranism today has followed synergism in its soteriology.

It is difficult to explain Luther's abiding respect for his colleague's doctrinal aberrations. Partly, of course, Melanchthon taught these views only after Luther had died. But the seeds were being sown during Luther's own lifetime. Perhaps it was out of respect for a colleague who had stood by his side. Perhaps it was a failure of a man, worn with work and the cares of the Reformation, to discern the direction Melanchthon was going. Whatever the reason, true Lutheranism disappeared under Melanchthon's guiding hand, and his apostasy ought to be a warning to all who similarly depart from the glorious truths of the Lutheran and Calvinist Reformation in its doctrines of sovereign and particular grace.

CHAPTER 18

AGRICOLA AND ANTINOMIANISM

INTRODUCTION

When God provides men of great ability for the church in times of crisis, God gives to these men a breadth of understanding of his word that it is not always easy for others to comprehend fully. Great men are able to hold all the nuances of the truth of Scripture in a proper and biblical balance, so that their theology remains consistently biblical. But some followers of these men, unable to see the scope of their leaders' theology, latch on to one aspect of it and make only that one aspect the be-all and end-all of orthodoxy.

An example is found in the work of some who find common grace and the well-meant offer of the gospel in John Calvin. One must admit that there are passages in Calvin's writings that would lead one to suspect that Calvin may have believed in these wrong doctrines. But one who understands the breadth of Calvin's thought will also understand soon enough that Calvin never intended by these passages what theologians of the nineteenth and twentieth centuries make of them.

It is easy also to find examples in more recent history. Some, claiming to be ardent followers of Herman Hoeksema in years gone by, but failing to grasp the breadth of his thinking, latched on to one aspect of the truth, carried it to extremes, and insisted that their narrow view of what Hoeksema taught is the full truth.

Presumably this happens with every great man of God whom God uses to bring the faith of the ages to fuller development. It happened to Luther even during his own lifetime.

Luther's central doctrine was the wonderful truth of justification by faith alone without the works of the law. During the later years of Luther's reformatory work, some latched on to Luther's insistence that the works of the law had nothing whatsoever to do with the believer's justification, but they carried it to erroneous extremes and became what today we call antinomians. They turned their backs on the law altogether, cursed the law, and insisted that a justified man had nothing more to do with the law. They even went so far as to accuse Luther of abandoning his own theological position when Luther condemned them. They claimed to be true to the genius of the Lutheran position and charged Luther with going back to the error of Rome.

Luther never taught such a view and despised those who taught it. But Luther from time to time made statements that, taken by themselves, could easily lead one to think that Luther threw the law out of the church window and considered it to be Old Testament refuse. But when Luther made these statements, he was speaking of the damnable error of Rome that works of the law served in part as the basis for justification. Luther could also preach and teach in most vigorous language the absolute necessity of the law and of the believer's obligation to keep the law. But narrow men took hold of just one aspect of Luther's thought and built a whole theological system out of it.

One of Luther's critics, Johann Agricola, was an antinomian.

AGRICOLA'S LIFE

Johann Agricola is to most people an unknown figure. He seems to have dropped off the stage on which the drama of the Reformation was taking place; or, if not that, he seems to be such a bit player in the drama that few notice him. Yet he played an important role and caused Luther no end of grief.

Agricola was born in Eisleben in Prussian Saxony on April 20, 1494, under the name Johann Schneider. Eisleben was also the birthplace of Luther, although Luther had been born eleven years earlier. Their paths did not cross in this village, however, for Luther's parents moved to Mansfeld when Luther was but six months old.

Agricola entered the University of Leipzig in the winter of 1509–10 to study medicine. Somewhere he became acquainted with Luther's thinking even before Luther nailed his theses on the chapel door of the church of Wittenberg. This must have been sometime during his studies at Leipzig, for in the winter of 1515–16 he went to Wittenberg to study theology under Luther.

We have some evidence here of the fact that Luther's theological breakthrough came several years earlier than the actual beginning of the Reformation in October 1517. Agricola's contact with Luther's theology demonstrates that Luther's views were being circulated before Luther publicly opposed indulgences and launched the Reformation proper.

After studying under Luther in Wittenberg, Agricola became thoroughly Lutheran in his thinking and joined an ardent band of men who were captivated by Luther's thought. Agricola was held in highest esteem for his theological acumen and his loyalty to the cause of reformation. He was present when Luther nailed his ninety-five theses on the chapel door; he witnessed the Leipzig Disputation where Luther, in debate with the powerful Roman Catholic apologist John Eck, committed himself wholly to the authority of sacred Scripture. He became Luther's private secretary and formed a close friendship with Melanchthon. He was in the inner circle of Wittenberg's reformers and contributed his own understanding to the movement as under God's guidance and blessing it gained momentum and started to turn Europe upside down.

So respected was Agricola that he was appointed to teach Latin classics and Latin grammar at the University of Wittenberg. Later he was appointed to teach dialectics and rhetoric; later still he was given the important chair of New Testament studies.

In August of 1525 Agricola was entrusted with the responsibility of the headship of a new Latin school in Eisleben, the city of his birth. The appointment demonstrated how much confidence the reformers had in him, and it served as some measure of his ability. A list of his accomplishments is impressive. He wrote two catechetical books that were widely used. He gathered and edited three collections of German proverbs, giving explanations of them. This work became immensely popular and spread his fame throughout Germany. He translated Melanchthon's commentaries from Latin into German. He became a preacher (although his ordination was always somewhat suspect) and was apparently one of the most powerful preachers of the Reformation, for he was appointed to preach the opening sermons at the Diets of Speyer in 1526 and 1528 in the presence of all the ruling princes and counts of Germany.

AGRICOLA'S BREAK WITH REFORMATION THOUGHT

But Agricola had one fatal flaw. Perhaps his success went to his head. He became proud of his own theological abilities and acquired a vanity that proved to be his downfall. In 1526 he applied for the position of theological professor at the University of Wittenberg. He did not receive the appointment, but Melanchthon, his close friend, was given this now very prestigious post. Agricola was jealous of Melanchthon and became bitterly antagonistic.

What the relationship is between Agricola's pride and his subsequent error is known only to God. Of this we may be sure: throughout the history of the church, as often as not a heretic introduces false doctrine in the life of the church not so much because he does not understand the issues involved, but because he has become a proud man. Pride frequently lies at the bottom of a heretic's doctrinal aberrations. Dorothy Sayers, a writer in the late twentieth century, said that the underlying sin of Judas Iscariot was intellectual pride. If so, he was followed by a legion of others, outstanding men in the church who betrayed their Lord by sacrificing his truth for their own thirty pieces of silver: the acclaim of men.

When Agricola began to teach his wrong views, he attacked not Luther, first of all, but Melanchthon. This attack, though a defense of antinomianism, was made in a jealous rage against a friend who had acquired the position Agricola coveted.

If this were not so serious, it would be ludicrous. It is like a pygmy aspiring to become a giant, or like a man who cannot balance his own checkbook aspiring to be the head of the mathematics department at M.I.T. Agricola had his gifts. Contentment with them and a humble effort to use them in God's kingdom would have enshrined him in the company of those heroes of faith who restored to the church the great gospel of salvation by grace alone. Pride got in the way, however, and an ignoble heresy of his own invention destroyed his effectiveness.

In 1527 Agricola publicly attacked Melanchthon on the place of the law in the Christian's life. Agricola did this by driving a wedge between the law and the gospel. Luther was disturbed by this attack on Melanchthon, but he considered Agricola's abilities to be useful in the cause of the Reformation. Luther, therefore, worked hard to mediate a truce between the views of Melanchthon (which views were also those of Luther) and the aberrations of Agricola. It seems as if Agricola backed down—something he was to do repeatedly in subsequent years when things got a bit too hot. Peace lasted for a while.

Not only did Agricola take over Luther's place in the church and university in Wittenberg while Luther was gone on church matters, but Agricola also began openly to attack Luther's views. For this he was arrested upon Luther's return, but he escaped. Then followed a series of retractions when Agricola really saw his position endangered, yet these retractions proved to be insincere at every turn of the way. Luther really never trusted Agricola again.

In a limited way Agricola continued to have influence. In 1541 he became court preacher of Joachim II of Brandenburg. He was appointed to a commission at the Diet of Augsburg to prepare an interim agreement between Protestants and Roman Catholics. And he continued to be a preacher of some note.

He died in Berlin on September 22, 1566, at the age of seventy-two.

AGRICOLA'S ANTINOMIANISM

Agricola was a thorough antinomian. He gained a following within Lutheran circles that supported him and developed his views. Both Agricola and his followers claimed to represent true Lutheranism. They claimed that Luther had departed from his own teachings and had taken a giant step back toward Rome. In fact, Agricola was so bold as to insist that in the controversy, he was Paul correcting Peter in Antioch, Luther, of course, being Peter.

What was it that Agricola taught? The controversy really centered around the question of the necessity of good works. Are good works necessary for the Christian? Agricola answered with a sharp No! Luther said, with equal or greater vehemence, Yes!

But Agricola's position generated other statements and doctrines. He taught that the law and the gospel were totally opposed to each other and that only the gospel ought to be preached in the church. Luther said that the law could not be preached without the gospel and that the gospel could not be preached without the law.

Luther claimed that through the law one comes to a knowledge of sin. Agricola claimed that while this was probably true, the only knowledge of sin that the law stirred up in man was the knowledge of damnation.

Agricola claimed that repentance, the consciousness of sin that saved, and the fear of God all arose out of the gospel, not the law. Luther taught that it is by the law that the believer comes to the knowledge of sin, which leads to repentance.

Jacob Schenk, an ardent follower of Agricola, carried his mentor's views to their extreme. He said, "All who preached the law were possessed with the devil; . . . do what you will [live as you please], if you only believe, you are saved," and "to the gallows with Moses!"[1]

Luther took up certain propositions of Agricola and held a disputation against them on December 18, 1537. Agricola failed to show up for the disputation, but Luther defended his position anyway. It might be profitable to quote some of the important propositions of Agricola.

1. Repentance is to be taught not from the decalogue or any law of Moses, but from the suffering and death of the Son through the gospel.
2. For Christ says in the last chapter of Luke: "Thus it behooved Christ to die and in this manner to enter into his glory, that repentance and remission of sins might be preached in his name."
3. And Christ, in John, says that the Spirit, not the law, convicts the world of sin.
7. Without anything whatever the Holy Spirit is given and men are justified: this thing [the law] is not necessary to be taught either for the beginning, the middle, or the end of justification.
8. But the Holy Spirit having been given of old is also given perpetually, and men are justified without the law through the gospel concerning Christ alone.
13. Wherefore, for conserving purity of doctrine we must resist those who teach that the gospel is not to be preached except to those who have been crushed and made contrite through the law.
16. The law only convicts of sin and that, too, without the Holy Spirit; therefore it convicts unto damnation.
17. But there is need of a doctrine that not only with great efficacy condemns, but also at the same time saves: but that is the gospel, which teaches conjointly repentance and remission of sins.[2]

While there are surely statements in Luther's writing and teaching that, if wrested out of context, could be quoted in support of this blatantly antinomian position, nevertheless, Luther never taught any such thing. He steadfastly maintained the important place of good works in the life of the believer even though justification is by faith alone without the works of the law. He insisted, and rightly so, that Agricola's position led directly to a profane and godless life in which a man could live in every fornication and sin and yet go to heaven. "Let us sin that grace may abound" is the conclusion of antinomianism.

The controversy continued after the deaths of Luther and Agricola and was not officially settled until the adoption of the Formula of Concord in 1576–77. Article 5 of this confession defines the Lutheran position.

CONCLUSION

It is no wonder that the Heidelberg Catechism, written in Germany, enters into this issue in some detail. It outlines the Reformed position in an entirely biblical way. The law, the catechism insists, is necessary for two reasons. By the law is the knowledge of our misery because it brings us to the knowledge of our sin (Lord's Day 2). And the law is the rule of gratitude by the keeping of which we express thankfulness to God for such a great salvation as he has given to us (Lord's Days 32 and 33). Gratitude makes good works necessary, says the catechism, not as the ground of our justification (Lord's Day 24)—a doctrine that the catechism condemns in almost violent language—but because thankful children are obedient children.

The law is indeed, as Luther said, inescapably attached to the gospel. In fact, Scripture makes clear that the law *is* gospel, for it has the power to convert the soul, to make wise the simple, and to enlighten the eyes (Ps. 19:7, 8). David loved God's law (Ps. 119:97) and ascribed to it many blessings of salvation, such as an understanding of God's ways that came to the psalmist through God's precepts (v. 104).

The law always requires obedience of all men on pain of death, but the law becomes gospel as the perfect law of liberty, or as James calls it, the royal law, that is, the law of the kingdom of heaven. As such, it is the law that, though broken by man in his transgression, is fulfilled in the perfect obedience of Christ who kept the law when he suffered the torments of hell. By his perfect obedience Christ fulfilled the law for his people, so that the law is written in their hearts as their rule of gratitude, and the ability to keep that law is given by grace.

This is the gospel that smashes all antinomianism and protects the great truth of justification by faith alone without the works of the law.

CHAPTER 19

ANABAPTISM: THE RIGHT WING OF THE REFORMATION

INTRODUCTION

The Reformation was, of course, a return to the doctrine, liturgy, and church government of Scripture over against the departures and apostasy of Roman Catholicism. As difficult a task as the reformers had in their opposition to Rome, they faced the additional problem of radicals within the reformation movement itself. In some ways this radical movement was a greater threat to the success of the Reformation than Rome itself. All the reformers, though they had their differences on some points of doctrine, were united in their opposition to these radicals. The reformers had to guide the ship of the Reformation between the dangers on the left wing in the Roman Catholic Church, and on the right wing in the influential radical movement. It was the Scylla of Rome and the Charybdis of the radicals.

The basic problem was relatively simple. The reformers were wise men, endowed by God with extraordinary gifts of discretion and moderation. They knew that the evils in the Romish church were many and great: wealth of the clergy; fornication in the monasteries; concubinage among the priests; simony, bribery, and political intrigue in every level of church life; and evils of formalism, image worship, and idolatry of the mass in the worship services. But they also knew that all these evils were rooted in more fundamental doctrinal departures from the truth of Scripture, and that if reform in morals, worship, and church government were to be brought about, this could take place only through doctrinal reform. If the church, by the grace of almighty God, were to be led back to the truth of Scripture, the rest of the reform would follow.

They also knew that the power of reform lay not in men's efforts, but in the power of God's grace revealed through his promise to preserve his church so that the gates of hell would never prevail against it. That is, they knew with total certainty that the power of reform was in the preaching and teaching of the pure gospel and nothing else. God worked through the gospel by his Spirit. God alone could reform.

Translated into practice, this meant that reform, especially in the area of the church's liturgy and church government, had to be brought about slowly and carefully. The people had to be instructed and taught from the Scriptures. They had to have time to make what for the majority of the populace were momentous and earth-shaking changes. They had to learn to shift their blind trust in the institute of Rome and the pope to enlightened confidence in Christ alone as their Savior. They had to learn that the worship of God was not in liturgical functions, ceremonies, and rites, but that God is pleased with worship that is in spirit and in truth. This would take time, patience, and much, much instruction.

The radicals wanted everything changed at once. They wanted purity from the first moment of reform. They wanted to force change on the people, if not by the force of precept, then by the power of the sword. They believed the reformers were weak, lacking in courage, hesitant in the work, afraid of antagonizing the secular power, and thus unfit for the work that had to be done. They were convinced that the reformers never went sufficiently far in their reformatory work. This position, not at all uncommon in the church, led these radicals into excesses of every kind.

The radical reformation is commonly called the Anabaptist movement. The radicals themselves were called Anabaptists because nearly all of them repudiated infant baptism and insisted on *anabaptism*, which means "[adult] rebaptism."

Nevertheless, the movement was not unified. One student of the Anabaptist movement divided it into three distinct branches: the Anabaptists, the spiritualists, and the rationalists.

The Anabaptists were characterized especially by their desire to return the church to apostolic purity. They wanted to help the church jump back a millennium and a half and become what, at least to their minds, was the character of the church during the time of the apostles.

The spiritualists were the wild radicals who gave Luther such major problems in the reformatory work in Wittenberg and who were guilty of the worst sort of excesses. They took the position that all externals in worship were sinful and that the only true worship was the communion of the soul with God through visions, dreams, inner revelations, and private conversations between God and the human heart.

The rationalists were of a far more sober kind but are probably designated as rationalists because they denied many cardinal doctrines of Scripture.

The Anabaptist movement is thus a diverse one, difficult to describe, and yet in all its many forms a grave threat to the Reformation. We shall treat the different aspects of Anabaptist thought separately with special attention to the main characters in the drama as the movement played itself out in Germany, Switzerland, and the Netherlands.

CARLSTADT AND THE ZWICKAU PROPHETS

The radical branch of the Reformation was known by various names. Luther called them *Schwärmer,* a term that suggests the uncontrollable buzzing of bees around a hive, an apt description.

Carlstadt was the leader of the Reformation in Wittenberg and a close friend and colleague of Martin Luther. He was born Andrew Bodenstein but took the name of his birthplace. His advanced education was acquired in Rome, where he studied theology and canon law. In 1504 he went to Wittenberg to study, for already at this early date Wittenberg had gained a reputation for scholarship. Carlstadt was an able student and, upon the acquisition of his degree, was hired to teach at the University of Wittenberg in the chair of theology. It is not surprising, therefore, that he came under the influence of Luther, was persuaded of Luther's teachings, and joined forces with Luther in the reformatory movement.

Carlstadt was such a trusted friend that he went with Luther to the Leipzig Disputation in 1519 and engaged in a debate with John Eck over the issues of human freedom and divine grace. Eck was perhaps Europe's most able debater, and Carlstadt was soon out of his depth. He had to be rescued by Luther's intervention—something that hurt Carlstadt's pride.

After his courageous stand at the Diet of Worms, Luther was whisked away by friends in an apparent kidnapping and hidden in the castle at Wartburg. This opened the door for Carlstadt to assume leadership of the Reformation in Wittenberg. That in itself would not have been all bad, but Carlstadt was becoming increasingly radical, and he seized the opportunity of Luther's absence to steer the Reformation in a different direction than Luther had intended.

Luther was conservative. In the early part of the Reformation, he had no intention of leaving the church, and his idea of effecting changes in the church was to do so slowly and carefully, teaching and preaching the pure gospel. In fact, Luther's general position on change was to retain everything that Rome practiced except that which was explicitly contrary to Scripture.

But Carlstadt would have none of this. He began to attack every Romish practice that he could think of. First it was monasticism, then the mass, then the practice of administering the Lord's supper with the bread only, then the use of Latin in the liturgy. In close conjunction with all this, he attacked the celibacy of the priests, and he himself married. He wrote an entirely new church constitution, and he stirred up the people to engage in wild and frenzied iconoclastic mob action in which crowds of people would enter churches, tear down images, smash painted glass windows, drag all the trappings of liturgy into the streets to be burned, and gut the inside of church buildings.

But all this was not the worst. Even before Worms, Carlstadt began to shift his thinking from the admittedly dry and sterile scholasticism of the Middle Ages to a blatant mysticism. He began to scoff at learning as being an impediment to knowing God. He spoke of the inner work of the Spirit as being sufficient for all knowledge necessary to salvation, and he began to repudiate infant baptism as a practice in the church.

The movement was given impetus by the visit of two "prophets" from Zwickau, whose ideas we shall explain a little later. Even Thomas Münzer, a wild-eyed Anabaptist prophet, paid Wittenberg a brief visit. The city was ripe for anarchy.

It is not surprising that these matters should soon come to Luther's attention. He considered his isolation in Wartburg to be reprehensible to Christ and to himself while the village and his university were going up in the flames of Carlstadt's wild excesses. His elector, Frederick the Wise, refused him permission to return, so fearful was he of the dangers that Luther faced from the Roman Catholics. But in a beautiful letter Luther informed Frederick in no uncertain terms that he had to obey God rather than men.[1]

Luther went to Wittenberg in disguise and spent three days in the city without anyone knowing. He then came openly into the church where he preached and worshiped and delivered a series of eight sermons that were so utterly biblical and moving that by their power alone, peace was restored and the *Schwärmer* were driven from the city. It was a remarkable performance and an act of courage probably as great as, if not greater than, Luther's stand at Worms. The sermons were delivered in a calm, almost matter-of-fact way, without histrionics, anger, condemnatory language, or abuse of those who were systematically wrecking the Reformation. They were quiet but forceful expositions of the word of God. Let preachers today, who so quickly are dissatisfied with the fruit of solid expository preaching, take note!

Of these sermons Schaff writes,

> He [Luther] preached eight sermons for eight days in succession, and carried the audience with him. They are models of effective popular eloquence, and among the best he ever preached. He handled the subject from the stand-point of a pastor, with fine tact and practical wisdom. He kept aloof from coarse personalities which disfigure so many of his polemical writings. Not one unkind word, not one unpleasant allusion, escaped his lips. In plain, clear, strong, scriptural language, he refuted the errors without naming the errorists...
>
> The ruling ideas of these eight discourses are: Christian freedom and Christian charity; freedom from the tyranny of radicalism which would force the conscience against forms...; charity towards the weak.[2]

It was an astonishing demonstration that Luther was right. Man cannot perform the work of reformation. Only God can do that. And God's instrument then and now is the preaching of the word of God. These sermons may still be read today. They can be found in *Luther's Works*.[3]

Luther's evaluation of the power of the word was this:

> I will preach, speak, write, but I will force no one; for faith must be voluntary. Take me as an example. I stood up against the Pope, indulgences, and all papists, but without violence or uproar. I only urged, preached, and declared God's Word, nothing else. And yet while I was asleep, or drinking Wittenberg beer with my Philip Melanchthon and Amsdorf, the Word inflicted greater injury on popery than prince or emperor ever did. I did nothing, the Word did every thing. Had I appealed to force, all Germany might have been deluged with blood; yea, I might have kindled a conflict at Worms, so that the Emperor would not have been safe. But what would have been the result? Ruin and desolation of body and soul. I therefore kept quiet, and gave the Word free course through the world. Do you know what the Devil thinks when he sees men use violence to propagate the gospel? He sits with folded arms behind the fire of hell, and says with malignant looks and frightful grin: "Ah, how wise these madmen are to play my game! Let them go on; I shall reap the benefit. I delight in it." But when he sees the Word running and contending alone on the battle-field, then he shudders and shakes for fear. The Word is almighty, and takes captive the hearts.[4]

Carlstadt lost his effectiveness as a reformer. For a time he submitted to Luther and Luther's policy for reformation, but he did so sullenly. For a brief time he continued to lecture in the university but soon found this intolerable, for his heart was filled with revenge against Luther. After retiring, he lived simply and alone, but gave himself over to mystical inspirations and subjective revelations. He was in some contact with other radicals, but at last in 1532 he settled in Basel, where he seemed to regain some spiritual balance. At least he became pastor there and a professor in the university and died peaceably in 1541.

THOMAS MÜNZER

All the radicals had in common the notion that Christ was about to return to establish his kingdom here on earth, and these radicals thought they had been entrusted with the obligation to prepare the way by establishing that kingdom prior to Christ's coming so that it would be there ready for Christ when he actually came. They were premillenarian. They looked for Christ to establish an earthly kingdom.

Thomas Münzer was born in 1490 (a year for the birth of radicals, for several of them came into the world in that year). His home was in the German town of Stolberg. He studied in Leipzig and Frankfurt and became a gifted linguist, a literary scholar, and a learned theologian. He early came to appreciate and believe the ideas developed by Martin Luther and received a pastorate in the city of Zwickau in 1520. When Carlstadt made his move to assume the leadership of the Reformation in Wittenberg, two radicals—Nicholas Storck, a weaver, and Marcus Stübner, who had studied under Melanchthon—came from Zwickau, attracted by the possibility of mischief. Already by 1520 Zwickau was a hotbed of mysticism, and the radicals in Germany became known as the Zwickau prophets. Thomas Münzer was one of them. He, too, paid a visit to Wittenberg during the iconoclastic riots, but fled when Luther appeared on the scene.

I must interject at this point another aspect of the Reformation in Germany, which is important for an understanding of what follows. Luther's doctrines and reforms had a special appeal to the peasants in Germany. There were, I think, especially three reasons for this. Luther, though an educated man, nevertheless could talk in the language of the peasants and easily bring himself down to their level. He was their man, one of them who understood them and spoke to them in their own coarse and uninhibited German. The second reason was that a keystone in Luther's thought was the doctrine of the priesthood of all believers. The lowest peasant, Luther said, when he believed, became a prophet, a priest, and a king in his own life. This was heady tonic if the true nature of such an office were not clearly understood. In the third place, the peasants in Germany, as well as most other places in Europe, were terribly oppressed. The remnants of the old feudal system gave princes enormous powers to exercise over the peasants, and these poor struggling people had all they could do to keep body and soul together for the thirty-five or forty years prior to their premature deaths.

Put all those things together and one has a huge pile of tinder-dry brush. Add the spark of Anabaptist fire, and you have a conflagration. The radicals preached their inner-revelation doctrine and scorned learning. They spoke of the peasants as being closer to God than the princes. Because the peasants lacked learning, and because they became convinced that their calling was to prepare the way for Christ by establishing his kingdom here in the world, thousands upon thousands of them, moved by the rhetoric of Luther, looked upon the Reformation as an opportunity to overthrow the princes' power and to rule themselves. Thus all Germany burst into one mighty holocaust—a tragedy known in history as the Peasants' War.

While first the peasants were successful in their rampaging, rioting, and slaughter, soon the princes organized their armies, united their forces, and with Luther at their backs urging them to restore order, they destroyed the peasants in the Battle of Frankenhousen on May 15, 1525. Luther hated disorder, had preached for years that the word of God was the power of reformation, and clearly understood that no matter how much one could sympathize with the terrible plight of the peasants, rebellion against authority was contrary to the will of God. It was a sad day in the history of the Reformation. The peasants lost confidence in Luther, and Luther lost confidence in the peasants. This never changed in Luther's lifetime.

Münzer was the chief architect of the Peasants' War. With his fiery preaching, his promises of a high place in the kingdom of Christ, and his vision of deliverance from the oppression of greedy princes, he stirred the people into a frenzy.

Thomas Münzer was captured, tortured until he recanted his heretical views, and then unceremoniously put to death. He was thirty-five years old.

JOHN OF LEIDEN

There were other radicals who left their imprint on Europe. Hans Hut engaged in that favorite pastime of radicals: the prediction of the date of the Lord's return. He claimed that this momentous event would take place on Pentecost Sunday, 1528. He was imprisoned for leading people astray and burned alive when he set the prison on fire in an effort to escape.

Melchior Hoffmann was another such radical, but we will combine his story with that of John of Leiden.

John of Leiden was much like Thomas Münzer in his beliefs. He was also a radical of the worst stripe and firmly believed not only that the kingdom of Christ was to be established on earth, but that it was the solemn responsibility of those belonging to that kingdom to overthrow existing kingdoms, by force if necessary. John was from the Lowlands and remains a blot on the history of that place to this day.

John was born in 1509. Soon he turned to the most radical teachings of the radical reformation. He gathered a circle of people about him who were persuaded by his fiery style and somewhat charismatic personality. The establishment of Christ's kingdom here on earth in anticipation of the Lord's coming required that the true believers go back to early apostolic Christianity and practice religion according to the early church.

John had learned his lessons well, for he had learned them at the feet of Melchior Hoffmann, who believed himself to be one of the two witnesses mentioned in Revelation 11. He also claimed to be Elijah of whom the prophet Malachi had spoken in the last words of his prophecy (Mal. 4:5). He believed, too, that Strassburg was to be the New Jerusalem and the seat of Christ's universal kingdom. Direct revelation was to be the pipeline through which the citizens knew the will of God. Hoffmann asked to be imprisoned, thinking that this would make a greater impression on Christ, who was to return at any moment. Hoffmann died in prison. John of Leiden, whose actual name was John Matthys, a baker from Holland, seized the opportunity. If Hoffmann was the first witness, then he, John, was the second. If Hoffmann was Elijah, then he was Enoch. He moved into Strassburg and took Melchior's place, but he soon moved the "New Jerusalem" from Strassburg to Münster.

There John set up his kingdom, referred to himself as the King of Righteousness, and began to set up a theocracy. Three times weekly he appeared in the marketplace in royal robes to converse with his subjects, receive their homage, and direct their lives by means of the revelations given him by God. He established a type of communism, for this is what the early church practiced. He introduced polygamy and took the lead himself in marrying a number of women. The moral excesses that went on in that city under the guise of its being the kingdom of Christ are beyond telling.

Spain was still the ruling power in the Lowlands, but in this instance Spanish and Protestant forces joined to dig out this rot from Europe. Münster held out for a long time but was finally taken when some of its own citizens betrayed it. The carnage unleashed by the capture of the city was terrible. John himself was caught and tortured beyond endurance until at last death rescued him from his tormentors. The year was 1535. John was twenty-six years old.

CONCLUSION TO THE STRUGGLE WITH THE RADICALS

The radical movement had a profound effect on Luther. Earlier I mentioned that the Peasants' War brought about a break between Luther and the common people that was not healed in his lifetime. But Luther's commitment to the objective authority of the word of God was unwavering. Because these radicals, who had all but destroyed Wittenberg and who had stirred up the peasants to war, proclaimed a despised gospel of subjective illumination, Luther's hatred of their views was fierce and unmitigated. He despised all subjectivism and took every opportunity to oppose it.

There is a reference to these radical Anabaptists in the Belgic Confession of Faith. Although this confession was written in 1561, nearly thirty years after the debacle at Münster, the Roman Catholic authorities were still painting all Protestants with the same brush and insisting that all Protestants were as rebellious and politically treacherous as John of Leiden and his followers. They should, therefore, be eradicated.

To distinguish between these radicals and the true Calvinistic Protestants in the Lowlands, Guido de Brès added to Article 36 of the Belgic Confession these words: "Wherefore we detest the error of the Anabaptists and other seditious people, and in general all those who reject the higher powers and magistrates, and would subvert justice, introduce a community of goods, and confound that decency and good order which God hath established among men."[5]

EARLY SWISS ANABAPTISM

Another division of the Anabaptists was born in Switzerland and was the primary concern of the Swiss reformers, particularly Zwingli, Bullinger (the reformer of Basel), and Calvin. It was not the radical Anabaptism of the Zwickau prophets, Thomas Münzer, and John of Leiden. These Swiss Anabaptists did not stir up rebellion against government or preach a divine revelation that came through dreams, visions, and other forms of divine illumination independent of the Scriptures. They held more or less to a work of the Spirit that enlightened reason and informed reason with Scripture. Nevertheless, special revelations by means of the inner speaking of the Spirit were never far from their thinking. Menno Simons was the leader of this movement, and the sect called Mennonites is directly traceable to Simons' teaching. The early Anabaptist movement in Switzerland had its own share of radicals, and Thomas Münzer visited Switzerland to spread his views. In fact, the more peaceful movement of which Menno Simons later became a leader arose out of the more radical Swiss brand of Anabaptism. Nevertheless, the movement of which we now speak was not characterized by the excesses found in Germany and the Lowlands. The Peasants' War never spilled over into Switzerland. The millennial ravings of Melchior Hoffmann and John of Leiden were but distant rumblings. These Swiss Anabaptists were characterized more by a simple piety and a rigid morality.

The chief issue within the Zwinglian movement that gave rise to Anabaptism was the issue of the baptism of infants. There were men in the Swiss Reformation who repudiated this doctrine. Zwingli tried to convince them of their error in private conferences but did not succeed. A public disputation was held by order of the magistrates on January 17, 1525. Zwingli answered the arguments of the Anabaptists but failed to persuade them.

In February the first instance of rebaptism took place. At a private worship service an Anabaptist named Blaurock asked another member of his group, Grebel by name, to baptize him on confession of faith. This was done, and Blaurock in turn baptized all the others at the meeting.

The Swiss authorities banned Anabaptist teachings, and when the Anabaptists refused to obey, they were imprisoned and sentenced to death by drowning. Six were actually drowned between 1527 and 1532. Drowning was chosen as the cruel and ironic means of execution because of the Anabaptist practice of baptism by dipping. "Those who dip shall be dipped." Such persecution followed the movement as it spread throughout Europe.

ANABAPTISM IN THE NETHERLANDS AND MENNO SIMONS

Anabaptism in the Netherlands, and really throughout Europe, owed its more definite form to Menno Simons and his work. He was born in 1496, the son of a dairy farmer in Witmarsum, Netherlands. He had a fairly good education and became quite versed in the church fathers. He was ordained a Catholic priest, but as was true of so many priests, he ignored his parish duties and spent his time in drinking and playing games of chance.

During his life Simons began to have doubts about the truth of transubstantiation, the Romish doctrine that the bread and wine of the Lord's supper actually become the body and blood of the Lord. In his studies of the matter, he began to move in the direction of the Zwinglian position: that the Lord's supper was more a memorial ceremony than an actual sacrament. Pondering these subjects also brought about his conversion, and he now forsook the priesthood, abandoned his wicked ways, and turned to the cultivation of a life of holiness.

Simons' deviations from the doctrines of the Reformation did not end with his acceptance of Zwinglian views on the Lord's supper. He soon came to agree with the Swiss Anabaptists on the repudiation of infant baptism. The tragedy of Münster made a deep impression on him, partly because he had lost a brother in the massacre.

Because Simons had adopted a position contrary to the magistracy's decisions to support the Reformation, he became an itinerant preacher, forced to wander about from place to place, preaching and baptizing in secret. He was a hunted heretic. During the years of his wandering, he married a woman named Gertrude and had three children with her. They endured the sufferings that were his lot. He wrote many books during these years of wandering and in them defined the position of this branch of Anabaptism. He died peacefully at the age of sixty-six.

The chief emphasis of these Anabaptists was very similar to the mystics who were so influential in the Lowlands. Their concern was that many in the church contradicted their confession by a life of worldliness and carnality. These Anabaptists, therefore, as the mystics before them, emphasized the new birth, the inner life of fellowship with God, and the sanctified walk of the believer in the world.

ANABAPTIST ERRORS
There can be, of course, no error in emphasis on piety if it is placed within a biblical, doctrinal framework. This the Anabaptists failed to do. They erred, first, in failing to avoid the pitfalls of mysticism. Not only did the extreme radicals rely on inner illuminations, but this same subjectivism characterized all branches of Anabaptism to a greater or lesser degree. Such emphasis on subjective experience resulted in a certain mistrust of, and even scorn for, outward observances required by Scripture, such as formal worship services, the preaching of the word, the sacraments administered according to their true intent as means of grace, and well-defined church government. Their wrong legacy is carried on today among the Mennonites.

Second, they erred in other crucial doctrines of the faith. While there was undoubtedly some disparity between individual Anabaptists, generally speaking this sect repudiated forensic justification, which Luther taught, as being a barrier to godliness. They had a strong aversion to predestination and to the bondage of the human will apart from grace.

The Anabaptists also denied the true nature of the incarnation of Jesus

Christ. They taught that Christ formed his own human nature, independent of Mary's human nature, although he formed his human nature in Mary's womb. Article 18 of the Belgic Confession refers to this serious error:

> Therefore we confess (in opposition to the heresy of the Anabaptists, who deny that Christ assumed human flesh of his mother) that Christ is become a partaker of the flesh and blood of the children; that he is a fruit of the loins of David after the flesh; made of the seed of David according to the flesh; a fruit of the womb of the Virgin Mary; made of a woman; a branch of David; a shoot of the root of Jesse; sprung from the tribe of Judah; descended from the Jews according to the flesh; of the seed of Abraham, since He took on him the seed of Abraham, and became like unto his brethren in all things, sin excepted; so that in truth he is our IMMANUEL, that is to say, God with us.[6]

The detailed description of Christ's work in taking on himself the flesh of his mother emphasizes how seriously our fathers took this heresy of the Anabaptists.

The error for which the Anabaptists are best known, however, is their denial of infant baptism. The reason for this is their claim that the New Testament Scripture contains no proof for infant baptism. In their judgment the New Testament proves only that baptism must be on the grounds of confession of faith in Christ, something possible only for an adult. This argument is still the chief argument of Baptists today.

There were various historical reasons also for the Anabaptists' repudiation of infant baptism. They saw that the establishment of a state church (something common to Lutheranism and Calvinism in the sixteenth and seventeenth centuries) led to the establishment of churches filled with unbelievers, unregenerated people, worldly and carnal people, and people who practiced religion only in an outward way. They feared that a state church did not discipline as it ought.

This had several consequences. Anabaptism claimed that infant baptism was hopelessly tied to the idea of a state church, that in fact infant baptism was an innovation of the Romish church as Rome stretched its influence over the whole of Europe and set itself up as ruler in civil affairs as well as ecclesiastical matters. Infant baptism had to be repudiated along with all the other Romish trappings that had choked true spiritual life in the religiously dreary Middle Ages.

A state church, in its very nature, according to Anabaptists, encouraged formal religion and discouraged true piety. Thus a church ought to be composed of believers only. This ruled out children, whom they said could be incorporated in the church only upon confession of faith.

189

Thus Anabaptists struggled for a "pure church," that is, a church in which were to be found believers only. This idea is still inseparably connected to Baptist thinking in our day, and Baptists will usually argue for their position on the grounds of a pure church idea.

The Anabaptists certainly were right in their view that a state church necessarily leads to churches full of unbelievers in which no discipline can be practiced effectively, but their appeal to church history was dead wrong. Characteristic of all Anabaptists was their great sin of leaping over fifteen centuries of church history to return to the church of the apostles. Rome had many evils, but one of them was not their practice of infant baptism, even though Rome may have baptized infants for the wrong reasons. Anabaptists are wrong when they claim that infant baptism is an innovation of Rome. The fact is that infant baptism was practiced by the post-apostolic church throughout its entire history. There were those during that period who tried to cling to the pure church idea later espoused by Anabaptists, and who therefore baptized believers only, but they were the sects condemned by Scripture and history alike.

The Anabaptists really knew that the church always practiced infant baptism, and so they ignored all these centuries of the church's history to return to the apostolic era during which they said that their views had prevailed. This is a serious error and characterizes the Baptist movement to the present. By ignoring these centuries of church history, Baptists ignore the work of the Spirit of truth in the church and his mighty work of guiding the church into the truth, revealing the riches of the truth to every generation, forcing the church to develop that truth by living out of the past because of dependence on the past, and moving on into the future with the heritage of the truth as its legacy. Preaching on a creed, even the Heidelberg Catechism, is unthinkable to a Baptist.

Anabaptists and Baptists cut themselves off from the unity of the church in history. This is serious and has serious consequences. It means that Anabaptism is really individualistic in its thinking and has no conception of the organic relationships of the saints of all ages. No wonder Menno Simons denied predestination and total depravity. No wonder that he became basically semi-Pelagian in his thinking. No wonder that a great deal of the Baptist movement has continued along these same lines.

The separation that Anabaptists made between themselves and the church, and between the apostles and the Reformation, in their effort to return to the apostolic church also meant that they had no use for the church in the Old Testament. To this day, the church in the Old Testament is a conundrum to Baptists, so they make a separation between the Old and New Testaments and deny the unity of Scripture. As a result, they have had no conception of the biblical proof for infant baptism as it takes the place of circumcision in the New Testament era. The Anabaptist denial of infant baptism became the starting point of the Swiss reformers in their apologetics against Anabaptism. These reformers soon recognized that the error of Anabaptism was a repudiation of the unity of Scripture. From their battle with the Anabaptistic error emerged the budding doctrine of God's everlasting covenant of grace, a doctrine that forms the soul of genuine Reformed theology.

The Heidelberg Catechism says it all: "Out of the whole human race, from the beginning to the end of the world, the Son of God, by his Spirit and Word, gathers, defends, and preserves for himself unto everlasting life, a chosen communion in the unity of the true faith; and that I am, and forever shall remain, a living member of the same."[7]

CHAPTER 20

THE NICODEMITES

INTRODUCTION

With this chapter we turn to John Calvin's struggle against heretics of different kinds. Calvin was subject to countless attacks in the course of his work in Geneva and Strassburg, and in defense of the faith, he became a formidable polemicist.

Because of Calvin's influence throughout Europe and because the Reformation knew no more able defender of the faith, Calvin was subject to almost continuous attacks. It sometimes seemed that every enemy of the truth considered it his solemn duty to attack Calvin. If ever a man's life was filled with controversy, it was Calvin's, although we might add immediately that the devil well understands those who are particularly important in the defense of the cause of God, and they soon become the objects of the devil's attacks.

Without doubt, the Roman Catholic Church was Calvin's chief enemy, and Rome would have given much to silence his powerful pen. It was in the nature of Calvin's reformatory work that much of his polemical writings should be directed against the false doctrines and abuses of the church from which all the reformers parted ways. It is not, however, our intent to go into the errors of Rome and the answers to these errors that the reformers made. Our readers are, however, urged to read Sadolet's letter to the citizens of Geneva because this Romish prelate tried to lure the people of Geneva back to the Romish fold while Calvin lived in banishment from Geneva in Strassburg. And, having read Sadolet's letter, it is necessary to read Calvin's answer to Sadolet.[1] It is far and away the clearest, most forceful, and most powerful defense of the entire Reformation that came from any of the reformers, either on the continent or in the British Isles. It is a masterpiece.

There were various heretics who barked at Calvin and nipped at his heels, but I have chosen to write about a group of people, primarily found in France, who have come to be known as Nicodemites. They concerned Calvin throughout most of his lifetime, and he wrote six treatises against them. The most popular and best known is a letter to Nicholas Chemin with whom Calvin had stayed for a time and whose hospitality Calvin had enjoyed in Orleans.[2]

NICODEMITES' ERROR

The Nicodemites, found mainly in France, were not, strictly speaking, heretics. They taught no heresy but rather expressed agreement with Calvin in all his teachings.

To understand the position of these people, we must know, first of all, that the Calvin Reformation had had great influence in France. The Lutheran Reformation had touched the French people only slightly, but partly because Geneva itself was of French-speaking Switzerland, partly because Geneva sent preachers into France, and partly because Calvin himself was from France, Calvin's teachings had sunk deep roots and had produced, by God's work of gathering the church, an abundant harvest.

At the same time, Rome was firmly in control of France. The strongest and best Romish universities were in France, and the monarchy was under the control of powerful French prelates. The result was fierce persecution. With the possible exception of the Lowlands, no country in Europe knew such terrible persecution as the French Protestants. Every form of torture and cruel death was inflicted on them in a vain effort to destroy those who held to Calvin's teachings.

Because of the severe persecution, the Nicodemites attempted to escape persecution by hiding their faith. Theodore Beza, Calvin's successor, describes them in these words:

> In the year 1537 Calvin, seeing many persons in France, though they have a thorough knowledge of the truth, yet consulting their ease, and holding it enough to worship Christ in mind, while they gave outward attendance on Popish rites, published two most elegant letters, one on "Shunning Idolatry," addressed to Nicholas Chemin, whose hospitality and friendship he had enjoyed at Orleans.[3]

Calvin wrote this about the Nicodemites:

> When those who live in the difficult position which you now occupy perceive that they can neither maintain their tranquillity, nor live on harmonious terms with their neighbours, unless they make a pretence of indulging in Idolatry—amid the difficulties which thus beset and perplex them, they attend more to what may be expedient for themselves than pleasing to God—more to what may gain human

favour than secure Divine approbation. Meanwhile they devise a defence by which they may keep their consciences at ease in the view of the Divine tribunal, pretending that they are far from giving an internal heartfelt assent to any kind of impiety, but only have recourse to a little harmless pretence as a necessary concession to the ignorant, and also as the most promising means of gaining over persons who it were foolish to irritate by a course which could not lead to any beneficial result, and would be attended with the greatest danger.[4]

In brief, the Nicodemites, fearful of persecution, took the position that God was pleased if they confessed his truth in their minds and with their hearts, while they outwardly conformed to all the practices of the Romish church. Thus they received the name Nicodemites, because they were said to hide their faith as Nicodemus ostensibly did when he came to Jesus by night for fear of the Jews.

The Nicodemites defended their position with various arguments. They claimed that many of the Romish rites that they attended were indifferent matters that could be observed without sin. They argued that God looks on the heart and not on the outward appearance. They maintained, somewhat ridiculously, that they could be better witnesses to other Roman Catholics when they were not hounded and persecuted. And they appealed to the case of Naaman, who received permission from Elisha to enter the temple of Rimmon with his king and bow before the idol.[5]

There were different kinds of Nicodemites. There were some who, though they agreed with Calvin's teachings, stayed in the Romish church (as many today remain in apostatizing churches) and, for the most part, kept silence. There were some, like certain of the humanists (Erasmus, d' Etaples, Thomas More, etc.), who wanted reform in the Roman Catholic Church and who even expressed agreement with some of the teachings of the reformers, but who never left their church. Calvin's attention, however, was especially fixed on these folk in France who found the way of Nicodemus to be the better way to live their Christian life.

CALVIN'S CONDEMNATION OF THE NICODEMITES

Calvin had little patience with the Nicodemites and condemned them. Take, for example, what Calvin wrote immediately after the quotation given above in which he summarized their position: "By such beginnings they commence their own ruin." It was not as if Calvin did not appreciate the sufferings to which the French Protestants were subjected. Never, so far as I know, did he mention one of them by name, as if to spare them shame. When Calvin wrote to those imprisoned and awaiting death for the cause of the gospel, he wrote in the most tender way, fully aware of the agony of suffering martyrdom. Some of his most poignant letters were written to these persecuted saints.

But the deception practiced by the Nicodemites was, for Calvin, intolerable. He insisted that however unimportant Romish rites might seem to some (worship of relics, adoring images, and the like), all of these rites were in one way or another bound up in the mass, and the mass was an idolatry of the worst sort. Anyone who even outwardly engaged in these rituals was guilty of idolatry.

Calvin also maintained that the motive of these people was simply fear of persecution. And while he could understand this fear, he nevertheless pointed out that such fear drowned the fear of God by which Christians are to live. People who were threatened with suffering for Christ's sake had two options: either they could flee their land and live in exile, as Calvin himself had done and as the French refugee church in Geneva urged persecuted Protestants to do, or they could stay where they were, maintaining their faith and dying for it if that was required of them.

A major point that Calvin made in his condemnation of the behavior of the Nicodemites was that whether they liked it or not, they were approving the wrong and condemning the right in the eyes of all who knew them. Thus they were unfaithful witnesses to their faith and came under the terrible judgment of Christ himself, who said, "Whosoever shall deny me before men, him will I also deny before my Father which is in heaven" (Matt. 10:33).

In other words, Calvin took the firm position that one cannot separate what one believes in his heart from what one confesses in the whole of his life by his words and conduct. If one hides his faith from others, especially when the occasion demands a firm and clear testimony to the truth, one does not really believe in his heart what he claims to believe.

And cowardice with respect to persecution is in flat contradiction of the words of the apostles after they had been beaten by the Sanhedrin. They considered it an honor and singular favor of God that they were counted worthy to suffer for Christ's sake.

CONCLUSION

It seems to me that there are many instances when the term *Nicodemites* could with justice be applied to us. Even in our daily contacts with the world about us, we are hesitant to confess what we believe and live as Scripture requires because we fear the hatred, mockery, and laughter of wicked men. We justify our conduct before our own consciences, if not before God. It all comes down to cowardice.

The term *Nicodemites* can with justice also be applied to all those who remain in apostatizing churches. Whatever may be their reasons for doing so, they necessarily put themselves in a compromising position, for if they condemn the false doctrine of the church of which they are a part, they will be expelled. They cannot escape the same judgment Calvin pronounced on the Nicodemites of his day.

God's people are called to join themselves to the true church of Christ. They must do this because it is their solemn obligation in obedience to Christ. They must join themselves to the true church of Christ for their salvation and that of their children.

Finally, because much of the church today already lives in persecution, and persecution is right around the corner for us all, it is well that we read what Calvin had to say about the Nicodemites who denied the Lord because they were unwilling to suffer for his sake.

CHAPTER 21

BOLSEC AND PREDESTINATION

INTRODUCTION

Although many doctrines of the reformers came under the furious attacks of enemies of the Reformation, and although many doctrines taught by Calvin were opposed by heretics of every sort, no single doctrine was more bitterly hated than Calvin's teaching of sovereign predestination, including both election and reprobation.

The passing of the centuries has not brought an end to attacks against this doctrine. One would have some difficulty counting the supposed Calvinists who are resentful of Calvin's teaching on predestination. Some forthrightly deny the doctrine. Others claim to agree with Calvin but insist that he never taught sovereign and double predestination. Some professed Calvinists attack Calvin's doctrine by silence; they never speak about or preach election and reprobation. And some professed Calvinists grudgingly express a cool loyalty to Calvin's doctrine of election, but violently disagree with his doctrine of reprobation.

No doctrine of Calvin has been so frequently repudiated as the truth of sovereign reprobation. So true is this that one can very well make this one doctrine the dividing line between true Calvinists and pseudo-Calvinists. Indeed, every claim that Calvin taught a universal atonement, a well-meant gospel offer, a grace common to all men, and a free will of man is a claim smashed on the rock of Calvin's insistence on the biblical truth of sovereign predestination, including sovereign reprobation.

Perhaps no single controversy in the life of Calvin brought out more clearly his insistence on the absolute sovereignty of God in predestination than his controversy with Jerome Bolsec. To that controversy we now turn.

BOLSEC'S LIFE AND TEACHING

Not much is known of Bolsec's early life. He was probably born in Paris in the early part of the sixteenth century. He entered the Carmelite monastic order but soon began a pattern that was to characterize his entire life. He had a quarrelsome and turbulent character and was bold beyond the boundaries of discretion. These characteristics came out in his sermons, and he was soon expelled from the monastery.

Embittered by the treatment he had received, he left the Romish church, embraced Protestantism, and sought refuge with the Duchess of Ferrara, where he stayed for a few months. Schaff writes about this extremely interesting lady:

> She was a small and deformed, but noble, pious, and highly accomplished lady... She gathered around her the brightest wits of the Renaissance, from Italy and France, but she sympathized still more with the spirit of the Reformation, and was fairly captivated by Calvin. She chose him as the guide of her conscience, and consulted him hereafter as a spiritual father as long as he lived.[1]

Things did not go so well with Bolsec, however. The duchess admitted him to her home as an almoner, that is, one who distributes money to the poor on the behalf of others, whether a king or queen, a rich member of the nobility, or a monastery. During his stay with this gracious woman, Bolsec acquired an education in medicine and proudly bore the title of "Doctor of Medicine" the rest of his life. But again his temperament got him into trouble, and he was forced to leave the duchess' home. Theodore Beza, the colleague and successor of Calvin, claims that Bolsec deceived the duchess.[2] Whether it involved his position as almoner or something else, Beza does not say.

In 1550 Bolsec settled in Geneva, became the private physician of M. de Falais, and confessed to be an ardent admirer of Calvin. M. de Falais was a nobleman who lived in Geneva and was a personal friend of Calvin.

If Bolsec had left well enough alone and stuck to his profession, things might have been different. But he was too proud for that, and his pride led him to dabble in theology. The more he became acquainted with what Calvin taught, the more he came to question Calvin's doctrine of predestination. He was not content to learn more at the feet of one of the pastors in Geneva; he openly launched a frontal attack on Calvin and the truth of predestination, especially reprobation. He publicly asserted that Calvin's god was a liar and a hypocrite who encouraged the basest criminals and operated as Satan.

Such blasphemy could not go unpunished. The Venerable Company of Pastors admonished him for such folly, and Calvin attempted to instruct him on the biblical teaching concerning this doctrine. But it is impossible to teach God's truth to a proud man. Although he seemed for a time to submit, he soon reverted to his public opposition and blasphemy against God. The Venerable Company of Pastors brought him before their body. They examined him concerning his views, and in their assembly he boldly expressed what he believed. Schaff sums up Bolsec's position:

> He acknowledged that a certain number were elected by God to salvation, but he denied predestination to destruction; and, on closer examination, he extended election to all mankind, maintaining that grace efficacious to salvation is equally offered to all, and that the cause, why some receive and others reject it, lies in the free-will, with which all men were endowed. At the same time he abhorred the name of merits. This, in the eyes of Calvin, was a logical contradiction and an absurdity; for he says, "If some were elected, it surely follows that others are not elected and left to perish. Unless we confess that those who come to Christ are drawn by the Father through the peculiar operation of the Holy Spirit on the elect, it follows either that all must be promiscuously elected, or that the cause of election lies in each man's merit."[3]

Bolsec, as so many others who have followed him in his views, piously repudiated the whole idea that man could merit with God. But Calvin says, correctly, that the position Bolsec took necessarily implies merit. If Bolsec wanted an election dependent upon the choice of man's will whether to take God's offer of the grace of salvation or reject it, then those who chose to receive that grace merited with God, all their pious protestations to the contrary notwithstanding.

THE RESOLUTION TO THE CONFLICT

It seemed for a time that Bolsec was willing to accept the admonition of the Venerable Company of Pastors, who exhorted him to be silent about his views and submit to the discipline of the church. But Bolsec was a proud man. He did not alter his position, and he refused to listen to his pastors.

The episode in his life that brought his case to a head was very dramatic. It was the practice in Geneva to hold a meeting on every Friday in St. Peter's church to instruct the people more fully in the truths of God's word. It was conducted much like a worship service. At the meeting held on October

16, 1551, John de St. André preached on John 8:47: "He that is of God heareth God's words: ye therefore hear them not, because ye are not of God." It is clear on the surface that this verse teaches sovereign reprobation because it ascribes the Jews' unbelief to the fact that God has not chosen them to be his people. St. André understood the text and explained it to mean that those who are not elect will never believe God's words but will oppose God until they die, because God gives his grace only to the elect.

Bolsec could not restrain himself. While St. André was preaching, he suddenly arose and began a long harangue against the preacher. He shouted that the everlasting destination of all men was not decided by God before they were born, that God did not determine that some go to hell and others to heaven, but that man's eternal fate was in his own hands and God only willed to punish those who refused his overtures of love, while blessing only those who accepted his promises. Bolsec piled verbal abuse upon the clergy of Geneva and, turning to those who were present, warned them to reject the false teachings of their pastor.

What Bolsec did not know was that near the beginning of his harangue, Calvin had walked into the sanctuary and was standing in the doorway listening to everything Bolsec said. He permitted Bolsec to speak his piece. Then Calvin stepped forward and began an address to those present in which he refuted every argument of Bolsec with Scripture, showed that Scripture teaches reprobation, and demonstrated with many memorized quotations from Augustine that the truth of sovereign predestination was not an innovation but had been the teaching of the venerable church father Augustine. Beza said about this event and Calvin's thorough address: "All felt exceedingly ashamed for the brazen-faced monk, except the monk himself."[4]

The lieutenant of the police was also present. He arrested Bolsec and put him in prison for publicly abusing the ministers and for disturbing a worship service and the public peace.

Preparations for Bolsec's trial were made the same afternoon. The Venerable Company of Pastors drew up a summary of Bolsec's theological position and submitted it to the Council, the ruling body in the city responsible for the enforcement of civil law. They requested the Council to try Bolsec and required him to give an account of himself. Bolsec prepared his defense of his theological position and asked the Council to place Calvin and the pastors before questions to which they were to give specific answers.[5]

Bolsec's five errors as defined by the Council were that faith depends not on election, but election on faith; that it is an insult to God to say he abandons some to blindness, because it is his pleasure to do so; that God leads to himself all rational creatures and abandons only those who have often resisted him; that God's grace is universal and some are not more predestinated to salvation than others; and that when Paul says in Ephesians 1:5 that God has elected through Christ, he does not mean election to salvation, but election to discipleship and apostleship.[6]

The Venerable Company of Pastors decided to ask the Council to seek the advice of the other cantons in Switzerland that had, primarily under the influence of Zwingli and Bullinger, become Protestant. Accordingly, the Council sent a letter to the churches in the Swiss cantons outlining the errors of Bolsec's position and asking their position on the matter.

These churches demonstrated their weaknesses with respect to the truth of sovereign predestination. For the most part the churches advised the church of Geneva to be more tolerant of the views of others and to deal more gently with those who denied what they regarded as a mysterious and perplexing doctrine. The majority of the Swiss churches agreed with the ministers in Geneva on the doctrine of unconditional election, but they wavered on reprobation and wanted no condemnation of those who opposed it. Bullinger, perhaps the greatest theologian among the Swiss churches (other than Geneva) and the author of the Second Helvetic Confession, was more emphatic. He took exception to the doctrine of reprobation and expressed displeasure with the position Geneva had adopted. He, too, warned against the conclusions that one could draw from the position that God is sovereign in reprobation. Bullinger's unwarranted criticism of the position of Calvin and the other Genevan pastors was the occasion for a disruption of the otherwise cordial relationship between Calvin and Bullinger, although their relationship was restored before Calvin's death when Bullinger moved closer to Calvin's position. Only the canton of Neûchatel where William Farel ministered the word of God endorsed Geneva's position.

It is not surprising that Luther's colleague Melanchthon also took vehement exception to Calvin's position. For Melanchthon's synergistic position that salvation is a cooperative effort between God and man was not in agreement with Luther himself, who had written in his great work *The Bondage of the Will* what was almost identical to Calvin's position.

THE END OF THE MATTER
The Council refused to accept the advice of the churches from the neighboring cantons and condemned the views of Bolsec. The Council also ban-

ished him from Geneva on December 23, 1555 under penalty of being whipped if he ever returned.

Bolsec never returned to Geneva, but he did return to the Roman Catholic Church, where he rightly belonged, for his doctrine was that of Rome, not of the Reformation, and his views were semi-Pelagian and not Calvinistic.

Before he died he wrote a biography of Calvin full of slander, evil stories, and terrible accusations. The biography would have died at birth if the Romish church had not taken hold of it and promoted it as a genuine story of Calvin's life. At last, however, even Roman Catholic scholars, bound by scholarly integrity, killed it.

Calvin wrote a treatise entitled *God's Eternal Predestination and Secret Providence,* in which he set forth his mature and fully developed views on sovereign, eternal, and double predestination.[7] This treatise is sometimes called the *Consensus Genevensis* (Genevan Agreement) because it expressed the position of the Genevan churches.

CONCLUSION

It is difficult to imagine that there are men within the Reformed churches who come to Bolsec's defense and criticize Calvin for the Bolsec affair.

For example, they ignore Calvin's disagreement with Bolsec's theological position and charge Calvin with hating Bolsec because Calvin was determined to defend his position as dictator of Geneva. Calvin is charged with seeing in Bolsec a threat to Calvin's domination in the city and church and with using his power and influence to rid Geneva of someone whom he considered a challenger to his absolute sway within the city. One cannot take such a stand without calling into question Calvin's theology. The enemies of sovereign predestination also charge Calvin with gross error with regard to his position on predestination, and they honor and set forth as the truth of Scripture Bolsec's position.

More seriously, Reformed and Presbyterian writers would prefer that the entire episode of Calvin's dealings with Bolsec remain unknown. These, and there are many, claim that a position similar to that of Bolsec was Calvin's position; that Calvin never taught what is said to be Calvin's theology; and that later theologians, such as Theodore Beza, the fathers at Dordt, the Westminster divines, Francis Turretin, Abraham Kuyper, and Herman Hoeksema, to name a few, have rashly and wrongly twisted Calvin's theology into something Calvin never taught and intended. These writers do not want to mention the Bolsec controversy, for they are unable to explain Calvin's condemnation of Bolsec because they believe that Calvin's views were almost identical to Bolsec's.

And if that bit of historical legerdemain is not sufficient, even the theologians present at the Synod of the Christian Reformed Church in North America in 1924 claimed support for the well-meant gospel offer as being taught by Reformed writers in "the most flourishing period of Reformed theology."[8] In fact, that very doctrine was part and parcel of Bolsec's views so strongly condemned by Calvin.

Anyone who disputes this analysis needs to read *God's Eternal Predestination and Secret Providence.* It is all there. While Calvin does not name Bolsec but mentions Pighius, another enemy of sovereign predestination, the fact remains that Calvin's writing was occasioned by the heresy of Bolsec and the sympathetic treatment of Bolsec by the other Swiss theologians.

Every genuinely orthodox theologian from Calvin to today has agreed that Calvin's teachings on election and reprobation are the teachings of the word of God. All who have even a superficial understanding of the great church father Augustine also agree that Calvin did not bring into theology an innovation, a new doctrine, something invented by him, but that he taught nothing more than Augustine himself had taught and insisted was crucial to the truth of the sovereignty of God in his work of grace in salvation. Within a few years of each other, the great Synod of Dordt and the Westminster Assembly, both representing the best theologians that the age knew, and perhaps that the world has ever seen assembled, put their stamp on Calvin's teaching as being in all parts biblical.

Why do men refuse to accept what is so obviously true, namely, that election and reprobation are biblical, confessional, and the teachings of the reformers? The answer can only be that man wants no part of the absolute sovereignty of God. He prefers to salvage some remnants of his tattered pride and place some responsibility for his salvation in his own hands. He refuses to admit that God is sovereign also in the damnation of the wicked. He refuses to acknowledge that God does all his good pleasure and reveals in all the works of his hands that he alone is God.

The church has never claimed that this is an easy doctrine. It is not easy to understand, to preach, or to hold and confess. It crushes all human pride. It leaves man nothing and God everything. It insists that not man rules, not even in his own affairs, but that God—the creator, the sustainer of all—is the potter who is sovereign over the clay to make vessels of honor and dishonor as it pleases him. God wills the salvation of the elect in Jesus

Christ, and that decree of election is the "fountain and cause" of faith, of all good works, and of the fullness of salvation in Christ. But God also wills the damnation of the reprobate to everlasting hell in the way of their sin as the manifestation of his supreme justice and infinite holiness.

It is, in the final analysis, impossible to maintain the sovereignty of God in election and at the same time to deny the sovereignty of God in reprobation. To deny the latter will result in a denial of the former. Calvin understood that. Dordt understood that. Dordt insisted that election and reprobation were *one decree,* although with two sides: "That some receive the gift of faith from God, and others do not receive it, proceeds from God's eternal decree."[9]

Let those churches and ministers who preach the whole counsel of God and claim to be Calvinists preach also the doctrine of eternal, unchangeable, and sovereign reprobation and maintain it against all opposition.

CHAPTER 22

SERVETUS AND THE DENIAL OF THE TRINITY

INTRODUCTION

Calvin and Servetus—what a contrast! The best abused men of the sixteenth century, and yet direct antipodes of each other in spirit, doctrine, and aim: the reformer and the deformer; the champion of orthodoxy and the archheretic; the master architect of construction and the master architect of ruin, brought together in deadly conflict for rule or ruin. Both were men of brilliant genius and learning; both deadly foes of the Roman Antichrist; both enthusiasts for restoration of primitive Christianity, but with opposite views of what Christianity is.

They were of the same age, equally precocious, equally bold and independent, and relied on purely intellectual and spiritual forces. The one, while a youth of twenty-seven, wrote one of the best systems of theology and vindication of the Christian faith; the other, when scarcely above the age of twenty, ventured on the attempt to uproot the fundamental doctrine of orthodox Christendom. Both died in the prime of manhood, the one a natural, the other a violent, death.[1]

Thus writes Schaff as he introduces the struggle between John Calvin and Michael Servetus.

But Schaff also writes the following, as he introduces his subject:

The burning of Servetus and the *decretum horribile* are sufficient in the judgment of the large part of the Christian world to condemn him [Calvin] and his theology, but cannot destroy the rocky foundation of his rare virtues and lasting merits... Human greatness and purity are spotted by marks of infirmity, which forbid idolatry. Large bodies cast large shadows, and great virtues are often coupled with great vices.[2]

Schaff is referring here to Calvin's doctrine of reprobation and Calvin's participation in the burning of the heretic Servetus. He is sadly mistaken in his analysis of Calvin's theology, but his verdict on the burning of Servetus is worth examining.

In Calvin's time there were others who, while claiming to be a part of the Reformation, denied the truth of the Trinity, as Servetus did. They sometimes attempted to engage Calvin in a debate over these questions and sometimes used the platform of the Reformation to disseminate their views. With most of them Calvin did battle. Servetus was one of them. Servetus lived the most colorful life of them all and came in closest contact with Calvin. To Servetus we turn to discuss this particular heresy as one with which the Reformation had to deal.

SERVETUS' EARLY LIFE

Servetus was born in either 1509 or 1511 in Spain. That made him a contemporary of Calvin and about the same age. According to his own claim, Servetus was born from nobility. Although his first inclination was to enter the ranks of the clergy in the Roman Catholic Church, his interests soon turned to law until at least 1528, when he was about eighteen years old. He was an extremely intelligent young man with mental powers bordering on genius. At fourteen he became the secretary of the royal chaplain, a position that gave him opportunity to travel. Although all his travels are not clearly outlined (when speaking of the details of his own life, Servetus was accustomed to change his story to meet the circumstances under which he found himself), he was in Germany with his patron, the chaplain, and may have met Luther. He may also have seen other reformers, notably Bucer and Capito in Strassburg.

SERVETUS' ATTEMPT AT THEOLOGY

It was when he was still in his teens that Servetus began to dabble in theology, a venture that was in time to be his undoing. Although he continued to study law, he began to read and study the Bible along with the writings of some of the reformers, especially Melanchthon. This study particularly attracted his interest and gradually took the place of his preparation for a career in law.

It is never a bad thing, of course, to study the Bible. Nor is it a bad thing to study the Bible on one's own and learn what the Bible teaches. But one must be very careful, and Servetus was not careful. He was not careful because he was a very proud man, proud to the point where it was his damnation. In studying the Scriptures, one ought, surely, to recognize that no matter how much intellectual ability God has given him, at eighteen or nineteen years old, he is but a novice in biblical interpretation. More importantly, one ought to recognize that the Bible is God's word to his *whole church,* and that countless thousands of saints, of equal or greater ability, and frequently with greater spirituality, have also made the Bible the object of their most intent scrutiny and meditation. We never may come to Scripture *alone,* but must always come as a part of the church to which we belong with a great throng of other saints. We study Scripture in the context of the church that for hundreds of years since Pentecost has had the Spirit of Christ, who leads the church into all truth. We benefit from their studies, learn at their feet, find treasures in Scripture discovered earlier by them, and thus experience in a real way the communion of saints with those who have now joined the company of just men made perfect. Further, in our studies we subject ourselves to the preaching of the gospel and we test our ideas with fellow saints with whom we share our faith. All this requires an attitude toward Scripture of humility and willingness to hear what God says to us.

When we go to Scripture on our own, we reveal a towering arrogance that will lead to heresy and ultimately to hell. We despise our fellow saints, pull up our noses at people of God of earlier years, and slap the Spirit of Jesus Christ in the face. Who can ever learn what Scripture says while doing these things? That is, however, what Servetus did. He believed he could ignore all that anyone else had ever said about Scripture, learn on his own the truth, and produce his discovery as the last word on God's revelation. This is a pride that makes any child of God cringe.

This does not mean that Servetus did not read what others had written. He became an expert on the ancient church fathers and on the declarations of the councils of Nicea, Constantinople, and Chalcedon, all of which had addressed themselves to the doctrine of God. Precisely at that fundamental point of the Christian faith Servetus launched his attack. He attacked the doctrine of the Trinity and of the divinity of the Lord Jesus Christ and criticized the church fathers and the councils that had laid down the early creeds. He claimed to be the sole spokesman of original and primitive Christianity of the apostolic age. He claimed to be *the* reformer, thereby rejecting all the work of the many reformers who were his contemporaries.

It was not enough that Servetus took exception to the doctrines of the Trinity and of Christ. He also wrote *Errors of the Trinity,* in which he not only attacked the doctrines of the Trinity and of Christ, but also mocked them in such blasphemous language that one shrinks from reproducing his blasphemies in print.

Many, including some of the reformers, read Servetus' book. Without exception, they not only criticized the book, but also deplored it as the ravings of a religious fanatic. In fact, there was no one, either Protestant or Roman Catholic, who agreed with his writings. This seems to have sobered him a bit, and he decided, at least temporarily, to embark on another career.

SERVETUS' CAREER IN MEDICINE

Servetus took up the study of medicine and was uncommonly successful because of his unusual abilities. The record of this period in his life seems to indicate, however, that his main motive for a new career was fear for his life. It was an age when both Protestants and Roman Catholics killed men for heresy. When the storm of objections against his book seemed to threaten him, he abandoned his theological aspirations to take up the work of a physician. As if to ensure his safety, he went under the new name of Michel de Villeneuve.

Servetus' accomplishments were many as he moved about France, living in different places. He became a geographer of note and wrote books on the subject; he was a scientist and astrologer; and as one skilled in medicine, he discovered the circulatory system of the human body, explaining how blood passed between the heart and the lungs and to the extremities of the body. His reputation as a physician and scientist spread throughout France.

SERVETUS' RETURN TO THEOLOGY

Finally settling in Vienne, south and a bit east of Paris, he went back to his first interest: theology. He could not leave theology alone. He was, I think, too proud to see his views go down to public defeat by his silence. Some of the events of importance are quickly described.

He challenged Calvin, who was still in France shortly after his conversion to Protestantism, to a public debate in Paris. When Calvin showed up at the designated meeting place, prepared for the debate, Servetus failed to appear.

Soon afterward he began a long period of correspondence with Calvin in which he not only attempted to defend his views on the Trinity and the doctrine of Christ, but also began to question other articles of the Christian faith, such as justification by faith alone, the baptism of infants (showing strong leanings toward Anabaptism), and other doctrines concerning God's work of salvation. All this was done under his new name; apparently he hoped to evade detection, but Calvin soon guessed who was the real man.

At first Calvin answered his letters and attempted to refute and persuade Servetus of the truth, but finally the Genevan reformer wearied of it all. Servetus would consider nothing Calvin wrote. He went his own way, railing against, openly mocking, and arrogantly blaspheming all the sacred doctrines of the church that the faithful had believed since the Council of Nicea had drawn up the Nicene Creed. In disgust and with a sense of futility, Calvin refused to answer any more letters even though he continued to be bombarded with them. Calvin did write Farel, his colleague, that if ever Servetus should show himself in Geneva, Calvin personally would see to it that he did not leave alive.

Servetus wrote another book, though anonymously, called *Restitutio.* It was an attempt to demonstrate that the primitive apostolic church's views had been corrupted by the councils and that he, Servetus, had been especially called by God to return the church to its true doctrine.

One more important event took place at this time. Servetus was arrested and imprisoned by the Inquisition while he was in Vienne. At his trial Servetus first of all denied that he was Servetus, claiming to be an innocent physician by the name of Michel de Villeneuve. When that lie failed, he offered to retract what he had written, because he feared for his life. Some scholars claim that this trial took place at the instigation of Calvin, who knew that Servetus was in Vienne and knew that the Roman Catholic Church considered him as much a heretic as Protestants did. There is little evidence for this, however. Servetus' views were as much a criticism of Roman Catholic orthodoxy as they were of Protestant teachings, and Calvin never showed any interest in letting others do what he thought ought to be done, especially not the Romish church.

After his trial had gone on for some time, Servetus escaped from prison and fled to Italy. He was tried and condemned *in absentia,* and an effigy of Servetus was burned along with his books.

For some strange reason, Servetus chose to pass through Geneva on his way to Italy. This decision sealed his doom, for Calvin had been bothered and harassed by Servetus and had threatened to secure his condemnation. Yet Servetus went to Geneva when there was absolutely no necessity of doing this.

SERVETUS' CHARACTER
Schaff has an interesting description of Servetus:

> Servetus...was one of the most remarkable men in the history of heresy. He was of medium size, thin and pale, like Calvin, his eyes beaming with intelligence, and an expression of melancholy and fanaticism...
>
> His mental endowments and acquirements were of a high order, and placed him far above the heretics of his age and almost on an equality with the Reform-

ers... He knew Latin, Hebrew, and Greek... as well as Spanish, French, and Italian, and was well read in the Bible, the early fathers, and the schoolmen. He had an original, speculative, and acute mind, a tenacious memory, ready wit, a fiery imagination, ardent love of learning, and untiring industry... He had much uncommon sense, but little practical common sense. He lacked balance and soundness. There was a streak of fanaticism in his brain. His eccentric genius bordered closely on the line of insanity. For "Great wits are sure to madness near allied, / And thin partitions do their bounds divide."

His style is frequently obscure, inelegant, abrupt, diffuse, and repetitious. He accumulates arguments to an extent that destroys their effect. He gives eight arguments to prove that the saints in heaven pray for us; ten arguments to show that Melanchthon and his friends were sorcerers, blinded by the devil; twenty arguments against infant baptism; twenty-five reasons for the necessity of faith before baptism; and sixty signs of the apocalyptic beast and the reign of Antichrist.

In thought and style he was the opposite of the clear-headed, well-balanced, methodical, logical, and thoroughly sound Calvin, who never leaves the reader in doubt as to his meaning...

He labored under the fanatical delusion that he was called by Providence to reform the Church and restore the Christian religion. He deemed himself wiser than all the fathers, schoolmen, and reformers. He supported his delusion by a fanciful interpretation of the last and darkest book of the Bible.[3]

Servetus' towering pride more than anything else was his undoing.

Every man who knows and loves the creedal heritage of the church knows that the creeds are not on a par with Scripture; they are made by men.

To say that the creeds are man-made, however, does not rob them of authority. Christ promised to give the Spirit of truth, who would guide the church into all truth. This guidance of the Spirit in producing the creeds is carried out by men who search the Scriptures, consult with each other at synods, discuss Scripture's truths, defend them against enemies, and formulate them into precise theological propositions. Although the church that follows the formation of these creeds must compare them anew in every succeeding generation, the church recognizes the creeds as prized possessions, special gifts of Christ's Spirit, the fruit of intense work by great men, and born out of the thunder of the spiritual battlefield. Servetus rejected all of this.

SERVETUS' ARREST AND TRIAL

When it became known that Servetus was in Geneva—he made no effort to keep his presence a secret—the Council ordered his arrest on the ground of public heresy and blasphemy. He was imprisoned, and preparations were made for his trial.

The trial of Servetus took almost a month and a half. The Council proceeded slowly, determined to prove beyond doubt that he was guilty of the charges. During the trial Servetus, in an attempt to take the offensive, charged Calvin with false doctrine and many other serious charges. Schaff gives these "specimens":

> He calls Calvin again and again a liar, an imposter, a miserable wretch..., a hypocrite, a disciple of Simon Magus, etc. Take these specimens: "Do you deny that you are a man-slayer? I will prove it by your acts. You dare not deny that you are Simon Magus. As for me, I am firm in so good a cause, and do not fear death... You deal with sophistical arguments without Scripture... You do not understand what you say. You howl like a blind man in the desert... You lie, you lie, you lie, you ignorant calumniator... Madness is in you when you persecute to death... I wish that all your magic were still in the belly of your mother... I wish I were free to make a catalogue of your errors. Whoever is not a Simon Magus is considered a Pelagian by Calvin. All, therefore, who have been in Christendom are damned by Calvin; even the apostles, their disciples, the ancient doctors of the Church and all the rest. For no one ever entirely abolished free-will except that Simon Magus. Thou liest, thou liest, thou liest, thou liest, thou miserable wretch."[4]

Because he attacked Calvin's teachings, Calvin himself was brought to the trial to debate with Servetus in public. This took time, although Servetus used the opportunity to load additional curses on Calvin's head. The Council decided to write Vienne for further information. When the authorities in Vienne heard that Servetus was imprisoned in Geneva, they requested the Genevan authorities to extradite Servetus so that he could be tried there. The Council in Geneva gave Servetus a choice between being tried in Vienne by the Roman Catholics, or in Geneva by the Protestants. He chose the latter. It is difficult to know why, although it seems he thought he had a better chance of gaining his freedom from Protestant authorities than from Roman Catholic inquisitors. In addition, Calvin was at this time embroiled in controversy with the Libertines in the city of Geneva. These Libertines were ancient families in Geneva who had long ruled the city and who resented the influx of refugees from all over Europe and the change in Geneva from Roman Catholicism to Protestantism. They were desperately fighting for control of the city and were literally persecuting Calvin. Servetus was friendly with these Libertines and hoped that they might gain control of the rule of the city and secure his freedom.

The Council also decided to consult four other cantons in Switzerland, much as they had done in the case of Jerome Bolsec. They contacted Bern,

Zurich, Basel, and Schaffhausen, all of which, unanimously and without hesitation, condemned Servetus.

At this point Servetus filed formal charges of heresy against Calvin in the hopes that his countersuit would delay his sentence. But the Council would have none of it, and Servetus was found guilty of heresy, blasphemy, and public dissemination of dangerous denials of Scripture. He was sentenced to be burned at the stake in 1553.

Calvin tried to get the Council to execute Servetus by beheading, a less painful and less cruel death; but the Council refused. Both Calvin and Farel pleaded with Servetus to retract his heresies and sins, but to no avail. He was adamant, although he begged for mercy.

The heresy of Servetus ended in his being burned at a stake.

SERVETUS' HERESIES

The heresies of Servetus were many. For example, he tended strongly to a mystical pantheism, a heresy that deifies the creation and identifies it with God. He denied infant baptism and mocked the practice. But his chief heresies struck at the very foundation of all the Christian faith: the doctrines of the Trinity and the absolute divinity of our Lord Jesus Christ. He taught a vague Sabellianism in which he made the three persons of the divine Trinity three different manifestations of one divine being. In doing so, he also had to repudiate the truth that Jesus Christ is the Son of God, "true God of true God"—to use the well-chosen words of Nicea. That the heresies he promoted had been taught early in the history of the church and strongly repudiated by the church meant nothing to him. He brushed it all aside with a wave of the hand.

Servetus not only attacked the doctrines of Nicea, but he was also guilty of the terrible sin of blasphemy. He defined the doctrine of the Trinity as confessed by the orthodox in such terrible terms and with such blasphemous language that I cannot bring myself to print his words.

His heresies were recognized as such by all Christendom. Without dissent, Roman Catholics and Protestants, professors in Europe's universities and common folk on the street, old and young, condemned Servetus' views and saw him as a heretic and blasphemer of the worst sort. But nothing deterred him. Servetus is the father of all post-Reformation unitarianism and denials of the divinity of our Lord.

EVALUATION OF SERVETUS' DEATH

Though Calvin did not play a decisive role in the burning of Servetus, Calvin's name will always be associated with that funeral pyre outside

Geneva. Even Schaff calls it a dark blot on Calvin's name. All condemn Calvin for his part in the drama that ended so tragically. Enemies of Calvin gleefully latch onto this event as proof of Calvin's innate cruelty, and some even are so bold as to trace this condemnation and burning of Servetus to Calvin's theology. Sometimes, when one reads the stories, one gets the impression that Calvin was almost exclusively responsible for the execution of this heretic and was a greater sinner for burning Servetus than Servetus was himself. A statue of Servetus has been set up in Geneva as a kind of confession of guilt on the part of Protestantism.

The suppression of heresy by fire and sword is always wrong. This is true when the church executes heretics. But even the state may not engage in such activities. The power of salvation lies not in the sword, but in the work of the Holy Spirit, who works where and how he wills through the preaching of the gospel. The sword cannot do what the gospel does. Those err who rely on the sword to promote truth and suppress heresy. Rome tried for centuries and would do it again if given the chance. The Reformed have come to understand that they who fight with the sword perish with the sword—also in efforts to suppress heresy.

Nevertheless, the burning of Servetus must be understood in its context. The act cannot be excused or condoned, but it can be properly understood.

Some accuse Calvin of being no better than Roman Catholics in this regard. But let it be noted that Calvin once—only once—gave approval to the burning of a heretic, although he did not publicly object when, in other parts of Switzerland, a few Anabaptists were being imprisoned and drowned. Rome's murders are legion. The blood shed by the Inquisition over nearly five hundred years is a river engulfing all Europe. Insofar as Protestantism has been guilty of similar crimes, though on a far lesser scale, Protestantism soon abandoned this policy and saw the wrong of it. Rome would once again kill "heretics" if the opportunities were there and the "climate" right.

It must not be forgotten that Servetus' heresies were dreadful. He directly corrupted the truth of God's own person and being. He did this not only by denials of the truth, but also by blasphemies too terrible to print and by public dissemination of his views in an effort to persuade the multitudes. Let no one use the crime of the burning of Servetus to soften the horror of his heresies.

All Europe agreed with Geneva's sentence. There was no dissenting voice at the time. Roman Catholics and Protestants, reformers and laity, kings and rulers, professors and students—all agreed that Servetus justly received what he deserved.

That there was unanimity on this question is, of course, due to the fact that all Europe agreed that it was the solemn duty of the civil magistrate to "promote the true religion" by the suppression of heresy as well as by positive policies. The Council in Geneva was doing what the church and the states in Europe had done for hundreds of years. The dawn of a new day had not come. It was not far off, but it would be some time before the church as well as the state saw that each man must himself answer to God for the things he holds to be truth. The church must exercise the keys of the kingdom, but these keys are spiritual. The state must use the sword, but not to kill heretics. Policies that were painfully learned were slow in being put into practice. And still today the lessons are not learned. Piously proclaiming the separation between church and state, the state promotes its own agenda proclaiming evolutionism and favoring abortion and homosexuality. Liberal theologians, most gleeful in pointing to this error of the Genevan reformer, will be precisely the ones who turn in fury against the true church and those who confess the faith. They will be the first to wield the sword once again, but this time against the people of God. The "tolerant" are the most intolerant on questions of the truth. The "peaceniks" are the most warlike against those who oppose them. The opponents of forceful promotion of the true religion are the most violent against the truth. The days are near when policies of suppression of the true religion will be implemented once again.

Never allow Calvin's mistake to obscure the evil of Servetus' blasphemy.

PART 4
POST-REFORMATION PERIOD (1577–1900)

Contenders for the Faith and Historical Events		Promoters of Heresy
		Jacobus Arminius 1560–1609
Franciscus Gomarus 1563–1641		
		John Davenant 1576–1641
Formula of Concord 1577	1577	
		John Cameron 1579–1625
Arminianism first taught in England by Peter Baro 1595		Moïsé Amyraut 1596–1664
Johannes Cocceius 1603–69	1600	
Five Articles of the Remonstrants formulated 1610		
Synod of Dordrecht 1618–19		
Canons of Dordrecht 1619		
Westminster Assembly 1643–52		
Westminster Confession and Catechisms 1647		Thomas Boston 1676–1732
	1700	Jonathan Edwards 1703–58
		John Wesley 1703–91
		Charles Wesley 1707–88
General Assembly of the Church of Scotland condemned *The Marrow of Modern Divinity* 1722		
American Revolution 1775–83		
French Revolution 1789–99		Charles Finney 1792–1875
	1800	
		Charles Darwin 1809–82
De Afscheiding under Hendrik DeCock 1834		
Abraham Kuyper 1837–1920		
Christian Reformed Church founded 1857		Williams Heyns 1856–1933
Publication of Darwin's *On the Origin of Species* 1859		
American Civil War 1861–65		Walter Rauschenbusch 1861–1918
		Charles Fox Parham 1873–1929
Herman Hoeksema 1886–1965		
De Doleantie under Abraham Kuyper 1886		
	1900	

CHAPTER 23

ARMINIUS AND ARMINIANISM

INTRODUCTION

The Arminian controversy took place in the Netherlands, and the glorious triumph of the Synod of Dordt over Arminianism is part of the heritage of the Reformed churches. Yet if one would survey the ecclesiastical scene today, one would almost be driven to the conclusion that although Dordt was a great victory in the battle of faith, Arminius the heretic won after all. Dordt won a battle; Arminius won the war. One must not, however, look at the matter from a purely earthly viewpoint. The truth of it all does not lie open before our eyes. Faith, which is the evidence of things not seen, confesses that God always preserves his church and the truth of his sovereign and particular grace.

The Reformation came to the Netherlands very soon after it began in Germany and Switzerland.

The Netherlands was a part of a larger area known as "The Lowlands," comprising what is now the Netherlands, Belgium, and Luxembourg. The entire area was under the rule of the emperor of the Holy Roman Empire, who was, at the time of the Reformation in the Lowlands, a Spaniard named Charles V. The Lowlands were permitted a great deal of independence, to which they had become accustomed. In this area a strong mercantile and seafaring class had developed, making the Lowlands more prosperous than any other region in continental Europe.

The Lutheran Reformation had been the first reformatory influence in the land, and the first martyrs of the Reformation were two men of Lutheran conviction who were burned at the stake and in memory of whose martyrdom Luther had written a hymn. But Calvinism had quickly followed, and Lutheranism all but disappeared.

A strong Reformed church had been established in the Lowlands. The churches held their first synod in 1571 in Emden, outside the borders of the Lowlands in Germany. This was necessary because Charles V and his successor, Philip II, were determined to drive the Reformation from the Lowlands. To accomplish this Spain began a period of persecution during which people suffered horribly and many of the Reformed faith were killed.

Subsequent synods had been held in Middelburg and Dordrecht at which a church order had gradually been formulated and the Heidelberg Catechism and the Belgic Confession of Faith had been adopted as the confessional basis.

The church was a state church, as was the case in almost every other country in Europe. The result was that many in the Netherlands church were not genuinely reformed. Among these were several important leaders. Caspar Coolhaes was disciplined for teaching the free will of man and a general atonement of Christ. Dirk Coornhert was a humanist who opposed predestination. He had many supporters both in and out of government. John van Oldenbarneveld, the head of the government, favored a policy of religious and doctrinal freedom, which in practice meant that heretics were tolerated in the church.

Into this situation Jacob Harmsen, later to be known as Jacobus Arminius, was born and educated.

ARMINIUS' EDUCATION

Arminius was born in Oudewater in 1560. His parents had been killed by the Spaniards, and his education was supported by a guild in Amsterdam. He studied at the University of Leiden from 1575 to 1582. That university had been a gift from the government of the Netherlands to the city for its heroic resistance during the Spanish siege some years earlier.

At twenty-two years of age Arminius went to Geneva, sent there by the guild, to study under Beza, Calvin's successor. He was in this city for five years, heard Beza lecture on the book of Romans, and learned the system that is now called Calvinism. There is some evidence that he was already in trouble for his views and conduct in Geneva. Samuel Miller claims that already in these years Arminius began to disagree with the teachings of the Genevan reformers, particularly the doctrine of predestination, and that he began to meet secretly with fellow students to propagate his views. In fact, it is possible that he was expelled by the Academy for his conduct.

Arminius went from Geneva to Italy, where he visited Padua and Rome. No one seems to know why he went to the stronghold of Roman Catholicism and what he did there, but it certainly was strange conduct for one supposedly committed to the Reformation.

ARMINIUS' MINISTRY IN AMSTERDAM

In 1587 Arminius returned to the Netherlands and, after licensure, was ordained minister of the church in Amsterdam. His colleague was Plancius, a staunch defender of the Reformed faith. It was not long before Arminius was in trouble for his views. Strangely (though perhaps deliberately), Arminius began a series of sermons on the book of Romans. In his exposition of Romans 7:14–23, he said that Paul was speaking of himself in his unconverted state. The implication of this was, of course, that Paul, prior to his regeneration and conversion, could will to do the good. When Arminius came to Romans 9, he proved to be no better. He openly denied reprobation.

About this same time Dirk Coornhert also attacked the doctrine of predestination, and Arminius was asked to write a refutation of Coornhert's error. Apparently the request came to him because his views were not widely known and his reputation for learning was recognized throughout the churches. Arminius never wrote this refutation although he never informed anyone that he did not intend to write it.

ARMINIUS AS PROFESSOR OF THEOLOGY

Trouble was brewing in Amsterdam, and Plancius was the leader of the opposition to Arminius. But while the controversy was going on, Arminius received the appointment to the chair of theology at the University of Leiden, his alma mater. Arminius was actually the second choice for the position. The appointment had originally been given to Vorstius, a German theologian of note. Vorstius was, however, a known Socinian who denied the divinity of our Lord Jesus Christ. His appointment can only be explained by remembering that the universities were under the control of the government, and the government was, generally speaking, opposed to the Reformed faith. The opposition to Vorstius was fierce. Perhaps the one point that changed the minds of the government officials and the curators in the school was a letter from James I in England. Although James himself was not in any sense interested in true religion, he had counselors who were, and England was an ally of the Netherlands in the war against Spain. James objected to the appointment of Vorstius, and the government, concerned about keeping England as an ally, revoked the appointment and gave it instead to Arminius. It is doubtful whether the choice of Arminius was better.

Two staunchly Reformed theologians, Plancius and Gomarus, objected to the appointment of Arminius, but were overruled, and Arminius was installed. However, he was installed only after he had assured the curators of the soundness of his views and had promised to abide by the creeds.

Franciscus Gomarus was born in Bruges, a city in what is now Belgium, in 1563. He was a refugee from the Palatinate and had studied in Strassburg, Oxford, Cambridge, and Heidelberg. In 1587 he became minister of the Reformed church in Frankfurt, and in 1594 he was appointed to be theological professor at Leiden. He vigorously opposed the teachings of Arminius, attended the Synod of Dordt, and finally resigned from his post in Leiden and served as pastor of the church in Middelburg until his death in 1641. He may surely be called Arminius' chief opponent.

Arminius had sealed his appointment with a promise not to propagate his views, but this was a lie. Although he refrained from teaching his views in the classroom to keep them from becoming public, he taught them in private meetings in his home with select students whom he knew to be sympathetic to his position. These men were the future ministers in the Reformed churches, and the result was that the churches became filled with disciples of Arminius.

ARMINIUS' CHARACTER

Within the university and throughout the churches, controversy was increasing, and disputes over the teachings of Arminius were threatening the unity of the church. Although conferences were called and pleas for a national synod to settle the matter were made to the authorities, nothing was done, chiefly because the government authorities, alone empowered to call a synod, were sympathetic to Arminius and favored toleration of dissenting views.

In the midst of it all, Arminius died. The date was October 19, 1609.

Arminius was everything Gomarus was not. Gomarus was outspoken, tactless, and blunt to a fault, with no patience for the subtleties of those introducing false doctrine into the church, but he was profoundly committed to the Reformed faith. Arminius was of a meek and quiet spirit. He was an able scholar, well educated, refined in manners and appearance. He was an effective instructor and capable of gaining a loyal and devoted following. Yet he was something of a superficial thinker and lacked the depth of thought of his opponent Gomarus. He was a charismatic man to whom people were easily attracted, and he was noted for his camaraderie, especially with his students.

Nevertheless, all these favorable traits mean nothing in the light of his dishonesty. He was not a man of integrity. He knew that he was teaching ideas contrary to the Reformed faith. He knew that his views were contrary to the adopted confessions of the church. In spite of this, he attempted to introduce his views in secret and in unethical ways. He clothed his views in seemingly Reformed terminology so as to deceive people. He taught his views in secret, even when he had promised not to do this. He lied without compunction and was not afraid, hypocritically, to call on the name of God in defense of his abhorrent actions.

In short, he was what heretics frequently are. Rarely do heretics openly and boldly state their views within the church. One could wish that it were different. I often wonder why a man who deep down inside himself does not want the truth that a particular church confesses nevertheless refuses to state openly and frankly his disagreements with the doctrines of the church. Upon ordination he promises to do this very thing, but he prefers to break his vow. Always insisting that he is in agreement with the doctrine of the church, he nevertheless teaches false doctrine in subtle and devious ways. In this way he gains a following in the church, causes the church to be troubled to no end by his heresies, and complains of injustice when he is condemned.

How much more honorable it would be if a minister, having come to the conclusion that the church is wrong in some part of its confession, would bring his views to the assemblies, have them judged by his peers, and abide by the decisions of his colleagues. If he was persuaded that his views were wrong, well and good. If he was still convinced that he was right and the churches wrong, he could and should, without rancor, leave that denomination to join a church more in keeping with his views.

There are, I think, especially two reasons a man rarely does this. The first reason has to do with his sinful nature. Heresy arises out of pride—intellectual pride more than anything else. In his pride a heretic does not want to admit his wrong but wishes instead to persuade others of his position and gain a following of people sympathetic to him. A following enables him to justify his own error.

The second reason is that heresy has its origin in Satan's evil plots to destroy the church. Satan knows that the way to destroy the church of Christ is to rob the church of her confession of the truth. A church without the truth is a "synagogue of Satan" (Rev. 2:9; Rev. 3:9). But deceit is the order of the day if the ultimate goal is the destruction of the cause of Christ. Many must be persuaded that the lie is truth, that black is white, that error is confessional, and that wrong can be justified. Such persuasion requires deceitful tactics and a shameless lack of integrity.

ARMINIUS' VIEWS

Arminius died at the age of forty-nine, but his teachings lived on in the preaching of his students, and his heretical views were disseminated throughout the churches.

As far as his views are concerned, Arminius made the doctrine of predestination the primary object of his attack. He taught that God had ordained Christ to be the mediator and that, having done this, God determined to accept in Christ all penitent and believing sinners, but to condemn all impenitent and unbelieving sinners who remained such, even though the gospel was preached to them. In addition to this, God, foreknowing who would believe and who would not, foreordained the former to salvation.

This was an open attack on the truth of sovereign predestination and an introduction into the church of a false doctrine that made both election and reprobation dependent upon man's will. God's decree of election and reprobation thus was conditioned on man's faith or unbelief. Man's faith determined whether he was elect, and man's unbelief determined his reprobation. God's decree, then, was only a prediction of the future conduct of a man.

THE REMONSTRANTS

The death of Arminius did not stop the spread of his teachings. In fact a distinct Arminian party was formed in the church. Probably because the Arminians felt themselves to be sufficiently strong to make their views the official teachings of the Reformed churches in the Netherlands, and because they knew they had the sympathy of the magistrates, they frequently asked for a national synod. Their purpose in asking for this was to change the two creeds of the Reformed churches, the Heidelberg Catechism and the Belgic Confession of Faith, so that the confessions reflected their own views.

It is not at all uncommon for heretics, even today, to operate in much the same way. They follow a program that goes like this: As they begin to teach their views, they clothe their views in Reformed language and make their views sound as much like the truth as they possibly can. In this way they deceive the unwary.

When it begins to become apparent that they are not succeeding altogether in deceiving the churches, and when sound and orthodox men begin to expose their errors, they ask for their positions to be tolerated since they are unable to deny that their views are different from what is accepted in the church. Toleration becomes their motto. They plead that their views can be held without damage to the truth of Scripture. They claim that the confessions allow room for their position. They plead that they only want discussion of their proposals and that they are willing to be proved wrong. They speak of the value of a certain elasticity in various areas of doctrine. They are more than willing to allow those who disagree with them to maintain their own position, for they say that they are not trying to cram their views down the throats of anyone. They ask for themselves the toleration that they say they are graciously willing to give to others.

These are devious stratagems for which people easily fall. When the heretics gain power in the church and a sufficiently large following to press their position, suddenly they are the most intolerant of all and insist that the church conform to their position. Suddenly there is no room any longer for those who disagree with them.

So it was with the Arminians. When their numbers were sufficiently large, they began to agitate for a national synod for the purpose of revising the creeds. They were confident that the government, sympathetic to their cause, would control the synod and stifle opposition to them. Then the creeds could be modified to suit their own views, and the Reformed could be expelled.

All these efforts were successfully resisted by the orthodox, who objected that no synod could legally be called for the purpose of revising the creeds.

The government commission authorized to call a synod decided that if a synod could not be held, the particular synods ought to be informed to drop all discussion and debate concerning the differing views within the churches on the grounds that the differences were insufficient to warrant dissension. The churches were thus warned not to agitate against the teachings of the Arminians. This, in itself, was a triumph for the Arminian cause.

Emboldened by this decision of the government commission, in 1610 the Arminians came together in the Hague, the capital of the Netherlands, to draw up a document in which they set down their theological views. It was submitted to the government commission in the hopes that this document would settle the controversy. This document became the well-known "Five Articles of the Remonstrants."

This is an important document, because it was the basis for the condemnation of the Arminian position at the Synod of Dordt. The five chapters of the Canons of Dordt are each an answer to one of the five articles that the Arminians drew up.

The articles teach a conditional election based on foreseen faith. They flatly deny irresistible grace and speak of a universal atonement of Christ. They are ambiguous on the topics of total depravity and preservation of the saints.

The Arminians made an attempt to sound Reformed by using Reformed language and by including several Reformed views, but they omitted certain important doctrines from their articles that are important to the Reformed faith, particularly the doctrine of sovereign reprobation. They appealed only to Scripture and deliberately rejected the confessions. The Arminians knew that the confessions condemned their views, and therefore they wanted no part of them. In a direct appeal to Scripture alone to bolster their heresy, they could appeal to individual texts apart from their context and the teaching of the whole word of God.

THE POLITICAL AND ECCLESIASTICAL SITUATION

While all this was happening, the political and ecclesiastical situation was deteriorating. In the churches many Arminian preachers were in control. Faithful people of God who decried Arminian error were also present in these congregations, but their protests only resulted in persecution. Frequently, in parts of the Netherlands, the faithful were forced to meet separately on the Lord's day for worship. Nevertheless, they did not leave the Reformed Church, for there was no other church to which they could go. They spoke of themselves as *dolerende kerken,* that is, Reformed churches that were grieving over the sad state of affairs in their church, which they could not leave.

The political situation was also in disarray. Technically the nation was still at war with Spain, although there were no hostilities. Because of the constant threat of renewed fighting, a strong and united Netherlands was necessary. But now the nation was torn in pieces by the deep divisions between the Calvinists and the Arminians. Further, the government under Oldenbarneveld favored a loose confederation of provinces, each of which was more or less responsible for its own rule, while Prince William favored a more centralized form of government as being better able to cope with the Spanish threat.

Pressures were growing for a national synod to be held. Many of the provinces urgently requested a synod to ease the turmoil that was becoming increasingly harmful to the unity of the nation. Prince William pressed strongly for it, although his motives were political. Where a provincial government did not favor the Arminian party, the Arminians threatened to take up arms against the authorities, and outright rebellion loomed. Strangely, King James I of England wanted a synod in the Netherlands and instructed his ambassador to convey his wishes to the Dutch government officials. James' request was given considerable weight, because the Netherlands badly needed the support of England in its war with Spain.

When Oldenbarneveld was arrested for entering into secret peace negotiations with the Spanish, the time came for an overthrow of the government and the calling of a national synod. The government came under the control of Prince William, and one of his first decrees was the ordering of a national synod. The classes were instructed to choose delegates to meetings of the provincial synods, and the provincial synods were instructed to choose delegates for a national synod, which was held in the city of Dordrecht in the Netherlands.

THE SYNOD OF DORDT

It is not our purpose to give a history of the Synod of Dordt in this chapter, but we do wish to sum up the work of the synod, particularly its composition and adoption of the Canons, and the significance of this synod for the history of the Reformed faith.

Over the years a debate has been carried on between defenders of the Westminster Standards and people loyal to the three forms of unity over the question of whether the Westminster Assembly or the Synod of Dordt is the greatest assembly of divines in post-Reformation times. I am not interested in entering the debate, nor is there any answer to the question that will satisfy. The meetings were for different purposes, brought about by different circumstances, producing different types of documents, and of significance for different parts of the Calvinistic church world. Nevertheless, the Synod of Dordt was one of the great ecclesiastical assemblies of all time. To note a few reasons this is true would be worth our while.

First, the Arminian controversy itself is instructive and enlightening, because it gives an insight into the way heretics usually operate in the church. Heretics attempt to clothe their erroneous positions in ambiguous and outwardly orthodox language. Their motive is deception. They attempt to present aberrations from the faith as genuine Reformed doctrine. They plead that they are simply stating old truths in new and fresh ways, or that they are giving the people of God fresh and innovative insights into long-cherished doctrines. But they lie.

Of Arminius, Samuel Miller, the noted Presbyterian theologian of the last century, writes:

> This [the Arminian controversy] is a painful narrative. It betrays a want of candour and integrity on the part of a man [Arminius] otherwise respectable, which it affords no gratification even to an adversary to record. It may be truly said, however, to be the stereotyped history of the commencement of every heresy which has arisen in the Christian church. When heresy rises in an evangelical body, it is never frank and open. It always begins by skulking, and assuming a disguise. Its advocates, when together, boast of great improvements, and congratulate one another on having gone greatly beyond the "old dead orthodoxy," and on having left behind many of its antiquated errors: but when taxed with deviations from the received faith, they complain of the unreasonableness of their accusers, as they "differ from it *only in words*." This has been the standing course of errorists ever since the apostolic age. They are almost never honest and candid as a party, until they gain strength enough to be sure of some degree of popularity.[1]

As heretics spread their views in the church and attempt to persuade others, they plead for toleration, but toleration only as long as they are in the minority. As soon as they detect that other are ready to receive their views into the church, heretics become most intolerant toward those who oppose them. A plea for toleration by heretics usually only means their desire for freedom to persuade others of their false views until they gain sufficient power to secure approval from the church.

Second, the significance of the synod lies in its international character. Delegates from every Reformed country and province in Europe were present, with the exception of delegates from France, who were refused passage out of their country. The intellectual and spiritual gifts of the delegates are astounding. The delegates' names read like a "Who's Who" of Europe's outstanding theologians. And they were all devoted to the Reformed faith, although some to a greater degree than others. The only real sympathizers of the Arminian position were the delegates from Bremen and two of the delegates from England. The Canons are an expression of what Europe, one hundred years after the beginning of the Reformation, considered to be the truth of Scripture, of the Reformed confessions, and of the Reformed churches of Europe.

Third, the Canons are a sharp and unambiguous condemnation of all forms of Arminianism. It would be difficult to improve on the Canons in any respect, for their negative refutation and positive statement of the truth are unexcelled in the history of the church. One will not find a clearer statement of the error of Arminianism than in the declarations of the synod that met in Dordrecht.

The Canons drawn up at the great synod connect unmistakably the error of Arminianism with the error of Pelagianism; indeed, they call Arminianism the old Pelagian heresy resurrected out of hell.[2]

The Canons repudiate all the implications of the Arminian error, even a conditional salvation. The late Dr. Fred Klooster, professor of dogmatics at Calvin Theological Seminary, can say that the Canons refute an "Arminianism [which] is characterized by conditionalism."[3] The word *condition,* when it appears at all in the Canons, is found in the mouth of the Arminian party.

The Canons repudiate every effort to smuggle Arminianism into the church under the guise of a grace common to all men and a general desire on God's part to save all men. And while the Canons are devastating in their repudiation of the Arminianism in these doctrines, they do not become hyper-Calvinistic or radically one-sided. They insist that the gospel must be preached to all to whom God is pleased to send it. They teach clearly that in the gospel are both the promise of salvation to all who believe and the command of God that men turn from their sins and believe in Christ. When dealing with predestination, the Canons are careful to point out that election and reprobation are one decree, that the one decree is absolutely sovereign, but that the conclusion may not be drawn that as election is the fountain and cause of faith, reprobation is "in the same manner" the cause of unbelief and impiety.[4]

The Canons are solid in their discussion of the extent of the atonement. In their statement concerning this doctrine, they specifically state that the extent of the atonement, also in the purpose of God, is limited to "all those, and those only, who were from eternity chosen to salvation."[5] This is somewhat stronger than the Westminster Confession of Faith. While limiting the extent of the atonement to the elect, the Westminster Assembly, in full awareness of what Dordt had decided, deliberately dropped the exclusionary phrase "and those only," at least in part, because of serious objections to it by the Amyrauldians who were present at the assembly.

The significance of the Canons lies further in the fact that they are explanations of some points of doctrine found in the Belgic Confession and the Heidelberg Catechism. The Arminians wanted the confessions to be revised so as to make them more congenial to their heresies. The Reformed churches at Dordt insisted that these confessions were the truth of the Scriptures and that the Canons only made explicit what was implicit in the Belgic Confession and the Heidelberg Catechism.

Yet the Canons appeal as proof of their statements to Scripture alone. The synod was forced to do this. The Arminians insisted on it, and the government laid this down as the one restriction that the synod was to observe. This does not mean that the synod wanted to separate the Canons from the other two creeds, nor does it mean that the fathers at Dordt conceded the point that doctrine had to be proved from Scripture alone. The Formula of Subscription that the Synod of Dordt drew up stated that all office bearers must agree with the Belgic Confession and the Heidelberg Catechism, *"together with the explanation of some points of the aforesaid doctrine made by the National Synod of Dordrecht, 1618–'19."*[6]

Finally, the Canons are eminently pastoral. Much has been written about this, and we need not develop the idea beyond stating it. In this respect the Canons are more appealing than the Westminster Confession of Faith. The Westminster Confession is objective in its doctrinal statements; the Canons are intended for pastoral use in the churches and for demonstrating to the faithful the remarkable comfort that is to be derived from a firm commitment to the truths of God's sovereign grace as they apply to all areas of life. Although all the Canons speak to the heart of the believer as well as to his mind, the last chapter on the perseverance of the saints is so alive with the warmth of God's great faithfulness to us in all our unworthiness that I find it strengthening and encouraging to read for personal devotions at times of great temptation. They have brought solace to the hearts of many troubled, doubting, anxious souls.

All these characteristics of the Canons make them an insurmountable barrier against Arminianism. The Canons served that purpose in the seventeenth century, and they continue to serve that purpose today. The only way to introduce Arminianism into the church is to bypass the Canons.

God used the great heresy of Arminius to give to the church this remarkable document.

I began this chapter by saying that although Dordt was a mighty victory in the battle for the truths of God's sovereign and particular grace, Arminius won the war. So it would seem. Nevertheless, there is now, and there will always be until the Lord returns, faithful people of God who love and cherish the Canons.

88

8

88888

8888

CHAPTER 24

AMYRAUT AND AMYRAULDISM

INTRODUCTION

Shortly after Dordt a heresy arose that cast a long shadow over subsequent history of doctrine. It originated and was found primarily in France, but it also spread to England, where it had considerable influence. It is a heresy with which much of the church is burdened today. It is the heresy of Amyrauldism with its special emphasis on a universal grace in the preaching of the gospel in which God expresses his desire to save all who hear the gospel. It is known today as God's gracious and well-meant gospel offer. It is not just a pervasive heresy of modern times, but it also has a long history.

AMYRAUT'S LIFE

Moïse Amyraut was born in Bourgueil, Anjou, France, in 1596. He came from an influential Protestant family, which enabled him to receive an excellent education in France's leading French schools. After first studying law, Amyraut turned his studies to theology, fascinated by Calvin's *Institutes of the Christian Religion*. This is interesting because his later heresies were consciously directed against Calvin's teachings on the particularity of grace. It is also interesting because many defenders of a gracious, well-meant gospel offer appeal to Calvin in support of their views. Amyraut knew better and consciously rejected Calvin's views to develop his version of a gracious offer of the gospel to all men.

Having turned to theology, Amyraut studied at the University of Saumur under John Cameron. The University of Saumur was gifted with able professors and attracted students from all over Europe, although especially from Switzerland.

Amyraut and his teacher were much attached to each other. Everything Amyraut later taught came from his teacher and mentor, so Amyraut's views and heresies really should not be called Amyrauldism.

Having thoroughly imbibed the teachings of his master, Amyraut became a preacher in the Reformed church of Saint-Aignan. But his stay in Saint-Aignan was brief, for he was called in 1633 to become professor of theology in Saumur, his alma mater, along with two outstanding seventeenth-century theologians, J. Louis Cappel and Joshua de la Place. Amyraut succeeded a staunchly Reformed man by the name of Jean Daillé, although Daillé later became more open to Amyraut's views. Amyraut proved to be as popular as his mentor, if not more so. His skill as a teacher and his pleasing personality won wide acclaim throughout Europe and raised the school in Saumur to a glory that it had never had. It was also the forum for which he was waiting, and he used it with skill to promote his views. His position of prominence in the Reformed Church of France led to his appointment by the Synod of Clarenton to bring various requests to the attention of Louis XIII. Even in the royal court he made a good impression.

In general, Amyraut had as his motive the reconciliation of Lutheranism and Calvinism, but he attempted to achieve his goal by means of a serious compromise of Calvin's teachings. He was well aware of the fact that Lutheranism had adopted a synergism that described the work of salvation as a cooperative venture between God and man. He knew this was totally incompatible with Calvin's emphasis on sovereign and particular grace in the work of salvation. If reconciliation was to take place, Calvinism had to be modified; and this Amyraut set out to do.

Although the Reformed Church of France had been weakened by persecution and the flight of many Huguenots, there were still men who stood strong in defense of an uncompromised Calvinism. The events that surrounded the public propagation of Amyraut's heresy took place but a short time after the decisions of the great Synod of Dordt, which met from 1618 to 1619, and the first objections to Amyraut's teachings were filed with the synod of the Reformed Church of France in 1637, less than twenty years later. What Dordt had decided was well-known in France, and its strong statements of biblical truth regarding predestination and sovereign grace were widely published. Andrew Rivett, a delegate from France, had been forbidden by his king to be present at Dordt, but Rivett had followed the proceedings closely and contributed many ideas and objections to the Arminian position when the Canons were being formulated.

An influential and well-known French theologian named Du Moulin, along with some others, brought charges against Amyraut's teachings to the Synod of Alençon, which met in 1637. It was a measure of the weakness of the Reformed Church of France that the synod was unable to condemn Amyraut in spite of the objections to his views brought by the church's most gifted and prestigious theologians. Amyraut was acquitted of heresy.

This was not the end of the matter, for Amyraut's opponents continued to seek an official condemnation of his views, but nothing availed. The Synod of Charenton in 1644 reaffirmed the decisions of Alençon, and although the Synod of Loudun in 1659 condemned Amyraut's teachings—a decision that at last appeared to be a victory for the orthodox—the same synod, strangely and inconsistently, appointed Amyraut to the extremely important task of revising the Church Order. No censure, only encouragement. Such are the strange ways of synods that are afraid to stand unequivocally for the truth.

Amyraut died in 1664. Perhaps his death brought a sigh of relief to the French churches, for with his death the controversy over his views also died. His heresies, however, lived on.

Amyraut's Views

The views of Moïse Amyraut—called hypothetical universalism—are strange. Their strangeness, however, is not due to their novelty but to their obviously contradictory ideas.

Amyraut was a good student. It is almost certain that he was aware of the bitter controversies that had raged in the fifth century, first between Augustine, the bishop of Hippo, and the Pelagians, and later between Augustine and the semi-Pelagians. These controversies had raged in the church even after Augustine's death and had only finally been settled at the time of Gottschalk, that courageous defender of Augustine's views who had rotted in prison for his faith. Rome adopted a semi-Pelagian position.

Among the similarities between the views of the semi-Pelagians and Amyraut were the following: a general love of God for all men; a general grace given to all, flowing from God's universal love; a universal atonement made by Christ that extended to all men; and God's universal appeal in the gospel to all men, expressing his desire to save them. Rome ultimately opted for this heresy, so contrary to Augustine's views, in the interests of preserving its own heretical position, the merit of good works. Amyraut followed Rome.

Amyraut presented a position similar to the inconsistent and contradictory position of those who maintain a well-meant gospel offer and still claim to be Reformed.

The chief propositions of Amyraut were these: God's grace is universal in the sense that God desires the happiness and blessing of all men—provided they will accept his overtures of love; none can be saved without believing in Christ; God does not refuse to any man the ability to believe, but God does not give to every man his assisting grace, which improves a man's ability to believe; none can receive this assistance to believe without the Holy Spirit, whom God is not bound to give to anyone, and indeed gives only to the elect; Christ died for all men, a teaching that Amyraut insisted was the view of Calvin, as many wrongly do today; and the universal grace that God shows to all men is not sufficient to save them, because it is an objective grace that offers salvation to all men only on condition of repentance and faith, while subjective grace changes the heart.

In other words, Amyraut believed in universal grace *and* particular grace; in universal atonement *and* particular atonement; in an offer of salvation to all men *and* a work of the Spirit only in some; in a will of God to save all *and* a will of God to save the elect; in the necessity of the work of the Spirit to be saved *and* the ability of man to fulfill the condition of faith. It is like a man walking with one leg on the sidewalk and the other in the gutter. He limps, staggers from the sidewalk to the gutter and back again, and halts between whether the sidewalk or the gutter is the better place to be. He drifts rapidly back and forth between Calvinism and semi-Pelagianism and does so in the name of being Reformed. He accepts contradiction as desirable and finds delight in antagonistic doctrines that no one can understand.

Spiritually this is impossible, of course. The inevitable result is a drift into a totally Pelagian and Arminian position and an abandonment of even a semblance of being Reformed. The spiritual reason for this is defined by the Lord in these words: "He that is not with me is against me" (Matt. 12:30). One cannot sit long on a theological fence and totter between an orthodox position and Pelagianism. He falls off the fence on the wrong side.

Amyrauldism became a curse to the churches influenced by it.

JOHN CAMERON AND DEVELOPMENTS IN SCOTLAND

John Cameron was born in Glasgow, Scotland in 1579, and he spent the years 1600–1621 in France. Because of his vast knowledge, he was appointed professor of theology at the University of Saumur, where Amyraut obtained his degree. It was at the feet of Cameron that Amyraut became acquainted with the universalism that he later popularized.

In 1621 the school of Saumur ceased to exist because of the civil wars in France, and Cameron returned to Glasgow. He remained in his hometown for only three years before returning to France, where he was killed in 1625 during political rioting.

John Cameron is important because he carried Amyrauldism to Scotland, although similar teachings may very well have come earlier and from a different source. Some claim that Bishop Ussher from Armagh in Ireland, the author of a widely accepted chronology of the Bible, may have held similar views. John Davenant was already infected with errors similar to Amyrauldism prior to the Synod of Dordt. Four delegates to Dordt were sent by the English king: Davenant, Balcanqual, Carleton, and Goad. The latter three were sound men; Davenant was not. His ideas were so inimical to his colleagues at Dordt that there was constant debate within the English delegation. Davenant frequently agreed with the Dordt delegates from Bremen, who openly sided with the Arminians during the deliberations of that synod. Amyrauldism, or an earlier form of it, was represented at Dordt, although it could hardly be called by that name and could better be known as Cameronism after its founder.

However that may be, the views of Cameron came to England, and the influence of his views was wide. At the Westminster Assembly, Amyrauldism was represented by a party consisting of nine men, among whom were Seamen, Arrowsmith, and Sprigge. The particularism of Calvinism was also defended on the floor of the assembly, especially by the Scottish theologians Rutherford and Gillespie. The debates were long, but never anything other than amiable.

Although Amyrauldism was defended on the floor of the assembly, the Westminster Confession itself does not include Amyrauldian statements. Nevertheless, there is some reason to believe that the confession is not as strong as it could have been on the extent of the atonement.

In a paper that discusses universalism in Scotland, the statement is made that the amicable "attitude of the [Westminister] Assembly to the Davenant School was confirmed later in the same year on 4th December, when the Assembly defended the reputation of Moses Amyraut against the complaints of one Andrew Rivett."[1] However, an examination of the minutes does not seem to support this contention. The pertinent part of the minutes of December 4, 1645, reads: "Upon a motion made by Mr. Dury, according to the desire of Mr. Rivett, that the Assembly would purge him from a charge of complaining against Amyrauldus to this Assembly, *Ordered*—The Prolocutor and scribes do sign a certificate that neither in his name nor in any other man's name any such complaint hath been brought into this Assembly."[2]

Apparently the assembly had received a charge against Amyraut in the name of Andrew Rivett, whether he brought the charge himself or whether it was brought by someone else in his name. This charge was, at the request of Rivett himself, withdrawn from the assembly, and the record of it was expunged. How all that happened is not clear from the minutes. It is true, however, that the assembly had an opportunity to condemn the views of Moïsé Amyraut and did not do it.

In connection with this latter point, Philip Schaff takes the position that the Westminster Assembly was equivocal on the point:

> Nevertheless, behind the logical question is the far more important theological and practical question concerning the extent of the divine *intention* or *purpose,* viz., whether this is to be measured by God's love and the intrinsic value of Christ's merits, or by the actual result. On this question there was a difference of opinion among the divines, as the 'Minutes' show, and this difference seems to have been left open by the framers of the Confession.[3]

After pointing out the statements in the Westminster Confession that indicate that the divines at Westminster incorporated strong statements defending particular redemption, Schaff goes on to say,

> Ch. VII.3 teaches that under the covenant of grace the Lord "freely offereth unto *sinners* life and salvation by Jesus Christ, requiring of them faith in him, that they may be saved; and promising to give unto all those that are *ordained unto life* his Holy Spirit, to make them willing and able to believe." This looks like a compromise between conditional universalism taught in the first clause, and particular election taught in the second. This is in substance the theory of the school of Saumur, which was first broached by a Scotch divine, Cameron (d. 1625), and more fully developed by his pupil Amyrault, between AD 1630 and 1650, and which was afterwards condemned in the Helvetic Consensus Formula (1675).[4]

Schaff's argument here is not strong. In effect he claims that the Westminster Assembly left the door open to Amyrauldism by the use of the word *offereth* "the Lord ... freely offereth unto *sinners* life and salvation." But what was in the mind of the assembly when it approved this article is another question. The assembly might very well have meant (and it is clear from the minutes that many did mean) *offer* in the sense of "present" or "set forth." It may also have meant *offer* in the sense of a gracious expression of

God's intent and desire to save all who hear the gospel. Subsequent events revealed that it was eventually taken both ways.

Compare this, for example, with the statement of the Synod of Dordt:

> It was the will of God, that Christ by the blood of the cross, whereby he confirmed the new covenant, should effectually redeem out of every people, tribe, nation, and language, *all those, and those only,* who were from eternity chosen to salvation, and given to him by the Father.[5]

The Westminster Confession does have an exclusionary expression in an article dealing with election:

> As God hath appointed the elect unto glory, so hath he, by the eternal and most free purpose of his will, foreordained all the means thereunto. Wherefore they who are elected, being fallen in Adam, are redeemed by Christ, are effectually called unto faith in Christ by his Spirit working in due season; are justified, adopted, sanctified, and kept by his power through faith unto salvation. *Neither are any other redeemed by Christ, effectually called, justified, adopted, sanctified, and saved, but the elect only.*[6]

But this article speaks of the fruits of election and not of the atonement as such. The exclusionary statement of the Canons of Dordt was omitted by the Westminster Confession, even though the divines at Westminster were well aware of Dordt's statement. Westminster left room for the Amyrauldian position, which taught a universal atonement in some sense. Indeed, the Amyraldians interpreted the article as room for their position. Richard Baxter, author of *The Reformed Pastor,* was an Amyrauldian who refused to sign the Westminster Confession unless room was left for his universal atonement. He did sign it.[7]

As a result, Amyrauldism took deep root in the British Isles, along with Calvinism.

REACTIONS TO AMYRAULDISM IN SWITZERLAND

Theologians in Switzerland were not as charitable to Amyraut as England's theologians were. The Swiss theologians rejected Amyraut's views out of hand, and they withdrew the Swiss students who were studying under Amyraut. In addition to this withdrawal, the *Formula Consensus Helvetica* was drawn up. This creed was "composed at Zurich, AD 1675, by John Henry Heidegger, of Zurich, assisted by Francis Turretine, of Geneva, and Luke Gernle, of Basle, and designed to condemn and exclude that modified form of Calvinism, which, in the seventeenth century, emanated from the theological school at Saumur, represented by Amyrault, Placaeus, and Daille; entitled 'Form of Agreement of the Helvetic Reformed Churches Respecting the Doctrine of Universal Grace, the Doctrines Connected Therewith, and Some Other Points.'"[8]

There are various articles dealing with the error of Amyrauldism, but we quote here a few of the more pertinent ones.

As Christ was from eternity elected the Head, Prince, and Lord . . . of all who, in time, are saved by His grace, so also, in time, He was made Surety of the New Covenant only for those who, by the eternal Election, were given to Him as His own people, . . . His seed and inheritance. For according to the determinate counsel of the Father *and His own intention,* He encountered dreadful death instead of the elect alone, *restored only these* into the bosom of the Father's grace, and *these only he reconciled to God,* the offended Father, and delivered from the curse of the law. For our Jesus saves *His people* [italics in the original] from their sins (Matt. 1:21), who gave His life a ransom for *many sheep* [italics in the original] (Matt. 20:28; John 10:15), His own, who hear His voice (John 10: 27, 28), and *for these only* He also intercedes, as a divinely appointed Priest, and not for the world (John 17:9). Accordingly in the death of Christ, only the elect, who in time are made new creatures (2 Cor. 5:17), and for whom Christ in His death was substituted as an expiatory sacrifice, are regarded as having died with Him and as being justified from sin; and thus, with the counsel of the Father who gave to Christ none but the elect to be redeemed, and also with the working of the Holy Spirit, who sanctifies and seals unto a living hope of eternal life none but the elect, the will of Christ who died so agrees and amicably conspires in perfect harmony, that the sphere of the Father's election, . . . the Son's redemption . . . and the Spirit's sanctification . . . is one and the same.[9]

Article XVI is a sharp condemnation of the views of Amyraut:

Since all these things are entirely so, surely we can not approve the contrary doctrine of those who affirm that of His own intention, by His own counsel and that of the Father who sent Him, Christ died for all and each upon the impossible condition, provided they believe; that He obtained for all a salvation, which, nevertheless, is not applied to all, and by His death merited salvation and faith for no one individually and certainly . . . but only removed the obstacle of Divine justice, and acquired for the Father the liberty of entering into a new covenant of grace with all men; and finally, they so separate the active and passive righteousness of Christ, as to assert that He claims His *active* righteousness for himself as His own, but gives and imputes only His *passive* righteousness to the elect. All these opinions, and all that are like these, are contrary to the plain Scriptures and the glory of Christ, who is *Author and Finisher* of our faith and salvation; they make His cross of none effect, and under the appearance of augmenting His merit, they really diminish it.[10]

The above are only two articles in the confession that repudiate in unambiguous language the whole of the Amyrauldian system, even condemning the view that "the call unto salvation is so indefinite and universal that there is no mortal who is not, at least objectively, as they say, sufficiently called . . . , and finally denying that the external call can be said to be serious and true, or the candor and sincerity of God be defended, without asserting the absolute universality of grace."[11]

This latter statement is especially important in our day. The Protestant Reformed Churches in America and others repudiate the gracious well-meant gospel offer but insist, in keeping with the Canons of Dordt, that the external call is serious and true on God's part. Those who take this position are accused of denying the sincerity of the external call that is heard by all and are scornfully called hyper-Calvinists. The same charge was made by Amyraldians against the Reformed, although the pejorative term *hyper-Calvinist* was not yet invented. This confession throws that charge away.

CONCLUSION

Most scholars insist that Amyrauldism is not Arminianism and that the two are so different that they must be sharply distinguished. One wonders sometimes whether such a distinction is insisted upon by those who wish to be Amyrauldian in their theology but cringe at the charge of being Arminian. The Canons condemn Arminianism so sharply as to call it Pelagianism resurrected out of hell. One can, I suppose, attempt to dodge such sharp condemnation by repudiating Arminianism and adopting Amyrauldism. But it won't work.

There are differences in details between the two, obviously. But on the essentials both are in fundamental agreement. Both hold to a universal grace shown by God to all men. Both hold to a well-meant gospel offer as a manifestation of that grace. Both speak of a universal atonement of our Lord that makes salvation possible for all. Both insert conditions into the work of salvation, conditions that must be fulfilled for a salvation merited for all to be given to those who fulfill the conditions. Both take the work of salvation out of the hands of a sovereign God and put the work into the hands of man. And both are, therefore, compelled to introduce conflict and contradiction into God's eternal will and purpose that he determined from all eternity. This is a deadly error in whatever form it appears and has been the death of true gospel preaching throughout the centuries that followed its introduction.

It is good to know that those who repudiate the errors of Arminianism and Amyrauldism are in good company throughout the ages. They, and they alone, are in the company of Augustine, the opponents of Rome, the reformers, the fathers of Dordt, and the Swiss theologians. These are the faithful who hold uncompromisingly to the sovereign and particular grace of almighty God.

CHAPTER 25

COCCEIUS AND BIBLICAL THEOLOGY

INTRODUCTION

It would be a mistake to call Johannes Cocceius a heretic and to include him in a series of portraits of those who introduced heresy into the church. Cocceius was wrong in some aspects of his theology, but he was also very right in other ideas, particularly in his doctrine of the covenant. His wrong ideas sparked a bitter controversy in the church, and it lasted beyond his own lifetime. His wrong ideas introduced into the thinking of the church a way of studying and teaching theology that has had extremely detrimental consequences in the church, even today. That is why his ideas are worth our study.

A BRIEF SKETCH OF COCCEIUS' LIFE[1]

Cocceius was born in Bremen, Germany, in 1603; he was, therefore, a contemporary of the Synod of Dordt, although he was too young to attend. He was an outstanding scholar, especially trained in the original languages of Scripture, and his scholarship was widely recognized. He taught in his hometown of Bremen, Germany, and in Leiden and Franeker, two of the most prestigious seminaries in the Netherlands. Although the University of Franeker has since become a rest home for the aged, Cocceius' name is still carved in the stone about the main entrance.

Cocceius lived during one of the most flourishing periods of Reformed theology in the Netherlands and the entire continent of Europe, and he was one of many towering defenders of the Reformed faith, most of whom were present at the great Synod of Dordrecht. It was the age of the development of the truths of Calvinism and the systematization of these truths in dogmatical works.

Yet Cocceius was always "odd man out." Of German extraction, he never quite felt at home among the Dutch. He was noted for his piety in an age of somewhat loose living (partly because the Reformed Church was a state church, and all the citizens of the country were included on its membership rolls). In a time of systematic theology, he introduced a new way of dealing with dogmatics.

COCCEIUS' CONCERNS

Cocceius was primarily an Old Testament scholar, although his abilities in languages qualified him to teach New Testament as well. In the course of his studies, he became convinced that the church was responsible for serious errors when theologians wrote and taught theology as a systematic body of doctrine. He was of the opinion that the wealth of biblical truth, along with its rich teachings and its emphasis on piety, were obscured in theological treatises such as systematic theologies or volumes of Reformed dogmatics. He developed what has become known as "biblical theology."

It seems as if Cocceius' major concern was his fear that systematic theology omitted Christian piety. The works on dogmatics that had been written were so committed to a systematizing and analysis of all the truths of Scripture that the godliness, the Christian life, the subjective experience of the faith, and the piety that ought to be a part of the life of every child of God were all ignored. One was left with a cold, abstract, complicated, and involved theology that appealed to the intellect and not to the heart. It left a person with a head full of knowledge but did nothing for his own inner life of faith and his walk as a child of God in the world.

Cocceius had other concerns, too—all related to the dangers of systematic theology. He was concerned that the study of Scripture had become, in large measure, a matter of "proof texting." Theologians developed individual doctrines of Scripture, such as justification by faith alone, eternal and sovereign predestination, and the perseverance of the saints, and then they sought to prove these doctrines by citing texts found throughout Scripture. Cocceius argued that the Bible was used for proof texts and little else. The major task of the theologian, then, became discovering proof texts, building doctrines on them, and proceeding in a very rational and coldly intellectual way to analyze, dissect, and parse every doctrine so that it could be laid bare in all its implications.

Another serious danger arose from this approach, according to Cocceius. Texts from Scripture were misused as proofs for given doctrines. They were frequently torn out of context. Their place in Scripture went unrecognized, and exegesis did not take into account the historical circumstances under which a given text was written. To give an example (my own), in proof of the doctrine of the resurrection of the body, not only is Paul's powerful description of our bodily resurrection in 1 Corinthians 15 used, but also Job's words in Job 19—"I know that my Redeemer liveth" —are quoted as proof of the resurrection. Cocceius would have charged systematic theologians with the error of giving no significance to the fact that Job lived around two thousand years before Paul, that he was a contemporary of Abraham and could not have understood the truth of the resurrection as well as one who lived after the outpouring of the Spirit. Job's words simply become, in Cocceius' thinking, one more "proof" for a doctrine; but the meaning, the limited understanding, the power, and the force of them in Job's life were lost.

It is well that we grant Cocceius the point that a systematic approach to Scripture in the interests of Reformed dogmatics can indeed result in these errors. The method of the interpretation of Scripture that has been adopted by the church since the third and fourth centuries is called the grammatical-historical method. The use of that method implies that each passage of Scripture must be interpreted *in its own historical context,* and the question must be asked, "What did this passage mean to the saints at the time it was given by God?" Cocceius pointed to a real danger.

COCCEIUS' METHOD

In place of systematic theology, Cocceius proposed another method of developing doctrine—that of biblical theology, although he did not give it that name. His method was the study of Scripture from the beginning to the end, book by book, taking each book individually and separately, developing the theology in each book or each part of a book, and then moving on to the next section of Scripture.

Cocceius was convinced that this way of doing theology was far to be preferred. It dealt honestly with each text and explained it in its own historical setting. It was faithful to the character of revelation; God, as Cocceius was fond of pointing out, did not reveal himself in giving to the church a Reformed dogmatics, but God made himself known in and through history by means of a continual flow of revelation that gradually developed through time until it was all fulfilled in Christ. God added to, further explained, and enriched by new revelations the one great truth of salvation in Christ. Cocceius' historical approach did justice to that obvious fact of Scripture.

At the same time, because the emphasis fell on God's revelation in and through history, proper emphasis could also be placed on godliness and piety as the truths of Scripture were interwoven with the lives of saints and sinners and God's dealings with them.

It was this approach, for all its value, that made Cocceius a *covenant* theologian. Cocceius saw, in his study of the gradual development of God's promise throughout the old dispensation, that the covenant stood out in bold relief and was, in fact, the unifying truth in the whole of God's revelation. Although Cocceius never completely escaped the idea of the covenant as a pact or agreement between God and man, he nevertheless spoke of the covenant as a bond of friendship between God and his people.

COCCEIUS' SEPARATION OF THE TESTAMENTS

The approach to the doctrine of Scripture that Cocceius took led him, nevertheless, to serious mistakes.

Cocceius is considered the father of dispensationalism. Certainly he did not develop dispensationalism in the way and to the extent that it is developed today in dispensational premillennialism. But Cocceius, by his approach to Scripture, tended to separate the Old Testament from the New. This separation between the two testaments is fatal for correct Bible teaching.

One can understand how it goes. If a given passage in Scripture must be interpreted in its immediate context, the Old Testament passages must be interpreted as such, and any correct interpretation of them must take into account that Christ had not yet come, that the Spirit had not yet been poured out, and that the church lived in the "dark ages" of types and shadows. From such a view emerges the idea of two different dispensations and two different ways in which God deals with his people. That kind of separation between the Old and the New Testaments is the cornerstone on which all Baptistic thinking is built.

Cocceius applied this distinction between the two dispensations in another way: he applied the distinction to the moral law of God in general, and to Sabbath observance in particular. With consistency, Cocceius said that the fourth commandment was fulfilled in the work of Christ; therefore, it no longer applied to the new dispensation. He said that in our age no single day ought to be set aside as the Christian Sabbath, and that it is not necessary to make Sunday a day in which the church observes the fourth commandment and meets in divine worship services. It may be, Cocceius said, wise and expedient, but not a requirement of the law.

There is an irony here. Cocceius lived in an age of some looseness in Sabbath observance, yet he himself, in spite of his views, kept the Sabbath holy. His theology did not affect his life in this respect. Nevertheless, his views had their effect, and the fruit of his views is seen today, even among "conservative" evangelicals who desecrate the Sabbath on much the same grounds that Cocceius developed.

THE ERROR OF BIBLICAL THEOLOGY

Biblical theology is frequently the theological method employed in seminaries today. In more extreme cases, systematic theology is scorned and even accused of doing great harm to the truth.

There are many books that claim that while Calvin developed a theology that was biblical and interwoven with genuine piety, Theodore Beza, Calvin's co-worker and successor in the Academy of Geneva, began a trend of developing theology systematically. His practice, it is claimed, was followed by such outstanding Reformed theologians as the men at the Synod of Dordt, Francis Turretin, Abraham Kuyper, Herman Bavinck, and Herman Hoeksema. These theologians are often scornfully and mockingly called scholastics. This name is employed to designate them as being of the same ilk as the medieval, Roman Catholic Scholastics, who prided themselves in picking apart the truth, discussing abstract questions, such as how many angels can dance on the head of a pin, and rationally analyzing and dissecting truths in a coldly intellectual way.

But is biblical theology the desirable method it is said to be?

We cannot argue with the important principle of Bible interpretation that requires every text of the Bible to be explained in its historical context. This principle of interpretation is rooted in the truth that Scripture is the infallibly inspired record of God's revelation in and through history in which he shows himself as the God who sovereignly saves his church in Jesus Christ, his Son. Never may this truth be violated.

Nor may we dispute the fact that Scripture is vitally interested in godliness and genuine piety. Genuine piety arises out of doctrine. The two are inseparable. True doctrine deals with piety, and piety pleasing to God is confession in word and life of sound doctrine.

But theology is one thing, and preaching is another. The church needs both. Preaching—even the systematic preaching of doctrine—has to be woven through with the golden threads of godliness, or it is simply not preaching. And although a solid textbook on Reformed dogmatics will not ordinarily incorporate into itself biblical ethics, there is no reason for not doing this. In the teaching of "Systematics," a faithful professor can and must point the way to preaching godliness from doctrine. But a dogmatics is not a book on ethics any more than a book on ethics is dogmatics. Both are needed, and the blending of both into a whole is the business of the whole church.

THE IMPORTANCE OF SYSTEMATIC THEOLOGY

Systematic theology, as it is set down in a book on dogmatics, is important and crucial for the life of the church. The reasons are not difficult to understand.

God is truth. God is all truth. He is truth itself, and all truth is in him. He is one God, and because he is all truth, the truth is one.

God's revelation of his truth is one in Jesus Christ, for all revelation is in and through Christ and his work.

The record of that revelation in Holy Scripture is one. Even though Moses wrote a part, Isaiah another part, and Jude yet another part, the one author of Scripture is the Holy Spirit. Scripture's unity lies in infallible inspiration. Frequently the plea for biblical theology arises from those who make light of divine inspiration.

Thus Scripture teaches one doctrine of God, and all other doctrines as subheadings, in such a way that the whole teaches the same truth, and never can there be found any contradiction. The Spirit does not contradict himself. Job 19:25–27 agrees perfectly with 1 Corinthians 15:42–53, for the Spirit wrote them both. And Genesis 1 and 2 agree completely with the fourth commandment and Romans 4:17b, because the Holy Spirit was the divine author of all these passages.

It is this unity of Scripture that biblical theology denies. The principle of interpretation—"Scripture interprets Scripture"—is minimized or lost completely. With the loss of this principle, the *regula fidei* (rule of faith) is ignored.

This latter is especially important. The whole of the truth that the church has confessed in the past and confesses today is a truth based upon the whole of Scripture. When we seek to know what God has said about a given truth, then we search the whole of Scripture to find this out. If we want to know whether the will of God revealed in Scripture requires that infants be baptized, we go to both the New Testament and the Old to learn concerning this doctrine. We hold steadfastly to the dictum, "The New is in the Old contained; the Old is in the New explained." Scripture does not give us an exhaustive treatment of one doctrine in one given text. We must search the entire Bible.

Our confessions contain this *regula fidei.* They bring together what all of God's word says about a given doctrine. That is their beauty, their power, and their importance in the church. No wonder that Baptists do not like confessions. They prefer to prove their points by jumping about from text to text and refusing to interpret any given text in the light of the whole of Scripture. Arminians are cut from the same cloth. They will always appeal to John 3:16, but they refuse to interpret John 3:16 in the light of Romans 9. Well-meant offer defenders jump on 2 Peter 3:9 or Ezekiel 33:11. And when it is shown that their interpretation of these verses contradicts John 12:37–41, they weakly fall back on paradox, but they refuse to acknowledge that Scripture interprets Scripture.

Systematic theology is nothing else but taking the whole of Scripture as one's textbook, discovering what the whole word of God teaches about a given truth, and relating all the doctrines to each other so that they form one whole. In this way we come to know the living God in all his glory and perfection.

If, for example, one possesses a beautiful portrait of one he loves, he does not study each small part of the portrait by itself, or he will never come to see the portrait as a whole. Each section, taken by itself, gives no information. Only when each small bit is studied in relation to the whole can one see the portrait in all its beauty. Biblical theology thinks that by studying Genesis 17:4 in separation from Luke 2:7, one can come to a knowledge of the portrait of our Lord Jesus Christ, which portrait is in the Holy Scriptures. This is obviously nonsense.

Comparing Scripture with Scripture does not preclude the historical-grammatical method of interpretation; indeed, following this method enriches one's understanding of systematic theology and gives a full and broad view of the one truth of God in Jesus Christ.

THE DANGERS OF BIBLICAL THEOLOGY

Biblical theology, in distinction from systematic theology, leads to many dangers. Some of these dangers appeared in the thinking of Cocceius. He became somewhat dispensational in his thinking because he considered the Old Testament by itself and not in its relation to the New Testament. This, in turn, led him to a wrong view of the Sabbath.

Biblical theology has had its proponents over the years. A new chair in biblical theology was established in Princeton Seminary for the express purpose of giving the renowned Gerhardus Vos a professorship. Many seminaries have followed the practice by abandoning systemic theology and have taught only biblical theology. This has led to strange positions.

One devastating result of this type of approach to Scripture has been an emphasis on the human authorship of various books. While some proponents of biblical theology have refused to go so far as to deny (in whole or in part) the divine authorship of Scripture, it is not difficult to see how the jump can be made from biblical theology to higher criticism.

The Scriptures are one because they have one author, God the Holy Spirit. The Holy Spirit, through infallible inspiration, painted the portrait of our Lord Jesus Christ. Every part must be explained in the light of every other part. The unity of Scripture leads to an understanding of the *one* portrait of Christ, through whom we know the one true God. It makes no difference that the Holy Spirit painted this portrait of Christ over a period of more than a thousand years. He alone is the divine artist, and he never changes.

But when one breaks Scripture into parts and studies each part in relative isolation from the whole, one must concentrate in some measure on the human instrument, the man God used to write the Scriptures: Amos, Jude, Obadiah, Matthew, Paul, and all the rest. One must determine how the writings of each one differ from the writings of the others. Then one must determine how the theology of one differs from the theology of the others. The result is that one gets (I use familiar clichés found in most seminaries) "a corpus of Johannine literature," that is, the writings of the apostle John, and "Pauline eschatology"—frequently in distinction from and perhaps somewhat different than the eschatology of Isaiah. I recall vividly a discussion in a class I was taking in which the professor insisted that any passage in Paul was irrelevant to a discussion of the meaning of a similar passage in John, because we are, after all, dealing with a "pericope in Johannine literature."

I am fundamentally uninterested in anything that is Pauline or Petrine eschatology. I am deeply interested, when I come to Scripture, to learn the Holy Spirit's eschatology. If this is not true, then all I can do is read Scripture as I would read a *Festschrift* in which many authors write glowing essays in praise of some renowned theologian.

If one's interest is solely in what the Holy Spirit writes, then one must study the whole of Scripture and each part in relation to all the rest, for the Holy Spirit is the author of it all. One must follow the principle of "Scripture interprets Scripture," because the Holy Spirit, who wrote it all, alone can interpret his own book—something he does by means of the book itself.

Biblical theology can be deadly. This method of interpretation has recently been employed by the Auburn Four in defense of the heresy of justification by faith and works.[2] In the first chapter of *The Auburn Avenue Theology*, Douglas Wilson argues strenuously against confessions.[3] It is understandable that he does, for our confessions give what the church of the past, under the guidance of the Holy Spirit, found in Scripture concerning any one doctrine. The church brought the teaching of the whole of Scripture together concerning each doctrine of Holy Writ. The confessions are what Luther called the *regula fidei*.

Steve Schlissel argues against knowledge through propositions. He claims that faith is in a person, not in a proposition. Strangely, he writes, "If Truth is raw rationality, then one must tidy up all one's propositions. But if Truth is *personal*, then one must get to know the Person better. And you get to know a person better by knowing his character. His character is revealed in the degree of correspondence between his words and deeds. That is why the Bible is given in the form of a story rather than a systematic theology."[4]

To such strange ideas, set forth with the express purpose of denying the truth of Scripture, does biblical theology lead.

It is hard to understand what Schlissel means, but it is clear that he employs the biblical theology method to destroy knowledge through propositions. How else can we know anything? By inner feeling? By mystical contact? By an intuitive sixth or seventh sense? The fact is that all our knowledge is through propositions, even our knowledge of things earthly, including our acquaintance with people.

Scripture speaks of a personal, experiential knowledge of God that is the knowledge of faith. But the knowledge of faith that is personal and experiential consists of "a certain knowledge whereby I hold for truth all that God has revealed to us in his word."[5]

Herman Ridderbos' popular and widely read book, *Paul: An Outline of His Theology*, proceeds from the perspective of biblical theology. It seeks to understand what Paul believed concerning the truth of God.[6] The author claims that what Paul believed is quite different from what John and Peter believed. What then? What saint of God cares what Paul believed? His interest (and everlasting salvation) is in what the Holy Spirit taught, be it through the instrumentality of Paul, Peter, or Moses. The search of what the Holy Spirit teaches leads us to the whole of Scripture. That way is the way of systematic theology, not the wandering heretical paths of biblical theology.

CHAPTER 26

THE MARROW MEN AND THE MARROW CONTROVERSY

INTRODUCTION

The Marrow controversy arose in the Presbyterian Church of Scotland in the early part of the eighteenth century. The controversy gets its name from the book *The Marrow of Modern Divinity*, written by Edward Fisher. Although this book was republished soon after it was written in 1644, it never had a great deal of influence until, under rather peculiar circumstances, it became a subject of bitter debate that had to be settled by the broadest judicatories of the church.

The teachings at issue were many and complicated, and they were often framed in ways that are foreign to us and difficult to understand. But at bottom these debated questions concerned the nature of the preaching of the gospel, particularly whether preaching may be construed as a well-meant offer by God to all who hear it. The controversy had great influence on Presbyterian thought in subsequent years.

Because of the close contacts between the Presbyterian Church of Scotland and the Reformed Churches in the Netherlands, the Marrow controversy also had an impact on Dutch thinking. In fact, it is likely that the idea of the gospel as a well-meant offer first entered Dutch thinking under the influence of the Marrow men. If this is true, and there is reason to believe that it is, this Marrow controversy cast a long dark shadow also over Dutch Reformed thinking and is chiefly responsible for the introduction into Reformed theology of the heresy of the gospel as a well-meant offer.

BACKGROUND

Arminianism appeared early in the Church of England (Anglican Church), the church that emerged from the Reformation in that country. Arminianism was first taught in 1595 by Peter Baro, Margaret Professor of Divinity at Cambridge University. In fact, the Lambeth Articles were written as supplements to the Thirty-nine Articles of the Church of England because these articles, while Calvinistic, were not strong on the doctrine of predestination and sovereign grace. Attempts were made officially to add the Lambeth Articles to the creed of the Anglican Church, but this was never accomplished. Nevertheless, Peter Baro was forced to resign from his teaching position in 1596. The Anglican Church was sufficiently strong to combat this deadly heresy.

Arminianism had, however, taken root. And along with Arminianism, Amyrauldism was also taught.

From that time on, the struggle of the English church, along with the church in Scotland and Ireland, was a constant battle to resist the teachings of Arminianism and its blood brother, Amyrauldism. Especially the Stuart kings, deeply committed to Episcopalian church government and always attempting to nudge the Anglican Church closer to Rome, were ardent supporters of Arminianism. This is not surprising, for Arminianism is a blood brother of Pelagianism, the official doctrine of the Roman Catholic Church.

Of greater concern was the fact that Richard Baxter, author of a popular book *The Reformed Preacher* and a contemporary of the Westminster Assembly, taught an Amyrauldian doctrine of the atonement of Christ and of the preaching of the gospel. He claimed that it was necessary to hold to such a doctrine because of creeping antinomianism in the church. However, Baxter became a neonomist with his doctrine of justification by faith and works. His doctrine of universality in the atonement of Christ opened the door to later heresies.

The chief defender of Calvinism was John Owen, known primarily for his magnum opus, *The Death of Death in the Death of Christ.* Owen fought against Arminianism and Amyrauldism and vigorously defended the doctrine of the particular redemption of Christ. It is probably true that at the time John Owen wrote his masterful defense of the particularity of the atonement and the sovereignty of God's grace, Davenant, Baxter, and Bishop Ussher had not come out publicly with their views. Nevertheless, Owen's defense of this truth over against Arminian and Amyrauldian errors clearly indicated how widespread these heresies were in the English churches.

Because the nature of the preaching was closely connected to the controversy over Christ's atonement, Owen paid close attention also to this doctrine. He taught that the preaching proclaimed that Christ had died for sinners, and that all who confess sin and believe in Christ will be received by Christ. At the same time, he insisted that those who believe in Christ are the elect.

Owen did not shirk the command of the gospel, and he insisted that in the gospel all men are confronted with the command to forsake sin and believe in Christ. This is their duty before God, and those who refuse bring upon themselves God's dreadful judgments.

Thus Owen taught that Christ is offered in the gospel. He repeatedly used the word *offere,* which is the Latin word from which the English word *offer* is taken. But he did not use *offere* in the sense of a well-meant offer of God to all who hear the gospel, but as a presentation of Christ crucified and the one who thus accomplished satisfaction for sin.

In pressing home the commands of the gospel, Owen said that God's commands are given in utter seriousness: God means what he says when he commands men to repent of sin and believe in Christ. To press home to men the seriousness of God's commands, and to bring forcibly to the consciousness of sinners that Christ has accomplished salvation for all who believe, Owen did not hesitate to speak of an invitation by which Christ urges upon sinners the calling to believe in him, and Owen maintained that the minister of the gospel should do this with the tenderest of entreaties and most urgent pleas; in this way the minister would be conveying properly Christ's demands.

THE MARROW OF MODERN DIVINITY

While the Westminster Assembly was in session, Edward Fisher published *The Marrow of Modern Divinity,* hereinafter referred to as the Marrow.[1] The first part is a conversation among three hypothetical characters: Neophytus, a new convert to the faith; Nomista, who represents the position of legalism; and Evangelista, a pastor who speaks the views of the author and what he considered to be the truth of Scripture. The book was purported to be a discussion of the relation of the gospel to the law, but actually it was a vendetta against what the author perceived to be a characteristic of the church at this time: a dangerous and deadly antinomianism.

The book did not attract any significant attention until more than a half century later, although the question of whether antinomianism was truly representative of a weakness in the church is another question. It would be well worthwhile to consider the matter briefly.

We must remember that the Marrow controversy took place in Scotland, and that we are dealing from now on not with the Anglican Church, but with the Presbyterian Church of Scotland. After Cromwell defeated the royalist forces under Charles I, and after the Westminster Assembly had met, the Presbyterian Church became the national church in the British Isles. It remained such in Scotland, although its existence as the national church in England was brief. This Presbyterian Church of Scotland was the church of the covenants, the church that had fought fiercely against the Stuart kings and their doctrine of prelacy, the church that had endured persecution when thousands were martyred for the sake of the gospel, and the church that struggled to remain faithful to the Westminster Standards. Its credentials were solid.

Faithful to the Westminster Standards, the Presbyterian Church of Scotland maintained strongly the doctrine of justification by faith alone. This important truth was fundamental to its doctrine of salvation and the pivot on which turned the whole truth of sovereign and particular grace. I mention this because enemies of the doctrine of justification by faith alone always accuse those who hold to this truth of being antinomian. They claim the doctrine makes careless and profane Christians. They maintain that the doctrine is detrimental to preaching the gospel and makes it impossible to bring the gospel to sinners with passion and a sense of urgency and love for the lost. When, therefore, the Presbyterian Church of Scotland was accused of antinomianism, one does not accept that accusation without some strong proof.

It was equally true, however, that the Presbyterian Church of Scotland was a national church. As such it had to harbor in its fellowship and retain on its rolls wicked men who infrequently came to church, lived worldly lives, and scorned things spiritual. Such a state of affairs opened the church to the charge of antinomianism and undoubtedly, at least in some respects, justified the charge. It is doubtful whether antinomianism was an officially held position within the church. I know of no one who taught, in so many words, the antinomian teaching that good works are unnecessary for the Christian. But there was a sort of "practical antinomianism" in the church because, being a national church, she had to harbor ungodly men in her membership, and discipline was very difficult to exercise.

The Marrow men offered a solution to the problem of a perceived antinomianism. Was the proposed solution of the Marrow men the biblical solution? Or was it treating a case of food poisoning with a dose of tainted meat?

THE OCCASION FOR THE MARROW CONTROVERSY

In 1708 John Simson was appointed professor of divinity at Glasgow, one of the schools in which students from Scotland and Ulster received their theological training. In 1715 he was charged with teaching Arminianism, and the General Assembly of the Presbyterian Church of Scotland appointed a committee on purity of doctrine to investigate the charge. The committee reported in 1717 and informed the assembly that Simson had indeed used questionable statements but insisted that he intended to teach only what was taught in the Westminster Confession of Faith. On the grounds of his intention, he was acquitted but warned "not to attribute too much to natural reason and the power of corrupt nature to the disparagement of revelation and efficacious free grace." Only a few years later Simpson was charged with Arianism, that is, a denial of the divinity of Jesus Christ.

On the day the assembly acquitted Simson of charges of Arminianism, the assembly also treated a case involving what seemed to be an opposite point of doctrine. This case involved an appeal to the General Assembly by William Craig against the Presbytery of Auchterarder in the Highlands of Scotland, which had examined Craig for licensure. Among the questions put to him in the examination was one that asked him to assent to this proposition: "It is unsound to teach that men must forsake sin in order to come to Christ."[2]

The wording of the statement is unfamiliar to us and is, for that reason, not so easy to decipher. Put in simpler language, William Craig was asked to declare that it was heresy to teach that a sinner had to forsake his sin in order to come to Christ. Or, to put it in a slightly different way, "It is biblical to teach that a sinner need not forsake his sin to come to Christ."

William Craig refused to agree to that statement and was denied licensure. Therefore, he appealed to the General Assembly. The assembly was not pleased with the highly irregular conduct of the Auchterarder Presbytery and summoned the presbytery to appear before it. The assembly decided, first, that the presbytery could not require subscription to any statement that the General Assembly had not approved. The Auchterarder Presbytery was, therefore, reprimanded for going beyond anything the General Assembly had required of its ministers. Second, the assembly condemned as antinomian the Auchterarder "creed because it taught that repentance was not necessary to come to Christ. The assembly expressed abhorrence of the creed as most detestable, tending "to encourage sloth in Christians and slacken people's obligation to Gospel holiness."[3] Third, the General Assembly warned against the evils of denying the need for holiness in the lives of people (antinomianism) and warned against the prevalent teaching in the church that good works are the basis for salvation (neonomism).

In an attempt to avoid a heresy trial, the presbytery tried to to give a good interpretation of the statement by insisting that it meant only that a sinner cannot go to the cross of Christ for forgiveness unless he takes his burden of sin with him. If he does not take his sins with him, he has no need of going to Christ. If he has forsaken sin, he has no sin to carry along to the cross. The assembly accepted this explanation, but in 1718 forbade the use of such dangerous expressions in the future.

Both antinomianism and Arminianism had been condemned, although some wryly noted that antinomianism had been condemned with greater ferocity than Arminianism.

THE PROBLEM WITH THE AUCHTERARDER CREED

The Auchterarder creed was condemned because the General Assembly said it was antinomian. Its argument was that it taught that a man could continue in his sin, have no sorrow for it, and yet come to Christ. It was not necessary to forsake sin and confess sorrow for sin in order to seek forgiveness in the cross. One could, therefore, go to Christ, find forgiveness for sin, and continue in sin.

This is contrary to all that Scripture teaches and is, indeed, an antinomian statement.

However, the delegates of the Auchterarder Presbytery also argued cogently that if repentance from sin and sorrow for sin were conditions to come to Christ for forgiveness, then sorrow for sin and fleeing from sin are the grounds for forgiveness, and forgiveness is conditioned on the works of the sinner, namely the works of sorrow and contrition. This is Arminianism and makes forgiveness (justification) dependent on the works of the sinner.

The debate is illustrative of the battle in the church between those teaching an Arminian doctrine and those tending toward antinomianism. The debate over the Auchterarder creed highlighted the differences and dangers.

THE SOLUTION

Must a sinner forsake sin to come to Christ? Of what does repentance from sin—repentance that brings the sinner to Christ—consist? It is important to emphasize, first, that the repentance of a sinner is the work of the Spirit of Christ in the hearts of his people, a work of the Spirit that is the Spirit's means of bringing the elect sinner to the cross. This needs to be stressed because, as we shall note later, many in the church did not ascribe sorrow for sin to the saving operation of the Spirit.

The sinner does not follow a pattern something like this: First he comes to see his sin as it truly is. Seeing sin as it truly is persuades him that he ought to abandon this sin. At this point he decides that he must seek forgiveness from sin. He then proceeds to go to the cross to seek such forgiveness.

Nor does the sinner go to the cross to seek forgiveness without having any desire to forsake sin and to be obedient to God. This is what the Auchterarder Presbytery wanted William Craig to say. That was wrong.

Rather, as the Spirit works in the sinner, all these things take place together. Under the Spirit's working and by the power of grace, a sinner sees the horror of his sin, recognizes that he has come under the judgment of God, desires holiness that he is unable to attain by his own efforts, learns of forgiveness in the perfect satisfaction of the Son of God, hears the promise of forgiveness in that cross when he comes by faith, and flees in faith to seek all his salvation in the cross. It all happens at the same time, and efforts to sort it out in some kind of time chart fail to recognize the power of the Spirit's work in a sorrowing sinner. But it is the Spirit's work and his alone. The sorrow of one with a broken spirit and a contrite heart gives no thought to a neatly packaged list of duties and to what comes next on the list.

WHERE THE MARROW ENTERED THE CONTROVERSY

From a certain point of view, the issues in the Marrow controversy were not the issues that had been decided by the General Assembly, but the Marrow controversy cannot be understood without knowing something of these things.

Actually the controversy itself had a different origin. During the lengthy debate on the Auchterarder creed at the General Assembly, Thomas Boston leaned over and whispered in the ear of John Drummond, a fellow delegate, that he knew of a book that answered admirably all the points that were under discussion on the floor. The book he referred to was Edward Fisher's *The Marrow of Modern Divinity*. Thomas Boston had seen this book on a shelf in the cottage of one of his parishioners and, being unacquainted with it but interested in it, had borrowed and read it. He had been impressed.

The book was read by some, and James Hog, a friend of Thomas Boston and pastor at Carnock, decided to have it republished. He added a highly commendatory preface to it. This gave the book wider circulation, and many within the Presbyterian Church of Scotland read it. Both Thomas Boston and James Hog were ministers in that church. Boston is still famous for his book *Human Nature in its Fourfold State,* which has become something of a classic in Presbyterian literature. He was pastor of the church in Ettrick, where he spent most of his career.

Because of the popularity of *The Marrow of Modern Divinity* and because of its doubtful teachings, the book soon became the object of official scrutiny. Principal Haddon of St. Mary's College, St. Andrews, condemned the book in a sermon opening the Synod of Fife. He pointed out antinomian teachings in the book and quoted references from it that were contrary to the teachings of the Westminster Confession of Faith. James Hog printed a reply to the criticisms that Principal Haddon had made in his sermon, and in doing so, Hog defended the book. The scene was set for a bitter controversy.

The General Assembly of 1719 instructed its commission on purity of doctrine—by this time a very busy commission—to study the book and the pamphlets that had appeared as a result of the book, and to bring a report to the General Assembly. The committee reported and pointed out five separate heresies in the book; it also proved that the charge of antinomianism was justified. The assembly adopted the report, forbade ministers to use or recommend the book, and told them that they must warn their parishioners against it.

The commission on doctrinal purity found in *The Marrow of Modern Divinity* these errors: assurance is of the essence of faith (the Westminster Confession of Faith in 18.3 denies that assurance is of the essence of faith); there is a universal atonement and pardon in Christ's cross; holiness is unnecessary to salvation; the fear of punishment and the hope of reward are not allowed to be motives of obedience; and the believer is not under the law as a rule of faith.

Twelve men, who came to be called the Marrow men, including Thomas Boston, James Hog, and the two Erskine brothers, Ebenezer and Ralph, protested these decisions. The matter was further discussed by the commission as well as by the General Assemblies of 1720 and 1722, but the outcome was that the Marrow men were condemned by an overwhelming vote, although they were not disciplined—in spite of the fact that they informed the assembly that they would never live with nor be able to abide by these decisions. Their determination to maintain the doctrines of *The Marrow* is significant.

In 1730 the Marrow men, along with others, left the Presbyterian Church of Scotland to establish a Secession Church. It is not clear what role the Marrow controversy played in their secession. There were other issues that became the immediate occasion for secession, but it is striking that the Marrow men, for the most part, left the church.

CHRIST'S DEATH AND PREACHING

When the book *The Marrow of Modern Divinity* was officially treated by the General Assembly of the Presbyterian Church of Scotland, it was condemned for various errors contained in it. One error, however, is of particular interest to us. It is the error of defining the extent of the atoning sacrifice of Christ on the cross to include all men. The book was condemned for teaching that Christ's death was for all men. The Marrow controversy seemed to swirl around that point. And yet the controversy was not so much about the extent of the atonement of Christ as it was about the nature of preaching. A vast and crucial difference in the idea of preaching separated the Marrow men from the rest of the church.

It may not be immediately evident that the extent of Christ's atonement and the preaching of the gospel are related to each other so closely, but a further reflection will prove that this is indeed the case. The preaching of the gospel is the preaching of Christ crucified. Is Christ crucified as an atoning sacrifice for all men, or only for the elect? The answer to that question will determine the character of the preaching.

The Marrow men considered the preaching that was generally practiced in the Presbyterian Church of Scotland to be sterile, cold, distant, and conducive to a careless and profane manner of life among those to whom the preaching was addressed. The Marrow men wanted the preaching to address the evils of external religion, such as carnal security among those who were at ease in Zion and a spirit of smug self-satisfaction among the people who were content with the observance of outward ceremonies and requirements of the church. The Marrow men were concerned about a perceived antinomianism in the church. They wanted the preaching to address people on a more personal and experiential level, to press upon them the urgent demands of the gospel to seek one's salvation in Christ alone, to believe in him as Savior, and to flee to him for refuge from sin.

All of this sounds good, of course, and as such, it is true that there is a need for this emphasis in the preaching of the gospel. The Marrow men, however, firmly believed that this could not be done without making the gospel an expression of God's love for all who hear and an expression of God's desire to save all. What the Marrow men wanted was a general well-meant offer of the gospel, although it was not called that in those days.

In order to accomplish the purpose in preaching that these men strove for, they talked a lot about the "warrant" to believe. They distinguished between having Christ in possession and having Christ in warrant. This is a rather strange way of putting things, but it was language commonly in use in the first part of the eighteenth century in Scotland.

The idea was that while all those to whom the gospel came did not have Christ in actual fact, they possessed the warrant to have Christ, and therefore the warrant to believe. The best way to explain their use of the word "warrant" is to substitute the word "right": all who hear the gospel have the right to believe. They have this right to believe because God has expressed in the gospel that nothing can possibly stand in the way of their salvation. Those who hear the gospel have no excuse for not believing what the gospel proclaims. Even if they reject the gospel, they have the right to believe Christ is for them. Even if they are reprobate, when they hear the gospel, they have an objective right to believe that Christ died for them.

This means, of course, that when the gospel proclaims that Christ died for sinners, those who hear have the right to say, "Christ died for me; I have a right to believe that Christ died for me." It means, in fact, that when, more specifically, the gospel says that Christ died for his people, the individual hearer has the right to say, "I am one of God's people if I believe."

Now it ought to be clear that, according to Marrow teaching, the minister in his preaching must make this as strong as possible to his hearers. First of all, if the minister is to press home this "warrant" to believe, he must make clear that the promises of the gospel are *objectively* for everyone.

Second, the minister could press home the "warrant" to believe by stating emphatically that the God who promises Christ to all who hear, even objectively, can do so only because, objectively, Christ loves all and desires their salvation. The minister can thus say to everyone who hears, "God gives you the right to believe because he loves you and wants your salvation."

Third, as far as the hearer is concerned, when persuaded that he has a right (warrant) to believe, he possesses also the *promise* of God along with the assurance of God's love for him and God's desire to save him.

Fourth, the only reason that a man with this warrant to believe is not saved is because he will not believe. Everything hinges on his faith. To have Christ in possession rests on faith. He has Christ in warrant, but he has Christ in possession only at such a time as he "closes with Christ," that is, accepts Christ as the offered Savior.

Finally, this view of preaching opens the door to the minister's use of earnest pleading and passionate urging to close with Christ, that is, accept him by faith, because the hearer has the warrant to believe, and all that prevents him from being saved is his own sinful and stubborn heart.

Such a view of preaching as taught by the Marrow men is basically Amyrauldian. If it is true that the gospel says to all who hear it, "God loves you all and has provided you with all that is necessary to be saved, but you will be saved only if you 'close with Christ,'" then faith is man's work and not the work of God. This is Arminian and Amyrauldian.

THE EXTENT OF THE ATONEMENT OF CHRIST

It is quite obvious that the twelve Marrow men who opposed the decisions of the General Assembly and who did so because of their view of preaching also had to say something about the extent of the atonement of Christ. What they really wanted was a general and well-meant gospel offer. The General Assembly had condemned such an offer, and the Marrow men insisted that by this condemnation the assembly had made it impossible to fulfill the divine commission to preach salvation in Jesus Christ to all men without distinction.

But such a view required that the Marrow men say something about the extent of the atonement of Jesus Christ. The Marrow men denied that they taught a universal atonement, but their denials rang false. These men distinguished between a giving of Christ in possession, and a gift of Christ such as warranted men to receive him. Where did this warrant come from? It had to come from the atoning sacrifice that Christ completed on Calvary. The Marrow men approved of Fisher's book, which taught (and again we have a very strange distinction) that while Christ did not die for all, he is dead for all. They solemnly assured the assembly that they considered it heretical to teach that Christ's atoning sacrifice was for all men; but they approved of the expression that Christ is dead for all men.

The distinction is impossible to understand and can only be interpreted as a rather subtle way to introduce into the teachings of the church a universal atonement of our Lord. It was intended to teach, I think, that while Christ did not die to save all men, nevertheless his death has universal significance and benefit. Because Christ is dead for all, all have a warrant to believe. If everyone who hears the preaching has a "warrant" from God to believe in Christ, that warrant must have a juridical basis. That is, if I promise ten men a thousand dollars each if they will come to my house, I had better have ten thousand dollars available to me, or my warrant is a lie. If God gives everyone who hears the gospel a warrant to be saved if they believe in Christ, that salvation must be available. If it is not, the promise of God is false.

Thus the atonement of Christ was, in an important and significant way, for all men.

WRONG INTERPRETATIONS OF THE MARROW CONTROVERSY

There have been other interpretations of the Marrow controversy. Some have maintained that the Marrow men were concerned with various evils present in the church. Among these evils was a conditional grace. This interpretation was closely tied with the charge of hyper-Calvinism. Christ, so it was said, was being separated from his benefits in the preaching. The church could not offer the benefits of Christ to all, because they were only for the elect, and the church had to know who were the elect before these benefits could be offered to them. But those who were elect could be known as elect only by the manifestation of election in their lives. Thus Christ's benefits hinged on this manifestation of election in a holy and sanctified life. The conclusion is, so the argument went, that the offer of the gospel was made conditional. One receives salvation only if he is elect, that is, if he manifests election in his life and if he is assured of his election. Hence all the salvation was made conditional on the works of sanctification that prove election.

The Marrow men claimed to preach an unconditional salvation, according to this interpretation. They taught that God, moved by love to all, made a deed of gift and grant to all that whoever believed might have eternal life. This, so it was said, was the offer. This was not Arminian or Amyrauldian, it was claimed, but a gospel of free grace, offered freely to all, a grace that is not conditional. The defenders of the offer were, therefore, to be considered the orthodox, while the General Assembly was to be condemned for teaching a conditional salvation.

This interpretation, found among the defenders of the well-meant gospel offer, is an attempt to turn the tables by charging those who repudiate the offer as teaching conditions, while those who maintain the offer are the ones holding to sovereign and free grace. This interpretation is false, however.

The General Assembly never taught a conditional salvation. The assembly did maintain that the promises of the gospel were only for the elect, but it believed that the gospel had to be publicly and indiscriminately proclaimed along with the command to repent and believe in Christ. This, as we know, is the teaching of the Canons of Dordt.

Indeed, it was the Marrow men who taught a conditional salvation, and all attempts to turn the tables are failures. The Marrow men taught that everyone has a warrant from God that Christ is for him. This warrant from God is based on the cross in which Christ became dead for everyone. Why are not all then saved? All are not saved because the condition for having Christ in possession is faith in him, and all do not fulfill this condition. That is conditional salvation, pure and simple. It makes salvation dependent on the will of men and not on the sovereign grace of God.

The issues brought up in the Marrow controversy are still pertinent issues today, and the errors of the Marrow men are still destroying the preaching of the gospel today.

THE CONCERN OF THE MARROW MEN
The concern of the Marrow men was rooted in what they perceived as being an insufficient interest in the salvation of souls on the part of many within the church. The Marrow men detected a false security and a spiritual carelessness in many church members that indicated that they were unconverted, even though they were members in good standing.

There may have been something to this. The Presbyterian Church of Scotland was the national church, and many within it were indeed unconverted, and worldliness was rampant. This is an inevitable consequence of a national church.

Concern for these unconverted drove the Marrow men. They wanted a gospel that would press home as strongly as possible the demands of the gospel and leave people without an excuse to avoid what the gospel required. Briefly, this position was that the gospel is an offer.

AN IMPLIED VIEW OF PREACHING
In making the gospel an offer, the Marrow men were basing their view on a particular view of preaching. At that time, the current view of the church was of a national church. In a national church all the citizens of the nation technically belong to the church, and the church is responsible for the spiritual welfare of the entire populace. In a national church, the government promotes one denomination as the one to whom all the citizens ought to

belong, and everyone is, as a rule, baptized and married in the church, as well as buried by the church in a church graveyard.

It was apparent that many, if not most, in the church were unconverted. And the Marrow men, correctly, insisted that not mere membership in the church would guarantee salvation, but that conversion was necessary for a man to be saved. Conversion was the one point that ministers were called to press home on people.

However, even apart from the idea of a national church—an idea the Marrow men were willing to give up if necessary—they did not consider the church as the gathering of God's covenant people but as a gathering of mostly the unconverted.

This conception within the Presbyterian Church of Scotland had an effect on the preaching of the gospel. The Marrow men considered the preaching as giving men a warrant to believe and to close with Christ, but there were other ideas that we now need to notice.

The Marrow men held to a view of the law and the gospel that separated law and gospel. For them, the preaching of the law with its demands of obedience had as its purpose to bring people under the conviction of sin. The preaching of the gospel had as its purpose to show men the way of salvation.

This distinction led to other errors in the preaching. The Marrow men (and their successors) held to the notion that the preaching of the law could be in the service of the gospel, because the effect of preaching the law was a conviction of sin necessary to see Christ as the way of salvation. They believed, therefore, that conviction of sin could be present in the unconverted, that is, in the unregenerated. Some even spoke of a grace that came to all who hear the gospel, and that grace prepared them for the gospel by convicting them of sin apart from the actual work of salvation.

Such people could be so under the conviction of sin that they bewailed their sins, cried out in anguish over them, longed to escape from the chains of sin, and greatly dreaded the horrors of hell that were about to come upon them. But such conviction of sin did not necessarily guarantee that they would "close with Christ." They might be under such conviction for a long time, only and finally to reject Christ in the end and to turn away from Christ.

These people were called seekers, and the effect of preaching the law became a preparatory work to preaching the gospel. The gospel offer, it was said, had to be presented to these people. It had to be pressed on them in the anguish of their sin by gentle entreaties, earnest pleas, and a passion for souls that urged the sinner to "close with Christ" and find his escape in the arms of the Savior. To make these pleas and entreaties as forceful as possible, the sinner had to be told that he had a "warrant" of salvation, that God loved him, that Christ was dead for him, and that there was absolutely no obstacle to his clinging in trust to Christ.

THE ERRONEOUS VIEW OF PREACHING HELD BY THE MARROW MEN

Not only did the Marrow men have a wrong concept of the church as national in character and hence a largely unconverted body, but also they did not see that the church is a gathering of the covenant people of God.

The church of Christ as manifested on this earth is the gathering of believers and their seed, the assembly of God's covenant people. The church is not composed of *some* believing adults while the *majority,* especially the young people and children, are unbelievers. The church is the gathering of believers and their seed who are also children of the covenant. God saves believers and their seed. He saves the seed of believers as children, indeed as infants. The assembly of the church is the gathering of the converted people of God. The children of believers are, therefore, born into the church. They do not become members by joining the church nor by baptism. They are born into the church by virtue of God's covenant.

This does not mean that everyone in the congregation is converted. Unbelievers come into the church, though under false pretenses. Not all the children of believers are elect. But the church, organically considered, is the gathering of elect believers, be they adults, young people, or children. This is the truth of God's covenant.

The minister must address the congregation as a gathering of elect believers. He is not to start the service with an address such as "Esteemed audience" or "Honorable listeners." He is to address them as "Beloved in our Lord Jesus Christ." That address embraces adults, young people, and children. They are the beloved people of God, his covenant people.

This does not mean that the minister knows who the elect are. That is known to God alone. But it does not alter the fact that the preacher addresses the congregation as God's church, God's beloved, Christ's body, and the number of the redeemed. He does this even as a farmer speaks of his wheat field as a field of grain, even though it may have many weeds in it. A farmer speaks of his field from the viewpoint of his purpose in doing all the work the crop requires. God speaks of his church from the viewpoint of his purpose in saving it.

This does not mean that the minister never comes with the demands of the Scriptures that those in the audience be converted. Those who are the wicked in the congregation must be confronted with the command to repent of sin and turn to Christ. But more importantly, God's people must hear the call to conversion all the time, every day anew, for conversion means to turn from sin, to flee to Christ, and to walk in obedience before God. This God's people must do all their lives.

Does this mean that the minister need never warn the congregation of the severe judgment of God upon the unrepentant? No. God uses warnings, too, in order to summon his people from their sinful ways. Nor does the fact that the congregation is composed of elect mean that no admonitions need be preached. God's people are sinful saints who walk in every sin that arises in their sinful flesh. The admonitions of the gospel summon the ungodly to repentance in order that they may be without excuse, and they call the people of God to become what God has made them: his own covenant people.

Does preaching in the congregation mean that the minister is cold and indifferent toward the struggling saints? Does it mean that he has a coldness that finds no room for entreaties and earnest pleas rooted in his desire to see them walk in faithfulness? He cannot be a shepherd if this is the case. He must love his sheep and earnestly seek their salvation in all his ministry.

Does his preaching ignore the law? No, he preaches the law. He does so knowing that by the law is the knowledge of sin, a knowledge that is worked by the Spirit as a part of the work of salvation. That same law is a rule of gratitude in the keeping of which the believer shows his thankfulness to God for the great salvation he has received. The law is gospel. If anyone doubts it, let him read Psalm 19 and Psalm 119. Let him hear the words with which the law begins: "I am the LORD *thy* God, which hath brought *thee* out of the land of Egypt, out of the house of bondage" (Ex. 20:2). God comes with his law to his people whom he has saved.

The minister may not attempt to devise ways and means to make the gospel more effective. If he does, he is an unfaithful shepherd. He preaches in the humble awareness that all the fruit of the gospel belongs to God, for only God can make the gospel the power unto salvation that Paul claims it is (Rom. 1:16). God will use the foolishness of preaching to save his elect, but he will also use it to harden the impenitent and leave them without excuse.

The minister must not preach in the congregation as if he were on a mission field. If he wants to preach to the unconverted, then let him pray God to send him to a foreign field where the gospel has never been preached. Even there, however, he preaches not an offer of the gospel rooted in a universal atonement and expressing God's love for all, but the sovereign grace of God in salvation and the promise of eternal life to all who believe. And the minister accompanies his preaching with the command to turn from sin and flee to Christ, in whom alone is found salvation. He warns of judgment upon all those who continue in their sins, for God is a holy God who will surely punish the sinner.

The Marrow men had a wrong conception of these things, because they had no correct view of God's covenant and of God's church as the gathering of God's covenant people. Those who make of the preaching a well-meant offer have followed in the erroneous paths marked out by the Marrow men.

CONCLUSION

While the Marrow controversy was going on in Scotland, the *nadere Reformatie* (further Reformation) was going on in the Netherlands. This movement was a protest against the evils in the state church, also a national church, and an effort on the part of the godly to find food for their souls. Many, in addition to attending what were increasingly apostate churches, met with like-minded saints in homes where the Scriptures were read and discussed and prayers were made to God. To make such edification greater, and because there were few if any faithful shepherds, these troubled saints read from other writers who could build them up in the faith. Because the ties between Scotland and the Netherlands were so close, many of these writers were of the Marrow men. A chronicler of the *nadere Reformatie* wrote, "The *Nadere Reformatie* is in fact the Dutch counterpart to English Puritanism . . . The linkage between these movements is strong, historically and especially theologically."[4] This close association with the Marrow men brought the well-meant offer of the gospel into the stream of Dutch theology.

CHAPTER 27

WESLEY AND
ARMINIANISM

INTRODUCTION

While the Marrow controversy was going on in Scotland among the Presbyterians and the church in that land was struggling with the Arminianism latent in Marrow theology, England was developing its own kind of Arminianism within the Anglican Church.

Arminianism had been present in the Anglican Church from its beginning and had, more or less, been tolerated within the church. But it came to full-blown development during the work of John and Charles Wesley, the founders of Methodism. The impact that these two men had on England cannot be underestimated. Their influence continues to the present, and their influence is not limited to England. Methodism has been firmly established in the United States as well, and it was, in fact, the religion of the frontier when the American West was being settled. The theology of Methodism has penetrated into many other denominations that still hail John Wesley as a saint of the first rank.

WESLEY'S EARLY LIFE

John Wesley was born June 8, 1703, from Samuel Wesley and Susannah Annesley. The Wesley family was of ancient Saxon stock of some fame in the annals of early British history. Susannah was the twenty-fifth child of Dr. Samuel Annesley, and she brought into the world nineteen children of her own. John was the fifteenth child, but only five sisters and one brother had survived by the time he was born. Samuel Wesley was rector of the parish of Epworth, where life was grim and difficult. It was also dangerous. The people of the parish, though members of the Church of England (Anglican), were coarse, brutal, uneducated, and much inclined to violence, and the manse was not sacred ground. When the people thought that their rector was too godly and required too much of them, they were not only threatening, but they also endangered the well-being of the children with their violence.

Because the revenues of the parish were not great, and because of a series of crop failures, the Wesley family fell on hard times, and Samuel was briefly imprisoned for a debt of less than thirty pounds. During this time, riotous mobs with drums and guns paraded outside the rectory. The cows belonging to the rector were stabbed. The "people swore that if they got [their hands on] the parson...they would squeeze his guts out."[1] They even set the thatched roof of the manse on fire.

But Susannah was a gifted, strong-willed, capable, and pious woman who saw her family through the hard times to which they were subjected. She taught her children at home and gave all those who survived death an excellent education. She instilled in them an enormous respect for the church in which their father was rector.

Her strong will often clashed with that of her husband, who was no weak personality himself. When William of Orange from the Netherlands came to the throne of England, Samuel was elated, but his wife refused to support a foreign king. When Samuel prayed for William of Orange, she refused to say "Amen." Her husband, irritated by this lack of submission, said to her, "Very well, Sukey, if we are to have two kings, we must have two beds."[2] And with that he saddled his horse and rode to London. It was all, however, a bit of a bluff. He had business in London in any case, and he soon returned to the family and his wife, toward whom he was usually most affectionate.

John soon went off to school in London. He was about ten and a half years old, and the year was 1714. He entered the Charterhouse, a public school for boys. Here he remained for six years although he was not alone the entire time. In 1716 he was joined by his brother Charles, who was to be his companion and co-laborer through many years of his ministry. That same year his brother Samuel became an usher in Westminster Abbey, London. The three were now together.

Throughout his life, John was committed to mysticism in its unbiblical form. From these early years, many influences in his life seemed to drive him in the direction of mysticism. It was an important part of John's life and explains in some measure the direction that his theology took.

One influence was a most peculiar series of events in the rectory back in Epworth, to which John occasionally returned. Beginning in 1716, groans and knocks were heard at different times and were the beginning of many other different noises. The family was not unduly disturbed by them, which is probably evidence of the fact that spiritism was a regular part of the religious life of a superstitious age. At any rate, the boys who were away were told of these strange goings-on, and at the times when they were home, they were supposedly witnesses of them. These occult events made a deep impression on John and created in him a lifelong belief in spiritism.

WESLEY'S LIFE AT OXFORD

On his seventeenth birthday John entered, as a commoner, Christ Church College at Oxford University, one of the most prestigious universities in England and, along with Cambridge, one of the most influential in the entire continent of Europe. Oxford was to be John's home for many years.

During these Oxford years John's spiritual life began to develop. Whatever he himself expected from religious and spiritual development, he did not consider himself truly converted, even though he engaged in all the religious exercises required by the college.

About 1725, while John was at Oxford, another influence came to bear on him that turned him in the direction of mysticism. He became acquainted with the writing of Thomas à Kempis, the late medieval mystic and the author of *The Imitation of Christ*. John was heavily influenced by this book, and it stirred up his interest in other medieval mystics. This was also the year that he was ordained a deacon of Oxford and was licensed to preach.

In 1726 John was elected to Lincoln, another Oxford college known for its piety and learning. He was appointed Greek lecturer and moderator of the disputations. These disputations were somewhat like public debates in which students were grilled on an assigned thesis and required to defend it. In 1727 he acquired his degree of master of arts and spent some time in his father's curacy. His father was becoming increasingly infirm and was burdened with the great weight of the almost negligible influence of his ministry on the coarse and hardhearted members of the parish. John's father begged John to stay and take over the ministry of the parish in his place, but John refused and soon returned to Oxford, where he stayed for an additional six years.

Mystical influences continued to mold his theology. He spent a great deal of time reading and studying William Law's *A Serious Call to a Devout and Holy Life*. The book emphasized the importance of a personal and experiential relationship to God, but did so within an Arminianism that was becoming increasingly strong in the Church of England. In fact, John Wesley's father Samuel was a part of the Arminian party within the church. If one wonders why Arminianism was tolerated in what was intended to be a Calvinistic church, the answer lies in part in the fact that the Church of England was the established church authorized by the government to be the only church within the realm that had a right of existence. As an established church it had to have room in it for a diversity of views in order to keep all the ministers in England within its walls.

Slightly before 1729 Charles Wesley and two other men formed the Oxford Holy Club on campus for the purpose of improving the spiritual life of its members. John Wesley became their leader. The club never had more than twenty-five members, but it exerted considerable influence. The members met together to encourage each other and to discuss how to improve their lives in holiness. The way they prescribed among themselves was the way of self-denial, ascetic practices, and good works. They regularly visited prisons and poorhouses and helped the inmates as much as they were able. It seemed as if the club members actually sought their salvation in their good works and ascetic practices and minimized the cross of Christ, which should be the only hope of the believer. The Oxford Holy Club had a lasting effect on Wesley and on his theology.

The club caught the attention of the students and the Oxford officials. For their exercises in holiness, the members were ridiculed, persecuted, and called Methodists, a name scornfully given to the members of the Oxford Club for their methodical exercises in piety.[3]

John describes his goals:

> My one aim in life is to secure personal holiness, for without being holy myself I cannot promote real holiness in others. In Oxford, conversing only with a chosen circle of friends, I am screened from all the frivolous importunities of the world, and here I have a better chance of becoming holy than I should have in any other place. Many good works, already begun, depend upon me for their continuance. In Epworth . . . I should be of no use at all: I could not do any good to those boorish people, and I should probably fall back into habits of irregularity and indulgence.[4]

One cannot help but be struck with the constant emphasis on good works with no mention of the cross of Jesus Christ.

Wesley was again subject to mystical influences in 1735 when he crossed the Atlantic to minister in Georgia as chaplain to a colony of debtors, whom the British government had sent to Georgia as punishment for crimes. John went with his brother Charles, the hymn writer of the later Methodist movement. While on board ship in the Atlantic, a terrible storm struck, and the ship was in grave danger of foundering. John was amazed by the serene composure of a group of Moravians who prayed and sang while the storm raged. Wesley made the acquaintance of these Moravians and was influenced by their theology. At the heart of their religion lay the idea of making theology a mystical experience and little more, so that the true knowledge of God was confined to a personal communion with him.

WESLEY'S CONVERSION

John Wesley's stay in Georgia did not go well, and after three years he was forced to leave. He returned to England and to Oxford in 1738. It was during this stay in Oxford that Wesley had what he considered to be his decisive conversion experience. It took place in a small chapel on Aldersgate Street in London. The biographer C. E. Vulliamy describes the event.

> On the 24th of May, it seemed to him that he had really found the assurance of belief. On the evening of this memorable day he went "very unwillingly" to the meeting of a religious society in Aldersgate Street, in which James Hutton appears to have been the principal figure. Someone was reading Luther's *Preface to the Epistle to the Romans*. At about a quarter to nine, while he was listening to the reader, Wesley felt a warming of the heart. He felt that he did trust in Christ, and that he was actually saved from the law of sin and death. He began to pray fervently, and more particularly for his enemies. And then, he says, "I testified openly to all there what I now first felt in my heart." But the assurance was not complete, for he did not feel the joy which he believed to be inseparable from a true knowledge of salvation. "Then was I taught that peace and victory over sin are essential to faith in the Captain of our Salvation; but that, as to the transports of joy that usually attend the beginning of it, especially in those who have mourned deeply, God sometimes giveth, sometimes withholdeth them, according to the counsels of His own Will.
>
> After his return home, he was "much buffeted with temptations," which returned again and again. Two days later he wrote, "My soul continued in peace, but yet in heaviness because of manifold temptations." ... On the 6th of June, after a terrible encounter with his fears, he felt "a kind of soreness," and knew that he was not invulnerable. "O God," he cried, "Save thou me, and all that are weak in faith, from doubtful disputations."[5]

Robert Tuttle claims that one of the weaknesses of mysticism, especially as practiced in the Middle Ages, is a denial of the atonement of Christ or a bypassing of it in the interests of immediate union with God. When one reads of Wesley's Aldersgate experience, as well as his life previous to that, one cannot help but be impressed that the core of Wesley's so-called religious experience had very little to do with the cross of Christ. In the same book Tuttle argues that mysticism inevitably leads to Arminianism; and, of course, a reciprocal relationship exists between bypassing (to use the more charitable word) the cross and a salvation by good works.[6]

WESLEY'S ITINERANT MINISTRY

Shortly after his conversion, Wesley began to preach more actively than he had before, although sometime earlier he had been ordained a deacon. That a deacon preached was and is common practice in the Church of England, where deacons have a different role than they do in Reformed church polity.

Wesley's preaching differed markedly from that of the bishops, curates, and rectors in the Church of England. We must remember that this church was the established church and that all the citizens of the commonwealth were technically members of the church, or at least under the supervision of it. When Wesley began his preaching, the religious and spiritual state of the church was very low. Wesley's father, Samuel, had learned that it was almost impossible to get any religion into the heads and hearts of the churlish, stubborn, unruly, violent, and uneducated members of his parish. That condition prevailed throughout most country parishes. While in the cities people tended to have more education (with the exception of the poor, whose life in the cities was still more cruel and debased than their fellow citizens in the country), those with education tended to be worldly, cynically sophisticated, interested only in a religion that allowed them to be confirmed in the church, to be married in the church, to bring their children to the church to be baptized, and to be buried in a church graveyard.

The ministers were not much better. They received their livings from the holdings in the parishes, were more humanistic Renaissance men than learned in the Scriptures, and were followers of Erasmus and other Renaissance scholars rather than servants of Christ. A "good sermon" was usually considered a learned discourse on some aspect of ethics or philosophy with copious quotes from a wide variety of secular writings, preferably from ancient Greek and Roman authors.

Wesley was right that little holiness could be found anywhere in the church of his day. Wesley was also right when he said that holiness, above all, is pleasing to God. But Wesley's theology of holiness was for the most part far removed from the teaching of the sacred Scriptures. It was a holiness that came from man's own efforts and not from the cross of Jesus Christ.

In sharp contrast to current preaching in the Church of England, Wesley began to pattern his preaching after the medieval mystics, especially those of the late fifteenth century who had lived in the Rhine River valley. Wesley stressed the necessity of the new birth and the endeavor to attain holiness. His preaching was not well received in the church, and an increasing number of churches were closed to him. One can well mark this closure of churches as the beginning of the Methodist movement.

At a loss as to what to do, Wesley seized quickly on an invitation from George Whitefield to come to Bristol and work with him. Whitefield had developed into a preacher in his own right in the western parts of England and in Wales. He had, however, never gone in the direction of mysticism and Arminianism but had become a rather staunch Calvinist. He had adopted the open-air method of preaching to crowds assembled in fields, streets, graveyards, and forests. Although somewhat skeptical at first, Wesley soon saw the effectiveness of this method, especially when church doors were closed to him. From that day on Wesley was England's most famous itinerant open-air evangelist.

It has been estimated that Wesley traveled nearly a quarter of a million miles (approximately ten times around the earth at the equator) and preached in excess of forty thousand times. His travel was usually on horseback, although sometimes afoot. He traveled over unimaginably rough roads filled with holes and boulders, slippery and treacherous when wet and dusty when dry. He traveled in all kinds of weather, during every season of the year, and usually was reading a book as his horse plodded along. He preached almost every day, and most of the time two or three times a day.

WESLEY'S RELATION TO WOMEN

Wesley's relation with women was strange. He was a close friend of Lady Huntingdon, a wealthy lady who was a supporter of the work of Wesley and Whitefield. He nearly married another woman, even traveling with her across the Irish Sea to Ireland. She was his close confidant and personal friend, and Wesley seemed intent on making her his wife. Through a combination of strange circumstances and another man who pressed his suit, the marriage never took place. When Wesley finally did marry, the marriage was most unhappy. He was seldom home, traveling throughout the whole of Great Britain on behalf of the gospel. His wife, embittered and rightly so by his constant absences, and rather sour by nature, tended to be an example of Solomon's proverb that a nagging woman is like a continual dripping of water.

WESLEY'S RELATION TO THE CHURCH

Wesley's relation to the Church of England was also a strange one. He remained all his life in the Church of England and always considered himself a faithful son of the church. When separation from the church was suggested to him, he refused to do so. The church was antagonistic to Wesley and closed its doors to his ministry, but it never disciplined or censured him. It permitted him to conduct his ministry freely without official ecclesiastical censure.

This relationship becomes yet more strange when we consider that the entire movement that Wesley launched, although it remained in the church during his lifetime, was a separate movement. It had its own chapels and organization. Wesley ordained ministers to serve in the organized churches. In fact, contrary to the law of the Church of England, Wesley ordained women. No Methodist chapel would endure the presence of an Anglican prelate on its pulpit, and no Church of England parish would even consider having a Methodist minister on its pulpit. But both were part of the same denomination.

No one would deny that Wesley was busy. He never took a vacation and considered any idle moment as a sin.

> We see him more and more frequently riding upon the highways of England; not upon such roads as we ride over today, but on ways muddy, rocky and wet; grassy or marshy tracks, full of pits, deep-rutted, narrow, abounding in quags, covered with loose flint-stones, or not covered at all, darkened by overhanging, unlopped trees, or washed away on the open moors...
>
> Sometimes accompanied by a servant, Wesley rode hired horses. He could ride from London to Oxford in one day, in 1741, changing horses twice. In his later travels he covered much greater distances between morning and night; but a day for Wesley never meant less than eighteen hours... If his carriage travelling is included, he journeyed over more than a quarter of a million miles between 1738 and 1790. But he was never a good horseman. He used to read books while riding, and as this meant holding his hands close to his face and letting the reins drop on the horse's neck, it is not surprising that the horse occasionally fell down or ran away... His longest ride—ninety miles in one day—took about twenty hours.[7]

Wesley did much more besides his circuit preaching. He did the work that rightly belongs to ecclesiastical bodies: organizing new congregations, ordaining preachers after training and examining them, exercising discipline and ruling over the many churches he established. He also raised funds for various causes, ministered to the sick, counseled those with problems, wrote pamphlets and books (including commentaries) defending his theological position, attacked in print his enemies, and corresponded with many people.

Wesley was no stranger to opposition and persecution. He and his preachers often had to face mobs and unruly crowds, incited to violence by local prelates of the church and magistrates. Not only were the mobs noisy in efforts to disrupt the meetings, but also sometimes things got so badly out of hand that injuries resulted from mob action. Wesley's ministry was particularly among the poor, the working class—miners, diggers, industrial workers—and the uneducated. These people, frequently stirred up to hatred by the authorities, considered violence against preachers a worthwhile diversion from the daily grind of their lives. But as the Methodist movement spread and grew, and as these itinerant preachers became more common, opposition decreased and finally died altogether.

WESLEY'S RELATION TO OTHERS

Although John Wesley had many helpers, fellow ministers, and close friends throughout England, four men especially are important to understand his work.

The first man was his brother Charles. Charles was, with John, a member of the Oxford Holy Club. He continued to be close to his brother. He himself preached as an assistant to John and was his traveling companion. He never attained the popularity of John but is better known as the hymn writer of the Methodist movement. Some of his hymns, familiar to this day, gave vigor and spark to the movement, but they also directed the thinking of the people in Arminian paths. There is no easier way to introduce heresy into the minds of people than through singing. Even the Arminians of the sixteenth and early seventeenth centuries in the Netherlands were said to have sung their way into the church.

The second man of note is Howell Harris, well-known in Welsh Protestantism. He was an associate and close friend of Wesley but a consistent Calvinist. Wesley's Arminianism was the direct opposite of the theology of Harris, and the two eventually parted ways. Howell Harris is known as the father of the Welsh Calvinistic Methodist Church.

The third man was George Whitefield. He was a man of unusual oratorical abilities ideally suited to field preaching. Whitefield traveled frequently to America. He sparked, along with Jonathan Edwards, the New England revivals in the early eighteenth century before the colonies fought their war for independence, and he was acquainted with, if not a friend of, Benjamin Franklin. Along with Howell Harris, Whitefield is considered the father of the Welsh Calvinistic Methodist Church. Whitefield, too, was a Calvinist, and his Calvinism was the occasion for a temporary split with Wesley.

While Whitefield was in America, he embraced New England Calvinism. Wesley preached a sermon on "Free Grace" in which he repudiated predestination as a blasphemous doctrine that made God worse than Satan. Whitefield urged him not to publish the sermon or repeat it, but Wesley did both. This led to separation between them. Wesley was offended that the Calvinists held not only to predestination, but also to particular atonement instead of universal redemption. This, to Wesley, was anathema.

But it was not long before Wesley and Whitefield were friends again. Whitefield, however, was the compromiser. While never forsaking his Calvinism, already before his split with Wesley he had said, "Let us offer salvation freely to all," and he was silent on election. Silence is also a denial of God's truth, whatever a man may hold in his mind. And so, both men were soon on friendly terms and they remained such throughout their lives although they traveled different paths. Wesley was a teacher of false doctrine, but Whitefield was the grand compromiser, willing to sell his convictions for the price of peace with a heretic.

The fourth man was Augustus Toplady, author of the hymn "Rock of Ages." He and Wesley were sworn enemies. The issue here also was Calvinism and especially the truth of election and reprobation. Lady Huntingdon has already come to our notice. Her sympathies tended to be with the Calvinists more than the Arminians. When six students sympathetic to Lady Huntingdon were expelled from the Methodist movement, Toplady entered the fray with a strong defense of God's sovereign and double predestination. This so infuriated Wesley that he wrote a slanderous and blasphemous caricature of predestination and published it using Toplady's name. Part of it read,

> The sum of all is this: One in twenty (suppose) of mankind are elected; nineteen in twenty are reprobated. The elect shall be saved, do what they will; the reprobate shall be damned, do what they can. Reader, believe this, or be damned. Witness my hand. A——— T———.[8]

The debate was furious, and the pamphlets many in number. But one thing the controversy brought out: Wesley was thoroughly Arminian and wanted nothing of the doctrines of grace.

WESLEY'S MYSTICISM

Wesley was deeply influenced by mysticism, both the mysticism of the Middle Ages and mystical teachings in some English writers. Many different mystical influences directed Wesley's thinking in his formative years. While later in life he abandoned some of mysticism's teachings, he continued to be mystically inclined. Tuttle speaks of the fact that mysticism has remained an important part of Methodist theology.[9]

It is possible, however, to distinguish between the Arminianism of the Remonstrants in the sixteenth and seventeenth centuries as rationalistic Arminianism, while Wesley's Arminianism could be called a mystical Arminianism. Some have utilized this distinction to approve of Wesley's Arminianism while denouncing the Arminianism of the Remonstrants. This is wrong. Both the Remonstrants and John Wesley hated the doctrines of grace, and both substituted heresies that ascribed salvation to the will of man.

Mysticism influenced Wesley's thinking in different ways. First, Wesley was actually uninterested in doctrine. His biographer Vulliamy points out that Wesley did not want doctrinal formulation, a "system" of doctrine that could be embodied in a confession. He was, apparently, like those who today boast of having "No creed but Christ." Yet he became very angry when anyone disagreed with him. But the doctrines of Scripture all have their center and focal point in the cross of Jesus Christ. Insofar as Wesley's mysticism tended to emphasize direct union with God, it denigrated the cross; that denigration of the cross led to a disinterest in doctrine.

Second, Wesley's mysticism led to an overemphasis on the inner life. This error, the opposite side of doctrinal disinterest, says that all that counts in the Christian life is one's relationship to God and that doctrine is unimportant. It does not matter what a man believes; only his relationship to God is important.

Third, Wesley's mysticism led directly to his Arminianism. Wesley did not teach, although he understood it well, that all salvation is only in the cross of Jesus Christ. The error of not giving the cross its full due leads to an emphasis on human effort that denies the cardinal doctrine of sovereign grace.

Finally, Wesley's mysticism led him to approve of revivals.

WESLEY AND REVIVALS

The narratives of Wesley's life call attention to the fact that, at least in the early part of his open-air ministry, his preaching was frequently accompanied with the strange behavior that is characteristic of revivals and is evidence, so it is said, of special outpourings of the Holy Spirit. Wesley himself did not apparently give a lot of emphasis to these special outpourings of the Spirit, and later in his ministry they ceased. Yet the entire work of Wesley is frequently called the Wesleyan Revival, and George Whitefield's work in New England, along with that of Jonathan Edwards, has become known as the New England Revival. On this basis, and on the basis of other revivals in the British Isles and in America, evangelicals still are busy praying for revival and see revival as the only hope of the church.

The special outpourings of the Spirit that men call "revival" are generally characterized by such severe conviction of sin that the agonies of the consciousness of sin lead to bizarre behavior, and the deliverance from conviction of sin leads to such joy in the Lord that it, too, is manifested in unusual and strange conduct. An example of such an occurrence is described by Vulliamy. It took place during the preaching of one of Wesley's colleagues.

> Inside the church at Everton, while Berridge was preaching or conducting his service, some of the people fainted and fell quietly on the floor, others roared and screamed, sinking down in horrible contortions; at one moment they felt themselves dropping into the blazing cavity of hell, and at the next, they were rising in ecstasies of joy and gratitude. Those who were less affected stood on the seats of the pews in order to see the disturbed congregation. The noise was incredible. Rustic boots hammered against the boards, broke the benches and split the sides of the pews. Children set up a shrill wailing. Women shrieked horribly, clapped their hands, or fell upon each other's necks. Some uttered short ejaculations of praise, and others shouted in wild triumph. Below the louder sounds there was all the while a noise of hard breathing, as of men half strangled and gasping for life. And above all the appalling din could be heard the powerful voice of Berridge, praying and preaching and calling on sinners, louder and more unmelodious, and louder still, until no voice, no human head or heart, could bear the strain any longer, and he walked out through the stricken multitude.
>
> Berridge walked from the church to the vicarage, and there the work was continued. People were carried into the house like casualties from the scene of some hideous disaster. Children raved and struggled in passages. It was observed by a witness that "almost all on whom God laid His hand turned either very red or almost black." Some laughed foolishly "with extreme joy," tears of inexpressible emotion running down their pale, radiant faces.[10]

Such conduct is supposed to be the manifestation of conversion on a grand scale. It is not my purpose to criticize the whole concept of revivals, including their wrong view of conversion, their mysticism with its emphasis on feeling, their false description of the work of conversion and salvation in the hearts of God's people, their wrong exegesis in making the biblical basis of revivals the national conversions of Israel in the Old Testament, and their failure to take into account God's federal and organic dealings with men in the line of generations. It is more than strange that people who claim to be Reformed can continue to pray for such modern-day revivals as were supposed to have taken place in the past.

WESLEY'S ARMINIANISM

Although Wesley claimed to be uninterested in doctrine, he nevertheless was sufficiently interested to preach and teach a thoroughgoing Arminianism and to pour out his spite against and hatred of the Calvinistic doctrines of grace. He despised election and reprobation and blasphemed against it and the God who determined both. How it was possible for George Whitefield to continue to associate with Wesley has to be indicative of Whitefield's own weakness. Wesley repudiated utterly the truth that Christ died only for his elect people, and he spoke of particular redemption as a failure of the cross. He vitiated the doctrine of irresistible grace, which he claimed to maintain, by balancing all salvation on the needle-point of man's free will.

The evidences of Wesley's Arminianism are numerous. In his controversies with Howell Harris, Whitefield, and Toplady, he showed a bitter antagonism against the truth of the gospel and of God's sovereign and particular grace. After the controversy with Toplady, he felt compelled to publish a *Manifesto*.

We have leaned too much towards Calvinism. Wherein?

With regard to *man's faithfulness*. Our Lord himself taught us to use this expression...

With regard to *working for life*. This also our Lord has expressly commanded us...

We have received it as a maxim, that "a man is to do nothing in order to justification." Nothing can be more false. Whoever desires to find favour with God should "cease from evil and learn to do well."

Review the whole affair: Who of us is *now* accepted of God? He that now believes in Christ with a loving and obedient heart.

As to *merit* itself, of which we have been so dreadfully afraid; we are rewarded "according to our works," yea, "because of our works." How does this differ from *for the sake of our works?* And how differs this from *secundum merita operum?* as our works *deserve?* Can you split this hair? I doubt I cannot [that, is, I have no doubt I cannot].

The grand objection to one of the preceding propositions is drawn from matter of fact. God does in fact justify those who, by their own confession, neither feared God nor wrought righteousness. Is this an exception to the general rule? It is a doubt, God makes any exception at all. But how are we sure that the person in question never did fear God and work righteousness? His own saying so is no proof; for we know how all that are convinced of sin undervalue themselves in every respect.

Does not talking of a justified or sanctified *state* tend to mislead men? almost naturally leading them to trust in what was done in one moment? *Whereas we are every hour and every moment pleasing or displeasing to God, according to our works; according to the whole of our inward tempers and our outward behaviour.*[11]

Wesley put sanctification before justification; he made sanctification dependent upon the human will; he taught that man is not only able to do good works but also that he merits by them; and, therefore, the whole of man's salvation turns on man's own choice.

He maintained as well the totally Arminian doctrines of a universal atonement, an atoning sacrifice of Jesus Christ that only makes salvation possible. He defined the gospel, in close connection with his erroneous views of the atonement, as an expression of God's willingness to save all men. He believed that those who never heard the gospel could be saved by the proper use of what natural light they possessed. Although giving the doctrine his own peculiar twist, he also taught perfectionism, that is, that the sinner can attain perfection in this life.

> Wesley regarded the religious consciousness as advancing from a lower to a higher condition; he believed in a law of ascending evolution, with a corresponding ascending scale of moral values and responsibilities. It is possible, while in the body, to reach a state of Christian perfection; but not of sinless perfection, for that would make of no account the sacrifice of Christ. "By perfection," said Wesley, "I mean perfect love, or the loving of God with all our heart, so as to rejoice evermore, to pray without ceasing, and in everything to give thanks. I am convinced every believer may attain this; yet I do not say he is in a state of damnation or under the curse of God till he does attain. No, he is in a state of grace, and in favour with God, as long as he believes."[12]

This is a remarkable statement. The only need we have for the cross of Christ, according to Wesley, is for the sins that remain after we have attained Christian perfection. That does not leave much for Christ to do.

John Wesley has cast this long shadow: his views are held everywhere.

What is so troubling is that those who profess to be Calvinists honor Wesley but ignore his hatred of Calvinism with his whole being. What is also troubling is that Wesley's doctrine of justification by works is being taught today by many within Reformed and Presbyterian churches. How few they be who hold to the truth of God's great grace in Jesus Christ given to poor sinners, so that God himself may receive all the glory for the riches of his sovereign mercy and love.

CHAPTER 28

FINNEY AND REVIVALISM

INTRODUCTION

Among the churches in some parts of Europe, particularly in the British Isles, revivalism is a popular conception. Churches that where once strong and vibrant have become lethargic and small, and they look to revival for deliverance from their present woes. Spiritually weak churches think that revival will be the solution to all their problems, and many prayers are made for this special outpouring of the Holy Spirit.

While such countries as the British Isles, perhaps especially Wales and Northern Ireland, have been noted for revivals in the past, this phenomenon has not been quite as common in America. From a certain point of view, Charles Grandison Finney can be called the father of American revivalism.

By calling Finney the father of revivalism, I do not mean to imply that America had not seen revivals prior to his time. In the first half of the eighteenth century, when George Whitefield came to the United States and worked in New England with Jonathan Edwards, revival came to the colonies there. Charles Finney did his work in the first half of the nineteenth century. His method of revivalism and the theological aspects of his evangelistic preaching left their indelible mark on American evangelicalism. And insofar as some still hope for revival, it is mostly of the type associated with Finney.

If Finney's method and theology are ostensibly rejected by some conservative churches and preachers who pray for revival, their search for a "better" form of revival leaves one puzzled. Finney borrowed heavily from John Wesley, who received favorable treatment from conservative churches in the British Isles. Wesley's revivals have become something for which conservative churches long. To approve of Wesleyan revivalism is, therefore, to approve of Finney's revival teachings.

Finney's influence is widespread. He is frequently appealed to as a model for modern evangelistic preaching, and his methods are said to be just what the church needs if it is engaging in the work of "saving souls."

FINNEY'S PRE-CONVERSION LIFE

Charles Finney's early life was unspectacular, with few evidences of what he would someday become. He was born August 29, 1792, in Warren, Connecticut, into a family of farmers. He was the seventh son of a Puritan family, and he was born and raised among those who for more than 160 years had attempted to maintain a Calvinistic religion in New England, where the Puritans had originally settled. Jonathan Edwards had given the colonies a strong Calvinism, and because of Edwards' association with the Whitefield revivals, revivalism had made an early mark on Finney. But it was also a time of national turmoil and change. The country had just emerged from its battle for freedom, and the Constitutional Convention was still fresh in the minds of people.

It was also a time when doughty settlers were pushing the boundaries of the country farther west with each passing month. On the frontier, tent meetings, emotional religion, hastily organized churches, and circuit preachers were the order of the day. By comparison with the yeasty frontier, Warren, Connecticut, was staid and bland. But superb educations were available on the eastern seaboard—something not true on the frontier. The move of the Finney family to Oneida, New York, a town in the western part of the state and considered part of the frontier, had a profound effect on Finney's educational career and religious viewpoint. He never became a highly educated person, but he did become a religious man.

Although the family was a part of the Presbyterian Church, Finney considered most of the preaching to be doctrinally dry. Apparently the same was true of the family, for after moving to Oneida, New York, the family worshiped in a Baptist church. A great deal of the preaching on the frontier was revivalistic and emotional. This type of preaching seemed to be more appealing to Finney. A religion that emphasized the knowledge of the truth was to him stodgy; a religion with an emotional appeal, and therefore more exciting, suited his tastes.

Finney did make an effort to continue his education. He enrolled in Warren Academy in the town where he had been born and stayed for two years. He was a good student and became proficient in music: voice, violin, and cello. For four years, from 1814 to 1818, Finney taught school, but he soon turned his attention to law. He returned to his home in Oneida and became an attorney's clerk. Although once again Finney attended a Calvinistic church, he really had no interest in theology or religion. He did study the Bible, as he tells us in his autobiography, but his interest in the Bible was due to his interest in law and the influence the Bible had on jurisprudence.[1]

Finney claims to have been converted in 1821. He describes his conversion, probably at a revival meeting, in these words: "The Holy Spirit descended upon me in a manner that seemed to *go through me,* body and soul. I could feel the impression, *like a wave of electricity,* going through and through me. Indeed it seemed to come in *waves,* and *waves of liquid love.*"[2] He claims to have been made a different man.

FINNEY'S POST-CONVERSION MINISTRY

Finney was committed from the outset of his "new" life to the notion that the choice of the human will was decisive in the work of conversion. From this Pelagian position he never wavered.

Finney committed himself to the ministry. As is so often true of new "converts," his first impulse was to preach that which he had come to believe. From 1822 to 1825 he studied for the ministry under his Presbyterian pastor, George W. Gale, during which time he also engaged in preaching. Finney claims that the committee of presbytery responsible for preaching in the district where he lived wanted him to go to Princeton, but that he refused because he was convinced that the students who studied there were all wrongly educated. Finney's pastor, however, said that the school was reluctant to take him.

Finney's preaching soon aroused curiosity and some excitement, for it seems that almost from the outset it resulted in the conversions of many people and frequently sparked revivals.

It was not long before Finney began to disagree with fundamental Calvinistic doctrines, notably the doctrines of original sin and limited atonement. He considered them to be unreasonable, unbiblical, and impractical from the viewpoint of evangelical preaching.

When Rev. Gale became ill, Finney was invited to fill his pulpit. This required that he appear before the presbytery. Under questioning by the presbytery, he was vague on the question of his agreement with the Westminster Standards, but he said that he was in substantial agreement with them. On the grounds of his use of the word *substantial,* he got by. In fact, he had never read the creeds completely, much less studied them.

Finney prided himself in never preparing sermons prior to preaching.

In fact, he sometimes entered the pulpit without even knowing what text he intended to use as the basis for his sermon. He thought that the Holy Spirit would give him his sermons and that preparation would be nothing but an obstacle to the free work of the Spirit. Without seminary training, admittedly hostile to some key doctrines in the Westminster Standards, and without any fixed charge, he was nevertheless ordained into the ministry as a full-time evangelist on July 1, 1824. Such action speaks loudly of the state of Calvinism in the Presbyterian churches in those years.

In the fall of 1824, Finney was married to Lydia Root Andrews. With her he had six children, one of whom died in childbirth and another as a child. An interesting story is told of his early married life. Apparently Finney found it necessary to move to the northern part of New York State. He had to go a considerable distance to obtain a cart in which to pack their belongings. While going to fetch the cart, he preached here and there and began revivals wherever he preached. The result was that he did not return to his wife with his cart for six months.

As Finney's work gained in popularity, he was invited to more and more churches that were considered "dead," although the definition of dead was not always clear. He sparked revivals in almost every place and considered his work successful only if a revival followed his preaching. In his preaching Finney required of his audience immediate decisions for Christ. In fact, he began the practice of using an anxious seat, a row or two in the front of the building to which seekers could come, and in which seat they were pressed for a decision. This idea of an anxious seat was the forerunner of the invitation system or altar call so common in present-day revivalism.

Finney's revivals were accompanied by noise, which sometimes was so great that all Finney could do was move about and holler the gospel into one ear, then into another. Bellowing, roaring, weeping, shouting, holy laughter: all kinds of bizarre behavior were the results of Finney's preaching, and such bizarre behavior was considered a sure sign of the presence of the Holy Spirit and the success of revival. Such activity was not unique to the Finney revivals; it was characteristic of revivals in New England and in the British Isles as well.

Finney's method was to preach sometimes every day of the week, visit people in their homes, hold inquiry meetings, roam about through the audience assembled to hear him, and summon people to the anxious seat. This was thought to increase pressure on people to make immediate decisions. His *Memoirs* are frequently boastful of his success.

Finney was soon invited to the big cities to perform his revivalistic work.

Philadelphia was a target city, and in it he gained the support of the Dutch Reformed minister and the German Reformed minister. In New York City he began a chapel in the city's most depraved area. The chapel became a church that grew rapidly, but the overwork soon brought Finney to the brink of bad health. As a result, he went by himself on what was scheduled to be a ten-month cruise in the Mediterranean Sea. In his absence, troubles arose in the church he had founded, and the life of the church deteriorated rapidly. He cut his trip short but seems to have lost his popularity in New York. This decrease in his popularity sapped his energies, for he apparently fed on acclaim.

In 1835 the Oberlin Institute in Ohio offered him a professorship in theology. He accepted this offer and began what amounted to a new career. Although he attempted to keep up his work in New York City, this proved to be impossible. For reasons of health and finances, he could not do both. Before resigning from the church in New York, Finney left the Presbyterian denomination in which he had worked all these years, and he organized the New York church as a congregational church. From henceforth his labors were as a congregationalist.

Finney mixed his work in Oberlin Institute with revival work. In Oberlin meetings were frequently held in a tent, which seated as many as one thousand people. This was the beginning of the tent revivals common in America in the first half of the twentieth century.

Finney's wife died in 1847 after many years of poor health and many trials, including the care of a mentally handicapped girl, the death of a son-in-law, and her husband's own poor health. Finney married again in 1848, but his second wife, Elizabeth, died in 1863 in the middle of the Civil War. His third wife was Rebecca Allen Baze, whom he married when he was seventy-eight years old and Rebecca forty-one. Finney died in August of 1875.

THE STATE OF THE PRESBYTERIAN CHURCH

The Presbyterian Church in the United States had been the only strong representative in America of Calvinistic Presbyterianism. It was established prior to the Revolutionary War as early as 1611, and some Presbyterians were active in the struggle for independence from Great Britain. It was, on the whole, strongly Calvinistic and was faithful to the Westminster Standards after they were adopted in 1647. Princeton Seminary, founded in 1812, became the citadel of Calvinistic Presbyterianism under the leadership of Archibald Alexander and Samuel Miller.

Presbyterianism, however, had been seriously divided from the 1740s when Gilbert Tennant began what became known as "New Side Presbyterianism." For many decades a struggle went on within Presbyterianism between New Side and Old Side Presbyterians. The Old Side was strongly committed to the confessions of the church, taught and fought for a consistent Calvinism, and emphasized knowledge of the truth as essential for the Christian life. New Side Presbyterianism was much more loosely committed to the creeds, tended to be far more ecumenical in its thinking, and wanted to put the emphasis on church life, not in the local congregations, but on evangelistic efforts. The division was so sharp and deep that it eventually brought about a split within the denomination in 1837, a split that was healed in later years at great cost to the doctrinal integrity of American Presbyterianism.

Finney, in his evangelistic work, was influenced by many factors. Among the most important was the evangelistic labors of John Wesley with his emphasis on post-conversion holiness. He also read avidly, especially the works of Jonathan Edwards and his reshaped Calvinism. He was sympathetic, too, and in agreement with New School Presbyterians (which New Side people were sometimes called). In fact, Finney stayed in the Presbyterian Church as long as he did because he wanted to do battle with Old School members of the church.

New School Presbyterians readily embraced Finney and his evangelistic labors, but Old School men opposed him. These attacks came chiefly from Princeton, and some heresy trials were held of followers of Finney, but in every case Finneyites were acquitted. Presbyterianism simply could not summon the spiritual strength to condemn Finney and his teachings. It was a sad commentary on the denomination.

FINNEY'S THEOLOGICAL VIEWS

Soon after Finney's conversion he abandoned the doctrines of original sin and limited atonement. He considered them to be barriers to evangelistic work and unreasonable in any case. But once having committed himself to a Pelagian position, he could not stop there. In a debate with a universalist, Finney adopted the governmental theory of the atonement of Jesus Christ. This theory, first proposed by the Arminians in the Netherlands in the later part of the sixteenth century, taught that Christ's death was not a vicarious or substitutionary death nor a propitiatory death, but was simply an example of what God could have done to us if he had chosen to be strictly just. But now God forgoes his justice in the interests of his mercy and tells sinners that although he could do to them what he did to Christ, he will not punish them if they accept Christ as their Savior.

Such a view of the atonement, one that destroys the atonement altogether, is a necessary consequence of maintaining that Christ died for every man, head for head, even though all are not saved. And it fits in perfectly with the Arminian position of free will, for it makes man's freewill choice to accept Christ the decisive act of salvation. Finney's Arminianism reflected itself in his preaching; two of the favorite themes in his sermons were "Sinners Bound to Change Their Own Hearts" and "How to Change Your Hearts."

We must not conclude from all this that Finney was vitally interested in doctrine. Finney was an ardent ecumenist, as all defenders of revivalism must be. In his ecumenical frenzy, Finney was doctrinally indifferent. He did not care about differences in doctrine between churches, and he had no interest in studying and developing doctrine, even though he was professor of theology at Oberlin College.

Finney's reading of perfectionist literature, especially of John Wesley, led him to embrace the idea that a converted sinner could give perfect obedience to the law of God. This was in keeping with his denial of original sin. Finney, along with Pelagians throughout the ages, denied that sin was in the nature but said that it was limited to the actions of people. Hence "entire sanctification" is a matter of the activity of a person, not his nature. Entire sanctification does not imply any change in the powers of a person, good to begin with; only the right use of these powers is required and the sinner's successful efforts to put them to good use. This is a superficial view of sin that denies what every believer knows full well: that he is by nature prone to hate God and his neighbor. Finney did admit, however, that a man could make mistakes and not always feel at peace, even though he had attained perfection. Even New School Presbyterians balked at Finney's brand of perfectionism.

FINNEY'S MYSTICISM

Revivalism is inherently mystical. Finney claimed to have direct revelations from God and said that he was guided in what he did and where he went by inner voices or feelings that revealed God's will to him. When he faced opposition, he resorted to closet prayer and wrote that he met God as Moses did on Sinai: "The Lord showed me as in a vision what I had to pass through. He drew so near to me . . . that *my flesh literally trembled on my bones*. I shook from head to foot, like a man with an ague fit."[3]

Robert Evans, the chief figure in the 1904–1905 Welsh revivals, also claimed to have occasional conversations with God over a period of three or four months. Evans described the first such conversation in a letter to a friend in which he spoke of being awakened by God, visiting with God for three or four hours, and enjoying face-to-face conversation. Evans reported this in spite of the fact that John says in his gospel, "No man hath seen God at any time" (John 1:18).

Finney also spoke of a further baptism of the Spirit after conversion and thus paved the way for modern pentecostalism.

FINNEY'S SOCIAL GOSPEL

Finney was deeply involved in social betterment. Early in his work in various parts of New York, he adopted what can only be called an evangelistic and social-reform Calvinism. He established mission societies, frequently composed of women who supported and helped him in his work. In fact, a women's mission society was established in western New York State that commissioned Finney to preach and supported him financially. Finney encouraged women to be busy in missions and to participate so fully in the work that they also preached.

Finney was also busy in temperance work and joined with the temperance movement in any effort to rid the country of the evils of drinking.

As the Civil War approached, Finney began an abolitionist crusade and involved himself deeply in the efforts to secure the freedom of slaves. So strongly did he preach abolition in his church in New York that during his absence to the Mediterranean Sea to recuperate from exhaustion, his church was the scene of terrible riots between abolitionist and pro-slavery citizens of New York City.

REVIVALISM

Finney is noted above all for his revivals. His reputation as an outstanding teacher and preacher is staked on his success as a revivalist. Proponents of revivalism are ready to overlook his doctrinal aberrations, his poor preparation for preaching, his opposition to Calvinism, and his disdain for the established church in their support of his revivalistic teachings.

Totally apart from the question of the biblical condemnation of revivalism, Finney's views on revival were so contrary to Scripture that one wonders how anyone who has a semblance of understanding of Scripture can possibly approve of Finney's work.

In 1835 Finney published his *Lectures on Revivals of Religion.* He boasted in his *Memoirs* that the book enjoyed wide sales. In a book about Charles Finney, Charles E. Hambrick-Stowe writes,

> He [Finney] rejoiced in the *Memoirs* that the book did well in America (12,000 copies sold immediately), went through numerous editions in England (several hundred thousand copies were in print by the mid-1840s), and quickly achieved worldwide distribution. The Welsh translation sparked a notable revival in Wales, and it was soon translated into French as well...
>
> In his *Lectures on Revivals*, Charles Finney argued provocatively that just as "religion is the work of man" and "consists in obeying God," so a revival of religion is an essentially human activity. Contrary to the traditional Edwardsian view of them as a "surprising work of God" that could not be predicted or precipitated, Finney always believed that a revival was the "purely philosophical result of the right use of constituted means." In other words, if a preacher delivered the right gospel message, extemporaneously and with appropriate enthusiasm, and if the work was accompanied with faithful prayer, a revival could be expected. "A revival of religion is not a miracle," he wrote, in one of the most controversial sentences in American religious history; it is not "something above the powers of nature" but results from "the *right* exercise of the powers of nature." Old School and even moderate Presbyterian critics would have a field day with this, but Finney cared nothing for their opinion. In his view, he was simply updating the old doctrine of the "means of grace" with effective "new measures" and carrying on the spirit (if not the letter) of Jonathan Edwards's example, as his lengthy quotations from Edwards suggest.[4]

Finney was of the opinion that he alone was capable of bringing about revivals. He thought that he alone knew how to accomplish this, by which boasting he either left out the Holy Spirit altogether or considered himself a very special agent of the Holy Spirit.

Finney's entire work was fatally flawed by his departures from the teachings of Holy Scripture.

His life revolved around revivals. He developed a doctrine of revivals in which he claimed that revivals were brought about by men, seeming to eliminate the Holy Spirit's work altogether. He claimed that in his day, revival could only be brought by him, which was true. When he went on a cruise in the Mediterranean Sea, or when on three different occasions he went to England, revivalism in America disappeared and churches fell back into spiritual lethargy.

It is clear that many supporters of revivalism appeal to the divine origin of revivals on the grounds that there is no other explanation for what takes place at a revival than that it is the work of the Holy Spirit. I shall not attempt to engage in a religious or psychological explanation for the bizarre behavior that frequently characterizes revivals, or even for the mass turn-ings to religion that are supposed to be the fruits of revivals. Mass hysteria explains much of it, especially because of what the Welsh, famous for their revivals, call a *hywl*. This term is used to describe the peculiar tone of voice and inflection that a revival preacher uses to arouse people's emotions and to bring about what is truly a hypnotic state.

Hugh L. Williams writes the following concerning Finney:

> In the first quarter of the nineteenth century came the theology and practice of that arch-Pelagian Charles Grandison Finney, with his "new measures." Finney organized the "anxious seat" method, in which new converts were exhorted to come to the front of the meeting and make profession of their faith, a practice that still characterizes much of evangelicalism to this day. In addition, Finney was able to deploy certain personal characteristics he had developed, the virtually hypnotic state, the sustained emotional harangue, and the branding of local ministers and elders as failures and hypocrites because their churches were (by Finney's standard) "dead." This contagious egocentric wrote voluminously, and his literature on "revival" amounted to being a manual of "how-to-do-it."[5]

No Revivals in Scripture

If one attempts to find any evidence of revivals taking place in Bible times and recorded in Scripture, one's search is futile. Scripture gives no evidence of anything approaching revivals. Defenders of revivals attempt to show that Scripture does contain records of revivals by appealing to reformations brought about in Israel during the times of Samuel (1 Sam. 7:1–12) and reformations such as took place during the reigns of Asa (2 Chron. 15), Hezekiah (2 Chron. 29–31), and Josiah (2 Chron. 34, 35:1–19). But there are three reasons that an appeal to these reformations is spurious. First, they bear no resemblance to the revivals that have taken place in our dispensation. Second, modern-day revivals are defined as being special visitations of the Holy Spirit, but this could not have happened in the Old Testament times because "the Holy Ghost was not yet given" (John 7:39). Third, Israel was a picture not of a given nation such as America or Wales, but of the spiritual church of Christ. God preserved the church of Christ through the means of occasional good kings who brought about a measure of reformation so that Christ could come in the fullness of time, but such reformations have no resemblance to revivals.

Others appeal to Pentecost as a revival. How foolish such an appeal is. As the fulfillment of Christ's promise of the Spirit of truth in John 14, 15, and 16, the ascended Christ poured out his Spirit upon the church at Pentecost for the first time. That outpouring of the Spirit was not accompanied by bizarre behavior and strange conduct, but by signs that spoke of the work of the Spirit in the people of God and in the new dispensational church. It was a once-for-all event, though the Spirit continues in the church forever in the same way he was present with the church on Pentecost.

REVIVALS AND THE CHURCH INSTITUTE

Revivalists work in biblically wrong ways because of their disdain for the church institute.

Christ has established the church institute in the world for the sole purpose of preaching the gospel. The task of preaching the gospel is given to the church institute, and it is the only institution in the world that has the *right* to preach the gospel. By the preaching of the gospel through the church institute, Christ "gathers, defends, and preserves" his church.[6] This task the church performs through ministers who are sent by, are under the direction of, and are answerable to the church. Revivals were mostly carried on by itinerant preachers, holding office in no church, working entirely on their own, preaching without ecclesiastical credentials, and answerable to no ecclesiastical body. Christ does not work that way.

Revivalists, with their frequent indifference to doctrine, are almost always broadly ecumenical. Apart from their personal beliefs, they are willing to cooperate with anyone and everyone in spite of heresy and unbiblical teachings. Arminians, Pelagians, deniers of infant baptism—revival brushes these all aside in the name of restoring spirituality to the church. In other words, in their revivalistic work they believe that the Holy Spirit, the Spirit whom Christ has given to the church to lead her into all truth, no longer cares about truth.

Revivalists do not seek the unity of the church but are divisive in their work and frequently bring schism to the church. Charles Hodge makes this a major point in his scathing critique of revivals in the introduction to the book *The Constitutional History of the Presbyterian Church*. Revivalists damn the church as dead. They frequently enter congregations without the approval of the office bearers and begin to preach to the people, they charge the ministers with being unregenerate if they refuse to cooperate with revivalistic efforts, and they do their work independent of the church in which they are working.

Revivalists have a truncated view of the gospel and fail to distinguish between preaching in the established church and evangelistic preaching on the mission field. Hughes Oliphant Old, in discussing the preaching of Clement of Alexandria, calls attention to Clement's preaching that made no distinction between preaching in the church and "evangelistic" preaching.

> Our sermon [the sermon of Clement on which the author is commenting] ends by calling all who are present to repentance. The preacher begs his listeners to repent from the bottom of their hearts that they might be saved. Evangelism did not require a special message preached for the unconverted different from the one for the converted, nor did it mandate that the faithful hear and enthusiastically support again and again evangelistic sermons that were not really directed to them. Rather, when Christ is proclaimed as Lord and Savior, when God's promises are proclaimed and a witness is given that God is faithful and that in Christ those promises have been fulfilled, and will yet be fulfilled, then evangelism is done. When this kind of preaching is done, God's people hear this witness and believe it, and believing it they praise God that this is indeed true. Whenever the way of life which Christ taught his disciples is shown to be the fulfillment of the Law and the prophets, then evangelism is done. Whenever the beauty and the power and the sheer joy of holiness are proclaimed and God's people see that this is something for them, evangelism is done. When Christian preaching is done the way it should be done, then it is evangelistic.[7]

REVIVALISM AND THE COVENANT

Revivalism does not and cannot have any proper conception of the covenant of grace. This charge is true on especially two counts. It has no biblical conception of the place of children in the covenant, and consequently has a wrong view of conversion; it lacks a proper and biblical conception of how God works salvation organically in the line of the covenant. About both I must say something further.

Revivalism has no biblical conception of the place of children in the covenant. The teaching of Scripture and the Reformed confessions is that children, as well as adults, belong to the covenant of grace. This does not mean only that children of believing parents are born *outwardly* in the covenant and *outwardly* receive the privileges of the covenant. That children belong to God's covenant as well as adults means that the elect children of believing parents are in that relationship of friendship between God and his people, which is the essence of salvation, and thus are given all the blessings of salvation that adults have, though according to the measure of their understanding and faith. God saves such children.

Revivalism holds that most people are unconverted, whether in the church or outside it. Revivalists look upon the churches as dead, chiefly because they are filled with unconverted people, including office bearers and even ministers. They say that such a state of unconversion within the churches persists and seemingly grows worse. Revival is the one thing that can bring change. When revival comes, along with it come mass conversions. Hundreds and thousands are brought under the conviction of sin and are introduced to the happiness that forgiveness can bring. The whole process, brought about by the revivalists, is accompanied by mass meetings, emotional preaching, and the most outrageous behavior imaginable. Especially the strange and wrong behavior is supposed to be indicative of true conversion, although even then, experts in what constitutes true conversion are sometimes required to judge whether a person's experiences are genuine, for room is allowed for the deception of the devil, who likes nothing better than to give people a false sense of being converted, for that is the surest way to hell.

Add to all this mix the Arminian gospel of Finney along with his anxious seat, and you have a situation where true conversion is the work of man, brought about by the revivalist, who presses the claims of the gospel and demands an immediate decision, but who assures you that the final decision is yours to make.

How much more God-glorifying is the way the Holy Spirit saves. Without contesting the fact that sudden and remarkable conversions may take place on the mission field, especially in those foreign fields where the gospel has never been preached, we insist that even on the mission field, the Holy Spirit as the Spirit of Christ saves believers and their seed. He saves households, not individuals. He brings into the fellowship of the church covenant families, not solitary souls.

And when, within the covenant, the Holy Spirit works conversion, he does so in the elect children of believers in their infancy, or even before birth (Jer. 1:5). When the Holy Spirit works conversion, he works it in such a way that it is a quiet, all but unnoticed work in the heart of the elect sinner. He works not through the earthquake, the fierce wind, or the fire of revivals, but through the still, small voice of his irresistible power, transforming the heart and mind (1 Kings 19:9–18). He works through the elect believer's life so that daily the believer is brought to the consciousness of sin, flees to the cross, and finds peace in the blood of his Savior. He works so that the believer daily fights with sin within and without and finds in the cross strength for battle. He works like a fern that I once saw, the spore of which was buried beneath the asphalt road, but that slowly, without daily measurable growth, unnoticed, nevertheless was able to force its way through two inches of tarmac.

This was the lesson Elijah had to learn. He thought revival had come on Mt. Carmel when all the people shouted, "Jehovah, he is the God" (1

Kings 18:39). But he found that once Carmel's revival was over, Israel returned, as converts frequently do after revival, to their deadly normal way of life. He had to learn that fire, thunder, earthquakes, and wind will not accomplish God's purpose. The still, small voice of the Holy Spirit reserves to God seven thousand who refuse to bow the knee to Baal (1 Kings 19:18; Rom. 11:4).

REVIVALISM AND PREACHING

Because it is God's purpose to save in the line of generations and so to accomplish his decree of election, so it is also God's purpose to accomplish reprobation in the line of generations. God visits the iniquity of the fathers upon the children unto the third and fourth generation of them that hate him (Ex. 20:5). Thus when individuals forsake the church and turn their backs on the true gospel, these go lost in their generations. It is true that as generations go lost, God saves a remnant out of these generations. Much of home missions consists of that work. But the time comes when a church (or a family within the church), once having departed from the way of truth, becomes the false church in which the blood of atonement is denied. So it was in the northern kingdom of Israel; so it is today.

In this way God completes his work. He saves the true human race of eternal election. That human race must be and is gathered from all the nations of the earth. Jesus points to the fact that one of the signs of his second coming is that "this gospel of the kingdom shall be preached in all the world for a witness unto all nations; and then shall the end come" (Matt. 24:14). The end comes because the gospel, having gone throughout all nations, has gathered the elect from all nations. But God's work is always perfect. That same gospel has accomplished its sovereign purpose of hardening, and the whole world has, through its rejection of the gospel, become ripe for judgment.

God always performs his work in an orderly way. What is done in the church must be done decently and in good order because God does things in an orderly fashion. By contrast, revivalism teaches that God, through special outpourings of the Holy Spirit, returns again and again to a dead church to bring revival. In other words, a church dies; the Holy Spirit brings revival. The same church dies again, and revival comes again. And so it goes, on and on without any end. But God does not work this way. He does his work throughout history. He causes the gospel to be preached and saves, in the line of generations, believers and their seed. He also hardens, in the line of generations, unbelievers and their seed. In such a way the church is gathered from all nations and tribes and tongues, and the wicked are hardened in their sin and become ripe for judgment.

But the power is always the preaching. The Heidelberg Catechism makes part of the church's confession this statement: "That the Son of God, by his Spirit and Word, gathers, defends, and preserves for himself unto everlasting life, a chosen communion in the unity of the true faith; and that I am, and forever shall remain, a living member of the same."[8] It is not revival that the church needs, but preaching. It is not special out-pourings of the Spirit with strange manifestations of power; it is the pure preaching of the gospel. It is Christ-centered, biblical, confessional, ex-pository, lively preaching of the word. How sad it is when the church looks to revivals that will never come except in a form that does violence to all that Scripture teaches concerning God's way of saving his church. All the while, true preaching falls in the streets.

Let the church, then, tend to her task of preaching. When the church preaches, it is faithful to her divine commission. Then the Holy Spirit will work by the still, small voice of his efficacious power to save those ordained to eternal life, and God will accomplish his purpose to the glory of his name.

CHAPTER 29

DARWIN AND EVOLUTIONISM

INTRODUCTION

One of the great battles in which the church is engaged today is the defense of the doctrine of creation over against the theory of evolution. If secular and unbelieving science promoted evolution as an explanation of the origin of the creation, the church would not be unduly threatened; nothing of any value for the church comes from unbelief. But the church has sold out to this destructive heresy. One cannot find a major denomination that has not made its peace with evolutionary theory. This is disturbing and unsettling, for it is hard to imagine how a church that confesses that its faith is found in Scripture can so cavalierly and wickedly, like Esau, sell its birthright for a mess of distasteful and inedible pottage. This is what the church has done, thus bringing itself into agreement with secular humanism, ungodly scientism, and apostate Christianity. It is well, therefore, that we give some consideration to this subject of evolutionism and its evils.

CHARLES DARWIN, FOUNDER OF EVOLUTIONISM

It is actually incorrect to call Charles Darwin the "founder" of evolutionism. Some thinkers prior to Darwin had already suggested that life developed here on earth through slow processes over long periods of time, but their views never were widely accepted—partly because these thinkers were abstruse and difficult to understand, and partly because they had never given any good explanation of how such processes took place.

Furthermore, Darwin's theory did not spring from his head without other previously developed ideas by earlier scientists who profoundly influenced him. An example of such a scientist, and probably a most important example, is Charles Lyell, who developed the theory of uniformitarianism. I will discuss this later, for it enters into our discussion at critical points.

Yet Darwin did popularize the theory of evolution, made it widely known, and gave the first explanation of how evolutionary processes supposedly take place. He is, therefore, rightly given the credit for discovering it.

Darwinian evolutionism, as it is sometimes called, has been modified a great deal since Darwin published his famous work, *On the Origin of Species.* To describe Darwin's theory, therefore, is to open oneself to the criticism that Darwin's views have been outdated, that what he said is no longer applicable to evolutionary thought, and that one who criticizes his ideas is purposelessly waving his arms in the air. Nevertheless, the fundamentals of all evolutionary thought are to be found in Darwin's books, and we are interested in the fundamentals, not the details. We deal, therefore, with the ideas of Charles Darwin himself.

DARWIN'S LIFE

Charles Darwin was born of Robert and Susannah Darwin on February 12, 1809, in Shrewsbury, Shropshire, England. His mother died when Charles was eight years old, and he was raised by his sister Caroline.

Although he developed early an interest in collecting all sorts of things —pebbles, pieces of string, odds and ends found here and there—he was a very poor student in the local school in Shrewsbury. His father sharply reprimanded him for his disinterest in his studies: "You care for nothing but shooting, dogs, and rat-catching, and you will be a disgrace to yourself and all your family."[1]

The reprimand seemed to fall on deaf ears, even when Charles was sent to school in Edinburgh, Scotland, to study medicine. He failed his courses, far preferring to collect marine animals, go trawling with fishermen for oysters, and skin and stuff birds.

In desperation, Charles' father did what so many parents in similar circumstances did: he sent Charles to Cambridge to study for Orders in the Church of England. He was destined to become a prelate in this church. His professors left little mark on him, however, for Charles never did much studying, preferring rather to spend his time with his cronies riding and hunting.

There was one exception: a professor of botany sparked in Charles an interest in natural history. This was to be a turning point in his life. While continuing his careless or carefree ways, he did give himself to a diligent study of natural history, with much of his study done on his own initiative.

Charles succeeded in making himself so well acquainted with this subject that when a call went out for a naturalist to sail on a government-sponsored expedition to collect scientific data, Charles applied. With the help of others, he managed to get the appointment. In 1831, at the age of twenty-two, he sailed on the HMS *Beagle* to the coasts of Patagonia and to Tierra del Fuego, Chile, Peru, and some Pacific islands. The five-year-long journey of the *Beagle* brought him also to Tahiti, New Zealand, Australia, and Brazil.

While the ship was at the Cape Verde Islands, Darwin read Lyell's writings and learned of the principle of uniformitarianism, a principle that was to form the foundation for all his theories.

Darwin remained extremely busy on the entire trip. He collected specimens of species of all kinds: sea creatures, land animals, beetles, birds, vegetation, flowers, and the like. He also went on many long expeditions into the interior of the countries visited by the *Beagle*. These expeditions were frequently dangerous, but riding on horseback with others, he collected and indulged in his lifelong love, hunting with a gun. Yet when he discovered a poor creature wounded because his shot had not been fatal, he vowed never to shoot anything again—a vow that he kept.

During this long expedition Darwin wrote a number of books, most of which have been forgotten.

Returning from the expedition, Darwin worked for twenty years until, in 1856, encouraged by others, he began work on his book *On the Origin of Species*. He finished it in 1859, and it was an immediate success. The first edition was sold out in a few months, and by 1872 six editions had been published.

Darwin married and had ten children, two of whom died in infancy and one at the age of ten.

Darwin died of an undiagnosed disease. Since his death, by a study of the symptoms that his doctors had recorded, physicians are sure that he died of Chagas Disease, an infection that involves extreme fatigue, heart blockage, and intestinal discomfort. The infection was most likely brought on by a bug he caught while in South America. He died on April 19, 1882, at the age of seventy-three. The honor in which he was held can be measured by the fact that he was buried in Westminster Abbey in London.

DARWIN'S VIEWS

Darwin's evolutionary theories were much more limited than today's elaborate defenses and descriptions of evolution. Darwin knew nothing of the so-called big bang theory, and he was unconcerned with the universe prior to the appearance of life. His work was limited to the development of life on our planet, from early and simple forms of life to later and more complex forms.

Darwin was interested in explaining *natural history,* the history of living creatures. He was convinced that this history could be explained only in terms of the natural development of lower and simpler forms of life into higher and more complex forms of life. The question was, How did this take place?

Darwin's two principles, found in his *On the Origin of Species,* are the basic building blocks of all evolutionary theory. His first principle was natural selection, or the survival of the fittest. By this principle Darwin meant that some creatures, because of certain characteristics they possess, are more able to survive in a hostile environment, while some creatures are less able to survive and quickly perish. Those who survive pass on to their posterity those characteristics that enable them to survive the longest. The result is a strengthening of these characteristics and an improvement of the species' ability to adapt to their environment.

The second principle was that new species can be produced by earlier species. Darwin claimed that this is possible partly because the stronger a species became through its ability to adapt to its environment, the greater the likelihood that these stronger species will become new species. Also new species develop because, over long periods of time, genetic mutations take place that produce new characteristics in certain individuals in the species. Mostly these changes are for the worse, and those creatures that carry such changes soon perish. But if these mutations or changes enable a creature to survive better, they are passed on to its descendants, so that gradually new species emerge. Hence all living creatures develop from lower forms of life and, very far in the distant past, from one common ancestor.

Underlying these principles on which Darwin based his theory was a more fundamental principle, the principle of uniformitarianism, which teaches that one can learn how creatures operated thousands, millions, or billions of years ago based on the way those creatures operate today. To put it a bit differently, the laws by which creatures function are constant from their beginning to the present, without any variation whatsoever. What is most significant for our purposes is that evolutionism teaches that death did not come with sin and the curse as the punishment for sin, but was always present from the moment the first living organism evolved.

Theistic evolutionists, to whom we shall give some consideration a bit later in the chapter, spin out their theories on the same basis. All evolutionism, in whatever form it takes, presupposes that this present world has always been as it is now.

Peter, in the third chapter of his second epistle, expressly denies uniformitarianism. Peter reminds us that scoffers who deny Christ's coming are always present in the church (v. 3). The basis for their denial of Christ's coming is their assumption of the principle of uniformitarianism: "All things continue as they were from the beginning of the creation" (v. 4). Peter repudiates this claim and points to the flood to demonstrate that the earth is significantly different today than when God created it. The flood made vast changes in a world that was standing out of the water and in the water, while the world that now is, is reserved unto fire (vv. 5–7). We know from Paul in Romans 5:12–14 that an earlier catastrophe was the fall of Adam and resulting death because of the curse God pronounced upon the creation. The principle of uniformitarianism is invalid, and it is impossible to argue back to what the pre-flood and pre-fall world was like on the basis of its characteristics today.

DARWIN'S ATHEISM

Uniformitarianism naturally led Darwin to abandon the Christian faith. The *Encyclopedia Britannica* best describes Darwin's spiritual decline.

> The former candidate for Holy Orders had come to see that the Old Testament, "from manifestly false history of the earth, . . . and from its attributing to God the feelings of a revengeful tyrant, was no more to be trusted than the sacred books of the Hindoos, or the beliefs of any barbarian." The New Testament did not fare any better, and he could "indeed hardly see how anyone ought to wish Christianity to be true; for if so, the plain language of the text seems to show that the men who do not believe, and this would include my Father, Brother, and almost all my best friends, will be everlastingly punished. And this a damnable doctrine." The key to understanding Darwin's thinking is his horror of the imposition of suffering—on slaves by their masters, on animals by men, and by "the clumsy, wasteful, blundering, low and horribly cruel works of nature," as seen in the suffering caused by parasites and in the delight in cruelty shown by some predators when catching and playing with their prey. If God is as almighty, omniscient, and possessed of inexhaustible compassion as he is painted, "it revolts our understanding to suppose that his benevolence is not unbounded." So Darwin became a reverent agnostic.[2]

SUMMARY

Darwin's *On the Origin of Species* had more influence on subsequent thought than many other books of human writing, even though all the influence was bad. It was an extraordinarily clever tool in the determination of wicked men to drive God, the creator of all, out of his own world. No longer was a creator needed: evolution could explain how all things come into being without God.

Evolutionism has spread through the whole world and has been accepted by almost everyone who thinks about these things at all. In fact, so all-pervasive has evolutionary thought become that the church, called to defend the scriptural doctrine of creation, lives in an extremely hostile environment, in which it is fiercely threatened.

The theory of evolution has developed far beyond Darwin's description of it. All things that exist—not only living creatures—are now considered to be due to evolutionary processes. The whole universe, blown apart by one "big bang," has developed into its present form through evolution. Planet Earth, in all its rich diversity, has come from one infinitesimally small speck, and life itself was brewed by some natural processes when the first one-celled creature emerged from the soup of some primordial swamp. Powerful are the forces of darkness; small in number are those who still stand for God's truth.

THEISTIC EVOLUTIONISTS

Many in the church, and their numbers are legion, are convinced that evolutionism is perfectly compatible with the Christian faith. Such thinking goes back a long way. Even during Darwin's lifetime, some thought that Darwin's views constituted no threat to the church.

The Presbyterian tradition in this country, even in its days of strong Calvinism, was open to evolutionism. Charles Hodge, in the glory days of Princeton Seminary, allowed for the possibility of evolutionary development as an explanation for creation, and even J. Gresham Machen, the spiritual father of the Orthodox Presbyterian Church, would not commit himself on the question, arguing that the matter was one of science, not theology.

In Reformed circles the same has been true. The result is that today very few denominations can be found where evolutionism has not made its inroads. Some synods and general assemblies have openly gone on record as favoring some sort of evolutionism. One must go hunting with a strong spotlight to find creationists in today's churches.

In a discussion of evolutionism in the *Encyclopedia of Christianity*, several conclusions are drawn.

> Contrary to some opinions, Christian theology has been engaged with evolutionary ideas for two centuries, although that engagement has in many instances

been implicit, rather than explicit. In the 20th century that engagement has reached a high level of explicitness and sophistication...

Most important, even though there is a staggering variety of style and disposition among the thinkers in this survey, there is also one pervading concern and theme: that evolutionary ideas not be restricted to the materialist and reductionist interpretation that proponents of scientism tend to propound. Theologians in the main are convinced both that Christian theology can take the measure of evolution and that the idea of evolution is congenial to interpretations that bring ultimacy, transcendence, purpose, and moral earnestness into play. Scientific humanists deny this proposal, joined, ironically, by creationist thinkers; both groups insist that evolution is nothing but a materialist interpretation of the world. Interestingly, the theologians who offer a broad interpretation of evolution are joined by humanists and others of a naturalist bent who will not settle for a narrow, one-dimensional interpretation of evolution.[3]

In another paragraph, which discusses the views of Teilhard de Chardin, the French Roman Catholic paleontologist, such a synthesis of creationism and evolutionism is explained in more detail.

Teilhard comes as close as any thinker to a Trinitarian synthesis: the origins of the cosmos lie in God, who has set evolution into motion, giving it direction and meaning in Christ; the evolutionary process is in itself the providential working of God, who brings all reality, including what we call evil, to a divine consummation that is coincident with what is revealed in Christ. Teilhard invoked the "cosmic Christ" tradition, which is epitomized in Col. 1:17, according to which Christ himself "is before all things, and in him all things hold together." No other Christian thinker has used evolutionary ideas more powerfully and fashioned so full a Christian synthesis on the basis of evolution. Although his architectonic proposals are at points hardly more than a sketch and sometimes highly ambiguous and controversial, they rise as a monumental achievement of constructive Christian theological engagement with the idea of evolution.[4]

Del Ratzsch points out that while *"creationists and naturalistic evolutionists agree on very few things* ... [they] do seem to agree that theistic evolution is woefully—even perniciously—confused. Surprisingly enough, their reasons sometimes overlap."[5]

In short, theistic evolutionists try to "have their cake and eat it, too." They cave in completely to modern evolutionary thought while still trying desperately to hold on to the biblical doctrine of creation. They persuade themselves that they succeed by teaching that while evolution is an adequate and correct view of the origin of the universe, God controlled evolutionary processes.

THEISTIC EVOLUTIONISTS AND SCRIPTURE

Especially in conservative Reformed and Presbyterian circles, such a theistic evolutionism has to be justified with Scripture. In spite of the fact that Darwin himself considered this absolutely impossible, today's theologians each have their turn at attempting this hermeneutical legerdemain.

Some scientists simply separate their scientific activity from their religion. They claim to be evolutionists in the laboratory or observatory as they study the stars, but believers in Jesus Christ and in his word while in church on Sunday. This was the position of Howard Van Till in his book *The Fourth Day*.[6] If scientific theory and religion conflict, it is of no matter because science and religion need not harmonize, and life can, apparently, be easily categorized with compartments kept separate from the other. It is something like the "Sunday-go-to-church" Christianity.

Theistic evolutionists claim that it is necessary to believe in evolutionism because science has conclusively proved its validity. They point to the fact that this present creation is also created by the word of God and is, therefore, itself a word of God. God's word appears in two places: Scripture and creation. Because God is one, his word is one, and, therefore, his word in creation cannot contradict his word in Scripture. Since his word in creation speaks of a very old world (about 10 billion years), and since creation tells us things came into existence by development from lower and simpler forms of life to higher and more complex forms of life, our understanding of Scripture must be wrong. Scripture must obviously be reinterpreted.

It is something like a case of an honest, God-fearing grocery store owner being robbed at gunpoint by a murderous crook. Investigating the incident, the crook tells the police that the store owner gave him everything from the store, while the owner says that the criminal boldly threatened his life. The policeman, content to adopt the crook's version, tells the store owner that he must have been under the influence of a powerful narcotic when he gave all those things to the crook, or that his description of the robbery cannot be taken literally. The owner really meant that his gift to the robber can be construed as robbery because his conscience so smote him when he saw the poverty of the crook that it compelled him to give the store's contents to the crook. So theistic evolutionists are ready to sell out Scripture for evolutionism, and they do it by explaining that the scriptural narrative of creation cannot possibly be taken literally.

The numerous ways in which theistic evolutionists explain the scriptural narrative of creation in Genesis 1–3 are more than we can describe here. It seems that every few years a new idea comes along to explain away the first three chapters of Genesis. My first experience was with the gap theory, a claim that millions of years existed between Genesis 1:1 and Genesis 1:2. Then came the period theory, which interprets the "days" of Genesis 1 as long periods of time. Following the period theory came various theories that explained Genesis 1 as a doxology of praise to God for his participation in the work of creation. Genesis 1 was not the recitation of actual history; it was a symbolic hymn. Then we were told that the first chapters of Genesis were an attempt to give a Christian construction of ancient pagan myths concerning the origin of things. Howard Van Till introduced the packaging theory of Genesis 1. Next the framework hypothesis was introduced. I am sure that some fertile mind will propound yet another theory before long.

Theistic evolutionists have fatally compromised the biblical doctrine of creation and sold out to unbelieving science. To accomplish this, they have reinterpreted and misinterpreted Scripture, especially the first three chapters of Genesis. Realizing that these chapters are not the only parts of Scripture that need reinterpreting to defend their viewpoint, they have also come to reinterpret Genesis 4–11, not to speak of other parts of Scripture where creation in six days is clearly taught.

A WRONG VIEW OF FAITH

Before I make more specific criticisms of the position of the theistic evolutionists, there is one grave error that theistic evolutionists and many creationists make.

Del Ratzsch describes this error, but apparently does not dispute it, although it is wrong and leads to all sorts of confusion. After explaining both the creationist and evolutionist model of origins, Ratzsch writes,

> Both models, creationists claim, are beyond the reach of human proof—and consequently are not parts of *real* (inductivist) science. (Gish, though, sometimes appears to subsume both theories under "faiths," then claims that there is overwhelming evidence both for the creationist and against the evolutionist faith).[7]

Gish goes on to say, according to Ratzsch, "But since indirect, circumstantial evaluation does not either constitute proof or measure up to creationist definitions of science, the acceptance of either will constitute only *belief*."[8]

There is an important point here, not widely understood, but a serious point that we have to get straight.

The argument of many, also in creationist circles, is that neither the basic assumptions of the evolutionists nor the basic assumptions of the creationists can be proved. Both rest on faith; that is, both rest on unprovable assumptions that have to be accepted by faith. I was told the same thing: "You need not be ashamed of your faith; even the evolutionist rests his case on faith."

Now this sort of argumentation is not only dead wrong, but it is pernicious as well. If both the theory of evolution and the doctrine of Scripture rest on faith, then faith is nothing else but the blind acceptance of unproved and unprovable assumptions. But then the argument is reduced to a debate over who has the best line of argumentation and can summon the best proof for his position. God forbid that our defense of the doctrine of creation should ever come down to that.

The fact of the matter is that those who believe in creation have an iron-clad case that is unassailable. We have absolute proof for creation, and no stronger proof exists. That is that God himself tells us how he made the world. If that isn't proof, then I do not know what is.

I have sometimes used this illustration to describe the scientific view of creation. A group of men travel to a castle on the Rhine River in Germany to learn how the castle was constructed. Upon crossing the drawbridge over the moat and entering the castle, the men discover a book lying on the table, written by the architect and builder of the castle, explaining exactly how he accomplished this task. But these learned men, upon examining the book, decide that the architect and builder described his work in symbolic ways and therefore the book is of no use in their quest to learn how the castle was actually built. So they proceed through the castle, picking up a bag of dust here (to analyze in the laboratory), pulling out a stone in another place, examining under a magnifying glass various pits in the rocks, parts of broken walls, and ruins made almost meaningless by the erosion of time. They collect all their data and decide, after ponderous discussion, that the castle came into existence by itself, although some superintendent, ten thousand miles away, may have attempted from time to time to offer some guidance.

Faith is not blind acceptance of unproved assumptions. Faith is the bond that unites the elect child of God in a living connection with Jesus Christ. Faith is a complete change of the darkened mind into one able to think properly and correctly. Faith is a change of a stubborn will into one that makes a believer a humble servant of Jesus Christ. Faith gives a knowledge that no one without faith can possibly possess. Faith sees Scripture and Scripture's claim to be the word of God and believes it. And faith is such a power that when one believes the Scriptures, it brings him face-to-face with Christ himself to know him in a rich, blessed, wonderful, and saving way.

WHY FAITH?

Scripture tells us, "Through faith we understand that the worlds were framed by the word of God, so that things which are seen were not made of things which do appear" (Heb. 11:3). This passage teaches, among other things, that faith is the only way in which one can understand creation.

Why is that?

Man cannot know the truth because the curse is on the creation and on man himself, making him incapable of knowing truth. The fact is that although man can understand some things about the creation with respect to the earthly relationships in which various creatures stand to each other, he cannot see all things in their relation to God. Hence he cannot really know the truth. That kind of knowledge, which is the only true knowledge, is by faith. And faith has as its object the Scriptures, where believers learn all the truth of creation in its relation to God. Unbelief abandons the Scriptures and becomes mired down in unbelieving science. Worse yet, unbelief may piously acknowledge the Scriptures, but it sets science above the Scriptures and, of necessity, twists the Scriptures to make them fit unbelieving science.

The battle between evolutionists and creationists is not a battle between two different "faiths," the strength of each to be determined on the basis of scientific evidence. The battle between evolutionism and the truth of creation is between faith and unbelief. That puts the battle where it rightly belongs: not in the science classroom, where evidence for both can be examined, but in the forefront of the battle of faith waged in defense of the truth of God against all unbelief.

ERRORS OF THEISTIC EVOLUTIONISM

Theistic evolution accepts as truth the law of uniformitarianism, which teaches that the natural laws according to which the creation operates and develops have been the same since time began. Because it accepts that law as truth, theistic evolution believes (and must believe, to maintain its position) that there was death before the fall. How can one have a fossil record that is millions if not billions of years old unless death was present in the creation before man appeared on the scene and sinned, bringing down on him and the creation the curse of death? That death came into the world through the fall, Paul teaches in Romans 5:12: "As by one man sin entered

305

into the world, and death by sin; and so death passed upon all men, for all have sinned." Perhaps we cannot imagine a world in which there was no death, but "through faith we understand that the worlds were framed by the word of God" (Heb. 11:3).

Theistic evolutionists must deny the literal meaning of the first eleven chapters of Genesis. Let us be aware that if Genesis 1–11 can be interpreted in a way that is not literal, then any historical narrative, including the virgin birth and Christ's atoning sacrifice and bodily resurrection, can also be interpreted symbolically, doxologically, or whatever. And indeed, the force of logic compels those who will not take Genesis 1–11 literally, to reject many other parts of sacred Scripture.

Theistic evolutionists deny providence. In his defense of the framework hypothesis as an interpretation of Genesis 1, Lee Irons speaks of creation by "ordinary providence" rather than "special providence."[9] By ordinary providence, Irons means the laws of nature—creation takes place according to the laws of nature. That is a denial of providence. Providence teaches that God, who created all by the word of his mouth, continues to speak that same word so that the creature continues to exist. Providence teaches that God, who upholds the beetle and mosquito as well as the planet Jupiter by his almighty word, directs each creature in all its existence in the preordained way that he has determined. This includes man and his unbelief. God moves every drop of blood in my veins and guides the ant across the sidewalk at my feet. God brings rain to water the earth and water from the rock at Rephidim. God causes the deer to bring forth their young (Ps. 29:9) and brings about the conception of a new child in the womb of its mother. Theistic evolutionists deny Christ. That is a bold statement, but true. Already when I was taught the period theory in college, the class was told that it did not make any essential difference whether one was a creationist or an evolutionist, because neither had anything to do with our faith. We could believe in the period theory and in Jesus Christ as our Savior. Genesis 1 had nothing to do with the gospel.

This is a ploy to deceive the unwary.

Christ has everything to do with creation. Proverbs 8 claims for Christ, the Wisdom of God, "I was set up from everlasting, from the beginning, or ever the earth was . . . When he prepared the heavens, I was there . . . Rejoicing in the habitable part of his earth" (vv. 23, 27, 31). John 1 boldly says, "In the beginning was the Word, and the Word was with God, and the Word was God. The same was in the beginning with God. All things were made by him; and without him was not any thing made that was made" (vv. 1–3). Paul sings a doxology of praise to God in Christ, "Who is the image of the invisible God, the firstborn of every creature: For by him were all things created, that are in heaven, and that are in earth, visible and invisible... all things were created by him, and for him: And he is before all things, and by him all things consist" (Col. 1:15–17). Hebrews 1 introduces the whole book with the words, "God, who at sundry times and in divers manners spake in time past unto the fathers by the prophets, Hath in these last days spoken unto us by his Son, whom he hath appointed heir of all things, by whom also he made the worlds" (Heb. 1:1, 2).

When God pronounced his creation "good," he meant by that word that everything that he had made was perfectly adapted to the purpose for which he had created it. That purpose is the full revelation of his own glory in Jesus Christ, his eternal Son, through whom is the redemption of an elect church and the whole of the new heavens and the new earth. The original creation was perfectly formed to be the stage on which for more than six thousand years would be enacted the drama of salvation from sin and death in Christ.

To deny creation is to deny salvation in Christ. To believe in creation is to be saved by Christ.

CHAPTER 30

RAUSCHENBUSCH AND
THE SOCIAL GOSPEL

INTRODUCTION

The social gospel has come to dominate the thinking of the church. Characteristic of the social gospel is the idea that the work of the church can best be described as a concentrated effort to make this world in which we now live a better place so that the kingdom of God can be realized here on earth. If the church fails to work toward the alleviation of the sufferings of the poor, the oppression of the downtrodden, mayhem and murder, greed and hatred between man, war and its accompanying destruction, indeed, of all the social ills that afflict man, then the church has become a nonentity, an irrelevance, a useless institution not worthy of notice by those "called to a nobler task." We must, we are told, love all men. This is our calling. And without doubt, this means that the place where the action is cannot be found within the walls of the church sanctuary, but out on the streets, in the marketplace, and down in skid row.

Behind the social gospel is a whole set of beliefs, a sort of false theology, a terrible misinterpretation of Scripture. The social gospel speaks of the brotherhood of all men, a universal love of God, a suffering Jesus who gave us an outstanding example of suffering for one's beliefs, and a gradual transformation of this world into the kingdom of heaven.

Liberalism promotes the social gospel, but other theological positions share in the errors of a social gospel doctrine as well. Postmillennialism and reconstructionism, while speaking of the universal adoption of the Reformed faith, nevertheless share with social gospelers the dream of the kingdom of Christ here in the world. Those who follow the logic of Dr. Abraham Kuyper's view of common grace and the philosophy of Dooyeweerd and Vollenhoven have bought in to the social gospel and likewise find the calling of believers to be defined as working toward the kingdom of Christ here in the world.

The subject that we treat is an important one. Walter Rauschenbusch is considered by many the father of the social gospel. And if the name "father" is not apt, he is surely considered to be an outstanding leader in this movement, which has come to dominate so much of the religious thinking in our day.

RAUSCHENBUSCH'S BACKGROUND AND EARLY LIFE

Walter's parents were born and married in Germany. His father Augustus had a singularly good religious education He had studied under Augustus Neander, the noted church historian. Neander had, in turn, studied under Schleiermacher, had been heavily influenced by his theology, and had passed on Schleiermacher's influence to his students. Augustus Rauschenbusch was also a contemporary of Philip Schaff, another noted church historian with whose views Augustus was acquainted.

The Rauschenbusch family had produced five generations of ministers in the Lutheran Church, but it had also come under the influences of German pietism.

When Augustus took his family from Westphalia, Germany, to America, he did so as a missionary for the Lutheran church. His zeal and dedication to Lutheranism could not have been very strong, however, for he was in America only a short time when he became a Baptist. Augustus was only briefly in the pastoral ministry, for soon he was summoned to become a professor at Rochester Theological Seminary.

His son Walter, born October 4, 1861, in Rochester, New York, did not have much of a home life as a child. Walter's parents did not get along very well, and his mother took her children back to Germany in 1865, two months after the assassination of Abraham Lincoln. Augustus followed them after a few years but spent very little time at home. He was more interested in his research of the Anabaptist movement than in caring for his family and giving them the spiritual training they needed. In 1869 Walter's father moved the family back to the United States, where they lived the rest of their lives.

Walter was, not unexpectedly, a rebellious son who was frequently in trouble with his teachers. The tension in the home increased his tendency to rebel. Yet he completed his high school studies in 1879 and graduated second in his class. After his graduation, his father took Walter back to

Germany, where he studied for four years before returning to Rochester. In Rochester he completed his university studies, entered Rochester Theological Seminary for ministerial studies and was graduated from the seminary in 1886. He was ordained into the ministry in that same year.

INFLUENCES ON RAUSCHENBUSCH'S THINKING

A man's thinking and life are formed by his education and early life. So it was with Walter Rauschenbusch. Many different influences were instrumental in making him the father of the social gospel.

Walter's university training was conservative. In this country it was even Calvinistic to some degree. But during his seminary training his reading and studies led him in different paths. The seminary itself was probably not directly responsible for this shift in theology, because Walter's rather free-thinking style caused deep concern at Rochester Theological Seminary. In his reading he came across the writings of Horace Bushnell, an outstanding liberal thinker of the nineteenth century who had his roots in New England Puritan thought but who was in a measure responsible for the destruction of orthodoxy throughout the New England states.

It was from Horace Bushnell that Rauschenbusch acquired his view of the atonement. Bushnell and Rauschenbusch denied the substitutionary nature of the atonement; that is, they denied that Christ died on the cross in the place of those whom the Father had given him, so that he bore the sins and guilt of his people and satisfied God's justice by paying the price required for them. This denial strikes at the heart of the atonement and is, in fact, what Hebrews 6:6 calls crucifying afresh the Son of God and putting him to open shame. Yet denying Christ's substitutionary atonement is the necessary starting point for the social gospel.

In 1886 Rauschenbusch became minister of the gospel in the German Baptist Church in New York City. New York was the intellectual capital of the world at that time, and liberalism was beginning to make its mark, though mostly among the intelligentsia. Rauschenbusch took hold of their thinking and immersed himself in it.

Liberal thinking at this time was suspicious of capitalism, and it charged the economic theory on which the United States was founded with creating all the social, economic, and cultural problems that afflicted the country. Added to this unrest was heavy immigration, which brought tens of thousands of the world's poor to America's shores, and the industrial revolution, during which greedy industrialists became rich at the expense of the poor, who worked long hours for little pay and who had to put their little children in factories in order to have enough bread to eat. More and more, liberalism saw the gospel in terms of helping the poor.

At the time of his ordination into the ministry, Rauschenbusch was already worrying his parents by his liberal views, for their thinking had not gone that far, even though they were not what we would call orthodox. The pastorate that Walter Rauschenbusch assumed was in a tenement part of New York City adjacent to what was called Hell's Kitchen. It was the slum of the city, the high crime area, the core of poverty, oppression, and entrepreneurial tyranny. Rauschenbusch saw his work chiefly as helping these poor.

It did not help Walter's drift toward liberalism that his mother, finally unable to endure the constant warfare that went on at home, left her husband permanently and came to live with Walter, her unmarried son.

RAUSCHENBUSCH'S EARLY HISTORY
AS A SOCIAL REFORMER

Having committed his ministry to solving the problems of poverty in New York City, Rauschenbusch developed his social gospel.

He formed a fellowship with two other nearby pastors with similar views so that they could work together in social welfare programs among the poor. During this period, he was influenced by the social emphasis of John Wesley, Dwight L. Moody, and J. Hudson Taylor, who succeeded in combining what was thought to be a conservative theological position with social work and with an emphasis especially on helping the poor. So committed was he to this work that in 1888 Rauschenbusch turned down a request to take up professorial duties at Rochester Theological Seminary, where he had been trained and where his father had taught.

By the late 1880s Walter had suffered an extremely traumatic experience. He lost almost all of his hearing. Because of the severity of this handicap, he resigned from his pulpit, although his congregation refused to accept his resignation and insisted he continue his calling in Hell's Kitchen. He was plagued by this infirmity for the remainder of his life.

Walter became a friend of John D. Rockefeller, a Baptist who was instrumental in establishing the University of Chicago, and he persuaded Rockefeller to donate $8,000 toward the construction of a new church building in the Hell's Kitchen parish. During this same period he cooperated with Ira Sankey in preparing a new hymnbook by translating the old hymns into German, a language that was the only one many of his parishioners knew.

311

In 1891 Walter traveled to Germany, where he spent nine months drinking at the fountain of German higher critical thought. Upon his return, he married and produced five children. He seemed to have the same wanderlust that his father had, for he went to Europe without his family, content to live alone and leave family responsibilities behind. It is not surprising, therefore, to learn that all his children forsook the Baptist religion, turned their backs on their father's evangelical piety, and broke entirely with the church. He loved his neighbors in Hell's Kitchen so fervently that he had no time for loving his neighbors in his own home.

In 1897, partly because a growing family required an increase in his income, Walter accepted a position as professor of German in the Theological Seminary in Rochester. He was to remain in Rochester the rest of his life.

By 1912 both Walter and his wife were suffering from exhaustion and for a time were unable to do much work. Disillusioned by World War I and the smashing blow it gave to Walter's hope for a better world, he died of colon cancer in 1918 at the end of the war.

RAUSCHENBUSCH'S IDEAS

As I noted before, early in his college studies Rauschenbusch came to question the substitutionary atonement of Christ. In an essay he was required to write, he had the opportunity "to question 'ransom' or 'substitutionary' theologies of the atonement, that is, the deep-seated tradition that Christ's death occurred as a 'payment' for the sins of humanity."[1] In the same essay he wrote, "What was Christ's theology of salvation? He preached that men are sinful; that an entire change must take place in them by entering into a new and spiritual life; that God is very sorrowful over their absence from him and will be delighted to welcome them back to his love;...and if they do not come they will have to bear the terrible consequences of their refusal."[2] Christ died, so Rauschenbusch taught, not to pay for the sins of his people, but for his own beliefs, so that by his example man would be improved.

Such a view of the atoning sacrifice of the Savior is dreadful and a trampling underfoot of the blood of the covenant. It is, for all its denial of the miracle of the cross of Christ, an inevitable consequence of distorting the gospel by changing it from a gospel of salvation from sin to a gospel of salvation from material poverty. No atoning sacrifice of Christ who pays for sin is necessary to make a poor man rich.

During the time of his work in New York City, Walter and other likeminded ministers formed The Fellowship of the Kingdom, an informal group whose aim was to promote social consciousness in people so they would help alleviate social wrongs. This group remained active and influential for many years, and it proved to be a forum to develop the implications of the social gospel.

The social gospel, clearly, is not the proclamation of the cross of Jesus Christ as God's work of redemption and salvation through faith in Christ. Instead, the gospel is doing good to the outcast and downtrodden. The only obligation it laid upon men was to love their neighbor, not now in the sense of seeking his salvation, but by putting bread on his table, cleaning the filth from his home, finding a job for him, and enabling him to seek medical help when needed.

Conversion was abandoned, and taking a bath was substituted for it. The battle against sin became a battle against cruel industrialists and entrepreneurs; the banners under which the church marched had emblazoned on them, "Down with Unemployment."

As a matter of fact, the church as an institution was considered almost an irrelevance. It was of no practical use except to inspire the well-to-do to get out of the safety of the sanctuary into the teeming streets and slums where all the action was. "The institutional church," said Rauschenbusch, "is a necessary evil."[3] He believed that organizations, neighborhood meetings, and spirited group discussions could accomplish the same purpose the church strives to accomplish, and perhaps more effectively.

In 1907 Rauschenbusch published his book *Christianity and the Social Crisis.* This book was to be his definitive work and pushed him into the limelight and on up to the peaks of fame. From this book it became clear that Rauschenbusch had become a social reformer rather than a preacher. He insisted that he was only following in the footsteps of his lord and master Jesus Christ, for Christ himself was nothing more than a social reformer, although surely he was an outstanding example to us all when he was willing to suffer and die at the hands of callous church members who refused to fulfill the one precept of the law: "Love thy neighbor."

Rauschenbusch had no use for the Reformation, and more particularly, for Calvinism. He considered the churches faithful to the Reformation to be guilty of grossly distorting their gospel message. He scorned the great confessional heritage of the church, and he found the doctrines the whole church had confessed to be an albatross around the neck of those committed to these doctrines. He literally started the church in a new direction that was at right angles to the direction the church, under the leadership of the Spirit, had walked for eighteen hundred years.

RAUSCHENBUSCH'S VIEW OF THE KINGDOM

The keystone of a social gospel is the notion that Christ's kingdom must be understood in purely human terms. A succinct way of putting it was, "The leaven is the Kingdom. It is not in Heaven but it is here . . . The best way to get the self ready for Heaven . . . is to get this world ready for God."[4] Rauschenbusch put the matter more dogmatically in a speech to a 1894 graduating class at Oberlin College.

> Every department of human life,—the families, the schools, amusements, art, business, politics, industry; national policies, international relations,—will be governed by the Christian law and controlled by Christian influences. When we are bidden to seek first the kingdom of God, we are bidden to set our hearts on this great consummation; to keep this always before us as the object of our endeavors; to be satisfied with nothing less than this. The complete Christianization of all life is what we pray for and work for, when we work and pray for the coming of the kingdom of heaven.[5]

Rauschenbusch was confident that the whole world would be Christianized some day, at which time the kingdom of Christ would be established and all the promises of God would be fulfilled. He was the great optimist, and he held every hope for ultimate victory here in this sad world of sin.

The movement reached its apex just before World War I. That war was a major blow to Rauschenbusch's beliefs and his optimism, especially because he was confident that German culture would lead the way in the establishment of the kingdom, yet German culture had produced nothing but the chaos of a great and terrible war.

THE TRUTH OF THE MATTER

One need not have a profound understanding of today's ecclesiastical scene to know that although Rauschenbusch's dreams ended in the nightmare of World War I, his ideas live on.

His ideas live on in all liberal theology, which repudiates the atoning sacrifice of the cross and defines religion in terms of the do-goodism of a social gospel. From the viewpoint of a more conservative theological position today, Rauschenbusch's ideas also live on in postmillennial thinking, which promises us a better day when the Reformed faith will be held worldwide, when Reformed principles will determine the character of all society's institutions, and when the knowledge of God will cover the whole present earth from sea to sea. His ideas live on in the common grace tradition of Abraham Kuyper and the law philosophy of Amsterdam, made popular by the Institute of Christian Studies in Canada and taught in some major conservative colleges. Rauschenbusch's ideas live on as well in all teaching that defines a significant part of the Christian's life and calling as "making this world a better place to live." The shadow Rauschenbusch cast over today's church is long and dark.

I cannot set down in detail the biblical and confessional position over against all this corruption of the gospel. A brief outline of the main points will have to do.

The church of Christ is not an irrelevancy, but the only important institution in the whole world. I speak now of the church that bears the marks of the true church of Christ: the faithful preaching of the gospel, the proper administration of the sacraments, and the exercise of Christian discipline. It is the most important institution because it is the one institution that God has established to accomplish his own eternal purpose. All the rest of history has no meaning or importance except as it serves the church.

The church has only one purpose in this world: the preaching of the gospel. Every effort to involve the church in any other work but the preaching of the gospel is an attempt to distract the church from its only calling. If ever the church abandons that calling or no longer faithfully limits itself to that calling, then the church has become an irrelevancy. What a wide gap there is between Scripture and a social gospel. Rauschenbusch claimed that when the church preached the gospel, it was irrelevant.

The preaching of the gospel is the church's only task because the gospel is "the power of God unto salvation to every one that believeth" (Rom. 1:16). It is the one means that God uses to save a church that he has chosen from all eternity and that Christ purchased with his blood in a sacrifice on the cross. He paid the penalty for sin and satisfied God's justice, and the church bought with his blood will live with God in covenant fellowship in heaven.

The gospel proclaims that the human race is depraved, guilt-ridden, corrupt in all it does, unable to rescue itself, unwilling to go any way but toward hell. The gospel proclaims that faith in Jesus Christ is the way, the only way of escape from this dreadfully dangerous and hopeless world in which we live. The gospel puts a blanket curse on all man's endeavors and brands them as deeds that contribute to greater evil, greater trouble, greater condemnation. The gospel assures men that a future infinitely bright and glorious awaits those who believe in Christ Jesus.

The gospel causes a bright light to shine in this world in its present state and shows those who have received the gift of faith that to want a world here on earth is to be a fool of the worst sort, for here is only sin, and where sin is, there is suffering and trouble, violence and death. The bright hope of the future for the redeemed is in a great work of God when the wicked will be punished, the curse on this creation removed, and the earthly made heavenly. Former things will be no more.

The siren call of the social gospel is to love one's neighbor as oneself. The Reformed Christian would joyfully agree with those who preach love for the neighbor if only men would understand what love is. Is it love to put a drunk "on the wagon" when the wagon is on a steep hill that drops into hell? Is it love to feed an empty belly in which is found the bitter gall of the cancer of God's curse? Is it love to clean up the slums and make them glittering cities in which men carve out with their riches an inheritance in the gloomy and fiery abode of eternal destruction? What good is a social gospel in a world of sin?

The Reformed believer must love his neighbor as himself, as our Lord told us. Our neighbor is our wife or husband with whom we are called to live in our home in harmony and peace and not drag into a divorce court. Why is it that those who shout the loudest about loving their neighbors cannot love the one neighbor who lives next to them? How can we love the poor man in the ghetto if we cannot love our spouse? To love our neighbor is to love our children, our fellow saints, but also the man in the ditch alongside the highway on which we travel.

The towering command to love is a noble calling, but it is far from a mere do-goodism. It is not a clean-up-the-neighborhood campaign. It is not the formation of a Christian political party to end corruption in government. It is one thing and one thing only: to seek the eternal salvation of our neighbor whoever he or she may be. We must give groceries to the hungry and a thousand dollars to the one who cannot afford surgery for his child, but we must help our neighbor with groceries and our money only to show them the love and mercy of God toward sinners and to call them to repentance and faith in Christ that they may escape the wrath to come. All that material help is important only when we bring the gospel to the needy with and through the bag of groceries, and when we call that neighbor to a life of obedience to Christ. We love that neighbor when we do what we can to point that neighbor to the only hope there is in this world of sin. Then we truly seek our neighbor's good.

The believer knows with absolute certainty that this world will never be a better place. It will only become worse as sin develops and wickedness grows. Nothing can improve it, for the world's problems are the result of sin, and the solution does not lie in building affordable housing for the downtrodden, but in the cross of Christ. And while the base of the cross of Christ sinks down into hell where our Savior suffered hell's torments, it also reaches up to heaven to carry us out of hell's fiery abode into the splendor and sinlessness of the abode of the angels. To keep one's eyes fastened on this world is to fail to see the flames of hell licking around every human endeavor in this world. It is also a failure to see that there is no hope in this creation. Just as Rauschenbusch's dream for the future was shattered by the smoke and flames of World War I, so shall the hope of all those who dream of a kingdom of Christ here in the world go up in smoke when Christ comes again to judge man and deliver his beloved church.

PART 5

MODERN PERIOD
(1900–2010)

Contenders for the Faith and Historical Events		*Promoters of Heresy*
	1900	**Charles Fox Parham** sought pentecostal blessings to enliven churches in early 1900s
Abraham Kuyper prime minister of the Netherlands 1901–05		**Abraham Kuyper** published *De Gemeene Gratie* 1902
		William Heyns professor at Calvin College and Seminary 1902–26
Welsh revivals 1904–05		
Azusa Street Revival 1906		
World War I 1914–18		
	1920	
Henry Danhof & Herman Hoeksema published *Van Zonde en Genade* as a rebuttal to Kuyper's theory of common grace 1923		**Ralph Janssen** deposed as professor at Calvin Seminary 1922
Synod of Christian Reformed Church in Kalamazoo, MI, officially adopted the doctrine of common grace and deposed three ministers for refusing to subscribe to it 1924		
Protestant Reformed Churches founded 1925		
	1930	
		Norman Shepherd 1933–
World War II 1939–1945		
		Nicholas T. Wright 1948–
	2010	

319

CHAPTER 31

ERRORS CONCERNING
THE COVENANT

INTRODUCTION

Our concluding chapters on heresies that have appeared in the history of the church of Christ are a brief survey of more recent heresies that are present in the church in the twentieth and early twenty-first centuries.

The task of choosing which heresies to include in this book is not an easy one, and the choices are, admittedly, somewhat arbitrary. The difficulties are especially two. The first is that heresies are without number in post-Reformation times. If we were to describe and refute them all, we would have to write a number of volumes. Because of the sheer number of heresies, I have chosen to discuss, though briefly, those that have had an impact on the church of Christ, especially as represented in my Reformed tradition. By "impact" I mean not only heresies that have constituted a threat to the doctrinal integrity of the church and that have had to be warded off, but also heresies that have been a spur to further doctrinal development in the truth.

This choice led to another problem: many heresies have had an impact on the church, but much material and many books have been written about them already. I refer in a broader sense to such heresies as postmillennialism and preterism, and in a narrower sense to heresies that have produced a large amount of literature in the history of my denomination, the Protestant Reformed Churches. Examples of such heresies would be the gracious and well-meant gospel offer and a conditional covenant. Whether to write on all of these heresies or to refrain in the light of the wealth of written material has been a question not easy to answer.

In the interests of being as complete as possible, I have decided to say at least a few words concerning most of these heresies on which much has already been written. We begin these last chapters with the doctrine of the covenant.

SOME HISTORY

The doctrine of God's covenant of grace had its origins in Switzerland. The reformers Zwingli and Bullinger were especially involved in the early development of this doctrine. The occasion was their opposition to the error of Anabaptism, and they found that the scriptural truth of the covenant was the foundation upon which the doctrine of infant baptism rested.

The difficulty was that from the inception of the doctrine, the covenant was defined in terms of an agreement between God and man. Why this definition became the accepted one is not known with certainty. It may be that the Latin term used for covenant, *foedus,* which means "treaty," "compact," or "agreement," influenced the doctrine. Thus the biblical idea of the covenant that God establishes with his people was spoiled by the meaning of the Latin word for covenant.

Not that long after the Reformation the truth of the covenant was combined with what has become known as "federalism." The basic idea of federalism concerns the legal relationship between our first father Adam and the human race that came from him. In his position of federal head of the human race, Adam's faithfulness or transgression had legal consequences on the entire human race. If Adam remained obedient, his obedience would be imputed to all his descendants. If he sinned, the guilt of his sin would be imputed to the entire human race that he represented.

This federal idea was first advanced by theologians in the Palatinate of Germany between 1560 and 1590, the period during which the Heidelberg Catechism was written in 1563.

The combination of the covenant considered as a pact or treaty, plus the federal relationship in which Adam stood to the human race, led rather naturally to the idea of the covenant of works.

D. A. Weir, in his book on federalism, writes, "The *foedus* made with Adam before the Fall is a covenant which deals with creation and nature. Through it, man stands before God on his own merits."[1] Weir goes on to say, "The distinguishing feature of federal theology is the application of covenantal status to the paradisiacal state, with Adam as the responsible federal or covenant head who makes a decision for all the creation."[2]

The elements of the covenant with Adam, and by implication with all men, are as follows.

1. The conditions: Obedience to the command not to eat of the forbidden tree, and obedience to the command to rest on the seventh day.
2. The parties, which are God and man.
3. The conditions controlling both God and man. Ursinus believed that the covenant of grace was unconditional: man did not keep the covenant, but God keeps the original covenant in Christ.
4. The covenant was binding on Adam and his descendants, whether Adam sinned or remained obedient.
5. The sign of the covenant with Adam was the tree of life. After the fall, the sign was first circumcision, then baptism.
6. The promise of God to Adam, upon condition of obedience, was eternal life.

This view of the covenant dominated for centuries, although from time to time some differences in emphasis and/or ideas appeared. It was quickly adopted by Presbyterian theologians in the British Isles and continental theologians in Germany and the Netherlands. It is basically the idea referred to in the Westminster Confession, although we may be thankful that it does not appear in any form in the Reformed creeds.

A more recent view of the covenant of works differs very little from that of Ursinus. Louis Berkhof describes the covenant of works as including:

> *The Covenanting Parties.* A covenant is always a compact between two parties. In the case of the covenant of works there was ... the triune God ... And ... there was Adam, the representative of the human race ...
>
> *The Promise of the Covenant.* The great promise of the covenant was the promise of life in the fullest sense of the word, that is, not merely a continuance of the natural existence of man, but life raised to the highest development of perennial bliss and glory ...
>
> *The Condition of the Covenant.* The promise in the covenant of works was not unconditional. The condition was that of perfect, unconditional obedience ...
>
> *The Penalty of the Covenant.* The penalty that was threatened in case of transgression was death in the most inclusive sense of the word, physical, spiritual, and eternal ...
>
> *The Sacrament(s) of the Covenant.* ...In all probability the tree of life was an appointed symbol and pledge or seal of life.[3]

To sum up the doctrine, we conclude that the idea of the covenant of works includes the following basic premises:

1. The covenant of works is always related to the federal headship of Adam in his relationship to the whole human race.
2. It is based on the idea that any covenant between God and man is an agreement, contract, pact, or treaty.
3. It is always a conditional covenant; that is, it is established and maintained only

on the condition that man agrees to the provisions of the covenant and remains faithful. Unfaithfulness carries with it the penalty of death.

4. The promise of God to Adam is that, after a certain period of time, conditioned on Adam's obedience, Adam and his posterity would have gone to heaven.

It ought to be clear that the idea of a conditional covenant in general, and a covenant of works in particular, necessarily includes in it the idea of merit. The defenders of such a conditional covenant have frequently tried to avoid the notion of merit, but without success. Presbyterian defenders of the covenant of works have not been averse to the notion of merit, although they attempt to give it a sound interpretation.

DISSENTERS

Although the prevailing view of God's covenantal relation to man was almost universally defined in terms of a contract or agreement, some in the history of the Reformed churches spoke of somewhat different views of the covenant.

Calvin, for example, while speaking extensively of the covenant, emphasized its unconditional character and its relation to election. In speaking of the place of children in the covenant, Calvin was strong on the idea that elect children born in covenant lines belong fully to the covenant.

Olevianus, while also holding to the covenant as an agreement or compact, spoke of the covenant as also being a bond of friendship. The same was true of Cocceius, who even saw the truth that the covenant was rooted in the trinitarian life of God.

Herman Bavinck, a late-nineteenth-century Dutch theologian, also wrote of the covenant as a bond of friendship, an idea later to be fully developed by Herman Hoeksema.

Nevertheless, those who defined the covenant in terms of friendship added the idea that the covenant was an agreement or pact.

Even the covenant of works was not universally accepted. Thomas Goodwin, a Puritan, member of the Westminster Assembly and president of Magdalen College, Oxford, wrote,

> Much less can the grace of a mere creature (or ever could) merit a higher condition; to do which is more than to confirm the continuance of the present condition. Adam could not earn a condition of a higher rank, nor by all his works have bought any greater preferment than what he was created in. To compass it was *ultra suam sphaeram*, above his sphere; he could never have done it. As, for instance, he could not have attained that state in heaven which the angels enjoy. What says Christ? "When ye have done all that ye can, say, You are unprofitable servants," Luke 17:10. This he could no more do than other creatures by keep-

ing those their ordinances can merit to be "translated into the glorious liberty" which they wait for, and shall have at the latter day. The moon, though she keep all her motions set her by God never so regularly, yet she cannot thereby attain to the light of the sun as a new reward therefore. And thus no more can any pure creature of itself, by all its righteousness, obtain in justice a higher condition to itself. And therefore the angels, by all their own grace, have not to this day earned a better condition than they were created in. And yet all this falls short of satisfying for sin.[4]

It is not our intention to enter into a detailed criticism of the covenant of works. Perhaps Herman Hoeksema made the most complete analysis of the doctrine of a covenant of works in his *Reformed Dogmatics*.[5] It must be remembered, however, that Hoeksema's objections to the covenant of works are based on an entirely different conception of the covenant than underlies the covenant of works. I will briefly sum up Hoeksema's cogent and compelling arguments.

First, the doctrine of the covenant of works has no support in Scripture. Even Louis Berkhof, in attempting to find biblical support for the doctrine, is hard pressed to find it and simply deduces it from various other ideas that Scripture gives in connection with Adam's creation. One such biblical truth is God's command to Adam not to eat of the tree of the knowledge of good and evil, as the punishment for disobedience is death. On this command one can hardly base an elaborate conditional covenant that has the reward of heaven. Hoeksema points out that a command is no covenant.

Second, the idea of merit is foreign to Scripture, and most sound continental theologians have thrown it far from them in the interests of the sovereignty of salvation. Hoeksema quotes the same passage from Luke 17 that Thomas Goodwin quoted.

Third, the promise of eternal life creates all kinds of problems. How long would Adam have had to be faithful to earn eternal life? Would his posterity also have inherited eternal life? Would Adam have had to live on earth until the last of his posterity was born? Would the probationary command apply to all Adam's descendants, even though they were not in the position of federal head? But here also the promise of eternal life as the reward of obedience is contrary to Scripture. For Scripture is clear that eternal life is immortality, and that can be gained only through the perfect work of Christ, who conquers sin and death for his people (see 1 Cor. 15:50–58.)

Fourth, the covenant of works makes the covenant an incidental part of

Adam's life, added after his creation when he received the command of God not to eat of the forbidden tree.

Fifth, the covenant of works makes God's purpose in Christ to save his elect a sort of necessary alternate plan of God, when his original purpose to glorify himself in Adam's obedience met with disaster. Thus the covenant of works presents a view unworthy of God.

SERIOUSLY WRONG DEVELOPMENTS

Various erroneous ideas have developed from the wrong conception that the covenant is a treaty or an agreement. It is well to give brief consideration to these, so that we may see that a wrong principle leads to wrong conclusions and produces wrong doctrine.

In the development of the covenant among the Reformed churches, one of the great questions has been the place of children in the covenant. It is not a mystery why the place of children in the covenant is a matter of concern, for the doctrine of infant baptism goes back to the apostolic church and was held by the Roman Catholic Church as well as all the reformers. Furthermore, there has never been a question about the biblical truth that baptism is a sign of the covenant. When the conception of the covenant as an agreement is joined with the doctrine of infant baptism, it is obvious that the place of children in the covenant becomes a question, for if the covenant is an agreement ratified by two parties who agree to certain conditions, obviously infants cannot enter into the covenant.

Various solutions have been proposed over the centuries, and a large library of books has been written concerning this question. However, in general, orthodox theologians had no real problem with the place of children in the covenant but simply insisted that the elect children of the covenant belong to it from infancy and are usually regenerated in earliest infancy. The truth that the Protestant Reformed Churches hold today is thus not a novelty.

Calvin held this view. And it is incorporated into the Reformed confessions, both major and minor. The Form for the Administration of Baptism, a minor confession dating back to the middle of the sixteenth century, clearly contains this truth. The first question asked of parents who present their child for baptism is: "Whether you acknowledge that although our children are conceived and born in sin, and therefore are subject to all miseries, yea to condemnation itself, *yet that they are sanctified in Christ, and therefore, as members of His church, ought to be baptized?*"[6]

Further, in the prayer of thanksgiving with which the sacrament is concluded, the church prays, "Almighty God and merciful Father, we thank and praise Thee, that *Thou hast forgiven us and our children all our sins, through the blood of Thy beloved Son Jesus Christ.*"[7]

The Heidelberg Catechism asks, "Are infants also to be baptized? Yes; for since they, as well as their parents, belong to the covenant and people of God, and both redemption from sin and the Holy Ghost, who works faith, are through the blood of Christ promised to them no less than to their parents, they are also by Baptism, as a sign of the covenant, to be ingrafted into the Christian church and distinguished from the children of unbelievers."[8]

There has been a tradition throughout the entire development of the Reformed faith that has held firmly to the truth that elect children of believers are truly and fully members of God's covenant.

But if the covenant is a conditional compact, by virtue of this definition there is no place in the covenant for children of believers. Various ideas have been proposed to explain this anomaly. Professor William Heyns (1856–1933), who taught at Calvin College and Calvin Theological Seminary from 1902–1926, proposed the most common idea. After explaining a traditional view of the covenant of works, he went on to propose his ideas in his *Manual of Reformed Doctrine.*[9]

We give here a summary of Heyns' lengthy treatment of the covenant. We note that while he attempts to maintain a unilateral (one-sided), unconditional covenant, he nevertheless develops his ideas along different lines. He speaks of an objective (or external) and subjective (or internal) covenant. The former is established with all baptized children, and the latter is established only with those who accept and fulfill the conditions of the covenant. Thus all children born of believing parents are in the covenant externally and possess all the promises of the covenant. Only when they come to years of discretion and fulfill the conditions of faith and obedience do they actually enter the covenant in its full blessedness.

Heyns even speaks of a general subjective grace given to all the children of the covenant who are baptized, to enable them to accept or reject the conditions imposed on them at baptism. In this way, the administration of baptism becomes like the preaching when the preaching of the gospel is considered as a well-meant gospel offer to all who hear and in which all the hearers receive grace to accept or reject the overtures of Christ.[10]

In Presbyterian circles, Schenck has shown in an excellent book, *The Presbyterian Doctrine of Children in the Covenant,* that the Presbyterian view was sound and biblical in early Presbyterianism, especially, though not exclusively, in America. His contention is that a correct view of the place of infants in the covenant was altered significantly by New England theology as set forth primarily by Jonathan Edwards and that it was adversely influenced by the New England revivals during the time of Edwards and George Whitefield.[11]

CONSEQUENCES OF A CONDITIONAL COVENANT

The view of a conditional covenant has had serious consequences. I mention a few of the more serious ones.

It has led to a denigration of the importance of the covenant in the life of the church and the people of God. The covenant, because it is viewed as a conditional compact or agreement, is quite necessarily not the heart of the great gift of salvation that Scripture claims it is, but it is only a *means* to that salvation. It is the means by which God gives salvation only to those who accept the provisions of the covenant and fulfill the conditions, but it is not salvation itself. The covenant of grace is, therefore, as far as its central character is concerned, nothing but a general promise to all who are baptized that if they fulfill the conditions of the covenant, they will be saved. The covenant is reduced to a conditional promise rather than the essence of salvation itself.

Sovereign election as it is related to the covenant is denied. If the covenant consists of a conditional promise to all, election does not control the covenant and does not determine who are in God's covenant and who are not. Those who hold to the view of Professor Heyns insist that election has nothing to do with the covenant and must not be considered in connection with any discussion of the covenant.

But ultimately no one can deny that the covenant is salvation. The result is that those who hold to a conditional covenant hold also to a conditional salvation. And if they are forced to consider election, as Scripture compels them to do, they are driven to a conditional election. They say that all the baptized children are elect. Thus election is conditional and not determinative for salvation. Such conditionality in the covenant is pure Arminianism. The sovereignty of God in the work of salvation through Christ is denied, and the covenant blessings are made dependent on the will of man, who is free to make a choice for or against the covenant by the general grace imparted at baptism.

Such a position compels one to deny all the five points of Calvinism. Eternal election as the fountain and cause of faith is discarded. A general atonement as the judicial ground of a general promise becomes a necessity.

Total depravity is lost in the wilderness of this general grace given to all. Grace is resistible. Those once heirs of the promise and perhaps themselves elect can lose their salvation and election. Nothing is left. Only Arminianism and salvation by the will of man remain.

JUSTIFICATION BY FAITH AND WORKS

An extremely important consequence of a conditional covenant is the denial of justification by faith alone. This implication of a conditional covenant for the doctrine of justification by faith alone was popularized by Norman Shepherd.[12] The controversy over the doctrine of justification by faith rages fiercely today in the church world, and much has been written on it, also in the Protestant Reformed Churches, where the connection between a conditional covenant and the heresy of justification by faith and works has been clearly shown.[13] I will make only one comment: If the fundamental doctrine of the covenant as the great and glorious salvation of the elect is made conditional, then all salvation is conditional. If all salvation is conditional, then justification, too, is conditional. Then justification is not by faith alone but is conditioned on works, particularly the works of obedience. Then, too, the whole heritage of the Protestant Reformation is lost. Thus the way is paved to return to Rome's Pelagianism and idolatry.

THE TRUTH OF GOD'S COVENANT

Although the truth of an unconditional covenant has been held by Reformed theologians from the Reformation to today, an unconditional covenant is always difficult to maintain when the covenant is defined in terms of a compact or agreement. Herman Hoeksema, Henry Danhof, and George Ophoff, the fathers of the Protestant Reformed Churches are to be thanked for their development of the truth of God's covenant. The truth of God's unconditional covenant as a bond of fellowship and friendship with God has given the Protestant Reformed Churches their unique place as a separate denomination in the ecclesiastical world.

Herman Hoeksema took the lead in developing the doctrine of the covenant. He saw clearly that the theologians who had considered the idea of the covenant as a bond of friendship and fellowship were correct, but that such a conception of the covenant could not be maintained along with the idea of the covenant as an agreement. The latter had to be abandoned.[14]

The total abandonment of the covenant as an agreement was not as difficult as it might seem because there is no evidence in Scripture for such a conception of the covenant, and a closer examination of the supposed covenant of works that determines the character of the covenant of grace reveals, also, that a covenant of works is nowhere taught in sacred Scripture.

A brief summary of the truth of God's covenant as taught in Scripture would include the following elements:

First, the covenant of grace that God establishes with his people in Christ is the revelation of the covenant life that God lives in himself as the triune God, who is one in essence and three in person.

Second, God's covenant is a bond of fellowship between God and his people in Christ in which God takes his people into his own triune covenant life and dwells with them in a bond of peace and love as a husband dwells with his wife in the unity of one flesh.

Third, God created Adam to live in such fellowship with him, and God and Adam communed together at the foot of the tree of life. But Adam fell and alienated himself from God. As the head of the entire human race, he became a covenant breaker. But God maintains his covenant, for he is always faithful. He maintains his covenant with Christ and with the elect chosen eternally in Christ.

Fourth, God was and is always sovereign. Adam had to be moved aside so that the figure of him who was to come, our Lord Jesus Christ, could be revealed. In him the covenant of grace would be fully and perfectly realized with the elect.

Fifth, that covenant, rooted in eternal election, is solely God's work. God determined it from all eternity. God establishes it with his elect in the line of continued generations. God maintains it by his sovereign grace and in his own faithfulness. God perfects it in heaven, where the tabernacle of God will be with men. The covenant is one-sided and unconditional —the sovereign work of God alone.

This covenant includes in it the elect and their elect seed in the line of generations.

The Calvinism developed by the reformer of Geneva and set down in creedal form in the Canons of Dordrecht as the great biblical truth of the sovereignty of God in the work of salvation is now applied consistently and fully to the truth of the covenant. The two doctrines come together in perfect harmony in the organic unity of the truth of Scripture as confessed by the church.

It is frequently charged that those who maintain a view of the covenant that throws out conditions rob man of his responsibility before God. A few remarks will lay this charge to rest. First, the responsibility of man does not rest, as such, on man's spiritual ability. The totally depraved sinner, unable to do any good, is also responsible before God for his sin. Second, the charge is a wearisome repetition of the same charge that Arminians have always made against those who hold to the doctrines of sovereign grace. Third, nothing could be further from the truth than the charge that God's sovereign work of grace destroys man's responsibility, because as members of God's covenant, and representing the cause of God's covenant in the world, believers are called to fulfill what the baptism form calls "our part" of the covenant.

> Whereas in all covenants, there are contained two parts, therefore are we by God, through baptism, admonished of and obliged unto new obedience, namely, that we cleave to this one God, Father, Son, and Holy Ghost; that we trust in Him, and love Him with all our hearts, with all our souls, with all our mind, and with all our strength; that we forsake the world, crucify our old nature, and walk in a new and holy life.
>
> And if we sometimes through weakness fall into sin, we must not therefore despair of God's mercy, nor continue in sin, since baptism is a seal and undoubted testimony that we have an eternal covenant of grace with God.[15]

The view of the covenant as a compact or agreement is a cold and mechanical doctrine that has no intrinsic appeal at all. But the biblical truth of the covenant between God and his people in Christ as a unity of friendship and fellowship is warm, pulsing with life, moving the believer to doxologies of praise to the God of his salvation. It inspires every pilgrim in this world to seek the end of life's journey, the day when the tabernacle of God will be with men and he will dwell with them and be their God and they will be his people. It will be the full realization of God's covenant when God will wipe away all tears from their eyes, and when God will be praised forever for the greatness of his love and mercy.

CHAPTER 32

HIGHER CRITICISM

INTRODUCTION

Although heresies arise in the church of Christ for many reasons, one important reason for the rise of recent heresies is higher criticism. Higher critics ostensibly inquire into the origin of the sacred Scriptures; that is, they ask the question, How did the Bible come into existence?

The higher critics give varying answers to this question, but they are essentially one: Scripture is not, partially or in its entirety, the word of God. It has its origin, partially or entirely, in man's work. It is well that we look into their claim.

THE ORIGIN OF HIGHER CRITICISM

Higher criticism has its origin in modern philosophy, particularly in the Enlightenment of the eighteenth century. Modern philosophy, in turn, is a child of the Renaissance, which was antithetical to the Reformation of the sixteenth century. The beginnings of the Renaissance can be traced back as early as the publication of Dante's *Divine Comedy* in the early part of the fourteenth century. The Renaissance was a humanistic movement that exalted man's reason and made man the center of the universe, his happiness the reason for all things, and his mind the standard of truth. Although some have claimed that the Renaissance was one facet of the Reformation and that the two movements were two sides of the same coin, the fact is that the Renaissance was anti-God, while the Reformation was God's renewal of the true church of Christ and a rescuing of that church from the deadly embrace of Roman Catholicism.

Many modern philosophers, beginning with Malebranche and Descartes, claimed to be religious, but they separated faith from reason. They spoke of an area of faith, the object of which was contained in the Scriptures and could be accepted without proof, and they spoke of an area of reason in which only that which met the canons of rational proof could be accepted. For example, Descartes claimed that the truths of God, man, and creation could be rationally proved and ought to be accepted because they could meet the criteria of reason, but that reason is divorced from and not under the control of faith.

It is not hard to see that this view of the relation between faith and reason was utterly destructive of religion. One cannot, psychologically or spiritually, divide his mind into two compartments, whereby in one he holds to his faith and in the other he accepts what reason dictates as truth.[1] The inevitable result of such thinking is that faith disappears entirely, and reason is enthroned as the final standard of truth. That is, *man* is enthroned, and God is ruled out of his own universe.

That reason takes the front seat became evident in deism, a heresy that arose in Great Britain and was transported across the English Channel to the continent of Europe and across the Atlantic Ocean to America, where it formed the theoretical basis for the democracy imbedded in the Declaration of Independence and the Constitution of the United States of America.[2]

Deism teaches that the relation between God and his world is analogous to the relation between a watchmaker and the watch he makes. God created the world in such a way that it can run by itself, under its own power according to natural law, and does not need any providential guidance of God. God, so to speak, winds up the world and it continues to run mechanically under its own power.

Following this notion, deism accepted as truth only what could be proved scientifically, that is, by human reason. Everything that takes place in this world is explainable in terms of natural law; and whatever man may believe, if it cannot be demonstrated scientifically, has to be relegated to the area of myth, legend, or superstition. Thus, angels, devils, miracles, and anything supernatural were automatically ruled out as being untenable. The world is a closed system. It is not subject to outside influences. Those who claim that God intervenes in the world reduce him to a *deus ex machina,* an improbable being called into the world to resolve difficulties and problems for which man can find no solution.

In this general intellectual climate, higher criticism was born.

THE NATURE OF HIGHER CRITICISM
It was inevitable that the principles of rationalism and deism would be applied to the Bible and how it came into existence.

It is difficult to describe higher criticism because of its many different faces. The views promoted by higher critics run a wide spectrum from downright unbelief to various attempts to make Scripture's origin partially divine and partially human—the percentage of the divine and of the human varying with the particular higher critic.

Another element enters in at this point. In an effort to explain the fact that Scripture was written (though under divine inspiration) by different men, whose background, upbringing, personality, writing style, and individual characteristics are evident in their writings, Reformed theologians spoke of a *human element* in Scripture. Usually these theologians did not mean that the human element limited the divine inspiration of the Bible, but they wanted to emphasize that Scripture was not written by dictation, because the Reformed had often been charged with the error of maintaining a dictation theory of inspiration.

Nevertheless, speaking of a human element was unfortunate, because higher critics took hold of the idea and used it to prove that men had a sufficiently large role in preparing Scripture and, therefore, that the Bible contains human failures, errors common to men and wrong scientific ideas, such as the notion that the earth is flat.

However, when Scripture describes its origin it does not breathe a word about any human element and, in fact, repudiates the notion. "All Scripture is given by inspiration of God" or literally, "God-breathed," according to 2 Timothy 3:16. Any human element is also repudiated in 2 Peter 1:21: Scripture did not come "by the will of man" but by the Holy Spirit who "moved" men to write.

I will give brief descriptions of some of the more common higher critical explanations of Scripture, from the very liberal to the more conservative.

The most liberal higher critics do not consider the Scriptures to be written by God the Holy Spirit in any sense. If they speak of the inspiration of Scripture at all, they put it on the same level as the inspiration of Shakespeare in the writing of his sonnets. They look at Scripture as a human record of the history of religion as religion gradually emerged from pagan polytheism and superstition to more modern forms. While some critics admit that a man named Jesus lived and that he may have died on a gibbet, what the gospels say about him, including his birth, death, resurrection, and ascension, is mythology and legend.

Others also speak of the Bible with its myths and legends, but they explain the New Testament as an effort to put into mythological or legendary form what the author believed was true of Jesus. The early church considered Jesus to be a great teacher, a miracle worker, a man who died for his principles and whose spirit lives on in his followers. These followers of Jesus expressed their faith in Christ by means of stories of miracles that, though untrue, express eloquently what they considered Jesus to be.

Many higher critics reject the traditional authorship of various books. Some consider the Pentateuch to be the work of at least four different writers who lived at different times and had different reasons for writing what they did. Some critics claim that two different men wrote Isaiah; others claim that three or four authors wrote it. This denial of Isaiah's authorship is more pernicious than it appears. Higher critics do not believe that Isaiah, who lived long before Judah's captivity, could speak not only about the captivity, but also about the deliverance from the captivity, and could even name the Persian emperor Cyrus as the individual who would be instrumental in Judah's deliverance. Higher critics also deny that Matthew, Mark, Luke, and John are the writers of the gospel narratives named after them. These critics claim that the four gospels emerged in their present form over a long period of time through the work of many writers and editors who used one gospel narrative to compose another.

As we drift through the maze of what is euphemistically called biblical scholarship, we find those who promote what they call a *Sitz im Leben* view of inspiration. This German expression really means that the authors of Scripture reflect the conceptions of the universe of their time, the culture and superstitions of their day, and their mistaken ideas concerning the significance and outcome of events that took place in their lives. The result is errors in the historical narratives, geographical descriptions of places, and views of the universe, to name a few.

Yet others explain Scripture in strange allegorical ways in order to make the Bible harmonize with their preconceived notions concerning creation and the flood, thus introducing evolutionism into the church.

Dr. Ralph Janssen, who was deposed from his position at Calvin Theological Seminary in the early 1920s, believed that the miracle of the rock in Rephidim that spewed forth water was not a miracle, but Moses' fortunate discovery of water in the rock. Dr. Janssen taught many things current in the thinking of higher critics: that manna was a natural plant that grew abundantly in the wilderness; that the stories of Samson were myths that Israel invented in imitation of Greek mythology; that Moses' monotheism was developed from pagan sources during his years in the wilderness; and that much of Jewish religion was gleaned from heathen practices.

While Dr. Janssen was deposed for his views, they live on in the Christian Reformed Church.

All these higher critical views are efforts to destroy Scripture as the word of God.

Proceeding from a fundamental premise that the Bible is, at least in part, a human document, higher criticism has come up with many strange ways in which to explain Scripture. I am sometimes amazed at the fertility of human imagination, which can invent so many theories to deny that Scripture is the word of God. It makes one wonder when one discovers the literally hundreds of books that have been written, all professing to be learned treatises, all written by self-proclaimed scholars, but all having one message in common: Scripture is not verbally inspired.

Questions have been raised over the last two or three centuries over the authorship of various writings from antiquity, even whether Shakespeare actually wrote the plays ascribed to him. But no writing of ancient times has ever been subjected to the scathing criticism received by the Scriptures. No other body of writings has ever been challenged the way Scripture has. No other manuscripts from the past have been so ruthlessly torn to shreds and have occupied so much of the time of unbelieving critics as has the Bible.

THE SINFULNESS OF HIGHER CRITICISM

Why all this frenzy to disprove the Bible as the word of God if it is only a human book? Why write hundreds and perhaps thousands of unreadable tomes about a book that no one ought to believe in any case?

The only answer is that every critic knows that the Bible is the word of God, but he hates that truth and bends his efforts to discredit it and to destroy it and to persuade others to do the same. The Bible condemns him for his sin, and he will not repent. So he attempts to destroy the Bible to escape Scripture's condemnation of himself.

A striking example of this effort is the eschatological method of Bible interpretation. This method is used to justify women in the special offices of the church and homosexuality in its members. The theory goes like this: It is obvious that the Bible condemns women in the special offices of the church, and it is undeniable that the Bible condemns homosexuality; however, these were the opinions of Christians from long ago and opinions that may have had some validity in past centuries. But the Bible must be interpreted in the light of history moving toward the end where the ideal will exist. That ideal will be the equality of all, including male and female, and the acceptance of all sinners by a merciful God who loves them all. And so, as history moves irrevocably toward that end, we must move beyond Scripture's prohibitions and do all in our power to achieve now what Scripture says will someday be reality. In this way we confess our faith in a brighter and happier future.

SCRIPTURE'S INSPIRATION

The church of all ages has confessed that Scripture is the word of God and the standard of truth and holiness. Yet the bitter attacks against Scripture have forced the church to define more precisely what it means when it says that Scripture is the word of God. To do this involves defining more precisely the meaning of inspiration.

This the church has done. It is not my intention to define this doctrine in all its details in this chapter, but I will emphasize the main tenets of Scripture's teaching about inspiration.

Scripture is verbally inspired, fully inspired; Scripture is totally what the Holy Spirit wanted written. Scripture is given to the church by God, word for word. Hence Scripture is infallible and inerrant and emphatically God's own word. Attempts have been made to find a difference between the words *infallible* and *inerrant* to justify an infallible Bible that contains errors. These attempts have failed and ought to fail because they are word games meant to introduce error into God's word. The terms *infallible* and *inerrant* mean the same thing.

Scripture is, therefore, authoritative. It tells us what must be believed as truth and how we must live. To disobey the Scriptures in any respect is to disobey God. To disobey God is to incur God's wrath and just judgment. The doctrine of Scripture is not a doctrine the pros and cons of which can be argued in some intellectually enjoyable debate that makes no great difference in the end. The doctrine of Scripture is literally a life and death matter—eternal life or eternal death.

Even though Reformed theology has used the term *human element* in its doctrine of inspiration, the time has come to abandon the term and the idea. There ought not to be any regrets about abandoning the term and the idea, for it is impossible to find in Scripture anywhere so much as a reference to such a human element. The Scriptures from beginning to end—not only the classical proof texts—teach that the divine element is the only explanation for Scripture's existence. Nor ought the believer to be perturbed by the charge that such a view of Scripture is docetic. Docetism was an ancient heresy that denied the human nature of Christ. To deny the human element in Scripture is said to be docetic, the underlying premise being, of course, that there is an analogy between the union of the two natures of Christ in one person and of a human and a divine element united in one book.[3]

Does this mean that the Bible was mechanically written without any participation of men? Were they acting only as secretaries? Did God play on the keyboard of their minds in much the same way a rapid typist plays on the keyboard of a typewriter or computer? Or did the Bible perhaps fall complete from heaven as a gift of the angels?

Inspiration means nothing of the kind. The Bible, inspired by God through the Holy Spirit, gives us the infallibly inspired record of the revelation of God in Jesus Christ in the salvation of the church. This is the great miracle of the ages of which the other miracles recorded in Scripture were pictures. The inspiration of Scripture is organically connected to the miracle of salvation. This connection is there because the Scriptures are written for the church, the company of believers. It is Christ's love letter to his bride for her to carry with her while she is still absent from him. The Scriptures are also connected inseparably to the miracle of salvation, because salvation is, in fact, accomplished through the Scriptures. The gospel is preached from the Scriptures. The people of God derive their strength, their comfort, their hope, and their blessedness from searching the Scriptures. It is a mighty fountain of blessing from Christ himself. The Bible belongs to the miracle of salvation, and it belongs, along with salvation, to the church.

All I have said does not mean that Scripture has nothing to say to and about the ungodly. Scripture calls all men to repentance and faith in Christ. Scripture speaks a great deal of the wicked, but only in their relation to the church. So many today leave the impression that the word of God is chiefly for the unconverted.

The inspiration of the Bible is, therefore, a miracle planned in God's eternal counsel. God eternally determined to reveal himself in Christ. He determined to give the church an infallible record of that revelation as it took place in history and will reach its grand finale when Christ comes again. God determined how the Bible would be written; that is, he would use men who lived in different times and places, had different personalities, and were brought up under different circumstances. God would use these men in such a way that all their personal attributes would be reflected in what they wrote. Yet their role would be of minor importance. We do not even know the men whom God used to write significant parts of the Bible.

When every writer whom God eternally chose had, through God's sovereign control of his life, written by divine inspiration the part eternally assigned to him, the result was one book with one theme. It was perfect, complete, and exactly suited to the purpose for which God had intended it. It was the church's Bible. Because the Bible was prepared as a part of God's means to save his people through Christ, it is indispensable for salvation. To take it away as the word of God in any sense is to jeopardize man's salvation. To believe Scripture is to be saved; to reject it is to be damned.

The church has treasured the Scriptures. The reformers insisted that no work of reformation would be possible without restoring the Bible to God's people and that there was no hope of delivering the saints from the chains of popery without freeing the Bible from the shackles of Roman Catholic theology. The church produced men who understood the importance of the Scriptures and were willing to die a martyr's death to give Scripture to God's people in a language they could read. The roll call of martyrs is long and illustrious. They lived in constant peril of their lives because they insisted that Scripture alone was what they would believe. In heaven alone is known the number of times God's people have turned to his word in all the sorrows and sufferings of life and have found peace. In the desert of this life, Scripture is the cooling fountain of water in an oasis. From it God's people have drunk deeply and longingly to quench their parched souls.

The words of Theodore Beza to the king of France, though referring to the church, can be applied as well to Scripture and to the senseless and wicked attacks on Scripture by the higher critics: "Sire...it is an anvil that has worn out many hammers."[4]

CHAPTER 33

AZUSA STREET REVIVAL
AND PENTECOSTALISM

INTRODUCTION

Although modern pentecostalism is of fairly recent origin, the heresy that
the movement promotes has ancient precedents. Solomon uses as his theme
in Ecclesiastes the saying, "There is no new thing under the sun" (Eccl.
1:9). This truth applies to pentecostalism.

In the early church the error of Montanism arose, which while not in
all respects like today's error, was nonetheless a predecessor of pentecostalism. The Montanists were followed by various mystical sects that appeared throughout the Middle Ages when the church was enslaved by
Roman Catholicism. Even the reformers were not free from the bother-
some error of the Anabaptists, who in their theology resembled the pentecostals in so many ways.

Yet none of these sects was quite like modern pentecostalism. Perhaps
one of the chief distinguishing characteristics of today's pentecostalism is
its ecumenical nature. Almost always, whether tolerated in the church (as
were the mystical sects of the Middle Ages) or declared by the church to
be sectarian and heretical (as was true of the Montanists and Anabaptists),
these groups were separate from the church. Today the movement is more
like an amorphous spirit that has entered into the religion of many people.
The movement is not organized into one ecclesiastical body, but it has per-
meated almost every denomination. And it is the shame of these denominations, some of which claim to be Reformed, that they shelter in their
midst and give tacit, if not official, approval to a deadly error.

Pentecostalism is a grave threat to the church and will be the death of
the church unless it is eradicated.

THE HISTORY OF MODERN PENTECOSTALISM

After the Civil War ended in 1865, the churches in America emerged from this gigantic struggle in quite a different form than they had in the days of frontier religion. The difference was chiefly in more organization, more ecclesiastical control of the life of the church, more formal religion, and more of an intellectual orientation. Prior to the Civil War, frontier religion was free, loose from any organizational restraints, emotional rather than intellectual, and without a definite creedal basis. In response to what many regarded as the dead and cold life of post-war churches, the holiness movement arose, which put its emphasis on inner experience of religion, sanctification, and closeness to God.

In the early part of 1900, Charles Fox Parham, a teacher at Bethel Bible College in Topeka, Kansas, became increasingly dissatisfied with the coldness and formality of the churches in the area. Pondering the matter, Parham came to the conclusion that the problem lay in the churches' drift away from the simplicity and religious fervor of the early church in Jerusalem. He began to teach people and ministers to pray for a return of the Spirit and a renewal of the pentecostal blessing.

Agnes N. Ozman, a student of Parham, claimed that on January 1, 1901 she had received the baptism of the Holy Spirit and began to speak in tongues. Parham and his disciples, encouraged by this evident answer to their prayers, began in 1905 to preach their new discovery throughout the southwestern United States. They soon gained a large following and began to form groups of like-minded people to pray for divine renewal.

In the heart of the industrial district of Los Angeles, California, stood a small clapboard church in which Methodists had once held services. It was located at 312 Azusa Street and was called the Apostolic Faith Gospel Mission. It was led by William Seymour, a one-eyed Negro man, who had been influenced by Parham and was a former holiness preacher. At a public meeting in 1906, pentecostalism as a national and even international religion began. The group worshiping on Azusa Street experienced an outpouring of the Spirit that it claimed was a repetition of Pentecost. The people upon whom the Spirit came began speaking in tongues.

This church ministered to all classes and races of people and soon became a mecca for people from all over the United States. These people, sharing in the special outpouring of the Spirit in the Azusa Street meeting house, returned to their homes, spreading the word that another Pentecost had finally come. The movement spread like wildfire and grew by leaps and bounds.

341

ITS CHARACTER

Pentecostalism is not one denomination or an organized group of churches with a common confession and administration. It has always been, and is now, a movement.

This does not mean that there are not churches that have become thoroughly pentecostal in their church doctrine and life. The most well-known denominations are the following: the Church of God, with its emphasis on holiness, which may be the only church that practices foot-washing; the Assemblies of God; the Church of God in Christ; the Pentecostal Holiness Church; the Pentecostal Church of God of America; the United Pentecostal Church; and the International Church of the Foursquare Gospel, founded by Aimee Semple McPherson.

Pentecostalism is a movement with some common characteristics, although in practice wide differences exist between the groups. In other words, it is a movement that has infiltrated many denominations, and while such denominations differ radically in their doctrine, history, worship, and church government, they are, almost without exception, open to the presence of pentecostalism in their midst. The Roman Catholic Church and Reformed and Presbyterian denominations have been favorable to this movement. It appears as if the most powerful force driving ecumenicity and the union of all churches into one super church is the pentecostal movement.

The movement is known by various names. Some of the better known are the Azusa Street movement, the second blessing movement, the baptism of the Spirit movement, or the charismatic movement, whose name is taken from the Greek word *charismata*—the gifts of the Spirit Paul mentions in 1 Corinthians 12:4.

Pentecostalism is extremely appealing to today's churchgoers; its appeal is also its deceptiveness. When the church loses the power of the lively preaching of the word, the worship services become formal, cold, lifeless, and unsatisfying. There is a vacuum created in the lives of people into which almost anything that is appealing can come rushing in as a mighty wind. The vacuum left by dull and lifeless preaching is filled by the stormy winds of pentecostalism.

Add to this the reality of life in twentieth- and twenty-first-century America in which people began to emphasize more and more the necessity of feeling good. Under the leadership of powerful preachers who talked about a positive self-image, feeling good about oneself, and the power of positive thinking, a feel-good gospel was more and more attractive to people who found it too hard to do a little thinking and who were too intellectually lazy to try to master even the rudiments of the Christian faith.

THE TEACHINGS OF PENTECOSTALISM

When most people think of pentecostalism, they think of long lines of people waiting to be healed; of tongue speaking; of singing with rhythm and hand clapping; and of disorderly meetings with a lot of shouting, many verbal "Praise the Lords," and even rolling about on the floor. But these practices do not tell what pentecostalism is.

The core of pentecostal religion is the doctrine of the second blessing, or the baptism with the Holy Spirit.

This doctrine teaches that a child of God, regenerated, converted, believing, sanctified, and walking in the path of his pilgrimage, is at a lower level of salvation than he ought to be because he has not received all that is available to him in Christ. Although he may have been saved by the Holy Spirit of God at his conversion, God intends more for him. He must receive the second blessing, the baptism with the Holy Spirit. He can and must aspire to greater blessings and to a higher level of piety, obtainable only when he is baptized with the Holy Spirit.

After his conversion or his water baptism, whether as an adult or an infant, another baptism is required. This baptism with the Spirit sometimes comes unexpectedly, although usually an individual is actively seeking it through prayer. More frequently it comes through the agency of the ministration of others who lay hands on an individual and pray for this second blessing.

In some pentecostal circles the second blessing of baptism with the Spirit is accompanied by some startling behavior, which is also characteristic of revival meetings. The two have much in common, for revival meetings are conducted with the purpose of seeking special outpourings of the Spirit to bring renewal to a dead church. Such revivals are accompanied by bizarre behavior of all sorts.

A person who receives the second blessing is also suddenly endowed with special gifts. These gifts include speaking in unknown tongues, performing miracles, prophesying, and interpreting prophecy and unknown tongues. In more radical pentecostal circles the gifts also include handling of poisonous snakes. For proof of this latter gift, pentecostals appeal to Mark 16:18.

In the theory of pentecostalism, the second blessing, or baptism with the Spirit, is a reenactment of the first Pentecost and an ongoing fulfillment of the prophecy of Joel, which Peter quoted in his Pentecost sermon (Acts 2).

CRITICISMS OF PENTECOSTALISM

Pentecostalism is a dangerous threat to the church of Christ, which has the calling to hold fast to the truth revealed in the word of God. It is a measure of the spiritual and theological departure of much of the church world that pentecostalism is tolerated and approved within Reformed and Presbyterian churches. It is a destructive movement that contradicts Scripture's doctrine of the work of the Holy Spirit and comes close to being a blasphemy of the Holy Spirit, if it is not so.

We mention here, somewhat briefly, the objections to pentecostalism that arise out of Scripture's teachings.

Pentecostalism is seriously wrong when it speaks of the second blessing or baptism with the Holy Spirit as a power to bring the child of God to a higher level of spirituality and piety. By doing this, pentecostalism speaks scornfully of the ordinary life of the Christian who daily fulfills his calling in life in the home, the church, and the shop. The daily struggle with sin, the constant battle to live in obedience to God, the mundane and routine willingness to bear one's cross in patience—all this and so much more that belongs to the life of the Christian in the world is looked down on and denigrated. Such a Christian is, in the eyes of pentecostals, a second-class Christian who has not attained to the higher, nobler, more spiritual level of piety and Christian experience that belong to the spiritually elite. Such a wicked classification of other Christians smacks of Pharisaism and despises what is more than anything else pleasing to God, namely, a broken spirit and a contrite heart.

Pentecostalism speaks of gifts of the Spirit that belonged exclusively to the apostolic period as being still present today. This is a serious error, which completely lacks an understanding of the purpose of special gifts: God gave special gifts to the early church as signs of the truth of the gospel. This was necessary because the Scriptures were not written as yet, and those who were brought by the preaching of the gospel to faith in Christ had no complete Scripture with which to compare the teachings of the apostles to determine their truth. They could not perfectly do what the Berean Christians did in part: search the Scriptures to see whether these things were so. But when the Scriptures were completed, the need for signs and wonders was past. The church had the written word of God. That is not only enough, but far, far better than signs and wonders. In fact, to lean heavily on signs and wonders as a necessary part of the Christian's life is to speak disparagingly of God's word in the Bible. It is to say that the Bible is not enough; more is needed. It is to do what the rich man in hell wanted done when he pleaded with Abraham to send Lazarus to his brothers because he thought that a ghost from the dead would do what the Bible could not do. Let the pentecostals hear Abraham's words to the rich man: "If they hear not Moses and the prophets, neither will they be persuaded, though one rose from the dead" (Luke 16:31).

The fact that pentecostals teach the importance of signs and wonders is not strange. They really do not believe in the sufficiency of Scripture. They want to add to it, in contradiction of Scripture's words in Revelation 22:18. They want prophecies, additional revelation through those who speak in tongues, and special words from God through special revelations.

Pentecostalism stands in the tradition of mysticism. I need not go into this, for I have treated mysticism earlier. But let it be said, though briefly, that the mysticism of the pentecostals stands in the tradition of mysticism as it has raised its ugly head throughout the ages of the church since the Montanist movement in the third century. The Christian who has attained to a higher level of the Christian life supposedly has attained to direct and immediate fellowship with God through prophecies, visions, dreams, special revelations, and other mystical experiences.

Mysticism tends to bypass Christ, for it speaks of *direct* communion with God in meetings with God characterized almost entirely by spiritual ecstasy, highly emotional experiences, indescribable encounters with the divine, and a soaring of the soul to heavenly realms that submerge a person into the divine being. Here is where pentecostalism and revivalism meet. Leaders of revival speak of direct encounters with the triune God in which they talked with God, discussed with him various matters, and were given by God various bits of information that they proceeded to communicate to others.

Pentecostalism is deadly mysticism and denies that the only way to the Father is through Christ. Christ is set forth in the Scriptures, and only in these Scriptures do we know Christ and, knowing Christ, know God. But that knowing of God through Christ revealed in the Scriptures is an intellectual apprehension of the truth of the Scriptures and never a revelation apart from the Scriptures. Eternal life is, according to Jesus in his high priestly prayer, *to know* God as the only true God and Jesus Christ whom God has sent (John 17:3).

Finally, both pentecostalism and revivalism have an incorrect understanding of Pentecost. Pentecost was the outpouring of the Holy Spirit upon the church that marked the end of the old dispensation and the beginning of the new. According to John 7:39, the Holy Spirit as the Spirit of the ascended and glorified Christ did not exist in the Old Testament (see also Acts 2:33). The new dispensation differs from the old in significant respects because of the presence of the Spirit in the church. In the old dispensation, the church was limited to the Jews; in the new, the church is gathered from all nations of the earth; hence the sign of speaking in tongues. In the old, believers were utterly dependent on prophets, priests, and kings to know the will of God; in the new, believers have the Spirit and "need not that any man teach you" (1 John 2:27; Heb. 8:10, 11). In the old dispensation, the revelation of God was limited to types and shadows that enabled the saints to know only in part; in the new dispensation, through the Spirit they are led into all truth (John 14–16) and are able to understand things they did not understand before. Even on Mount Olivet at the time Jesus ascended, the apostles were still looking for an earthly kingdom (Acts 1:6), a misconception rooted in their failure to understand the work of Christ on the cross. Yet suddenly, after the Spirit was poured out, they understood it all clearly, and Peter was able to preach an extraordinarily insightful sermon in which he laid out the full meaning of Christ's perfect accomplishment of salvation in his cross, his resurrection, his ascension, and his pouring out of the Spirit.

Pentecost was a once-for-all event. Pentecostals and revivalists who speak of repeated Pentecosts in special outpourings of the Spirit sin greatly in denying the meaning and significance of that glorious event almost two thousand years ago.

Because pentecostalism is to be found in most denominations, it may very well be the one unifying factor in a false ecumenism that will eventually unite the church in the service of the beast.

CHAPTER 34

COMMON GRACE

INTRODUCTION

The controversy over common grace is of particular interest to the Protestant Reformed Churches in America (PRCA), for it was the immediate occasion for the existence of these churches as a separate denomination. The founders of these churches were expelled from the Christian Reformed Church (CRC) for refusing to agree with common grace as a doctrine taught in Scripture and the confessions. These leaders, Revs. Herman Hoeksema, George Ophoff, and Henry Danhof, refused to preach and teach it in their congregations as was required of them.

As the error of common grace was adopted officially by the CRC, it dealt with two ways in which the grace of God was said to be common to all men. One was the operative and powerful grace of God in the hearts of the reprobate through the Spirit of Christ by which sin in the reprobate was restrained and the unregenerate were enabled to do good works of value to God and the church. The second was a grace that was common because it was a general manifestation of an attitude of favor and love toward all men manifested not only in the good gifts that all men receive from God, but manifested especially in the well-meaning and gracious offer of the gospel that invites all men to believe on Christ. The common invitation of the gospel is an expression of God's heartfelt longing for all men to be saved.

There is a relation between these two views, for the grace of God toward all men that is manifested in the free offer of the gospel is also a grace given to all men in their hearts by which they are able to accept or reject the gospel offer. This is the same grace that supposedly makes it possible for an unregenerate man to do good.

THE COMMON GRACE OF THE GOSPEL OFFER

The idea of a gracious gospel offer and its associated doctrines was found from very early times in the history of the church of the new dispensation, although the term "gospel offer" was not used then. Already at the time of the great church father Augustine, in the last of the fourth and the first part of the fifth centuries, the issue between Augustine and Pelagius was sovereign and particular grace over against common grace. Augustine held to eternal and sovereign predestination. The followers of Pelagius held to a general desire of God to save all men and a universal atonement that made salvation possible for all men.[1]

Shortly after the great Synod of Dordt, the Amyrauldian heresy arose in France. It was named after its chief defender, Amyraut, who proposed the same ideas as the Pelagians of Augustine's time. The influence of this heresy, sometimes known as hypothetical universalism, was very influential in France and the British Isles, and to a lesser extent in the Netherlands.

Although the Westminster Assembly, which had a few Amyrauldian members, did not adopt the heresy of the well-meant offer, it nevertheless survived in two men, Richard Baxter and Edward Fisher. The Marrow men revived it in the Marrow controversy of the eighteenth century.

From Scotland, where the Marrow controversy took place, it was imported into the Netherlands. Close contact between the church of Scotland and the church in the Netherlands made a transfer of doctrinal ideas inevitable. The emphasis on a gospel offer and a certain universality of the death of Christ (Christ did not die for all men, but was said to be "dead" for all men) crept into the thinking of the more Reformed in the Netherlands. The state church in the Netherlands had become apostate, and the pious and orthodox people were forced to meet in conventicles to maintain their piety and orthodoxy. The emphasis on spiritual warmth of piety and experience that characterized the Marrow men appealed to the faithful in the Netherlands, who were left cold by the apostasy in their own church. But along with such piety came the idea of the offer of the gospel.

At the time of the Separation of 1834 (*De Afscheiding*) from the state church in the Netherlands under Hendrick De Cock and others, the idea of a well-meant offer had taken deep root. De Cock and Simon Van Velzen, did not hold to such an idea of the gospel, but Anthony Brummelkamp, and quite likely Albertus C. Van Raalte, did. And so it came into the thinking of the Reformed churches in the Netherlands and, through immigration, into America.

Although Abraham Kuyper was opposed to any notion of a well-meant gospel offer as was current thinking in parts of the Reformed churches, and although his followers in America did not teach such a view, many of those who had their ecclesiastical roots in the Separation of 1834 did believe this doctrine. And so it was freely taught in the CRC by various preachers from the middle of the nineteenth century on.

It thus entered the thinking of the CRC, and it is no surprise that when the CRC made decisions on common grace, it included a statement on the well-meant gospel offer.

The main ideas imbedded in the gospel offer are as follows.

The preaching of the gospel is and must be an expression on God's part to save all who hear the gospel. That is, God's will is that all who hear the gospel be saved. He earnestly desires this and expresses this desire in the preaching. Ministers who preach, therefore, are duty bound to tell all who hear that God wants them to be saved and does all he possibly can to assure them that salvation is available to them.

It is claimed by those who defend this view that it is impossible to do evangelism work and missionary work on foreign fields unless one can assure his listeners that God truly desires their salvation and that it is God's will that they be saved. Thus also the door is open for the minister to plead with sinners to accept Christ, to invite them to come to Christ, and to urge them to "close with Christ"—a phrase that had been popular with the Marrow men.

Such a desire on God's part to save all who hear the gospel is rooted in a certain favorable attitude of God toward all men. God is favorably inclined to all men and expresses that inclination in his will to save all. This is where grace enters in. God's favorable inclination is his gracious attitude toward all men. This gracious attitude toward all men is revealed in other ways, such as rain and sunshine, health and prosperity, and a good and prosperous life. But it is especially revealed in God's express statements to all who hear the gospel that God, on his part, really wants those who hear to be saved.

But grace is only one aspect of a favorable attitude toward God. Grace includes all God's attributes of love, kindness, longsuffering, mercy, and the like. And so God loves all men, is merciful to all men, is kind toward all men, and does nothing but that which will underscore his desire to save all men.

Because one necessarily must ask concerning the judicial ground for such an attitude of favor, this idea of common grace involves also a certain universal atonement. The judicial ground is the universal character and sufficiency of the suffering of Christ. God cannot want to save those for whom no salvation is available. God cannot offer blessings that are not in

God's storehouse. And so, a universal gracious gospel offer involves a universal aspect to the atoning sacrifice of Christ.

If the preaching expresses what God wants, it is obvious that whether a man is saved or not depends on what man wants. God does all he can, including atoning for sin in his Son; it remains to see what man will do. Thus a blatant Arminianism is tied to the gracious gospel offer. Salvation hinges on the free will of man. Those defenders of common grace who are still somewhat committed to Calvinism and its five points have attempted to preserve their Calvinism by insisting that man has no free will, but that God gives special and saving grace to his elect only. But such a harsh contradiction arises out of an idea of God who both wants to save and does not want to save. With such a contradiction, free will wins out, and those committed to a gracious and well-meant gospel offer have openly espoused the Arminian doctrine of free will.

Almost always, if not always, this common grace that comes through the preaching of the gospel is not only an objective statement of God's love for all men, but it is also a subjective bestowal of grace on those who hear the gospel. This grace is applied to the hearts of the hearers. This grace gives to those who hear the spiritual ability to choose for or against the offer of the gospel. It is a grace, therefore, that can be resisted.

OBJECTIONS TO THE GOSPEL OFFER
The objections against this view of the gospel, which have been brought throughout the centuries and particularly by the PRCA, are as follows.

The gospel cannot be and never is a mere offer, for it is "the power of God unto salvation to every one that believeth" (Rom. 1:16). A power unto salvation is quite different from an offer that depends on man's will for the reception of its contents.

Along with a well-meant and gracious gospel offer goes a whole package of doctrines that do dishonor to God by destroying the doctrines of sovereign and particular grace. Scripture and the confessions teach that God does all things for his glory as the sovereign Lord of all. In salvation, he determines who will be saved and who will not—for whom Christ died and for whom he did not die. God determines also in whom the Spirit works salvation and in whom the Spirit hardens the heart. God saves his own elect through the power of the cross, and his work of salvation is entirely his own. Thus, while the heresy of the gracious offer of the gospel is Arminianism, the Scriptures teach a sovereign and particular grace of God that gives all glory to God.

The whole concept of a gracious gospel offer introduces an impossible contradiction into God's own mind and will. It teaches (at least among those who claim to be Reformed) that God both wills the salvation of all men and does not will the salvation of all men. When confronted with such a contradiction, the defenders of this heresy fall back on the lame doctrine of paradox and apparent contradiction.

The view that the gospel expresses God's desire to save all men puts those who hold it into the camp of a long line of heretics beginning with the Pelagians of the fifth century. In contrast, sovereign and particular grace is the truth of the church from ancient times.

Such are the issues of the common grace of the well-meant gospel offer.

THE HISTORY OF KUYPERIAN COMMON GRACE

The other part of common grace has to do with God's grace, worked by the Holy Spirit in the hearts of all men, that restrains sin and enables man to do good.

This idea of grace was first proposed by Abraham Kuyper in a massive work *De Gemeene Gratie* (Common Grace). Kuyper gave this title to his book because he wanted to distinguish his common grace from the common grace of the gracious offer of the gospel, which he opposed.

When the followers of Kuyper came to this country in the latter part of the nineteenth and early part of the twentieth centuries, most of them joined the CRC. So there were really two camps in the CRC, both holding to a different view of common grace. These two camps did not get along very well, and the dissension between them was severe. But they found a compromise that restored peace and unity, a compromise expressed in the three points of common grace adopted by the Synod of the CRC in Kalamazoo, Michigan, in 1924. These three points were the occasion for the expulsion of Revs. Hoeksema, Ophoff, and Danhof, who refused to subscribe to them.

The Protestant Reformed Churches were organized from Reformed people out of the two groups within the CRC, one group from the De Cock camp and one group from the Kuyper camp. These members were, however, united in the PRCA in their mutual confession of sovereign and particular grace. They rejected both kinds of common grace as Arminian and contrary to Scripture and the confessions.

It is an interesting question why Kuyper developed his elaborate theory of common grace. The answer to this question lies in his view of the Netherlands and its role in the defense and propagation of the Reformed faith.

Prior to the Separation of 1834, the only Reformed church in the Netherlands was the state church (*Hervormde Kerk*). Many in the Netherlands, including Kuyper, believed that their country was destined to be the fountainhead of the Reformed faith in the whole world. The truth of the Reformed faith, issuing from the Netherlands as a mighty stream, they thought would sweep as a river through the world and have such influence that all nations would themselves become Reformed or would, at the very least, come under the influence of the Reformed faith and benefit from the prosperity and national well-being that would accrue to Reformed countries. The Netherlands would be in this powerful position because it was a Reformed country with a government that supported the Reformed church.

When Kuyper saw the possibility of organizing a political party that could control the government, he resigned from the ministry and entered politics. First his party, the Anti-Revolutionary Party, gained seats in the Dutch parliament, and then Kuyper saw the possibility that he himself could become prime minister. But he was able to become prime minister only by forming a coalition with another political party, since his party did not have an absolute majority by itself. This coalition was made with the Roman Catholic party, and as a result of the coalition, Kuyper did succeed in his goal of becoming prime minister.

Kuyper's coalition with the Roman Catholics was not a strange move on his part. It was obvious to all that although the Reformed Church was the government-sponsored church, not all the citizens of the nation were true children of God nor members of the Reformed Church. If, therefore, the Netherlands was to be the fountainhead of the Reformed faith as a Reformed country, it had to take into consideration the many who were not Reformed so that all could unite in a common cause of promoting the Reformed faith throughout the world.

Kuyper found the basis for such cooperation between all the citizens in his doctrine of common grace. Common grace was the one ground on which believers and unbelievers, indeed all the citizens of the Netherlands, could cooperate in a common cause of Christianizing the world, if not making it truly Reformed. It was the ground, therefore, for Kuyper's involvement in politics and for his coalition with Roman Catholics.

THE NATURE OF KUYPERIAN COMMON GRACE

Kuyper's idea of common grace worked out along the following lines.

The fall of Adam in paradise was of such devastating severity that without divine intervention, the creation would have become a barren wasteland and man would have become a beast or a devil. God, therefore, intervened with common grace, which he bestowed on all the descendants of Adam to preserve them from becoming beasts or demons. This same common grace was given to the creation at the time of the flood when God established a covenant with all creation and put the rainbow in the heavens as a sign of his common grace.

The result of this common grace is that man, through its power, is able to fulfill the original creation mandate of subduing the earth. Without common grace this would be impossible; with common grace, subduing the earth becomes a reality.

This calling to subdue the earth is given to all the descendants of Adam, and because all are able to engage successfully in this task, common grace forms a common ground for believers and unbelievers to cooperate in the common task of earth-subduing.

The cultural mandate implies the obligation of men to discover all the earth's powers and resources and to make use of them in ways in which these powers can be properly utilized. In subduing the earth, men discover the powers of the wind, the rain, electricity, the atom, etc. These powers are, in turn, put to use in ways that benefit mankind, make his life easier and more pleasurable, and give man leisure in which to develop the arts: painting, sculpture, music, architecture, and so on. Thus the human race progresses in the development of culture, which in turn can be used to solve the problems of disease, poverty, suffering, war, and racial and labor strife.

Because the unregenerate are striving for the same goals as the regenerate, cooperation is possible between both kinds of people, and the result is a huge area of mutual interest and concern in which the wicked and righteous work side by side to put the whole creation and all society's institutions in the service of Christ for the King (*pro rege*).

It all sounds a bit like a postmillennial dream. Although Kuyper would claim to be an amillennialist, the postmillennialists have claimed him as one of their own, and rightly so. Reformed churches have followed the Kuyperian dream in many instances, and the ideas of "making this world a better place to live," "subduing all things to Christ the King," and "putting everything in the creation in the service of Christ" are slogans of institutions and schools that still cling to the name *Reformed*.

Some thought this cooperation between godly and ungodly could take place in the world of ideas as well. Dr. Ralph Janssen appealed to Kuyperian common grace in support of his higher criticism of the Bible. He found many good ideas in the pagan worship of the nations surrounding Israel because of their common grace, and he saw Israel's religion as formed and molded by pagan thought and developed by common grace.

Evolutionism, openly taught in Reformed and Presbyterian schools, is justified on the grounds that unbelieving science, by the power of common grace, is able to determine how the world came into existence.

Regarding morality, the same is thought to be true. Worldly music, instead of being consigned to the generations and moral rot of Jubal, is viewed as God's fruitful work of grace in the hearts of otherwise wicked men. Any act or deed that in an outward way seems to be merciful, beneficial, skillful, or enjoyable is ascribed to the common grace of God, without any regard for God's own verdict: "Whatsoever is not of faith is sin" (Rom. 14:23).

Kuyper claimed that the good deeds of the unregenerate, because they were worked by grace, would be preserved for heaven and the fruits of the pagans would be found in glory. I find it difficult to imagine that hard rock will be played in heaven and that the walls of the new Jerusalem will be decorated with paintings by modern artists. Heaven would lose much attractiveness if such were indeed the case.

OBJECTIONS TO KUYPERIAN COMMON GRACE
Apart from the fact that Scripture is very clear on the crucial point that grace is always sovereign, the defenders of sovereign and particular grace, especially the PRCA, launched successful attacks against Kuyper's theory of common grace.

Kuyper's theory is not found in Scripture. One reads *De Gemeene Gratie* with amazement that Kuyper quotes so few scriptural passages in support of his position. But worse, the view is hostile to Scripture, because it goes against God's own pronouncement upon the "good" deeds of the unregenerate: "Whatsoever is not of faith is sin" (Rom. 14:23). That passage is unequivocal, all-embracing, and decisive for any evaluation of every deed of man. One gets the impression that in Kuyper's judgment, the ungodly are capable of far more good than the humble child of God who daily struggles with his sin, confesses that all his works are nothing, knows that even his very best works are corrupted and polluted by sin, and flees daily to the cross for forgiveness.

Herman Hoeksema predicted at the outset of the common grace controversy that if the theory of Kuyperian common grace were ever adopted, it would be the end of the antithesis between the people of God and the wicked. So it has proved to be. Common grace has been a hole in the dike of the antithesis, a hole that has grown larger with the passing of the years until it has become a yawning breach through which has poured a tidal wave of worldliness and evil. Look at the church about us today and weep.

The antithesis is not between the Reformed country of the Netherlands and the rest of the world, or between America and the rest of the world; it is between the elect and the reprobate in the Netherlands, in America, and throughout the world. The antithesis is marked by the fact that the totally depraved unbeliever, capable as he is of doing mighty deeds with the powers of God's creation, nevertheless uses everything he discovers and invents to promote the wicked kingdom of antichrist. He sins in everything he does, for his works are not out of faith but are in opposition to God and in the service of Satan.

The elect and regenerate child of God also lives in the world—the same world in which the wicked man lives—but the child of God lives in the world as a citizen of the kingdom of heaven. He thus uses God's world, insofar as he has any control over a part of it, to seek the kingdom of heaven. He seeks that kingdom as manifested in the world in his church, in his covenant schools, and in his walk as a faithful citizen who serves the Lord Christ and witnesses by word and life to the truth of the gospel. He seeks that kingdom by condemning all wickedness in the world about him and testifying of the certain judgment of God upon evil. And he seeks that kingdom by pursuing his earthly pilgrimage faithfully as it leads him ever nearer his eternal destination, the house of many mansions. The kingdom over which Christ his redeemer rules, and in which he is a citizen, is a heavenly kingdom.

CHAPTER 35

FEDERAL VISION THEOLOGY

INTRODUCTION

The new dispensation church, in its history of struggles to defend the truth of God's word, has had to defend one doctrine above all others, for it is the one doctrine that more than any other is subject to the unrelenting attacks of wicked men under the direction of Satan. This one truth is the doctrine of the absolute sovereignty of God, particularly in the work of salvation.

Although the threats against the doctrinal purity of the confessions of Presbyterian and Reformed churches in the twenty-first century are many, one of the most dangerous is the heresy of the federal vision. Much has been written on this subject. A brief summary of the heresy will serve the purpose of this book.

ITS NAME AND ORIGIN

Various names are given to this heresy. The most common name is the federal vision. This name indicates especially that it is closely connected with federal theology, that is, the doctrine of the covenant. Another name is the Auburn Avenue theology, a name given to it because a Presbyterian church on Auburn Avenue in Monroe, Louisiana, is the headquarters of this heretical thought.

The origin of it seems to have been the confluence of two lines of thinking that came together to form its chief features. The one line of thinking is the doctrine of justification by faith and works. Within conservative circles, this doctrine was first proposed by Norman Shepherd when he was professor at Westminster Theological Seminary in Philadelphia (1963–1981). The struggle over the doctrine went on for many years between Shepherd's supporters and critics. The battle took place in the late 1970s and early 1980s. It finally ended in Norman Shepherd's resignation from Westminster.[1] The irony was that his views were never officially condemned, and Westminster remains today a center for the propagation of the heresy.

The other line of thinking is, surprisingly enough, the theology of the late Prof. William Heyns of Calvin Seminary and the late Dr. Klaas Schilder of the "Liberated" Churches in the Netherlands. They emphasized the idea of a conditional covenant. Schilder taught these views throughout his ministry, although the idea of a conditional covenant was held more widely in the British Isles and on the European continent for many years prior to Schilder's work.

The idea of a conditional covenant is an inevitable consequence of an erroneous view of the covenant that many held from the time of the Reformation. The covenant of grace, in keeping with the notion of a covenant of works, was said to be a pact or agreement between God and man that depended for its adoption and maintenance on a number of promises and conditions.

The view of a conditional covenant included the idea that all the children who were baptized were included in the covenant and received the promise of God that they would be saved, but on condition that they would, in the future, accept the provisions of the covenant.

Although I wrote that the heresy of the federal vision was the "confluence" of these two lines of thought, that is not quite true since the idea of a conditional covenant is older, and the works-righteousness of the federal vision of more recent origin. The intrinsic relation between the two is definite and emphatic, however. To hold consistently to a conditional covenant must inevitably result in a doctrine of a conditional salvation. The federal vision theology carries out that conditional salvation idea to its necessary end.

Some of the chief defenders of this view, besides Norman Shepherd, are Steve Wilkins, a Presbyterian minister; John Frame, a professor in a Presbyterian seminary; Steve Schlissel and Douglas Wilson, two ministers in independent churches; and John Barach, formerly a minister in the United Reformed Church. Another vocal defender of this view is Don Van Dyken, a minister in the Orthodox Christian Reformed Church.

Almost every major Reformed and Presbyterian denomination has either approved of the heresy or refused to condemn it (an indirect form of approval). Some denominations, such as the Orthodox Christian Reformed Church, have struggled long with the doctrine, although one of its pastors openly taught it and has not been disciplined.

Opposition to the view seems to be increasing, however. The Reformed

Church in the United States (RCUS) has not only adopted a document condemning the federal vision, but it has also called to repentance those who hold to it. Two lengthy documents have appeared, as of this writing, condemning the view. One was prepared by a committee in the Orthodox Presbyterian Church (OPC), and another by the faculty of Mid-America. It is earnestly hoped that more churches will join in its condemnation.

The federal vision is, beyond any doubt, the gravest threat to confessional truth in general, and to the doctrine of the sovereignty of God in salvation in particular, that the churches have seen in many years. Innumerable modifications of the truth of sovereign grace have been introduced into the church since Dordt and Westminster, but there has always been something subtle and surreptitious about these earlier heresies. In the federal vision, we and the church world are confronted with an open and head-on attack against that one truth of sovereign grace in the defense of which so many in the past have suffered and died.

The attack is not camouflaged. It is, without apology, a rejection of Luther's justification by faith alone. It is a reiteration of what the Roman Catholic Church taught for centuries, and from which heresy the Reformation delivered us. It is a repudiation of the confessional heritage of the church. It is a bold and frontal attack on the salvation of the people of God.

THE TEACHINGS OF THE FEDERAL VISION

As I noted earlier, the federal vision has its roots in the heresy of a conditional covenant. It emphasizes that it is a doctrine having to do with the covenant that not only has its roots in covenant theology, but also defines the nature and essence of the covenant.

No matter what view of the covenant one may take, the doctrine of the covenant has to do with the doctrine of salvation. If the covenant is conditional in its very nature, salvation itself is conditional. This obvious fact is carried to its extreme by those who promote the federal vision.

If the covenant is conditional, it is conditional because it is established with more people than those who are actually saved. And this is what the promoters of the federal vision maintain. They take hold of the old covenant conception of Professor William Heyns, promoted and developed by Dr. Klaas Schilder, and carry it to its logical extreme. Heyns and Schilder taught that baptism is a sign and seal of the covenant and that God establishes his covenant, therefore, with every baptized child. Thus every child of believers is included in the covenant, fully and in such a way that all the blessings of the covenant are his.

Today's followers of the late Dr. Schilder maintain his views. They do not believe that election ought to be the controlling principle that determines membership in the covenant. They are adamant about separating the covenant from God's electing determination of his people. Dr. Schilder said that all born in covenant lines belong to the covenant. The men of the federal vision diverge from Schilder on this one point and even go beyond Schilder. They take the position that all born within covenant lines are elect: really, fully, and completely. They are all elect from all eternity, written in the Lamb's book of life, destined for eternal glory, and the objects of God's electing love. And because all are elect, all receive really, fully, and completely all the blessings of the covenant, which is to say that they receive all the blessings of salvation. They are regenerated, converted, justified, sanctified, and objects of saving grace.

Because not all are saved who are elect and are given the blessings of salvation, the covenant, with all its blessedness, has to be conditional. That is, all these blessings will continue to belong to the children of the covenant as long as they fulfill the conditions of the covenant. Should they fail to fulfill the conditions by not walking in obedience to God, they will lose their election, their conversion, their sanctification, and their justification. A conditional covenant results in a conditional salvation.

This conditional salvation is applied especially to the doctrine of justification. The result is a doctrine of justification by faith and works. And so we are back where the church started in 1517, for we are back to Roman Catholic theology.

One may object that the federal vision position vindicates the Roman Catholic Church. And so it does. One formerly Protestant author has justified his return to the Roman Catholic Church by an appeal to Shepherd's doctrine of justification by faith and works.

One may object that the reformers unanimously repudiated Rome's heresy and agreed that justification was by faith alone. The promoters of the federal vision are not deterred by an appeal to the reformers and scornfully repudiate them.

One may object that Luther called the truth of justification by faith alone the standing or falling of the church. It makes no difference. One promoter of the federal vision heresy simply wrote Luther off as wrong.

One may object that the Reformed confessions and the Westminster Standards are all agreed that justification is by faith alone. That, too, makes no difference to federal vision promoters. The confessions are dismissed as being wrong, or at best as being inadequate on this point. With a cavalier wave of the hand, they dismiss the entire tradition of the Reformation.

One may object that Scripture is clear, especially Paul in his epistles to the Romans and the Galatians, but this, too, is argued away. Here, however, we come to another aspect of the heresy of the federal vision. Since Paul is unmistakably clear that justification is by faith alone, these heretics had to do something about Paul. They now promote a new perspective on Paul. The leading figure in this effort to get rid of Paul is N. T. Wright, a theologian and Anglican bishop in Durham, England. He has invented the novel theory that Paul was not writing against justification by faith and works, but was rather combating a Jewish heresy that sought salvation in the works of the law. Paul's fierce denunciation of justification by faith and works, as well as his repeated insistence that justification is by faith alone, was simply a refutation of Jewish legalism. James in his epistle sets the balance right, so it is said, when James tells us that both Abraham and Rahab were justified by works.[2]

This is, admittedly, a brief summary of the teachings of the federal vision, but it is sufficient to give us some idea of the extent of its basic ideas.

THE ERROR OF THE FEDERAL VISION

The church of Jesus Christ is, with the rise of this heresy, confronted with a vicious and unprincipled attack against the truth of sovereign and particular grace. It rivals in danger anything the church has yet confronted in her entire history. This assessment is legitimate in light of the fact that it has come under the guise of the Reformed faith and in this disguise has deceived many within Reformed and Presbyterian churches.

The new perspective on Paul is born out of a higher critical view of Scripture that is destructive of God's word and insidiously deceptive. This "new perspective" is so necessary to the whole system of the federal vision that if it should be proved wrong, the whole system crumbles in pieces. Paul has to be reinterpreted by some sort of exegetical legerdemain in order to give credence to the view. We reject its higher critical view of Scripture as heresy.

The true children of the Reformation will be appalled at the arrogant dismissal of the teachings of all the reformers. There is a pride and conceit that staggers the imagination in such a dismissal of men whom God used to reform the church. Theological pygmies stand in the shadow of the giants of the sixteenth century and criticize them for being so tall.

But worse: the way is paved for a return to Rome, something many

Protestants have already done. If justification is not by faith alone, then the church can find no reason not to apologize to Rome for the sins of the sixteenth century and must rush back into the embrace of the pope. But let it not be forgotten that along the way back to Rome, one will have to pass by the graves of countless martyrs who died excruciatingly painful deaths in their commitment to the truth of sovereign grace. These graves will be the silent accusers of all who repudiate their glorious heritage.

To adopt the views of the federal vision is to repudiate every one of the five points of Calvinism, points laid down carefully by the great Synod of Dordt. For a particular, sovereign, and efficacious decree of *unconditional election,* the defenders of the heresy of the federal theology opt for the damnable Arminian doctrine of a universal and conditional election. For the doctrine of *total depravity,* the federal vision people teach that man has a free will and can do works by his own power. For *particular redemption,* we are now confronted with the age-old heresy of a universal atonement. If all baptized children have salvation in fact, this is because Christ died for them all. The church has fought for a particular atonement in vain if these views are accepted. Instead of *irresistible grace,* we are told that grace is resistible, since all baptized children receive grace although some successfully resist it. And no longer can the believer find refuge in the doctrine of the *preservation of the saints,* for he may once have been elect, once regenerated, and once justified; but he has no guarantee that he shall remain such. All hangs on his own obedience and good works.

God's everlasting covenant of grace—the one unifying truth of the gospel and the overarching doctrine of salvation—becomes a mere conditional agreement, dependent on our faithfulness and willingness to fulfill the conditions of it.

Why do so many want such poison pap instead of the rich and nourishing foods of God's sovereign and particular grace? The only answer can be that they are enemies of the gospel. Let the righteous beware, and let them thank God every day for the truth of his own everlasting covenant of grace.

NOTES

CHAPTER 1

1 "Irenaeus against Heresies," in Alexander Roberts and James Donaldson, ed., *The Ante-Nicene Fathers: Translations of the Writings of the Fathers down to AD 325,* vol. 1, *The Apostolic Fathers—Justin Martyr and Irenaeus* (Grand Rapids MI: Eerdmans, repr., 1987), 416.

2 Gnosticism was an early heresy that appeared in the church in the third century, although early forms of it may have been present in apostolic times.

CHAPTER 2

1 See Peter Jones, *The Gnostic Empire Strikes Back: An Old Heresy for the New Age* (Phillipsburg, NJ: P&R Publishing, 1992), which compares the New Age movement of modern times to the ancient gnostic movement.

2 Prof. Walther, quoted in Louis Berkhof, *The History of Christian Doctrines* (Grand Rapids, MI: Baker Book House, 1937), 47.

3 Iranaeus, "Against Heresies," quoted in Jaroslav Pelikan, *The Christian Tradition,* vol. 1, *The Emergence of the Catholic Tradition 100–600* (Chicago: University of Chicago Press, 1971), 87.

4 Charles Bigg, *Origins of Christianity,* quoted in Charles Williams, *Descent of the Dove* (Grand Rapids, MI: Eerdmans, 1939), 23.

CHAPTER 3

1 Philip Schaff, *History of the Christian Church,* vol. 2, *Ante-Nicene Christianity: AD 100–325,* 5th ed. (New York: Charles Scribner's Sons, 1910; repr., Grand Rapids, MI: Eerdmans, 1967), 426, 427.

CHAPTER 4

1 Adolph Harnack, *History of Dogma,* vol. 4, trans. E. B. Speirs and James Millar from third German edition (Eugene, OR: Wipf and Stock Publishers, 1997), 26, 27.

2 Schaff, *History,* 2:577.

CHAPTER 5

1 Nicaeno-Constantinopolitan Creed, in Philip Schaff, ed., *Creeds of Christendom with a History and Critical Notes,* 6th ed., 3 vols.ok (New York: Harper & Row, 1931; repr., Grand Rapids, MI: Baker Books, 2007), 2:58.

2 Eusebius, quoted in Schaff, *History,* vol. 3, *Nicene and Post-Nicene Christianity: From Constantine the Great to Gregory the Great, AD 311–600,* 5th rev. ed. (New York: Charles Scribner's Sons; repr., Grand Rapids, MI: Eerdmans, 1964), 624, 625.

3 Nicaeno-Constantinopolitan Creed, in Schaff, *Creeds,* 2:58.

4 Ibid., 59.

5 Ibid., 58, 59.

CHAPTER 6

1 Heidelberg Catechism, A 14, in Schaff, *Creeds,* 3:311, 312.

CHAPTER 7

1 Schaff, *History,* 3:721.

2 Schaff, *History,* 3:725.

3 Ibid., 728.

4 Symbol of Chalcedon, in Schaff, *Creeds,* 2:62.

CHAPTER 8

1 Benjamin B. Warfield, "Introductory Essay on Augustin and the Pelagian Controversy," in Philip Schaff, ed., *Nicene and Post-Nicene Fathers of the Christian Church,* 1st series, vol. 5, *St. Augustine: Anti-Pelagian Writings against the Pelagians* (Grand Rapids, MI: Eerdmans, 1987), xvii.

2 Ibid., xix.

3 Ibid., xiii.

CHAPTER 9

1 In the area of ecclesiology, the doctrine of the church, Augustine was weak. This was especially true of his views of the sacraments.

2 Quoted in Pelikan, *The Christian Tradition,* 1:320.

3 Conclusion to the Canons of Dordt, in Schaff, *Creeds,* 3:596, 597.

4 Pelikan, *The Christian Tradition,* 1:324.

5 Augustine, "The Enchiridion," in Philip Schaff, ed., *Nicene and Post-Nicene Fathers of the Christian Church,* 1st series, vol. 3, *St. Augustine: On the Holy Trinity, Doctrinal Treatises, Moral Treatises* (Grand Rapids, MI: Eerdmans, 1988), 268.

6 Ibid., 270, 271.
7 Herman Hoeksema, *History of Dogma* (Grandville, MI: Theological School of the Protestant Reformed Churches, 1982), 31.

CHAPTER 10
1 Schaff, *History*, vol. 4, *Medieval Christianity: From Gregory I to Gregory VII, AD 590–1073* (New York: Charles Scribner's Sons, 1910; repr., Grand Rapids, MI: Eerdmans, n.d.), 212.
2 Ibid., 212, 213.
3 Ibid., 31.
4 Ibid.
5 Ibid., 212.
6 Ibid., 227.

CHAPTER 11
1 Herman Hanko, *Portraits of Faithful Saints* (Grandville, MI: Reformed Free Publishing Association, 1999), 68–72.
2 W. Robertson Nicholl, ed., *Church History by Professor Kurtz*, 2nd ed., trans. John MacPherson, 3 vols. (London: Hodder and Stoughton, 1841), 1:547.
3 John McClintock and James Strong, *Cyclopaedia of Biblical, Theological, and Ecclesiastical Literature* (New York: Harper & Brothers, 1869–1881), *s.v.* "Gottschalk."
4 Reinhold Seeberg, *Textbook of the History of Doctrines*, vol. 2, *History of Doctrines in the Ancient* Church, trans. Charles E. Hay (Grand Rapids, MI: Baker Book House, 1958), 33.
5 Ibid.
6 Ibid.

CHAPTER 12
1 Schaff, *History*, 4:548.
2 Quoted in Ibid., 555.
3 McClintock and Strong, *Cyclopaedia*, *s.v.* "Berenger."
4 Ibid., 567.
5 Quoted in Ibid., 559.
6 Heidelberg Catechism, A 80, in Schaff, *Creeds*, 3:336.
7 Ibid., 430.

CHAPTER 13
1 For additional material on this topic, see Hanko, *Portraits*, 73–78.
2 Schaaf, *History*, vol. 5, David S. Schaff, *The Middle Ages, From Greg-*

ory VII, 1049 to Boniface VIII, 1294 (Charles Scribner's Sons, 1907; repr., Grand Rapids, MI: Eerdmans, 1967), 610.

3 Ibid., 611.

4 Ibid., 612.

5 Ibid., 620.

6 See Heidelberg Catechism, Q&A 12–14 and 16, in Schaff, *Creeds*, 3:311, 312.

CHAPTER 14

1 Schaff, *History*, 5:155.

2 Ibid., 156.

3 Ibid.

4 Ibid., 157.

5 Ibid.

6 Belgic Confession, Art. 29, in Schaff, *Creeds*, 3:421.

CHAPTER 15

1 Quoted in Schaff, *History*, vol. 6, David S. Schaff, *The Middle Ages: From Boniface VIII, 1294, to the Protestant Reformation, 1517* (New York: Charles Scribner's Sons, 1910; repr., Grand Rapids, MI: Eerdmans, 1967), 288.

2 Ibid., 284.

3 Ibid., 285.

4 Ibid., n. 2, 285.

5 Ibid., 284.

6 Ibid., 285, 286, 288.

7 Robert G. Tuttle, Jr., *Mysticism in the Wesleyan Tradition* (Grand Rapids, MI: Zondervan Publishing House, 1989), 22.

8 Ibid.

9 Ibid., 23.

10 J. H. Merle D'Aubigne, *History of the Great Reformation of the Sixteenth Century in Germany, Switzerland, etc.* (New York: William H. Colyer, 1844), 247.

11 Heidelberg Catechism, Q&A 1, in Schaff, *Creeds*, 3:307; emphasis added.

CHAPTER 16

1 Schaff, *History*, vol. 7, *Modern Christianity: The German Reformation*, 2nd ed., rev., (New York: Charles Scribner's Sons, 1910; repr., Grand Rapids, MI: Eerdmans, 1967), 401, 402.

2 Ibid., 408.

3 Quoted in Ibid., 426.

4 Schaff, *History,* 6:640; 7:414.

5 Schaff, *History,* 7:423.

6 Quoted in Ibid., 429.

CHAPTER 17

1 Schaff, *History,* 7:193.

2 Ibid.

3 Quoted in *The New Schaff-Herzog Encyclopedia of Religious Knowledge* (New York: Funk & Wagnalls, 1908), *s.v.* "Philipp Melanchton."

4 Quoted in Schaff, *History,* vol. 8, *Modern Christianity: The Swiss Reformation,* 3rd ed, rev. (New York: Charles Scribner's Sons, 1910; repr., Grand Rapids, MI: Eerdmans, 1958), 398.

5 Schaff, *History,* 7:701.

CHAPTER 18

1 Quoted in *The New Schaff-Herzog Encyclopedia of Religious Knowledge, s.v.* "Antinomianism and Antinomian Controversies."

2 Quoted in Ibid., 199 (footnote).

CHAPTER 19

1 Hanko, *Portraits,* 190.

2 Schaff, *History,* 7:388.

3 Martin Luther, *Luther's Works,* vols. 21–24, 51, 52, ed. Jaroslav Pelikan (St. Louis: Concordia Publishing House, 1956–61).

4 Quoted in Schaff, *History,* 7:389.

5 Schaff, *Creeds,* 3:433.

6 Ibid., 403.

7 Heidelberg Catechism, A 54, in Ibid., 324, 325.

CHAPTER 20

1 John Calvin, "Reply to Cardinal Sadolet's Letter," in *Calvin's Tracts and Treatises,* vol. 1, trans. Henry Beveridge (Grand Rapids, MI: Eerdmans, 1958), 25–68. Cardinal Sadolet's letter is found in *Calvin's Tracts and Treatises,* vol. 1, 1–22.

2 John Calvin, *Come Out from Among Them: Anti-Nicodemite Writings of John Calvin* (Dallas, TX: Protestant Heritage Press, 2001), 8n1. John Calvin, "On Shunning the Unlawful Rites of the Ungodly and Preserving the Purity of the Christian Religion," in *Calvin's Tracts*

and Treatises, vol. 3, trans. Henry Beveridge (Grand Rapids, MI: Eerdmans, 1958), 359–411. The tract was written in 1537.

3 Calvin, *Tracts,* 3:359.

4 Ibid., 361.

5 Calvin has a powerful refutation of this appeal to Naaman in *Come Out from Among Them,* 71–73.

CHAPTER 21

1 Schaff, *History,* 8:343, 344.

2 Theodore Beza, *The Life of John Calvin* (Albany, OR: Books for the Ages, 1998), 30, http://www.scribd.com/doc/24704173/THE-LIFE-OF-JOHN-CALVIN-Theodore-Beza

3 Schaff, *History,* 8:615, 616.

4 Quoted in Ibid., 616.

5 If one would inquire how the civil government could involve itself in religious and doctrinal questions, the answer is to be found in the unique relation between the state and the church in Geneva, but also in many other Protestant countries, such as the Netherlands and the British Isles. The civil magistrate was required to "promote the true religion." Nevertheless, Bolsec had disturbed the public peace and had come under civil authority with his tirades.

6 Schaff, *History,* 8:617.

7 John Calvin, "God's Eternal Predestination and Secret Providence," in John Calvin, *Calvin's Calvinism: God's Eternal Predestination and Secret Providence* together with *A Brief Reply* and *Reply to the Slanderous Reports,* trans. Henry Cole, ed, Russell J. Dykstra, 2nd ed. (Jenison, MI: Reformed Free Publishing Association, 2009), 15–203.

8 Herman Hoeksema, *The Protestant Reformed Churches in America: Their Origin, Early History and Doctrine* (Grand Rapids, MI: First Protestant Reformed Church, 1936), 84.

9 Canons of Dordt, 1.6, in Schaff, *Creeds,* 3.582.

CHAPTER 22

1 Schaff, *History,* 8:687.

2 Ibid.

3 Ibid., 786–88.

4 Ibid., 778.

CHAPTER 23

1 Samuel Miller, "Introductory Essay," in *The Articles of the Synod of Dort*, trans., Thomas Scott (Harrisonburg, VA: Sprinkle Publications, 1993), 16, 17.

2 Canons 2, Rejection of Errors 3, in *The Confessions and the Church Order of the Protestant Reformed Churches* (Grandville, MI: Protestant Reformed Churches in America, 2005), 165.

3 Peter Y. De Jong, ed., *Crisis in the Reformed Churches: Essays in the Commemoration of the Great Synod of Dort, 1618–1619* (Grand Rapids, MI: Reformed Fellowship, 1968), 56.

4 Conclusion to the Canons of Dordt, in Schaff, *Creeds*, 3:596.

5 Canons 2.8, in Schaff, *Creeds*, 587.

6 *Confessions and Church Order*, 326; emphasis added.

CHAPTER 24

1 *Universalism and the Reformed Churches: A Defense of Calvin's Calvinism* (Launceston, Tasmania: Magazine and Literature Committee of the Evangelical Presbyterian Church of Australia, repr., 1997), 6.

2 *Minutes of the Sessions of the Westminster Divines While Engaged in Preparing Their Directory for Church Government, Confession of Faith, and Catechisms (November 1644 to March 1649)*, Alex Mitchell and Fred Struthers, ed. (Edinburgh: William Blackwood and Sons, 1874), 167.

3 Schaff, *Creeds*, 1:772.

4 Ibid., 772, 773.

5 Canons of Dordt, 2.8, in Schaff, *Creeds*, 3:587; emphasis added.

6 Westminster Confession of Faith 3.6, in Schaff, *Creeds*, 609, 610; emphasis added.

7 Robert Shaw, *The Reformed Faith: An Exposition of the Westminster Confession of Faith* (New York: Oxford University Press, 1845; repr., Grand Rapids, MI: Baker, 1981), 71, 143; Benjamin Warfield, *The Works of Benjamin B. Warfield*, vol. 6, *The Westminster Assembly and Its Work* (Cherry Hill, NJ: Mack Publishing Co., 1971), 141; Schaff *Creeds* 1:770–73.

8 Formula Consensus Helvetica, in A. A. Hodge, *Outlines of Theology* (New York: Hodder & Stoughton, 1878), 656. Table found on 656; emphasis added.

9 Ibid., Article 13, 659.

10 Ibid., Article 16, 660.

11 Ibid., Article 20, 661, 662.

CHAPTER 25

1 For a fuller biographical sketch of Cocceius' life, a brief summary of his ideas, and the importance of his chief opponent, Gijsbert Voetius, see Hanko, *Portraits,* 328–40.

2 E. Calvin Beisner, ed., *The Auburn Avenue Theology Pros and Cons: Debating the Federal Vision: The Knox Theological Seminary Colloquium on the Federal Vision August 11–13, 2003* (Fort Lauderdale, FL: Knox Theological Seminary, 2004).

3 Douglas Wilson, "Union with Christ: An Overview of the of the Federal Vision," in *The Auburn Avenue Theology Pros and Cons,* 1–8.

4 Steve Schlissel, "A New Way of Seeing?" in *The Auburn Avenue Theology Pros and Cons,* 25.

5 Heidelberg Catechism, Q&A 21, in Schaff, *Creeds,* 3:313.

6 See Herman Ridderbos, *Paul: An Outline of His Theology,* trans. John Richard DeWitt (London: Holy Trinity Church; repr., Grand Rapids, MI: Eerdmans, 1975).

CHAPTER 26

1 There is some question about the exact date of publication of *The Marrow of Modern Divinity.* The Westminster Assembly began meeting in 1643. In 1647 the Scottish delegates left for home. The assembly did additional work until 1649.

2 John Macleod, *Scottish Theology in Relation to Church History Since the Reformation* (Edinburgh: Banner of Truth Trust, 1874), 156.

3 Ibid.

4 Joel R. Beeke, "The Dutch Second Reformation (*Nadere Reformatie*)," *Calvin Theological Journal* 28, no. 2 (1993): 302.

CHAPTER 27

1 C.E. Vulliamy, *John Wesley,* (London: Geoffrey Bles, 1931), 3.

2 Ibid.

3 Ibid., 48.

4 Ibid., 60.

5 Ibid., 85.

6 Tuttle, *Mysticism in the Wesleyan Tradition,* 122, 132, 133.

7 Vulliamy, *John Wesley,* 142, 143.

8 Ibid., 314.

9 Tuttle, *Mysticism,* 14.

10 Vulliamy, *John Wesley,* 277.

11 Ibid., 316.
12 Ibid., 357.

Chapter 28

1 Charles G. Finney, *The Memoirs of Charles G. Finney,* Garth M. Rosell and Richard A. G. Dupuis, ed. (Grand Rapids, MI: Zondervan Publishing House, 1989), 10.
2 Ibid., 22.
3 Ibid., 195.
4 Charles E. Hambrick–Stowe, *Charles G. Finney and the Spirit of American Evangelicalism* (Grand Rapids, MI: Eerdmans, 1996), 156, 157.
5 Hugh L. Williams, "The Free Offer Issue," *British Reformed Journal* (British Reformed Fellowship) 41 (Autumn 2004): 29.
6 Heidelberg Catechism, Q&A 54, in Schaff, *Creeds,* 3:324.
7 Hughes Oliphant Old, *The Reading and Preaching of the Scriptures in the Worship of the Christian Church,* vol. 1, *The Biblical Period* (Grand Rapids, MI: Eerdmans, 1998), 283.
8 Heidelberg Catechism, Q&A 54, in Schaff, *Creeds,* 3:324, 325.

Chapter 29

1 *Encyclopedia Britannica,* 15th ed., *s.v.* "Charles Darwin."
2 Ibid., 495, 496.
3 Geoffrey W. Bromeley, trans. and ed., *The Encyclopedia of Christianity,* vol. 2 (Grand Rapids, MI: Eerdmans, 2001), 235.
4 Ibid., 233.
5 Del Ratzsch, *The Battle of Beginnings: Why Neither Side is Winning the Creation–Evolution Debate* (Downers Grove, IL: Intervarsity Press, 1996), 180.
6 Howard J. Van Till, *The Fourth Day: What the Bible and the Heavens are telling us about the Creation* (Grand Rapids, MI: Eerdmans, 1986).
7 Ratzsch, *The Battle of Beginnings,* 181.
8 Ibid.
9 Herman Hanko, *The Framework Hypothesis* (Kalamazoo, MI: Evangelism Committee of the Kalamazoo Protestant Reformed Church, 2001), 5.

Chapter 30

1 H. Evans, *The Kingdom Is Always But Coming: A Life of Walter Rauschenbusch* (Grand Rapids, MI: Eerdmans, 2004), 39.

2 Ibid.

3 Ibid., 123.

4 Ibid., 90.

5 Ibid., 106.

CHAPTER 31

1 David A. Weir, *The Origins of the Federal Theology in Sixteenth-Century Reformation Thought* (Oxford: Clarendon Press, 1990), 62.

2 Ibid., 99.

3 Louis Berkhof, *Manual of Reformed Doctrine* (Grand Rapids, MI: Eerdmans, 1933), 131–33.

4 Thomas Goodwin, *Christ Our Mediator* (Grand Rapids, MI: Sovereign Grace Publishers, 1971), 82, 83.

5 Herman Hoeksema, *Reformed Dogmatics*, 2nd ed., 2 vols. (Grandville, MI: Reformed Free Publishing Association, 2004), 1:308–312.

6 "Form for the Administration of Baptism," in *Confessions and Church Order*, 260; emphasis added.

7 Ibid.; emphasis added.

8 Heidelberg Catechism, Q&A 74, in Schaff, *Creeds*, 3:331.

9 William Heyns, *Manual of Reformed Doctrine* (Grand Rapids, MI: Eerdmans, 1926), 67–72; for his idea of the covenant of grace, see 123–47.

10 Ibid., 136, 137.

11 Lewis Bevens Schenck, *Yale Studies in Religious Education*, vol. 12, *The Presbyterian Doctrine of Children in the Covenant: An Historical Study of the Significance of Infant Baptism in the Presbyterian Church in America* (New Haven: Yale University Press, 1940).

12 Norman Shepherd, *The Call of Grace: How the Covenant Illuminates Salvation and Evangelism* (Philipsburg, NJ: Presbyterian and Reformed Publishing, 2000).

13 See David J. Engelsma, *The Unconditional Covenant in Contemporary Debate* (Hudsonville, MI: Trinity Protestant Reformed Evangelism Committee, 2004); David J. Engelsma, *The Covenant of God and the Children of Believers: Sovereign Grace in the Covenant* (Grandville, MI: Reformed Free Publishing Association, 2005). See especially pages 135–209.

14 Herman Hoeksema, *The Covenant: God's Tabernacle with Men* (Grand Rapids, MI: Sunday School Mission Publishing Society of the First Protestant Reformed Church, repr., 1981), 8; Herman Hoeksema, *Reformed Dogmatics*, 1:470, 471.

15 "Form for the Administration of Baptism," in *Confessions and Church Order*, 258.

CHAPTER 32

1 While this view may appear as strange to the reader, we ought to remember that something similar is held by evolutionists who claim to accept Scripture. They argue that while the Bible teaches a creation in six days of twenty-four hours, science teaches an old earth. If one questions a theistic evolutionist about his faith in Scripture and Scripture's teachings, he will say something like this: "Sunday I worship in church and make use of the Scriptures, but in my laboratory or observatory I am a scientist." The impossibility of holding to such a division in the human mind is demonstrated by the fact that those who talk this way soon invent elaborate theories, such as the so-called framework hypothesis, to reinterpret Scripture so that it can be twisted in its meaning to agree with science. Science wins out; Scripture is destroyed.

2 Contrary to revisionist historians (to be found also in the reconstruction movement), such leading men as George Washington, Thomas Jefferson, James Madison, and others were deists. The very language of the Declaration of Independence is deistic.

3 This analogy was first suggested by Herman Bavinck, although he would have opposed the use to which it was put.

4 Schaff, *History*, 8:859.

CHAPTER 34

1 For a detailed study of the history of the well-meant offer of salvation, see Herman Hanko, *History of the Free Offer* (Grandville, MI: Theological School of the Protestant Reformed Churches, 1989).

CHAPTER 35

1 Subsequently Shepherd served in two churches of the Christian Reformed Church and wrote *The Call of Grace: How the Covenant Illuminates Salvation and Evangelism* (Philipsburg, NJ: P&R, 2000).

2 Nicholas Thomas Wright, *What Saint Paul Really Said: Was Paul of Tarsus the Real Founder of Christianity?* (Grand Rapids, MI: Eerdmans, 1997); Nicholas Thomas Wright, *Paul: In Fresh Perspective* (Minneapolis, MN: Fortress Press, 2005; Nicholas Thomas Wright, *Justification: God's Plan and Paul's Vision* (Downer's Grove, IL: InterVarsity Press, 2009).